HIGHBROW/LOWDOWN

THEATER, JAZZ, AND THE
MAKING OF THE NEW MIDDLE CLASS

DAVID SAVRAN

The University of Michigan Press / Ann Arbor

Copyright © by the University of Michigan 2009
All rights reserved
Published in the United States of America by
The University of Michigan Press
Manufactured in the United States of America
♾ Printed on acid-free paper

2012   2011   2010   2009   4   3   2   1

A CIP catalog record for this book is available from the British Library.

Library of Congress Cataloging-in-Publication Data

Savran, David, 1950–
    Highbrow/lowdown : theater, jazz, and the making of the new middle
class / David Savran.
        p.   cm.
    Portions of the text were previously published.
    Includes bibliographical references and index.
    ISBN-13: 978-0-472-11692-8 (cloth : alk. paper)
    ISBN-10: 0-472-11692-4 (cloth : alk. paper)
    1. Music—Social aspects—United States—History—20th century.
2. Jazz—History and criticism.   3. Theater—United States—
History—20th century.   4. Middle class—United States—History—
20th century.   I. Title.
ML3917.U6S28   2009
306.4'84097309042—dc22   2008051143

Earlier versions of a few sections of this book have been published as "Making Middlebrow
Theater in America," in *Codifying the National Self: Spectators, Actors and the American Dramatic
Text*, ed. Barbara Ozieblo and María Dolores Narbona-Carrión (Brussels: Peter Lang, 2006),
21–38; "The Curse of Legitimacy," in *Against Theatre: Creative Destructions on the Modernist
Stage*, eds. Alan Ackerman and Martin Puchner (Houndmills, UK: Palgrave Macmillan,
2006), 189–205; "The Search for America's Soul: Theatre in the Jazz Age," *Theatre Journal*
58.3 (October 2006): 459–76; and "The Canonization of Eugene O'Neill," *Modern Drama*
50.4 (Winter 2007): 565–80. I thank these publishers for permission to reprint these essays
here in altered form.

For Daniel Gundlach

We had the smiles,
We had the tunes . . .
—ED KLEBAN

[T]he American soul . . . is a combination that includes the wail, the whine and the exultant note of the old mam[m]y songs of the South. It is black and white. It is all colors and all souls unified in the great melting-pot of the world.

— GEORGE GERSHWIN

Only history itself, real history with all its suffering and all its contradiction, constitutes the truth of music.

— THEODOR W. ADORNO

ACKNOWLEDGMENTS

While writing this book, I was fortunate enough to receive the assistance of many people. I want first to thank my colleagues Marvin Carlson, Jean Graham-Jones, and Judy Milhous for the many fruitful conversations I had with them about this project and for their close reading of individual chapters. I am grateful to other colleagues at the Graduate Center for their help and support: Glenn Burger, John Graziano, Pamela Sheingorn, and Jeffrey Taylor. I want to thank the two anonymous readers for the University of Michigan Press and my friends in the profession who have given me invaluable feedback along the way: Alan Ackerman, Charlotte Canning, Tracy Davis, Jill Dolan, Rob Hume, Willmar Sauter, Rose Subotnik, and Stacy Wolf. LeAnn Fields has yet again proven invaluable for her encouragement, support, and suggestions for making the book more accessible to nonspecialist readers. I want to express my appreciation to my graduate students working in related fields, with whom I have had many stimulating conversations: Kevin Byrne, Kimon Keramidas, Ken Nielsen, and Constance Zaytoun. I especially want to thank my friends who nourished and sustained me during the five long years I was writing this book: Glenn Berger, Michael Cohen, Charles Curkin, David Hult, Richard Niles, Don Shewey, Brian Smith, Scott Teagarden, Paula Vogel, and KC Witherell. Finally, I owe the greatest debt to my sister, Shelley Savran Houlihan, for her boundless generosity and love, and to Daniel Gundlach, who helped and cheered me every step of the way, proofread the manuscript, and most important, gave me the confidence to write about music.

CONTENTS

PROLOGUE

Jazz . . . is an unforgivable orgy of voice, a riot of discord, usually perpetrated by players . . . who believe that random whoops, blasts, crashes and unearthly tom-toming is something akin to genius. It may often be associated with vile surroundings, filthy words, unmentionable danc[ing], and horrible plays.

—"Jazz at its Worst," *Musical Courier,* 14 February 1924

n the beginning, back when *The Birth of a Nation* was only a glint in D. W. Griffith's eye, live theater was the most popular form of entertainment in the United States. Before television and the talkie, before the Great Depression and the national syndication of radio, theater comprised a vast array of public amusements that included vaudeville, minstrel shows, and burlesque; circus and freak show; musical comedy and revue; as well as the so-called legitimate stage: drama, comedy, and tragedy. However, by the end of the decade F. Scott Fitzgerald dubbed the Jazz Age, the most popular and popularly priced entertainments (especially vaudeville and burlesque) were vanishing in part because they could not compete with the feature-length talking pictures being screened in luxurious new movie palaces. By the early 1930s, everything had changed. The range of theatrical offerings had shrunk dramatically just as for the first time American playwrights were being acclaimed as the creators of a serious, elevated drama.

In virtually every account of the American theater during the 1920s—a period of unprecedented cultural and social change—the decline of cheap, commercial entertainments is seen as a salutary purification. And one man is constructed as the savior who drove the money lenders from the temple of art: Eugene O'Neill. Casting out "horrible plays" and a hodgepodge of cheap and tawdry entertainments littered with "filthy words" and "unmentionable dancing," O'Neill allegedly invented a distinctively American literary drama. He was the first, the legend goes, to be able to hawk his wares abroad and so alert the European elders that the United States was finally mature enough to produce works of theatrical art guaranteed to be immortal and stunningly up-to-date. The tribute of poet and critic Benjamin De Casseres is typical of the testimonials thrown his way during the 1920s:

> Genius has its innings at last . . . and American genius at that! An American playwright—a revolutionist in form, a scathing ironist and a poetic pessimist in substance—is crowned in an era of brutal, materialistic babbittry![1]

Recent historians have been less hyperbolic in their assessments of O'Neill, a "heroic figure" if there ever was one, but the shape of the argument remains the same. Typical is Daniel J. Watermeier's explanation why the years between World War I and the Great Depression became, in his words, "the most dynamic period in the history of the American stage." Before O'Neill, the theater had been propelled by commercial rather than artistic interests, which ensured that "conventional taste . . . took precedence over innovation . . . or genuine literary merit." Watermeier never explains what "genuine literary merit" means, but it clearly has nothing to do with melodrama, farce, musical comedy, and, of course, genres like vaudeville and burlesque that fail even to register on his scale of merit. But with the founding of nonprofessional, nonprofit little theaters between 1909 and 1915 and the emergence of new journals devoted to modernist art and ideas, the "overall artistic quality of American theatre and drama" began to be "elevat[ed]." By 1920, Watermeier writes, "the New York stage was set, even primed, for O'Neill's theatrical ascent."

Watermeier's evolutionary narrative mystifies O'Neill by making him inevitable, a seemingly natural, irresistible force that miraculously birthed "a body of work that was both artistically and commercially successful."[2] Although Watermeier reflects on the critical and economic contexts for theatrical production, he ignores (in what, I must allow, is a very brief overview) the broader cultural field and, in particular, the performing arts that abutted and overlapped with the legitimate theater during the first three decades of the twentieth century. My goal in this book is to demystify O'Neill and, indeed, the other so-called literary playwrights of the 1920s, to consider them in relation to musicians, writers, performers, and critics working in related fields, and to analyze the changes in cultural production, distribution, and consumption that helped engineer the emergence of an art theater in the United States. O'Neill is most emphatically not the hero of this book. Although I examine him in the last chapter, I do so to try to answer a daunting question that has been formulated most simply and memorably by the great French sociologist, Pierre Bourdieu: "what authorizes the author?"[3] What agents and institutions grant an author power and legitimacy? What during the 1920s encouraged so many theatergoers to believe that O'Neill was indeed "the personal symbol of our awakening American drama"?[4] And why does he still hold the title "America's leading playwright"?[5]

The main purpose of this book is to answer these and more wide-ranging questions: Why did a literary theater arise in the United States during the 1920s that was able to pass muster as high art? That found a niche in the cultural hierarchy next to museums and symphony orchestras? That could secure the patronage of "the *élite* . . . in flashing tiaras and shirt fronts"?[6] That could compete with prestigious European theaters? That carefully distinguished itself from rival and, it was repeatedly emphasized, lesser genres like musical comedy and vaudeville?

Why did the 1920s engender a theatrical dispensation that continues, more or less intact, to the present day?

To begin to answer these questions, we might look at the development of the little art theaters in the United States and larger enterprises, like the Theatre Guild, that were instrumental in disseminating the new forms and styles. We could examine the increasing concentration of theaters and theatrical management in New York, and Broadway's relationship to production throughout the United States. We could study the enormous impact of motion pictures and their success in hijacking large segments of what had been the theatergoing public. We could analyze the developments in playwriting, design, acting, and direction that were linked to the "awakening" of American drama. We could investigate the changes in the class system and the increasing theater ticket buying power of white-collared, salaried workers, the so-called new middle class.

I do indeed take on these explanatory projects. But I do so by focusing on a cultural practice that, at first glance, would seem to have little to do with the emergence of a literary theater in the United States—jazz. One must bear in mind, however, that during the 1920s, jazz represented far more than a new musical style. For the producers and consumers of culture, jazz was the portal to a new world. It described and emblematized the most exhilarating and controversial ways of making music, love, poetry, race, and America. Jazz functioned, in other words, as a force around which coalesced what the British cultural theorist Raymond Williams calls a structure of feeling. A structure of feeling, he explains, is a fusion of the objective and the subjective; it is "as firm and definite as 'structure' suggests" even though it is "based in the deepest and often least tangible elements of our experience."[7] The new structure of feeling that emerged during the 1920s was characterized by both explicit and unspoken sets of conventions, rules, and habits as well as much less orderly assortments of emotions, sensations, desires, thrills, and revulsions. I turn to Williams because I cannot emphasize strongly enough that jazz was far more than music; it represented "a particular quality of social experience and relationship" that was so radically different from anything that had come before that it gave its name to the era: the Jazz Age.[8]

Given the overwhelmingly commercial nature of theater during the 1920s, jazz was eagerly appropriated by the theatrical forms that most catered to the working and lower-middle classes: vaudeville, musical comedy, variety, and burlesque. Indeed, for the many Americans, both white and black, who frequented dance halls, vaudeville shows, and musical comedy, theater was jazz—and jazz was theater. It was often very difficult to differentiate among musical comedy, revue, and an evening's entertainment at a cabaret. In a Vitaphone short, an emcee asks mischievously, "What's the difference between a theater and a night club?"[9] By what criteria could one distinguish the black musical comedy *Shuffle Along* (1921) or the Ziegfeld Follies from a floor show at the Savoy Ballroom or Cotton Club? Because the boundary between jazz performance and theatrical performance remained indistinct, theater professionals intent on the elevation of the legitimate theater were made distinctly anxious by the ubiquity of a low-class music that emerged from African Americans, eastern European Jews, and other immigrant groups. Because jazz was also a primary site for working out anxieties about racial difference, they became especially nervous about the refusal of jazz to know its place. How were they to respond to the obvious correlation between John Howard Lawson's play *Processional: A Jazz Symphony of American Life in Four Acts*, produced in 1925 by the prestigious Theatre Guild, and the contemporaneous rage for what was called symphonic jazz? Or the unmistakable family resemblance among jazz music, jazz poetry, and jazz theater? How were they to give ticket buyers what they wanted and at the same time prove that the United States was finally capable of producing a highbrow, world-class drama?

The large majority of playwrights who aspired to make what they called works of art tried to will jazz out of existence. The few who wrote plays that referenced jazz typically constructed it as a pesky incursion from below, the cacophony of those worthy of ridicule, segregation, or expulsion. One of the few plays to take jazz as its primary subject was *The National Anthem* by J. Hartley Manners (written for his wife, Laurette Taylor), which enjoyed what in 1922 was a comfortable Broadway run of 114 performances. In his foreword to the play, Manners paints a lurid portrait of "modern civilization's saturnalia":

Jazz!
What a mental picture rises as one sees the word in print.
Civilization chants its tune as an anthem.
    And bodies writhe and intermingle and brains rattle in skulls as the ghastly jigging procession circles under blazing lights to the cheap, deafening "music"(!) of the tire-less orchestras.

In Manners's overheated fantasy of a world upside down, the combination of tangled, mixed-up bodies and nonstop jazz describes what could be nightclub, ballroom, or theater. For in the blinding light, all distinctions vanish. Girls and young women become "harlot[s]," beauty turns "hideous," rudeness supplants "courtesy," and "blackguardism" becomes synonymous with manliness.[10] To Manners's list of carnivalesque inversions we might add other, even more threatening, forms of masquerade: white tricked out as black and upper class as working class.

In this book, I am using jazz as a kind of lever to prise open relations between and among the producers and consumers of a wide range of theatrical genres, the shifting class relations that were so deeply implicated in the rapidly changing shape of the cultural hierarchy, and the relationship between a revolution in music and a revolution in modes of industrial production. For jazz was persistently seen as the music of a new Machine Age that brought a profusion of skyscrapers, washing machines, radios, electric signs, and public amusements. Jazz's status as an art that rose from the laboring classes, "its rapid standardization and its speed," its widespread distribution by machines (phonograph and radio), and its emphasis on rhythm allowed it contradictorily to stand for both "mechanical determinism" and "the revolt of human free-will against" determinism.[11] Jazz, in other words, represented a *social relation*, a result of and analogue to new forms of labor, both mass production and reaction against mass production. A cultural practice around and through which a new structure of feeling and new class relations crystallized, it provided a touchstone for both old and new forms of theater. For jazz became an emblem of live performance itself, of an improvisation that can never be repeated and, like an exhilarating vaudeville turn, is "impossible to put in score upon a page of paper."[12]

In trying to banish jazz from the boards, the makers of a commercial theater that aspired to be an art theater ended up turning the symbol and epitome of liveness, of performance, into a kind of hated nuisance they couldn't quite get rid of. Some playwrights who trafficked in the written word—the only element of theatrical performance protected by copyright laws—attempted to quell the anxiety surrounding live speech by trying to kill live jazz: moving it into the wings, reproducing it mechanically (on radio or phonograph), or expelling it completely. (Even in *The National Anthem*, jazz is heard only from offstage.) The transformation of live music into dead sound was crucial for safeguarding the legitimacy of the legitimate theater and controlling this dangerous and seductive musical supplement.[13] Endeavoring to ensure that jazz would be, in Manners's words, a "Dance of Death," playwrights and producers intent on the elevation of the stage tried to mock and sabotage jazz's eminence as the most exhilarating instance of live performance.[14] Yet by keeping jazz at bay, reducing it to a mere supplement, they inadvertently revealed the slavish and mechanical structure of theatrical performance based on a written text to which performers are bound in a kind of indentured servitude.

Rather than focus narrowly on the legitimate theater, musical comedy, or vaudeville, I am trying to show how these categories were constructed in the first place and their boundaries policed. I have selected jazz because, as a performance practice, it cuts across laterally and disturbs the integrity of different genres and media. I want to emphasize, however, that I am using the word *jazz* as it was during the 1920s to describe virtually all new, popular music. Although most jazz historians since World War II consider 1920s jazz to be the work almost exclusively of African American composers, singers, and musicians, I am deliberately employing the term as it was then to describe a panoply of musical styles, most of which, in fact, are the product of European Americans associated with Broadway and Tin Pan Alley. I am using the wide range of performances associated with jazz to perform the kind of analysis that was pioneered seventy-five years ago by the Marxist sociologist and refugee from Nazi Germany, Theodor W. Adorno. A famously difficult theorist, Adorno (who was also a composer and musicologist) explained that criticism in the modern age should become "social physiognomy," an analysis that makes discernible the ways in which both "general social tendencies" and the interests of "the most powerful" are expressed in culture.[15] Given Adorno's notorious scorn for popular music, I realize there is something downright perverse about citing him as an authority for an analysis of the musical form he most detested. Yet Adorno is indispensable, I believe, because he was the first to identify music—all music—as a form of social mediation. "Society," he notes, "has been inscribed in [music's] very meaning and its categories," and music, as a result, reflects and mediates "the trends and contradictions of bourgeois society as a totality." Adorno argues that sociology can use music as a tool to "decipher" the world of which it is a part, a world saturated with music. But the process of deciphering must take into account the social being of music in modernist culture: its equivocal and always partial protest against the increasing regimentation of the modern world, its status as "a carefully cultivated preserve of the irrational in the midst of the rationalized universe." Although Adorno understands the potentially emancipatory power of music, he resists romanticizing the composer or musician. Debunking the fiction of the solitary artist-rebel, he points out that society, in all its complexity, inheres in the work of every composer. Be he George Gershwin or George Antheil, Eubie Blake or Aaron Copland, the "compositional subject is no individual thing, but a collective one. All music, however individual it may be in stylistic terms, possesses an inalienable collective substance: *every sound says 'we.'*"[16]

Trying to discern how every sound says "we," I am analyzing a broad range of theatrical practices, both those that take up jazz directly (either affirmatively or negatively) and those that pretend it does not exist. The most challenging part of this project, however, has necessitated my examination of the "we," the audiences that frequented different social amusements during a period of unprecedented social and economic change. This analysis has been especially daunting because the 1920s long predated the era of the audience survey. It has also had to confront a theoretical problem, the fact that social class and brow level were not (and are not) synonymous. The economic, social, and cultural hierarchies implicated in matters of taste are always interactive and always determined by many different factors. Thus, for example, highbrow taste is by no means the exclusive property of the upper classes or those with the most education. It is, in fact, more often than not associated with intellectual rather than economic elites. Moreover, in analyzing hierarchies of taste, I have come to believe that as important as racial, ethnic, and gendered differences are, they become intelligible only when linked to class relations. And in so many primary sources, social class, unlike other axes of identity, is unremarked, taken for granted, or invisible. The most important and most elusive of identities, it is the product of many different kinds of variables. When the other kinds of identity are assumed to be essential and unalterable, social class is considered relatively inessential because it is believed (usually wrongly) to be easily alterable. (How unshakable is the fairy tale that it only takes hard work or good luck to become a Gordon Getty or Bill Gates!) Like the elephant in the living room, social class is seen but ignored. And among scholars, it remains the most undertheorized of identities. (This was especially true in the social sciences before the publication of detailed quantitative and qualitative studies of social class in the United States by the sociologist W. Lloyd Warner and his associates in the early 1940s.)[17]

In order to tackle the problem of class head on, I have had to make a modest detour, putting jazz aside in what is, in fact, the central chapter of the book in order to examine both the history of the theorization of class in the United States and the class composition of audiences. Elsewhere, I try to analyze the shifting overlaps and disjunctions among the fields of legitimate theater, musical comedy, vaudeville, concert music, and jazz performance. And as much as I would like to be able to reach unimpeachable conclusions about audiences, that project is foreclosed by the lack of statistical data from the 1920s as well as by the impossibility of compassing (and in many cases, even describing) musical and theatrical performances of eighty years ago. Adorno emphasizes that the empirical study of musical effects is "hazardous" because of the difficulty of gauging their "unconscious and preconscious nature" and "of accounting for [them] in words."[18] Although the textual basis for some kinds of theater makes their effects more readily subject to description and analysis, performances from the 1920s are not accessible except in highly mediated forms.

In this book, I am attempting to write a political economy of culture during a key moment in U.S. history: an analysis of the relationship between particular theatrical and musical practices and the changing shape of social and economic resources. Rather than unthinkingly privilege what are now canonical texts, I have tried to understand how and why plays and musical pieces were or were not canonized. In all cases, I am striving to analyze what is taken for granted, the unspoken rules of art. Investigating a wide variety of texts and performances in search of these rules, I have chosen not to write a strictly chronological history in part because I am fascinated by the concurrence of events, the fact, for example, that John Alden Carpenter's jazz ballet, *Skyscrapers*, was a hit when performed at the Metropolitan Opera in 1926, while George Antheil's *Ballet mécanique*, performed a year later at Carnegie Hall, earned some of the most sneeringly contemptuous reviews I have ever read. Why? To answer this and many other questions, I have organized the chapters thematically. Each takes up a particular social and artistic struggle taking place during the 1920s and examines how this struggle played itself out and what its consequences and implications were for the shape of U.S. culture. Yet underlying all these brawls is the fight over the meaning of jazz.

In composing this book, I have strung chapters together as if I were assembling a vaudeville show or revue. A large cast of characters has emerged, with a handful of headliners and scores of bit players. Like a revue at the Palace Theatre, this book showcases a succession of colorful personalities who come from different worlds. They include playwrights Elmer Rice, John Howard Lawson, and Eugene O'Neill; composers George Gershwin, Eubie Blake, John Alden Carpenter, and George Antheil; and sociologists Robert S. Lynd, Helen Merrell Lynd, and C. Wright Mills. But the real stars of the show, somewhat improbably, are theater and music critics. Shining a spotlight on those who usually sit in darkness, I am arguing that a generation of immensely powerful critics born in the 1880s and 1890s worked to change the character of U.S. culture. The headliners include Gilbert Seldes, Walter Prichard Eaton, John Tasker Howard, and

George Jean Nathan. I want to emphasize that unlike these critics, I aim not to separate the admirable from the abominable. Rather, I am endeavoring to study how and why these men and women have been constructed—and in most cases, constructed themselves—as agents uniquely capable of explaining the shape of U.S. culture and discriminating between the real and bogus.

This book studies the first and arguably the most heated of the culture wars fought over music in the United States. For 1920s jazz inspired the intense adulation and furious attacks (on musical, racial, and moral grounds) that would find their echoes in the controversies over rock 'n' roll in the 1950s and hip-hop in the 1990s. During the Jazz Age, the musical culture wars played themselves out in a number of contests: between jazz and classical music, the legitimate theater and its illegitimate cousins, Jews and gentiles, African Americans and the blackface tradition, nationalist and international modernisms, the old and new middle classes, the champions and adversaries of the machine, avant-gardism and high modernism, and a theater inspired by jazz and one scornful of it. In determining the book's structure, I decided to move (albeit not in a straight line) from lowbrow to highbrow, from vaudeville, musical comedy, and other illegitimate forms of theater to unmistakably elitist attempts to construct highbrow jazz, ballet, and drama. The book begins with an examination of the contest over the meaning of jazz during the 1920s and moves on, in chapter 2, to a history of the terms *popular* and *legitimate* (as in *the legitimate theater*) and an analysis of the antagonism between the serious and lively arts. Chapter 3 focuses on George and Ira Gershwin's development of musical comedy in relation to debates over the racial and ethnic provenance of jazz, while chapter 4 studies how the influx of the so-called new middle class into the theater helped change its character. Chapter 5 examines expressionism, which many considered to be jazz theater par excellence, and its role in legitimizing the art theater; chapter 6, the centrality of jazz in fashioning a transatlantic cosmopolitanism and a highbrow music theater. Finally, chapter 7 studies the codependent relationship between Eugene O'Neill and his critics to expose how, in constructing a canon of American drama, they exercised symbolic violence against jazz, vaudeville, and melodrama.

To conclude this prologue, I want to return to the man whose spirit has presided over the composition of this book: Pierre Bourdieu. I would be hard pressed to name another social theorist whose work has been as groundbreaking, encyclopedic, and frankly challenging. Because he drew his methods from so many different disciplines, it is difficult to know how to characterize his approach. But one could do worse than to note that his work is centrally concerned with the claim that every field of culture—from philosophy and medicine to theatrical performance and gastronomy—is a site of struggle for power, for social distinction. In the United States, he is perhaps best known for his theory of the distribution of what he calls forms of capital. Employing the terminology of economics, he devised a theory to describe competencies in many different arenas. Economic capital refers to money and property, cultural capital to cultural knowledge and skill, symbolic capital to accumulated prestige and celebrity, social capital to acquaintances and social networks, and so on. And because these resources are everywhere unequally distributed, every society is structured by contests over forms of capital. Bourdieu's theory of capital is indispensable, I believe, for the demystification of what (except for religion) is probably the most mystified social domain: art. His best-known essay in this field, *Distinction*, an exhaustive ethnography of French society in the 1960s, maps the fields of culture by providing a painstakingly detailed analysis of the politics and economics of taste. I do not cite him as frequently as I do some other critics in part because his writing style is so notoriously difficult and his work so damnably specific. Because of this specificity, I cannot simply import his methods to analyze U.S. culture in the 1920s—or the 2000s, for that matter. I have, as a result, come to the conclusion that the way to be most true to Bourdieu is to be disloyal, to stray from his models and devise my own. This book, therefore, is an exercise in infidelity.

ONE

AMERICA'S MUSIC

What after all is this taking new thing [jazz], that, condemned in certain quarters, enthusiastically welcomed in others, has nonchalantly gone on until it ranks with the movie and the dollar as the foremost exponent of modern Americanism? Jazz isn't music merely, it is a spirit that can express itself in almost anything. The true spirit of jazz is a joyous revolt from convention, custom, authority, boredom, even sorrow—from everything that would confine the soul of man and hinder its riding free on the air.

—J. A. Rogers, "Jazz at Home" (1925)

During the 1920s, jazz was far more than a new musical style. For the makers, consumers, and arbiters of culture, jazz was everything. A weltanschauung, a personal identity, a metaphysics, an ethics, an eros, a mode of sociality—an entire way of being. Or rather, everything became filtered through a music that seemed more innovative, scandalous, and exhilarating than anything that had come before. Never had an artistic movement in the United States so galvanized—and exposed the cultural predispositions of—different classes and races. In a few short years, jazz became the symbol of a modernist revolt in a nation undergoing radical social and economic change. F. Scott Fitzgerald famously dubbed the 1920s the Jazz Age: "It was an age of miracles, it was an age of art, it was an age of excess, and it was an age of satire."[1] At its end, Isaac Goldberg, a musicologist and George Gershwin's first biographer, summed up the conflicting views of the emblem of the age:

> Jazz is all things to all ears. To the theological dogmatist it is a new guise of the ancient devil, to be fought as a satanic agency. To the pagan, if he is minded to interpret novelties in the language of social ethics, it is the symptom of a glorious release from the bonds of moral restraint. The musician, if he is one of the old school, looks upon it with mingled amusement and disgust; if he is of the modernist persuasion, he beholds in it rich possibilities of a new style.[2]

The impossibility of confining a discussion of jazz during the 1920s to musical particulars is highlighted by the sweeping social implications and associations of a new music whose name designated a vast array of musical styles. Any and every popular band (from Louis Armstrong's Hot Five to Paul Whiteman's Palais Royal Orchestra) or piece of music (from Bessie Smith's "Downhearted Blues" to Aaron Copland's *Music for the Theatre*) was at some time dubbed jazz. Whatever it was, jazz could not be defined, contained, or quarantined. It consistently muddled and challenged class-based, racial, and ethnic hierarchies—musical and otherwise—and quickly became a touchstone for a wide range of social and cultural issues. It was credited, moreover, by its supporters and detractors alike, with being the first distinctively American art form to disseminate American style and modernity across the globe, providing the commodity that, together with cinema, launched the United States as a cultural force to be reckoned with. Goldberg's discourse smartly dramatizes the easy slippage from the musical to the cultural to the moral to the racial that characterizes almost all discourse on the subject during the 1920s:

> Jazz was a fad that wouldn't last. Jazz was the salvation of the art. Jazz was the intrusion of the cheap dance-hall into the sacred precincts of the symphonic concert auditorium. Jazz wasn't so young as it pretended to be; it could be found in the classics, used to better advantage than it was used by the pounders and pluggers of Tin Pan Alley. Jazz came from the slums of music; it corrupted taste and manners. Jazz brought

to classical music a new, if vulgar, blood that would rejuvenate the art through this necessary alliance. Jazz was, literally and figuratively, a mésalliance, an example of miscegenation that worked to the detriment of the superior race [*sic*]. It was a subtle triumph of black over white.[3]

A revolutionary practice that threatened to overturn hierarchies of social class and racial identity, jazz was often likened to Bolshevism (e.g., by the *Ladies' Home Journal*!) in part because of its alleged link to the "protest[s] against law and order" associated with labor unions, the Great Red Scare, and the Palmer Raids (1919–21).[4] Because it doggedly resisted being confined to the musical field, it was habitually charged with either invigorating or demeaning (depending on one's point of view) virtually all the arts, from theater, poetry, and dance to those, like painting or sculpture, that seemed to have little or nothing to do with music. Given the extraordinary proliferation and range of theatrical activities during the 1920s, theater was arguably the most deeply impacted among music's sister arts. The most popular theatrical entertainments of the period, especially vaudeville and musical comedy, quickly cashed in on this new musical craze by using jazz as scoring or underscoring for songs, dances, and scenes. But even the so-called legitimate theater was not immune to the seductions of syncopated dance music, and jazz sometimes featured in more serious plays like Eugene O'Neill's *Diff'rent* (1920), J. Hartley Manners's *The National Anthem* (1922), George S. Kaufman and Marc Connelly's *Beggar on Horseback* (1924), Samson Raphaelson's *The Jazz Singer* (1925), and John Howard Lawson's *Processional* (1925). It thereby functioned as a benchmark, the sign of an impudent and seductive popular culture in relation to which playwrights carefully positioned their work, often by employing jazz as a divisive emblem of a new "Age of the Young" and constructing sympathetic or disagreeable characters who either loved or hated it.[5] But the impact of jazz went far beyond questions of characterization. For jazz—as style, emblem, inspiration, metaphor, and performance practice—represented a central point of reference and inspiration for a theater redefining itself during a period when the disposition of the entire field of cultural production in the United States was up for grabs. For playwrights and critics intent on legitimizing theater as an elite cultural practice, it was the source of tremendous anxiety and was, in fact, decisive in separating the newly emerging literary theater from its illegitimate cousins.

The relationship between jazz and theater is based on far more than jazz's function as musical scoring for, or as a topic of discussion within, a play, musical, or revue. The popular theater's rapid appropriation and absorption of jazz points to the overlap in conventions and performance practices between theater and jazz during the 1920s. Most obviously, both live jazz and live theater flooded the senses. During Prohibition, jazz cabarets and nightclubs would often stage elaborate floor shows to entertain patrons (who could participate as social dancers). As William Howland Kenney notes, these speakeasies provided a highly theatrical setting in which "new styles of personal liberation—clothes, insiders' slang, cigarettes, bootleg gin, marijuana (called 'gage'), sexual expressiveness, and interracial mingling" functioned "to add drama to the new music." Particularly in Chicago, Kenney reports, cabaret floor shows "put musicians on display and focused increased attention on visual dimensions of musical performance." In fact, the strategy adopted most often by saloons in an attempt to camouflage the illicit sale of alcohol was to "upgrade the entertainment into a small vaudevill [sic] show." Using jazz as a front for illegal activities, these cabarets often featured chorus lines of dancers as well as nonmusical performers, including actors and comedians, and so represented "an adaptation"—and extension—"of vaudeville comedy to the night club."[6]

As these descriptions of nightclub entertainments suggest, jazz was much more closely aligned during the 1920s with popular theater forms than with literary dramas and comedies. Like vaudeville and musical comedy, in which it was regularly featured, jazz is a partly improvisatory practice that happens in the space between performer and spectator. A jazz solo, a song, or a piece of shtick is a virtuoso turn whose effectiveness is dependent upon the skill and inspiration of the performer, who, if the chemistry is right, will be encouraged and egged on by the audience's spontaneous and often raucous participation.[7] During the 1920s, jazz, vaudeville, and musical comedy were performance practices that, Pierre Bourdieu notes, satisfied "a deep-rooted demand" of "the popular audience . . . for participation" that the formal experimentation of the art theater "systematically disappoint[ed]."[8] In vaudeville proper, orchestras routinely theatricalized jazz performance and undermined the distinction between music and theater by surrounding "the orchestra with expensive cycloramas and sets" and incorporating "in the act a song story, scenic exploitation, costume bit, singing numbers, dances, or other unusual features to put the act across."[9] Patently commercial forms, jazz and popular theater capitalized on innovation during a new Machine Age that witnessed the triumph of the assembly line in the workplace and the introduction in both the home and office of countless new inventions and consumer goods. Audiences no more wanted to hear a clichéd trumpet solo than watch a tired vaudeville routine. Musical comedies and revues would prove their modernity (a much prized characteristic for popular entertainments during the 1920s) by being as up-to-date as possible. Why croon a Victor Herbert song when you could just as easily syncopate a new ditty by Eubie Blake or George Gershwin?

Throughout the 1920s, jazz, the exemplary urban art form, was regularly described as being centered in the theater district, as the common turn of phrase, "the jazz-mongers of Broadway," suggests.[10] And Broadway, with its glittering, seductive, and often tawdry novelties, became a metonym for and emblem of jazz. Both were imagined as being the "expression of the times, of the breathless, energetic, super-active times in which we are living."[11] As an indignant guardian of high culture tartly put it, "If New York City, or rather a segment situated on Broadway is America, then jazz does represent the American soul."[12] Given its many manifestations, guises, contexts, and performance venues, jazz thus represented the most significant form of cross-mediated performance in the 1920s: a form that undermined the autonomy of dance and concert music, cabaret, social dancing, vaudeville, revue, and narrative theater. It was, in short, less a discrete style than a musical and social energy linking all these performance practices.

Although the legitimate theater eschewed improvisation and disdained shamelessly crowd-pleasing works, experimental, left-wing plays like *Processional* (subtitled *A Jazz Symphony of American Life in Four Acts*) used jazz as a metaphor or inspiration for innovations in both dramatic form and content. In *Processional*, Lawson explicitly attempted to mimic, that is, find a theatrical analogy for, the form, spontaneity, and unruliness of jazz. By turning jazz into drama, Lawson claimed "to reflect . . . the color and movement of the American processional as it streams about us," the processional whose "rhythm is staccato, burlesque, [and] carried out by a formalized arrangement of jazz music."[13] Although Lawson presents jazz as being both emancipatory and violent, *Processional* divided critics and perplexed audiences, running for only ninety-six performances despite the imprimatur of the prestigious Theatre Guild, America's foremost art theater. With its use of a live jazz band; appropriation of stereotypes derived from

Act 1 of the Theatre Guild's 1925 production of John Howard Lawson's *Processional: A Jazz Symphony of American Life*. Sadie Cohen (June Walker) blows the trombone while the members of the jazz band, most of them in blackface, look on. Scene and costume design by Mordecai Gorelik.

Credit: *Billy Rose Theatre Division, The New York Public Library for the Performing Arts, Astor, Lenox and Tilden Foundations*

vaudeville, burlesque, and minstrel shows; repeated rupture of the fourth wall; embrace of avant-gardist techniques; and left-wing politics, *Processional* proved the most controversial play of the 1920s, a "revolutionary prank," as Brooks Atkinson later described it, that was "the prototype of the left-wing political plays that flourished in the next decade."[14]

Even critics who were positively disposed to *Processional* did not know quite what to make of it. Heywood Broun, who in his review called it "one of the finest things which has yet come out of this native theatre," noted warily that the "scratch paper of a great American play was thrown last night in the face of an astonished audience."[15] One critic judged it "so novel in its outlook, so startling in its development, so daring in its conception, so desperate in its irony, that it must be seen more than once to be comprehended."[16] The many critics who disliked the play, like the notoriously conservative Alan Dale, made no attempt to disguise their contempt for what he called the "oleaginous conserve of tommyrot entitled 'Processional'" and the "consummate hypocrisy" of the Guild for "pretending that this ludicrous and incoherent inanity had some deep significance."[17] Not content with merely censuring the play, Percy Hammond personified it as a madman, "suffer[ing] from convulsions" and "writh[ing] all over the stage."[18] H. Z. Torres called *Processional* "chaotic," "puerile," devoid of "life" and "joy," and "un-American." It is composed, he noted, of "dull[,] drab and generally meaningless episodes, whose keynote is ugliness and depression."[19] Even the usually temperate Burns Mantle judged it "the weirdest jumble," all "satire and muttered ravings," "rough and primitive."[20] It is clear from surveying these reviews that the critics were in part responding to (and in some cases, seconding) what must have been a decidedly negative response from the opening night audience. Reviews repeatedly noted that the spectators sat "in stony silence" or "in glum affront at the temerity" of the playwright.[21] Even Broun admitted that he had "seldom seen first-nighters more mystified and annoyed."[22] With its "wild and discordant" performance, *Processional* quickly became a succès de scandale, "the play," the *Minneapolis Journal* reported, that "all America loved to argue about."[23] A public forum sponsored by the Theatre Guild attracted a standing room only crowd, some eminent defenders of the play (including Elmer Rice, Fanny Hurst, and Dorothy Parker), and "violent speeches from the balcony."[24]

It is clear from these testimonials that Lawson had hit a nerve, that his act of viewing "the American scene in the spasms of syncopation" had, if nothing else, roiled the high-status public that patronized the Theatre Guild.[25] *Processional* also clearly revealed what was arguably the decisive fault line in 1920s theater—between a jazz-loving, populist avant-garde and those who sought to institutionalize an elite, literary modernism. As Burns Mantle observed, it prompted a debate between "the more excitable" progressives who declared "it represented a gorgeous new form in the theatre" and "the more conservative" litterateurs who insisted its promiscuous mixture of high and low made for a "formless and incoherent entertainment" that was "repellent in its ugliness."[26]

For artists and critics less committed than Lawson to innovation and political radicalism, both jazzed theater and theatricalized jazz remained an even more controversial and troubling cultural performance. This was especially true for a legitimate stage attempting to survive the insurgence of a lowbrow art form (cinema), separate itself decisively from a jazzed-up vaudeville, absorb and Americanize the vital European modernism of Ibsen and Strindberg, boost its prestige in relation to its many illegitimate cousins, and, in Oliver Sayler's words, strive "seriously to become an art rather than a pleasant pastime."[27] Playwrights in pursuit of cultural and symbolic capital dismissed jazz as a low-class, immoral, mass-produced form. For example, Arthur Hornblow, the editor of *Theatre* (the most widely read magazine in the field), was a vociferous opponent of jazz, pronouncing it "stupidity, license," and "madness," a "devil's hell broth" that the crassly commercial, popular theater dished up to the "lecherous, amusement-thirsty mob."[28] For him and many others, it thereby served as the practice on which an emergent, would-be highbrow, literary theater looked with horror in part because it was providing the substance and style for vaudeville and musical comedy. As figured in both esoteric and exoteric plays, jazz provided the fulcrum that divided a heroic, universalizing modernism from its popular, mongrelized other. The action of *Beggar on Horseback*, for example, centers on the opposition between the cheap, silly "jazz tune[s]" of "damned cabaret orchestra[s]" and the inspired "highbrow music" composed by legitimate artists, like the play's protagonist, who must support himself by stooping to writing jazz.[29]

The best-known and most popular play of the era to tackle the subject, *The Jazz Singer* (which racked up 303 performances on Broadway before being made into the first talkie), adopts a more ambivalent attitude toward jazz than *Beggar on Horseback*. Portraying syncopated dance music as the "symbol of the vital chaos of America's soul," New York City–born playwright Samson Raphaelson describes jazz less as the devil's music than as a perverted musical practice, a "prayer" that modernity has rendered "distorted" and "sick." Because it represents the debris of elite, consecrated, European culture (with its "cathedrals and temples"), it can be celebrated only by "lost soul[s], dancing grotesquely on the ruins."[30] The play itself, however, with its decidedly ambivalent attitude toward assimilation, constructs jazz—and blackface performance—as the primary ingredient for the Americanization of Jack Robinson (né Jakie Rabinowitz). It is the sirens' song that makes him forsake his cultural and religious heritage ("I want to be part of America") in favor of Broadway glamour and an alluring shikse who happens to be "a big star in musical comedy."[31] Although Raphaelson adopts a patronizing attitude toward the musical revue being rehearsed in act 2, the force of the play depends on an identification between Jewish cantorial chant and Jack's rendition of "Dixie Mammy" (with its shameless plantation nostalgia). The latter, the stage directions protest, is "excellent jazz" that "has an evangelical fervor, a fanatical frenzy; it wallows in plaintiveness and has moments of staggering dramatic intensity, despite the obvious shoddiness of the words and the music." If Jack prevails, it is only because he has become "a Cantor in blackface" who has "intensified" but "cheapened his "religion . . . by the trappings of Broadway."[32] Raphaelson may stop short of vilifying jazz, but his presentation makes it clear that "Dixie Mammy" represents a bad copy: jazz can only degrade the sacred music it mimics.

The National Anthem, on the other hand, damns jazz utterly along with all those unfortunate souls who have come under its sway. The British-born Manners (who was then fifty-two years old) pillories youth culture, constructing jazz as the sign of decadence, moral turpitude, standardization, hypocrisy, and cultural miscegenation. The devil's music, it supplies the dreaded pretext for "bodies [to] writhe and intermingle and brains [to] rattle in skulls."[33] Even the stage directions drip with sarcastic contempt: "The beat of the tom-toms, the blowing of whistles, the mocking of the laughing-horn—all unite in a paean of glorification of modern joyousness."[34] The play's action centers on Arthur, a young, wealthy, charming, reckless, alcoholic, jazz-loving swell, who elopes with a wholesome, "breezy, fascinating, spoilt young lady," Marian, naive enough to believe that she can reform him after marriage. Predictably, the reverse happens and the play becomes increasingly melodramatic after the couple removes to Paris, where alcohol flows like water, and Marian, too, becomes a miserable drunk. This cautionary tale ends with Arthur's death in an automobile crash and Marian's slow recovery from alcoholism and an accidentally administered dose of poison. Because she is the corrupted innocent, the playwright allows her to live.

The National Anthem garnered strong reviews, enjoyed a healthy run of 114 performances, and became something of a cause célèbre.[35] In the New York Times, Alexander Woollcott described it as "an acrid sermon in four acts" but went on to praise it as "a good play, vigorous, direct, dramatic and interesting all the way through" and especially lauded the "superb performance by a great actress," Laurette Taylor (who would later create the role of Amanda in The Glass Menagerie [1944]).[36] Burns Mantle, too, thought it a "good play," if "over-preachy in its moral propaganda" and noted that it was a runner-up to what he reckoned the ten best plays of the season.[37] None of the critics, however, mentioned the intriguing way that the play

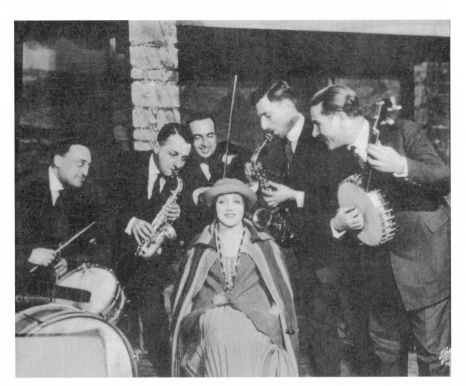

J. Hartley Manners's *The National Anthem*. Marian (Laurette Taylor) with the boys in the band.

Credit: Billy Rose Theatre Division, The New York Public Library for the Performing Arts, Astor, Lenox and Tilden Foundations

uses the gratuitous presence of a "serious" and "respectable" actress, Madeleine, Marian's friend, to critique both the popular theater and theatrical culture. Madeleine enables Manners to distinguish between the "theatre that matters," the "real theatre" (that, presumably, produces plays like *The National Anthem*), from jazz theater, the one with "brassy music, nudity, common jokes and the laughter of fools." If that were not enough, Manners also supplies the dissolute Arthur with a jazz-loving, degenerate friend who shuns "the theatre" in favor of "musical comedy and revue" and the company of the loose women who populate the musical theater, "the 'non-commissioned ladies of the stage.'"[38]

The emergent literary theater of the 1920s was of course dominated by Eugene O'Neill, who was repeatedly singled out as the inheritor of the mantle of Shakespeare, Sheridan, Ibsen, and Shaw and the chief native architect of what the critic Walter Prichard Eaton called "the true theatre, the true spoken drama."[39] O'Neill, more than any other playwright, succeeding in consecrating American drama and establishing "America's kinship," in the words of one of his earliest critics, "with the stage of the modern world."[40] But tellingly, despite being judged a "progressive," O'Neill nearly eschewed jazz in his work, in part because so many of his plays (not by accident) take place before 1920 or are set in locales into which jazz has not yet penetrated.[41] Even *All God's Chillun Got Wings* (1924) opts for spirituals and turn-of-the-century Tin Pan Alley songs rather than jazz. One of his two plays of the decade even to reference jazz, *Diff'rent* heaps ridicule on it on account of its association with one of O'Neill's most "revoltingly incongruous" and deceitful women characters whose pathological and perverted desires it epitomizes.[42]

Although playwrights who aspired to realize what Oliver Sayler called the American theater's "rich . . . potentialities for becoming an art theatre" undoubtedly represented a diverse lot, they seem to have tacitly agreed that despite jazz's distinctively American character, a music that issued from African Americans and the working classes was antithetical to a theater that increasingly catered to what was repeatedly dubbed the "intelligent minority."[43] And the more conservative arbiters of culture applauded the legitimate theater's studied dissociation from jazz. One critic stamped jazz "musical rowdy" and maintained that it "occupies the same relation to the art of music that 'burlesque' (on the stage) does to the 'legitimate drama.'"[44] Another expressed great relief that O'Neill was pursuing a heroic "dream" of an imperial America personified by a powerful "young conqueror" striding across the globe rather than a jazz-loving, "strapping swaggerer . . . doing the 'Charleston.'"[45]

SOME DEFINITIONS

Despite the difficulty of defining jazz, one cannot begin to investigate the relationship between the media called theater and jazz without analyzing the latter's contested meanings and genealogies. Max Harrison, the writer of the entry on jazz in the *New Grove Dictionary of Music and Musicians*, throws up his hands at the very beginning of his essay: "Attempts at a concise—even a coherent—definition of jazz have invariably failed."[46] Indeed, most writers on the subject could explain their positions by paraphrasing

Justice Potter Stewart's description of pornography: I don't know how to define it but I know it when I hear it. Even during the Jazz Age, jazz denoted many different kinds of music, including some that now seem quite unrelated to what has been classified as jazz since the 1950s. As Nicholas Evans points out, "from World War I into the 1920s, the lines separating what we now call jazz, ragtime, Tin Pan Alley, vaudeville music, and other relevant forms were quite unclear. . . . The emergence of 'jazz,' as such, was a messy, uneven, discontinuous process that *itself* was unclear—then, if not also now."[47]

If one nevertheless chooses to categorize the popular music of the 1920s, one could do worse than to begin with Charles Hamm's claim that there were three bodies of music called jazz. The first kind—and the only one considered jazz by virtually all post–World War II writers on jazz but rarely heard by the vast majority of white Americans during the 1920s—is "jazz (and blues) performed by black musicians for black audiences." Recordings of this music, sometimes called hot jazz, were "marketed as 'race records' by small independent record companies beginning in 1920," sold in black record stores, and enjoyed little mass distribution. (These are the salacious artifacts that Fitzgerald compares to forbidden spirits by describing them as "bootleg negro records with their phallic euphemisms.")[48] The artists in this group are the ones routinely cited as the first great jazz artists: King Oliver, Jelly Roll Morton, Bessie Smith, Louis Armstrong, and many others. The second type, which became prominent in the second half of the decade, is "jazz (and blues) performed by black musicians" like Cab Calloway and Duke Ellington for white audiences at the Cotton Club and other Harlem and South Side Chicago speakeasies. The third type, and the one that enjoyed widest distribution on recordings and the radio and signified jazz for almost all white Americans and Europeans, Hamm describes as "so-called jazz performed by white musicians for white audiences." This latter category, sometimes called sweet jazz, was the subject of "virtually all writing on 'jazz'" during the 1920s and early 1930s, despite the fact that, in the words of one contemporaneous critic, "the 'sweet' technique" is "hardly connected with true jazz save by its employment of saxophones and banjoes."[49] Irving Berlin, Jerome Kern, and George Gershwin numbered among the leading composers of sweet jazz for Tin Pan Alley and Broadway, while Paul Whiteman, who "made sweet jazz the Established Order," was the best-known among the band leaders, who included Vincent Lopez, Ted Lewis, and Ben Selvin.[50] For the vast majority of white Americans, the aptly surnamed Mr. Whiteman was indeed the (self-crowned) King of Jazz.

Although there is historical justification for Hamm's mode of categorization—which correctly points out the massive shift in the definition of jazz between the 1920s and 1950s—it tends to oversimplify a convoluted and racially fraught history. Indeed, jazz, and all that has been labeled jazz, remains one of the most heavily contested subjects among musicologists. As John Gennari emphasizes, "Jazz has never been just music—it's been a cornerstone of the modern cultural imagination, an archive of mythological images, and an aesthetic model for new modes of writing, seeing, and moving."[51] While minstrelsy has proven the most embarrassing (and in the main, repressed) cultural remnant of chattel slavery, jazz has been regarded almost universally as being rooted "in the black social experience and in African-American aesthetics."[52] It is accordingly the musical genre that most clearly represents resistance to (and triumph over) racial oppression. The racially charged nature of these histories—and the enormity of the cultural stakes—have ensured that race, as Evans points out, has tended from the 1920s to the present "to be the lightning rod for the most emotionally and ideologically charged arguments."[53] It has been decisive in distinguishing those historians (including Amiri Baraka, Stanley Crouch, Albert Murray, and Wynton Marsalis) who view jazz as essentially black from those (including Gene Lees, Richard Sudhalter, James Lincoln Collier, and William Howland Kenney) who argue that it is essentially hybridized and multiracial. Yet, as Evans argues, even those historians, like Sudhalter, who proselytize for the multiracial character of jazz end up falling back upon essentialized racial categories and emphasize "white and black cultures' separateness."[54] Purity in music may be "a myth," Ted Gioia cautions, but it is an extraordinarily resilient one.[55]

Despite their best intentions, many jazz critics inadvertently construct black and white as monolithic categories and in doing so, erase differences in social class, education, and region and marshal stereotypical characterizations of black music (which is coded as natural, highly rhythmic, and loosely constructed) as opposed to white music (which is supposedly more scrupulously organized both melodically and harmonically).[56] Musicologists also tend to apply different terms of analysis depending on their predisposition. Those who emphasize African roots tend to privilege rhythmic complexities (including those related to African dance forms), timbral idiosyncrasies and distortions, microtonal inflections, antiphonal structures, and "jazz's function as a form of communal bonding, ritual, and social interaction, . . . a way of living in the world."[57] Those who emphasize European genealogies tend to focus on more formal questions: harmonic structure, melodic shape, modal and pentatonic scales, instrumentation, and the adaptation of European dance forms.[58]

As useful as Hamm's typology is, he too categorizes jazz far too neatly and inflexibly because his system of classification is also defined in racial terms. The music business (like Broadway) was indeed segregated during the 1920s, but Hamm's classificatory scheme presupposes a large degree of racial homogenization. It erases differences between white ethnicities (Jews were not always considered a part of the so-called white race) and denies the fact that African Americans were even then considered to have a syncretic identity (by W. E. B. Du Bois and others). It also ignores class differences. As Kenney notes, black religious leaders in Chicago "and old time South Siders with . . . Victorian attitudes . . . disapproved of dance halls, cabarets, ragtime, jazz, [and] leisure time license."[59] Langston Hughes criticized the antipathy to jazz on the part of "self-styled 'high-class' Negro[es]," a position seconded by Gioia, who emphasizes that those portions of the black middle and upper classes committed to the project of racial uplift were "at best, ambivalent about embracing vernacular elements of African American culture—and often explicitly hostile."[60] Most important, any racially oriented theory of jazz must imagine a kind of pure, original jazz that is an essential product and expression of African (American) bodies. As William H. Youngren explains, ever since "jazz began to be taken seriously, the conviction that it . . . has been tainted or deformed" by European American culture has "sent critics and historians off on a quest for the unadulterated archetype: absolutely pure black (which usually means New Orleans) jazz."[61] And if not New Orleans, then Chicago or San Francisco or even Africa was singled out as the birthplace, especially by writers in the 1920s. Cesar Saerchinger, for example, writing in 1926, traced jazz back to "the lovely new barbaric dances" of "the dives of San Francisco" in which "the music was furnished by Negroes."[62] Another writer indulged a lurid fantasy (reminiscent of O'Neill's exactly contemporaneous play, *The Emperor Jones* [1920]) while listening to jazz: "there surges up before the inner eye, a tropical African glade at night, the queer trees all lit from below . . . , a circle of cannibal forms, [and] a great black pot."[63] But even the king of (sweet) jazz, Paul Whiteman, begins his history cum memoir titled simply *Jazz* by claiming it "came to America three hundred years ago in chains."[64] Isaac Goldberg, meanwhile, constructs a progress narrative that describes the form's evolution from its beginnings "in darkest Africa as a rhythm" to its end "in lightest America as an abandoned counterpoint."[65]

In the post–World War II era, James Lincoln Collier, Gunther Schuller, and Frank Tirro argue more coherently (if less vividly) than Whiteman and Goldberg that jazz has its roots in traditional African music, in slave songs, spirituals, and ragtime.[66] The focus on this racialized genealogy has been in part a result of the success of the civil rights movement in redefining and reclaiming what is arguably the most important and influential art form to have been developed centrally by African Americans. This reclamation was clearly linked to the development of black cultural nationalism and Afrocentrism in the 1960s. As Gennari emphasizes, jazz has been and remains "for African American musicians and audiences, a hugely important form of historical memory."[67] Although some writers in the 1940s identified jazz as uniquely black music, *Blues People: Negro Music in White America* (1963) by Amiri Baraka (then LeRoi Jones) was the first book to maintain that jazz is in essence the music of black Americans.[68] To back up his claim, Baraka makes the much-contested assertion that the blues is "the parent of all legitimate jazz" and "the product of the black man in this country," that is, of the "African captives" who became "American captives."[69] Because, in Gerard's words, "the black nationalist jazz-as-black-music perspective dominated jazz criticism for years," Baraka was followed and seconded by many of the most celebrated writers on jazz.[70] Scott De Veaux, for example, notes that jazz is "strongly identified with African-American culture, both in the narrow sense that its particular techniques ultimately derive from black American folk traditions, and in the broader sense that it is expressive of, and uniquely rooted in, the experience of black Americans."[71] In his magisterial history of early jazz, Gunther Schuller argues that "*every* musical element—rhythm, harmony, melody, timbre, and the basic forms of jazz—is essentially African in background and derivation."[72]

But no musical form, especially one developed over decades by different social groups in different locales, could possibly be unencumbered by outside influences. All music, like every form of cultural production, is syncretic. There is no such thing as cultural purity. African American traditions may represent the sine qua non of jazz, but various European American traditions, most of them ethnically particularized, from Irish clog dancing and minstrelsy to klezmer, also played a role in the development of what would be called jazz. As Youngren emphasizes, "the men who actually created jazz were not only surrounded from birth, as listeners, by Western tonal music; they also made their living by playing it."[73] Indeed, Sudhalter's list of antecedents and influences, to which most jazz scholars subscribe, includes the blues, "ragtime, Tin Pan Alley, late 19th-century European concert and dance music, grand opera, minstrel and vaudeville traditions of both [sic] races, the white folk music of Appalachia and, perhaps most of all, the concert bands so ubiquitous in turn-of-the-century America."[74] Even in its early years just after World War I, the music called jazz was a profoundly hybrid art, played by black, brown, beige, and white musicians.[75] With regard to its emergence in New Orleans, Gioia notes that "jazz remained primarily an African-American contribution to the city's—and, eventually, the nation's—culture; but like all such contributions, once given, it no longer remained an exclusive province of the giver."[76] Indeed, what is usually considered the first jazz recording, "Livery Stable Blues" (1917), is in fact the product of New Orleans' all-white Original Dixieland Jazz Band. And despite segregation, musicians and audiences of different races often intermingled at urban performances in the early years of jazz. Among musicians, especially in New Orleans and Chicago (the northern city to which southern jazz musicians first migrated), "there was a lot more mixing of the races," Willy "The Lion" Smith recollected, than in New York.[77] Yet just as virtually all the writings on jazz from the 1920s exclude African American musicians, so most postwar histories omit or mention only in passing the most celebrated white musicians of the 1920s who personified jazz for so many Americans and Europeans (Whiteman, Gershwin, Lewis, and many others). In other words, most discourses on jazz from the 1920s to the 1970s tend to emphasize racial categories. The earliest marginalize and demean African American music by constructing it, as Whiteman does, as "raucous," "crude," and "unmusical"—"a low noise in a low dive."[78] Later writers associated with black cultural nationalism, however, celebrate an African (American) musical essence that separates the real thing from its European American simulations.[79]

During the 1920s the universe of jazz—and of the many varieties of music that passed for jazz—in the United States was immense. (Despite the terminological problems, I will use the word *jazz* in the remainder of this book to designate all the music that was then called jazz.) Although African American musicians and composers unquestionably led the way, it is sometimes difficult to distinguish formally among the different kinds of jazz according to racial provenance. (A moderately well-informed aficionado of early jazz would find it difficult at times to discriminate between recordings of white and black jazz from the 1920s and early 1930s unless he or she knew the particular recording.) The jazz craze is usually dated back to the release of "Livery Stable Blues," which caused an international sensation. As Paul Lopes notes, the Original Dixieland Jazz Band's "particular style of jazz music which incorporated a heavy use of 'novelty' sounds, . . . in addition to the collective improvisation and syncopated rhythm common to black New Orleans musicians, caught on among white popular musicians and audiences."[80] The immediate and widespread popularization of jazz was in part an effect of the Great Migration that brought half a million African Americans from the South to the northern cities between 1916 and 1919.[81] This massive relocation, which continued through the 1920s, brought many southern black musicians in contact with professionalized northern black artists. (Black migration and cultural achievement, as well as a swell of Jewish and Catholic immigration from eastern and southern Europe, also spurred a terrible resurgence of the Ku Klux Klan.[82] By some estimates, there were three to six million Klansmen by 1923.)[83] It also coincided with and spurred on a post–World War I economic expansion, the growth of the black entertainment industry, an unprecedented popular dance boom, and the increasing mechanization of musical entertainments. For jazz was the first new musical genre to be widely disseminated by the phonograph (between 1914 and 1921 the sale of records increased from about 27 million to 100 million per year).[84] Black musicians like James Reese Europe, Eubie Blake, James P. Johnson, and Will Marion Cook quickly developed, transformed, and disseminated the new jazz styles.

Despite the impossibility of defining jazz with any precision, the range of music that was called jazz during the 1920s employs a number of distinctive devices that distinguish it from ragtime, coon songs, and the waltz-based songs (in triple time) that dominated Tin Pan Alley at the turn of the twentieth century.[85] First, 1920s jazz was as a rule performed in duple or quadruple time and at a faster tempo than waltz songs or ragtime. Second, jazz bands usually featured not strings (except in symphonic jazz) but brass and woodwinds, mainly cornet, trumpet, clarinet, saxophone, and sometimes a vocalist, as well as a vigorous rhythm section comprised of drums and other percussion (including the piano, which, as with ragtime, also provided harmonic anchoring). Third, jazz tends to spotlight syncopated rhythms in both melody and harmonic accompaniment which gave them a playfulness songs in 3/4 time lacked. Fourth, although usually performed in major keys, 1920s jazz often attenuated and undermined the major mode through the use of so-called blue notes, most commonly flatted thirds and sevenths. In the blues, a blue note was usually produced by bending the pitch; in so-called sweet jazz, it was as a rule played on the pitch. The use of blue notes has the effect of evoking the parallel minor, and some of the music that was called jazz in fact seems to alternate between major and minor modes more freely and impulsively than early Tin Pan Alley songs.

These harmonic complexities, combined with syncopated rhythms, lively counterpoint, and unexpected modulations, was especially important in giving jazz a richer emotional palette than earlier popular song and linking it to—and inspiring—countless modernist experiments by American and European composers of art music, from John Alden Carpenter and George Antheil to Maurice Ravel and Igor Stravinsky.[86] Gennari emphasizes the impeccable modernist credentials of early jazz, arguing that it is analogous to cubist painting because it "conveyed both the fragmentation and the wholeness of time and sound" through its use of "shifting rhythms, sliding harmonies, and instrumental juxtapositions."[87] When applied to Broadway songs, these various musical devices allowed for a mischievousness and irony that waltzes and ragtime usually shunned. They enabled composers and lyricists, like George and Ira Gershwin, to build more complex and supple musical-dramatic structures by exploiting provocative contrasts between music and lyrics as well as among different parts of songs. The music that Gershwin wrote may not have been considered jazz by postwar writers, but it multiplied exponentially the dramatic possibilities of the popular song and allowed the latter to develop as a popular analogue to the operatic aria or scena.

White writers on jazz during the 1920s almost invariably imagined what Baraka and others call real jazz to be a vigorous, untamed, natural music: "the antics of uncultured Negroes" with their "endless, senseless improvisations" and "'ad lib' playing."[88] For the black jazz musician was cast, as Gerald Early notes, as "a magical primitive, . . . making music without a score, producing art without a text, based entirely on the inspiration of the moment."[89] And while the construction of instrumental jazz as primal and brutish, as "merely crude 'nigger stuff,'" is a predictable move on the part of cultural conservatives, modernists and other defenders of jazz also argued for its primitive vitality.[90] Unwilling to challenge the assumption that nature and culture are utterly opposed (and that culture is superior), modernists like Picasso and Stravinsky inverted the terms in order to valorize the primeval essence that supposedly lay concealed in humankind's savage soul and the modern unconscious. Thus Gilbert Seldes, for example, the writer of a groundbreaking defense of the indigenous cultural practices he called the "lively" arts (and one of the most articulate white advocates for jazz), insisted that "the negro side" of jazz "expresses something which underlies a great deal of America—our independence, our carelessness, our frankness, and gaiety." Constructing "the negro" as passionately intense, he praised the "instinctive qualities" that come from being "a little more simple and savage than we [sic] are." But above all, Seldes, like most all of the early advocates of jazz, used racially marked discourse to champion a miscegenated art in which "an uncorrupted sensibility is *worked* by a creative intelligence."[91] The composer Percy Grainger also extolled a cosmopolitan jazz whose "excellence rests on its combination of Nordic melodiousness with Negro tribal, rhythmic polyphony."[92] John Tasker Howard, a composer and writer of one of the more sympathetic contemporary assessments of jazz coming from the world of classical music, noted that "the Negroid manner has permeated our music" and argued that "the Negro's [songs] . . . all show some phase of the undeveloped black man's childlike temperament." Although he recognized jazz to be "probably the most American thing we have yet produced," he noted that "the earliest known jazz bands" played "pretty crude stuff" that required the intervention of "skilled arrangers" like Ted Lewis and Paul Whiteman.[93]

In contrast, most postwar jazz historians—at least until the 1990s—either ignored Whiteman or else displayed as much discomfort with his jazz as Seldes, Grainger, and Howard did with the "savage" and "senseless" music of black Americans. Although once considered the most important and influential jazz musician, Whiteman is referenced in the *New Grove* entry on jazz only in passing. Tirro disregards him except to note that his band provided a springboard for several giants of early jazz, including Bix Beiderbecke and Frank Trumbauer. Gennari points out that Whiteman's symphonic jazz, "leavened by the 'sweet' sound of violins, carefully concealed its indebtedness to African American folk sources behind a façade of middle-class white respectability."[94] Finally, Gunther Schuller, hedging his bets, may have come up with one of the more accurate assessments by claiming in a footnote that Whiteman's music, except for fleeting moments, was something quite other than jazz: it "was not jazz, of course—or perhaps only intermittently so."[95]

The relationship between African American and European American traditions in the development of early jazz remains problematic in part because neither tradition is monolithic and because so many different musical styles converged to make jazz, styles (like ragtime, coon songs, and military marches) that are themselves the product of complex, multiracial evolutionary processes. And while there is no question that African American musicians and traditions were decisive for the invention of jazz, European American musicians and composers—especially Jews—were repeatedly cited, by both those attacking jazz and those extolling it, as the ones primarily responsible for its popular and commercial success with white audiences. These genealogical questions, I would argue, are closely linked to and influenced by two factors: the laws governing intellectual property and the economics of the music business. One cannot begin to evaluate the provenance of jazz without considering the legal differences in the 1920s between sheet music, which could be copyrighted, and performances, recordings, and styles, which could not. As Jane M. Gaines points out, "copyright in musical composition was based on the analogy with literary property . . . it was . . . presumed that music was a 'writing,' a 'work of authorship' that had its form in either a notational system or a performance. While one could 'author' a musical composition, one could not 'author' a mechanical reproduction of sound."[96] In other words, copyright law in the 1920s privileged writing over sound, the ostensibly permanent over the ephemeral. The Copyright Act of 1909 gave composers, lyricists, and playwrights ownership of "musical" and "dramatic or dramatico-musical compositions" as printed texts.[97] But not until 1972 were musicians granted copyright protection over their recorded performances. (As the *New Grove* points out, writing and performance were even then constructed in opposition to each other since "the copyright in sound recordings applies only to the actual sounds contained in them as distinct from the underlying musical compositions.")[98] Gramophones remained something of a curiosity during the first two decades of the twentieth century and less important than the parlor piano for the dissemination of popular song. But beginning in 1920, sheet music suddenly soared in price "following a 50% increase in production costs as a result of a printers' strike and a concurrent paper shortage." Almost overnight, Russell Sanjek notes, "the American public turned from sheet-songs to phonograph records."[99] During this period, however, records were granted a more precarious legal status than "other mechanically and electronically produced objects of culture."[100] And the phonographs on which they were played were not deemed writing machines because they "produced aural copies of writings, they performed, and they did so until the copyright code was revised again" in 1972 and extended to sound recordings. Because mechanical means of sound reproduction during the 1920s were considered not "talking machines" but "reading machines," reading, for the first time, was "severed from the human subject."[101] Phonographs produced not writings that could be copyrighted but merely disembodied readings, "unfixed, transitory 'performances.'"[102]

Because the Copyright Act of 1909 systematically devalued live and recorded performance in favor of written texts, the latter alone were considered of economic and cultural value, being the supposed transcription of the "intellectual creation which first exists in the mind of the composer."[103] This devaluation is especially challenging for jazz musicians (and jazz historians) because of the long-established preeminence in jazz of live performance. Indeed, in most forms of jazz (from the 1920s to the present) the so-called chart from which musicians play is usually more of a cue sheet (providing crucial harmonic and melodic changes) than a fully written out score. The many prejudicial judgments against jazz from the 1920s must be seen in light of a long intellectual tradition, reflected in copyright laws, that produces live performance as supplementary, contingent, and ultimately frivolous and that constructs the performer as a mere servant, a manual laborer, a feminine conduit in relation to the masculine creative genius who supposedly creates ex nihilo and whose melodies are legally protected. The legal depreciation of both recording and performance coupled with the necessary ephemerality of live music can thus be said to have defrauded musicians (including many, many African Americans) of their proprietary rights, which were transferred to composers, publishers, and distributors. As Isaac Goldberg candidly explains: "Jazz is essentially an American development of Afro-American thematic material. Its fundamental rhythm and its characteristic melody derive from the Negro; its commercialization belongs largely to the popular-song industry of the New York white."[104] The construction of European Americans (especially Jews) rather than African Americans as the real geniuses of jazz was thus in part a result of the economics of publishing, that is, of the dissemination of music as a form of writing. Jeffrey Melnick argues that the extraordinary level of success enjoyed by Jews behind the scenes (as music publishers and distributors, composers, theater owners, producers, and musicians) meant that they were able to exercise more and more control over jazz perfor-mance, "both in the crude sense of owning the means of production, and through the more complex process of gaining status as the best interpreters of African American culture." Having commandeered and promoted so many "representations of 'Blackness,'" from blackface comedy to jazz, Jews were able to "stake their claim as extraordinary translators of African American music."[105] The near ubiquity of Jewish performers, composers, and publishers during the 1920s—and the marginalization of African American musicians and the race records they made—encouraged writers like Gilbert Seldes to believe that jazz was essentially a Jewish art.

It is tempting to consider the jazz produced by white composers and band leaders during the Jazz Age a continuation of minstrelsy. And cer-tainly white singers like Al Jolson and Sophie Tucker and black vaudevil-lians like Bert Williams became stars precisely through blackface perfor-mances. But the minstrel paradigm was not invoked during the 1920s—"sweet" jazz was seen as something quite distinct from min-strelsy—and is not the only, or best, way of understanding the relationship between black and white musical traditions. Questions of racial imperson-ation are further complicated by recording technologies, which became far more technically accomplished with the invention of the electrical process in 1925. As Lisa Gitelman notes, "phonograph advertisements from the 1890s to the 1920s" "emphasize the changing visuality of music" (i.e., the absence of the live performer) by showing music lovers watching and lis-tening to the phonograph.[106] Gazing at the machine, listeners sometimes found it impossible to tell from the sound of a performance whether the musicians were black or white. For example, the popularity—and titilla-tion—of the coon song on record in the early twentieth century was to some extent predicated precisely on the difficulty of determining the race of the singer. Because the phonograph transformed the visual and perfor-mative orientation of minstrelsy, the "sound of white-constructed 'black-ness'" became more idiosyncratic, mutable, and disembodied.[107] It is thus hardly an accident, for example, that listeners often mistook Sophie Tucker "for a southern black girl" and that "Dutch fans who had heard her only on record were surprised to learn she was not black."[108] This confusion is in part the result of what Jane Gaines calls "the ineffability of sound that makes it so ideologically malleable, so responsive to the shape we want to give it; thus it is empirical proof at the same time that it is uncertainty and ambiguity."[109] It is also in part a consequence and symptom of the ongoing struggle over the meaning of "blackness," which *Plessy v. Ferguson* (1896) made even more elusive and perplexing by deciding it was defined by blood, not skin color.

The difficulty of ascribing a racial provenance to jazz is redoubled by the fact that it not simply a black and white affair. Because it also incorporates Latin American elements and traditions, it represents, in Gennari's words, nothing less than a pan-American, "New World mulatto music that carries forward the already Africanized, multicultural soundscape of the Spanish and Portuguese colonial powers."[110] It is, in sum, a diasporic art—the first world music—the product of multiple, aggregated genealogies. At the risk of suppressing a long and brutal history of love and theft, of racist and nativist violence and economic exploitation, I would respectfully disagree with Melnick and suggest that the jazz produced by white musicians in the 1920s was quite distinct from minstrelsy, which I understand to be a (white) performance that envies, mimics, and degrades the (black) originals it copies. (This is the condition Nietzsche named *ressentiment*.) Yes, publishers, record companies, and booking agencies were white-controlled, but the development of jazz was far more racially interactive and collaborative than minstrelsy ever was. In vaudeville, musical theater, and cabarets in both black and white entertainment districts, "the black vernacular and black artists were in demand." Eager to cash in on the jazz craze, many musicians quickly "adopted elements of the jazz vernacular in their performances and recordings."[111] In New York, the most successful band leaders went to Harlem to listen to jazz bands, mingled with black musicians and artists, and availed themselves of the services of professional black composers and arrangers. Whiteman, for example, was the first white bandleader to hire black arrangers like Don Redman and William Grant Still, who was also a distinguished composer of so-called classical music.[112] Vincent Lopez programmed music by both black and white composers and in 1924 alternated with Fletcher Henderson's black orchestra at Roseland Ballroom.[113] Gershwin especially, "more than any other composer (or critic, or historian) of his time, constantly sought out black musicians and listened to the widest possible range of black music."[114] But he was hardly unique. "[W]hite borrowers," one commentator noted in 1922, took up the "'blues' [that] came direct from the Negro field hand." And these borrowings were in turn borrowed by others. "Thus is American music made: the Negro borrows from the whites, puts his own interpretation on things, and then the whites borrow it back again and adapt it to their own uses."[115]

Mistrustful of the minstrel model, I would suggest that jazz developed in its early years as a copy of a copy of an original that never existed in the first place.

JAZZING POPULAR THEATER

Cultural critics and historians agree that the 1920s marked the decade when American artists (in music, theater, painting, poetry, and narrative fiction) for the first time succeeded in producing a distinctively American—and distinctively modernist—art that, in George Gershwin's words, was "nervous, hurried, syncopated, ever accelerando, and slightly vulgar."[116] This art, an expression of "the rhythms and impulses" emanating from a "Machine Age America," held irresistible fascination not only for American urbanites, but also for European artists and audiences.[117] For the first time, Europeans in droves were intent on learning and borrowing from America. Europeans listened to jazz, played it, wrote it, danced to it, made love to it. In the United States, jazz moved swiftly (if controversially) from vaudeville houses and nightclubs into more rarified climes. U.S. modernists of European descent (like Gershwin, Seldes, Lawson, and many others) who embraced their roles as both nationalists and cosmopolitans delighted in the ways that jazz disrupted musical norms; undermined stuffy, hidebound traditions; and shifted the center of international cultural gravity decisively westward. And while musicians may have invented jazz, they were only one among several groups of artists that were able to capitalize on its cultural and social power and allure.

The popular theatrical form that profited most from the arrival of jazz was vaudeville, which was revitalized by syncopated dance music. Variety entertainments of many kinds had captivated nineteenth-century Americans, but the term *vaudeville* came into common usage only in the 1870s to describe a kind of variety performed not in saloons or amusement parks but in urban theaters. Although a vaudeville show could feature a great diversity of entertainers—from dancers, jugglers, and equestrians to opera singers and actors from the legitimate stage—it was distinguished from other entertainments for working-class audiences (like burlesque) by its relative refinement, especially after the reforms instituted by Tony Pastor in the 1880s, which banished alcohol, vulgarities, and scantily clad women. Vaudeville became even more regularized with the founding that same decade of the Keith-Albee Circuit, which booked acts and controlled the-aters across the United States. By the end of the century, vaudeville was ubiquitous, a truly national culture that ranged from "small time," which rarely charged more than five cents admission and catered to rowdy, work-ing-class, often immigrant audiences, to the higher-priced "big time," which played in more respectable and sometimes lavish new theaters (most famously, the Palace Theatre in Times Square) to an increasingly middle-class clientele whose behavior was being carefully policed by theater man-agers and producers.

Despite the encroachment of cinema in the early 1920s, vaudeville re-mained the most popular form of live entertainment because it was able to offer, in Edward F. Albee's words, "something for everybody."[118] Indeed, many of the best-known entertainers of the first half of the twentieth cen-tury started in vaudeville, including Fred Astaire, W. C. Fields, James Cagney, Fanny Brice, Mae West, Eddie Cantor, Al Jolson, George Burns and Gracie Allen, the Marx Brothers, Milton Berle, and countless others. In 1924, Marian Spitzer noted that big-time vaudeville would usually fea-ture a nine- or seven-act bill "built around its headliner" in which a full-stage spectacle ("girl show," acrobatics, jazz bands, "sketch with a big name," animal act) would alternate with a performance "in one," that is, in front of the first curtain (song and dance team, "smart comedy talking act," "good musician," "strong comedy single").[119] Small-time shows were shorter, often five acts, and featured less starry and polished performers. And while a big- or small-time show was always put together as a series of disconnected episodes, it, like each of its individual acts, built toward a "wow finish" that would "lift roaring waves of applause to sweep toward the stage." Most important, vaudeville provided large working- and mid-dle-class audiences in the new urban business districts with the kind of thrill they could rarely get from the legitimate stage. For in vaudeville, where performers spoke and sang directly to the audience, the "illusions of the legitimate stage" were gone, especially its "attitude of superiority." "Actor and audience are closer together, know each other better."[120] It is little wonder that vaudeville was widely perceived as being "very Ameri-can" and very modern, the entertainment that epitomized "the era of the department store and the short story." An urban performance to be savored and forgotten, it was "a kind of lunch-counter art."[121]

Given the rise of cinema and the unprecedented economic and social changes that were taking place throughout the entire field of theatrical practice, both the popular and the legitimate stage (in very different ways) were revolutionized by a fascinating, syncopated rhythm, that "little rhythm, a rhythm, a rhythm / That pit-a-pats through my brain."[122] For producers of vaudeville and musical comedy intent on breaking with European models, jazz and jazz-inflected language, choreography, and design were the key to forging a uniquely American theater vernacular that could respond to and express the new rhythms and economies of the Machine Age. As Paul Whiteman exclaimed, jazz (like vaudeville) is "peculiarly American"; it is "the spirit of a new country. It catches the underlying life motif of a continent and period."[123]

Vaudeville was key to the dissemination of jazz because theaters retained live orchestras (whose numbers varied with the size of the house and admission charged) that accompanied all performances save comic routines and one-act plays. Observers noted that vaudeville audiences loved music "fervently" and that they were offered "a gorgeous variety of brands," from opera and symphony to jazz, ragtime, and novelties like barbershop quartets or faux-Spanish gypsies and toreadors.[124] After World War I, however, vaudeville became so strongly identified with jazz that one commentator turned to a vaudevillian for the etymology of the word *jazz*, noting that "the phrase 'Jaz [*sic*] her up' is a common one to-day . . . when a vaudeville act needs ginger."[125] In vaudeville and musical comedy, jazz was a revolutionary force that transformed structures, conventions, idioms, and performance practices. In 1923, *Metronome*, an orchestra and band monthly, found more than seventy-five jazz orchestras playing in vaudeville.[126] In 1926, jazz-mad New Yorkers alone spent "more than fifty million dollars a year for jazz music" played in theaters, hotels, cabarets, and movie houses (a whopping 2 percent of the 1926 federal budget).[127] On the legitimate stage, however, it was a dangerous commodity, condemned by the vast majority of artists but cautiously taken up by those few modernists, like John Howard Lawson, intent on producing a national, populist theater.

Few juxtapositions dramatize the differences between the two theatrical fields as clearly as the opposing critical responses to Lawson's vaudevillian "jazz symphony," *Processional,* and a play that opened a few weeks earlier, *Lady, Be Good!,* the first musical comedy with a complete score by George and Ira Gershwin. The longest-running Gershwin musical of the 1920s, it enjoyed 330 performances on Broadway before moving on to London in 1926 for 325 more.[128] Starring Fred and Adele Astaire in both New York and London, *Lady, Be Good!* boasts one of the Gershwins's most celebrated

Adele and Fred Astaire in the Gershwins' *Lady, Be Good!*
Credit: Billy Rose Theatre Division, The New York Public Library for the Performing Arts,
Astor, Lenox and Tilden Foundations

and virtuosic exercises in stumbling, breathless syncopation, "Fascinating Rhythm," and a collection of "tuneful, lively, gay and haunting" songs.[129] The reviewers pronounced the show "just about the best musical comedy in town." Besides Adele Astaire, the critics' darling, they especially praised the "bright and sometimes brilliant" Gershwin score.[130] The very same Alan Dale who would six weeks later massacre *Processional* offered that in the midst of "musical comedy season par excellence, . . . when we turn up our noses at anything that fails to toe the mark, . . . 'Lady, Be Good' can hold its own." He especially extolled Gershwin's "easy little songs set in his delightful network of harmony" as well as his "masterly" "orchestrations" (although the orchestrations, most now lost, were not by Gershwin, he almost certainly collaborated closely with the arrangers).[131]

While the New York daily press praised the score, it took a Philadelphia critic to analyze Gershwin's real achievement in his first musical to open after *Rhapsody in Blue* ten months before had given the composer a measure of high-cultural legitimacy. Describing Gershwin's music as elusive, Linton Martin deemed the piece a "Vital Contribution to American Music." Martin prophetically placed the composer's style squarely at the center of a newly emerging American popular modernism (that in fact anticipated and helped pave the way for the leftist populism of the 1930s). The songs that Gershwin wrote for Broadway during the 1920s undermine the opposition between the popular and the esoteric: "Right in the middle of a bit of bouncing jazz he will insert an echo of the whole tone scale, hitherto heard only in the ultra-modern music of symphony concerts." (In fact, the whole-tone scale is a hallmark of French impressionism, especially the music of Debussy, which was then no longer exactly "ultra-modern." But it was a rarity on the Broadway stage.) Like so many of his fellow modernists, Martin constructed Gershwin as an original, all-American, one-man melting pot, the inventor of a radically syncretic music that, in Gershwin's own words, expressed "the voice of the American soul."[132]

Why would a critic like Alan Dale who judged Lawson's "jazz symphony" a "ludicrous and incoherent inanity" be wholly disarmed by the brilliant senselessness of *Lady, Be Good!*? The "plot" of the latter "eluded me," Dale confesses, "as such plots invariably do, and I never worry." Why did Lawson's experimentation induce such feverish anxiety and disgust while the narrative absurdities of *Lady, Be Good!* charmed him completely? "Why worry with plots?" he asks, besotted with Gershwin's "exquisite" music. "Let 'em go, I say."[133] The stark discrepancies between these two reviews clearly signal the utterly different—and contradictory—criteria used during the 1920s to judge the legitimate stage as compared with musical comedy, vaudeville, and revue. Why was this disparity the rule? Why was jazz venerated in one field of culture and reviled in an adjacent one? What kinds of cultural work were legitimate plays and musical comedies expected to accomplish? To which classes of people were they addressed? Why did the legitimate stage, as it was rapidly and irreversibly losing ground to motion pictures, so carefully sequester itself from certifiably popular theatrical forms? Why was the Jazz Age the era in which American drama was invented? And why did musical comedy and this new literary drama fashion themselves as opposites, unlikely and unhappy dance partners locked in a feverish embrace—while the band played on?

TWO

THE STRUGGLE FOR LEGITIMACY

~~~~~~

The part of vaudeville that is pure . . . is rarely matched on our other stages. Certainly not in the legitimate, nor in the serious artistic playhouse where knowing one's job perfectly and doing it simply and unpretentiously are the rarest things in the world. Revue and musical comedy require and often attain the pitch of technical accuracy which vaudeville sets as a standard.

—Gilbert Seldes, *The 7 Lively Arts* (1924)

Historians of American culture routinely consider the 1920s a golden age of the theater. Although they may debate the quality of the ore, they cannot ignore its prodigious quantity. Despite the encroachment of cinema, theater flourished as never before during its long history in the United States. Broadway was the vibrant center of theatrical activities, a "paradise for playwrights," in Brenda Murphy's words.[1] On the average, more than 200 new productions opened each year on the Great White Way, peaking with 264 during the 1927–28 season.[2] That same year, there were seventy-six theaters in New York City used for so-called legitimate productions, twice as many as had been available only twelve years before.[3]

In New York and across the nation, the proliferation of the so-called little theaters, or art theaters (like the Provincetown Players), plus subscription theaters (like the Theatre Guild) nurtured a new generation of American writers and led to the somewhat belated invention of what is now regarded as a literary theater and the composition of the kind of plays that continue to fill anthologies and college syllabi. Pulitzer Prize–winning dramas like Sidney Howard's *They Knew What They Wanted* (1924), George Kelly's *Craig's Wife* (1925), and Elmer Rice's *Street Scene* (1929) became certified Broadway hits. But all American playwrights were overshadowed by one man, Eugene O'Neill, who racked up three Pulitzer Prizes during the 1920s and found his plays produced around the world, from Stockholm to Tokyo. With his long string of Broadway successes from *Beyond the Horizon* (1920) to *Strange Interlude* (1928), "American drama," Barnard Hewitt proudly announced, finally "came of age."[4] And he has since come to be re-garded by all those with a weakness for making lists (and a tacit aversion to Tennessee Williams's homosexuality) as "America's leading playwright."[5]

The prosperity of theater in New York during the Jazz Age could not, however, distract the keener cultural observers and theater professionals from the fact that its institutional foundations were shaky. The number of theatrical companies on tour had dropped from over three hundred at the beginning of the twentieth century to a yearly average of about sixty for most of the 1920s.[6] As one producer explained, "the motor [automobile], the movie, the radio, and managerial stupidity have all contributed to bringing about the *débâcle* of the road."[7] This national decline was further complicated by the rapid intensification of the hit/flop phenomenon (in Lee Shubert's words: "A production is either a knockout, or it is a failure"). As a result, the second half of the decade bore witness to what Jack Poggi describes as "an unprecedented number of failures" in the commercial the-ater.[8] As *Billboard* ominously foresaw, the 1925–26 New York season, de-spite 255 new productions, was promising to "turn out to be the most prolific and most disastrous on record."[9] One critic, meanwhile, conjured up an even drearier scenario: "I am of a disposition melancholy enough to suspect that the death-knell of the American theatre has been sounded—that it is time, indeed, to sound the dirge, and hang crêpe on the doors of the syndicate theatres."[10]

The contradictory position of theater during the 1920s—its prosperity and contraction, artistic triumph and economic distress—is symptomatic of profound changes taking place in the shape of American culture, the organization of leisure, and the composition of audiences. It is also a result of the fact that theater in the United States has never been a unified and coherent set of institutions and practices. During the 1920s, for example, the category of live theater included Broadway (with its plays, musicals, and revues), nonprofit theaters (both little and not, in New York and elsewhere), vaudeville (both big time and small time), burlesque, and road houses that hosted touring productions of all of the above genres—plus a host of other forms (some slipping swiftly into obsolescence) ranging from minstrel shows to Wild West shows to jazz cabarets. The rich diversity of offerings must not disguise the fact that the 1920s witnessed the consolidation of a new cultural settlement in the United States that has persisted to the present day—despite the shuffling of the cultural hierarchy, emergence of new media forms, and vicissitudes of social history. For by the beginning of the 1930s, theater was nearing extinction as a popular form, except for the one genre most closely linked to jazz, musical comedy, the genre that was then "the biggest money-making factor in the theatrical business" and remains the most lucrative and widely loved.[11] The theater, in other words, was becoming increasingly bifurcated into the so-called legitimate stage—deeply suspicious of jazz, cinema, and other popular forms—and everything else.

The word *legitimate* has since the nineteenth century been the principal term used to discriminate among theatrical practices. It represents not an unprejudiced descriptive but a value-laden metaphorical concept—one of the most loaded metaphors in the theatrical lexicon. It is highly unlikely that the legitimate theater's imprecisely defined adversaries would fancy themselves "illegitimate." Nonetheless, the category of the legitimate, as Richard Butsch reports, has been more or less continually "recruited into the discourse on the relationship of theater to art and to mass culture," two terms with which theater has long had a vexed and anxious relationship.[12] According to the *Oxford English Dictionary*, the word *legitimate*, when applied to drama, designates "the body of plays, Shakespeare or other, that have a recognized theatrical and literary merit." (The earliest example cited dates from 1855.) Alfred L. Bernheim in fact finds an earlier example, from an 1843 article in the *New Mirror* in which the "legitimate" theater is equated *tout court* with "the drama," which is housed in "the temple dedicated to the muses." It is opposed to diverse entertainments presented at "low prices" for "low audiences": "horses, dancing, negroes and magicians."[13] Butsch, meanwhile, references both an 1879 column in the *New York Dramatic Mirror* and the *Autobiography of Joseph Jefferson* (1890). In the

Dramatic Mirror, "the legitimate stage" is set in strict opposition to "the variety business." The columnist fails to clarify the former but describes the latter as "the money-making branch of the theatrical business." Variety— that is, vaudeville, burlesque, animal shows, minstrelsy, and the like—must be first and foremost a commercial enterprise that caters to "the popular taste" (or "low audiences"), unlike the legitimate stage which is supposedly unconcerned with making money because it is a sanctuary for a sacred art.[14]

The celebrated actor Joseph Jefferson, more interested in art than commerce, notes that "legitimate comedian" is "a somewhat technical term, usually applied to those actors who confine themselves as strictly as possible to the acting of characters in old English and Shakesperean [*sic*] comedies." Although these actors may on occasion impersonate "American characters," Jefferson sees them as interpreters of canonical English literature.[15] For the legitimate theater represents an elite cultural practice that (from the nineteenth century to the present) is linked to British traditions and understood to be text-based in comparison with performance-based forms: "spectacle, opera, pantomime, etc."[16] It remains forever haunted by "the luminous traces of the footsteps of Garrick, the Kembles, Kean, [and] Rachel," those "great actors . . . who compel the world to lose its wits in admiration of them by sheer force of their own noble gifts."[17] It is, as one actor-producer described it in 1926, a conservatory "of fine tradition and pure artistic expression."[18] If, to unpack this metaphor further, the legitimate theater is lawfully begotten, pure, artistic (i.e., beyond price), and Anglo-Saxon, its illegitimate cousin must be spurious, improper, indigenous, a commodity to be bought and sold, and if not "negro," then at least of questionable Anglo-Saxon heritage. It is merely and deplorably "popular," a "faddist, exotic" theater.[19] During the 1920s, the theatrical field in which the legitimate was opposed to its misbegotten competitor was analogous to the musical field in which European-made or European-inspired art music was opposed to jazz.

In order to compass the difference between the "legitimate" and its adversaries and to understand the development of a literary drama in the United States, we must first consider theater's uneasy relationship with its other rival, motion pictures, which had by 1920 become by far the most widely attended form of public amusement. If there is one thing on which cultural historians agree, it is that Hollywood has been the "largest single force" shaping the American theater since at least 1912, when "the first full-length commercial film was shown in America," *Queen Elizabeth*, starring (not by accident) the most famous stage actor in the world, Sarah Bernhardt.[20] The impact of Hollywood on the theater was—and remains—so difficult to gauge in part because it entails analyzing an extremely imbalanced economic relationship in which the two are sometimes in a productive rapport and sometimes at odds institutionally and aesthetically. During the 1920s, the tensions between them involved competition for audiences and capital; the theft by the movies of stage actors, playwrights, and directors; the optioning of successful stage properties; and investments by Hollywood producers in Broadway productions. Although I have couched these statements in terms that make the stage seem the injured party, these disputes could sometimes play to the advantage of theater, or at least certain kinds of theatrical practices. Nonetheless, to claim that Hollywood was primarily responsible for the contraction of the theater industries during the 1920s and that the Great Depression delivered the coup de grâce is by and large correct. But it is only the beginning of an interrogation of the relationship between theater and popular culture during the Jazz Age. It is only the first step in analyzing how the modern, legitimate theater emerged and why it has, at least since the mid-1920s, been in a more or less continuous state of contraction.

THEORIZING POPULAR CULTURE

With the rise since the 1960s of the academic field called cultural studies, a large body of theoretical and historical scholarship has been produced that analyzes the social, political, and economic foundations of cultural production. In both its British and U.S. versions, however, cultural studies has meant the study of primarily popular texts: film, television, music videos, advertising, hip-hop, comic books, and so on.[21] The founders of cultural studies (Richard Hoggart, Stuart Hall, and many others) reacted against the midcentury condemnations of popular culture on the part of Theodor Adorno, Max Horkheimer, and the New York Intellectuals (e.g., Clement Greenberg and Dwight Macdonald) and aimed to reassess (and often celebrate) an array of popular texts that, they argue, are not examples of "false consciousness" but sites of complex and contradictory social negotiation. Indeed, their focus on the popular is in large part what distinguishes cultural studies from a more traditionally inclined literary studies, despite the now widespread recognition that "literature" cannot be neatly separated out from other kinds of texts. Yet, with few exceptions (most notably Raymond Williams and Pierre Bourdieu), the founders and most celebrated practitioners of cultural studies have ignored theater. The reluctance by most U.S. cultural theorists to consider theatrical practices is doubtlessly linked historically to many different phenomena: the marginalization of drama in university English departments, the difficulty of obtaining and analyzing performance texts, theater's steady decline as a vital force on the American cultural scene, its increasing superannuation and subordination in elite graduate programs in relation to performance studies, and the seemingly irrepressible vigor of the antitheatrical prejudice. Perhaps most important, however, is the fact that in the United States, theater and what passes for popular culture have largely gone their separate ways since the 1920s. As the legitimate theater became increasingly and irreversibly literary and high modernist, the theatrical forms categorized as popular have declined or expired, with the important exception of musical comedy. In the following pages, I will analyze theorizations of the popular (and of the legitimate stage's relationship to the popular) up to and including the work of Gilbert Seldes, whose *The 7 Lively Arts* (1924) represents one of the most provocative and influential apologies for jazz and other forms of popular culture.

The legitimate theater can no more be disentangled from popular culture than twentieth-century concert music can from jazz and other vernacular genres. For the popular is an ever-shifting site of struggle. As Brecht insisted, "what was popular yesterday is not today, for the people today are not what they were yesterday."[22] The category of the people is a notoriously slippery one that can be and has been mobilized for myriad purposes. Adorno and company, coming out of an antifascist tradition, tend to conflate the people with the hapless, easily gulled, urban proletariat—the masses deceived by fascism. And they imagine twentieth-century popular culture as being synonymous with mass culture in order to signal the degraded, systematized, mass-produced, and commodified status of both. In Adorno's oversimplified formulation, jazz, like all forms of mass culture, represents a counterfeit rebellion and thereby helps to reconcile one to an intolerable world. It "converges with the equally standardized schemas of the detective novel and its offshoots, which regularly distort or unmask the world, . . . but which . . . charm away the seductive and ominous challenge through the inevitable triumph of order." Jazz fans are therefore narcotized, "castrated" consumers, the "vague, inarticulate followers" of stars, "intoxicated by the fame of mass culture."[23] Yet even Adorno (who, in fact, knew very little about the early development of jazz) admits that the concept of the popular long predates the assembly line, and he tries to rescue a relatively benign, pre-twentieth-century popular culture in order the better to condemn its corrupt, standardized offspring, mass culture.[24] And while it is useful, I believe, to consider the differences between the two, one must be wary of doing so, as Michael Kammen does, in order to salvage an allegedly salutary, early twentieth-century "participatory and interactive" popular culture from an anaesthetizing, privatized, postwar mass culture that merely "induce[s] passivity."[25] This substitution of moral judgment for sociological analysis makes it difficult to analyze the struggles that take place in all cultural productions, including mass-produced, mass-mediated, and mass-consumed forms.[26]

Adorno, Seldes, Stuart Hall, and countless others have heatedly debated the value of the culture of "the people." Indeed, this debate dates back to Johann Gottfried Herder and Jean-Jacques Rousseau and the rise of industrial capitalism in the West. At stake is the culture of those Stuart Hall identifies as "working people, the labouring classes and the poor," those, in other words, who had to be trained and disciplined to supply the manpower demanded by the industrial revolution.[27] Raymond Williams points out that the very word, *popular* (derived from the Latin, "belonging to the people"), has had contrasting connotations at least since the sixteenth century that, in one form or another, have persisted to the present day. On the one hand, it has long been derogatory, seen from the position of "those seeking favour or power from" the people. By this definition, "the people" are identified with the "'low' or 'base,'" as are those who are seen trying to curry favor with them. Although a more positive sense meaning "well-liked by many people" dates back to the same century, it did not become the primary meaning until the Romantic period.[28] It was during this age, as Peter Burke notes, that popular culture was constructed in opposition to "learned culture" (some hundred years before the terms *highbrow* and *lowbrow* had been coined). In revolt against the neoclassical rules of art, early-nineteenth-century intellectuals (especially in Germany) extolled the virtues and artifacts of peasant life. "Hence the rise of terms like *Volkslied* ('folksong'), which Herder was one of the first to use, or 'folklore,' a word coined by William Thoms in 1846."[29] According to the Romantic critics, fairy tales, folk songs and tales, and rough-hewn, vernacular poetry were works that came not from civilization but from nature and could be used to legitimate the nationalist projects and liberation movements that arose throughout Europe and the Americas.

With rapid industrialization and urbanization in the United States after the Civil War, the first generation of professional critics emerged who were eager to educate, discipline, and uplift the working classes. As a result, they were far more suspicious of popular cultures than their Romantic, nationalist forebears. These were the genteel critics whose "emphasis on moral and aesthetic 'training,'" Joan Shelley Rubin notes, "shaped their understanding of their public role" as well as their taste in art and culture. They strove, for example, to "instill 'a taste for good reading,' an objective connected with mastering 'control of the will' and 'the quickening and growth of the moral sympathies.'"[30] During this period, the words *highbrow* and *lowbrow* were coined, Lawrence Levine reports, the former "first used in the 1880s to describe intellectual or aesthetic superiority" and the latter "first used shortly after 1900 to mean someone or something neither 'highly intellectual' nor 'aesthetically refined.'"[31] These terms, borrowed from a racially inflected, nineteenth-century phrenology, were used to accentuate the differences between a Europeanized, morally and spiritually uplifting art and a vulgar, primitive, commercialized, sensual art; the culture of the intellectual and economic elites ("the hardy northern races") as opposed to that of the working classes, especially recent immigrants from southern and eastern Europe (African American culture hardly figured in the social calculations of these critics). Opera houses, concert halls, and museums were constructed to look like classical temples to guarantee that certain kinds of art could be "in effect 'rescued' from the marketplace, and therefore from the mixed audience and from the presence of other cultural genres." As Levine emphasizes, the championing of highbrow represented a kind of rearguard assault "on the part of the older elites who were losing their grip on political and economic authority."[32] The elite's fervor for cultural order thus provided them with an important weapon in their drive to organize and rationalize the social and economic realms and to buttress their own power. For in certain respects, the ability to fashion a hierarchy (cultural or otherwise) and police its boundaries is far more important than the specific content of categories like highbrow and lowbrow.

During the first decade of the twentieth century, the genteel critics were challenged by social reformers and progressives (like Jane Addams and Frederic Howe) who attempted to resolve the contradiction between the genteel critics' crusade for social uplift and their less explicitly articulated wish to shield highbrow culture from the unwashed masses. The progressives (almost all of them hailing from upper-middle-class families) believed, as Paul Gorman notes, that urbanization and the assembly line anaesthetized the laboring classes and drove them to seek out "shocking amusements."[33] In their paternalistic zeal, they attempted to educate the working classes to appreciate highbrow art and to abandon popular forms (like cinema, variety, and ragtime) for legitimate culture or prettified versions of folk culture. They decried the sensationalist character of public amusements, especially, in the words of Jane Addams, "the vaudeville shows" and "the five-cent theaters . . . full of the most blatant and vulgar songs."[34] In place of these crude amusements, the progressives advocated a theater that promoted social uplift, and they were instrumental in founding the art theater movement in the United States. Addams herself reorganized the Hull House Theatre in 1907 to present plays by Ibsen, Galsworthy, Shaw, Synge, and other now-canonical playwrights.[35] For these social reformers, the so-called little theater was a key institution for the training of bourgeois audiences. Accordingly, it devoted itself, as Thomas H. Dickinson then wrote, to "the encouragement and support of an American drama, the giving voice and tongue to a neighborhood, the production of the great masterpieces of the world, [and] the elevation of taste of the community."[36]

Despite the differences between their missions, the genteel critics and the reformers set popular cultural forms in opposition against highbrow art and implicitly defined "the people" as the urbanized working classes, classes that were increasingly composed of immigrants who were expected to renounce their particular cultural heritage in favor of a universalized aesthetic standard. Rembrandt, Tennyson, or Beethoven may not have stirred them, but they were nonetheless required to appreciate the logic that separated highbrow from lowbrow. For both sets of critics, as for their many successors, the construction of ostensibly universal principles of culture thereby gave them a way to assert their own importance as intellectuals in a nation in which their leadership was being rapidly usurped by the captains of industry. For until the end of the nineteenth century, as Janice Radway notes, there remained a close link between "those who commanded economic capital" and the "dominant ecclesiastical, educational, and cultural institutions." In cities like Boston, a "tightly knit, Brahmin, genteel elite" was able to control "both the economic and cultural spheres."[37] But by the beginning of the twentieth century, economic elites had become more and more estranged from the progressive intellectual class, a trend that became accentuated with the development of American modernist art.[38] Although progressive intellectuals may have been writing about the working classes, they were directing their campaign of cultural uplift less to those who frequented the dance halls than to the respectable, moneyed, white, middle classes that read the journals in which they published and anted up for their books.

With the ascendance of rationalized modes of production in the United States in the early years of the twentieth century, the Machine Age commenced in earnest. Two years after Frederick Winslow Taylor's *Principles of Scientific Management* (1911) was published, Henry Ford built the first assembly line at his plant in Highland Park, Michigan. Mass production aligned human beings and machines by abstracting and coordinating "a manufacturing project," in Ford's words, dedicated to "the principles of power, accuracy, economy, system, continuity and speed."[39] The triumph of the rationalized workplace and the development of new communication technologies corresponded to an almost frenetic growth of new popular forms, most notably jazz and motion pictures. Many younger, radical critics argued that the project of cultural uplift was not succeeding because mass production was creating a standardized mass society. The recognition of this failure was one of many factors that spurred the development of modernism in the United States as a reaction against both the genteel and progressive traditions. Cultural critics were dismayed that despite the extraordinary success of American industrial methods and technologies, American culture remained a backwater. So-called little magazines like the *Dial* and *Seven Arts* were committed to a nurturing a distinctively American, Machine Age art that would decisively cast aside nineteenth-century conventions. Thus, for example, Randolph Bourne exclaimed in 1915: "I feel a certain unholy glee at this wholesale rejection of what our fathers reverenced as culture."[40] His delight, however, did not impel him automatically to embrace the entertainments that were replacing it. But it was symptomatic of a cultural radicalism that was reassessing the value of popular forms. No longer disdaining the mass-mediated arts of the industrial age, a band of modernist populists embraced a brand of democratic Americanism in the "spirit of Walt Whitman." "What we are seeking," claimed a 1917 *Seven Arts* editorial, "is what he sought: that intense American nationality in which the spirit of the people is shared through its tasks and its arts, its undertakings and its songs."[41] These populists hoped that inspired U.S.-born artists would come along who could harness "the spirit of the people" to produce an American art that would take its place on the world stage.

Although respectful of the "arts" of the working classes, the *Seven Arts* editorial, like much populist writing, ends up championing a highly abstracted and idealized version of the people and its culture. For as Stuart Hall rightly insists, terms like *the people* and even *the working class* are categories that wield enormous discursive and social power and are always used for political ends. Most important, "there is no separate, autonomous, 'authentic' layer of working-class culture to be found," no sacred preserve of pure, indigenous, popular entertainment untouched by other forms (like an unadulterated New Orleans jazz). Every "popular recreation" is saturated by what Hall calls "popular imperialism," the power of dominant culture.[42] Because no social group develops in a vacuum, especially one that is by definition a dominated class, the working class and its amusements cannot represent a site of pure resistance to capital. Rather, to cite Hall again,

> there is a continuous and necessarily uneven and unequal struggle, by the dominant culture, constantly to disorganize and reorganize popular culture; to enclose and confine its definitions and forms within a more inclusive range of dominant forms. There are points of resistance; there are also moments of supersession. This is the dialectic of cultural struggle.[43]

In the second decade of the twentieth century the struggle over the value of art heated up as ragtime metamorphosed into jazz and more and more intellectuals hearkened to the sirens' songs of popular culture. Among the radicals, R. J. Coady epitomized a kind of utopianism that associated the people with progress, youth, kineticism, mass production, and America itself. In a 1917 essay entitled "American Art," he rejects the highbrow culture that comes "from the Academy or the money old ladies leave." To discover "something new, something big," he turns "outside of our art world" to look for an American art that does not yet exist. He finds "enormous possibilities," however, in industry, the modern city, and popular entertainers, among them the black vaudevillian Bert Williams singing his signature song, "Nobody." "It's in the spirit of the Panama Canal. It's in the East River and the Battery. . . . It's coming from the ball field, the stadium and the ring. . . . To-day is the day of moving pictures, it is also the day of moving sculpture." To fulfill the utopian promise of America is to fulfill the promise of modernity and the working classes whose machines and labor will be blissfully transformed into art. If "taste," he argues, "equalled the creative construction of the [steam hammer] we'd have a mighty art!"[44]

The most celebrated and influential radical analysis of U.S. culture was Van Wyck Brooks's essay "'Highbrow' and 'Lowbrow,'" first published in 1915. Born in New Jersey, Brooks was educated there, in Europe, and at Harvard and, in the words of one critic, introduced "a cosmopolitan experience unmatched in American criticism of that day."[45] For Brooks, as for Coady, an authentic people's culture did not yet exist in the United States.[46] Rather, he argued that every aspect of American life was perverted by the pervasive binary opposition between highbrow and lowbrow, between "transcendent theory" and "catchpenny realities," ideals and dollars, and a "desiccated" but elevated art and "stark utility" (6, 7, 14). Although he attacked both positions, between which "there is no community, no genial middle ground," he was intent on envisioning some kind of imaginary solution to the problem (7). "On the economic plane," he wrote, "that [middle position] implies socialism; on every other plane it implies something which a majority of Americans in our day do not possess—an object in living" (34). Although Brooks was barely able to articulate it, he seemed to prize above all a genuinely popular, democratic culture. Just as "priggishness . . . paralyzes life," so does the opposition between high and low squelch "a popular life which bubbles with energy and spreads and grows and slips away ever more and more from the control of tested ideas" (29, 15). More explicitly than Coady, Brooks extolled the modernist vision of "a popular life 'with the lid off'" that finds its expression in vernacular modes of writing, "slang, journalism, and unmannerly fiction" (15). For just as socialism would guarantee an idealized, coordinated collective, so does the popular—a popular whose very improbability points yet again to its abstraction from the working classes—promise to redeem America and its culture.

THE GREAT, THE LIVELY, AND THE BOGUS

Almost a decade after the essays of Brooks and Coady, Gilbert Seldes published *The 7 Lively Arts*, which is widely regarded as the most important work on Jazz Age entertainments. Widely and lavishly praised in the press, Seldes's mapping of American cultural production in 1924 would prove enormously influential and prescient. Not only was it revolutionary (and hence emblematic of its historical moment), but it also sketched out the contours of a cultural hierarchy that has had remarkable longevity. For 1924 was a banner year in U.S. culture. Marking the end of the economic slump of the early 1920s, it was the year of Gershwin's *Rhapsody in Blue;* O'Neill's *Desire Under the Elms;* the first George and Ira Gershwin collaboration, *Lady, Be Good!;* the formation of Columbia Pictures and Metro-Goldwyn-Mayer; the opening of Saks Fifth Avenue; and the first volume of Burns Mantle's *Best Plays* to include only American plays. It was the year symphonic jazz became the rage and American concert composers turned for inspiration to syncopated dance music.[47] Even today, many of the distinctions Seldes draws between the "lively" and the "great" arts remain unexpectedly relevant. This feat is all the more remarkable when one considers that the book was written when radio was in its infancy, before the advent of sound-synchronized motion pictures, before the supersession of the acoustic by the electrical recording process, and before writers like George and Ira Gershwin, Jerome Kern and Oscar Hammerstein II, and Richard Rodgers and Lorenz Hart had revolutionized the Broadway musical and produced so many of its undisputed masterpieces.

Seldes, born in 1893 into a middle-class, liberal, secularized Jewish family—like so many of the producers of the "lively" arts he champions—first hoped to become a playwright, having been from an early age, Michael Kammen reports, "enchanted with the works of Ibsen and Shaw."[48] After Harvard College, however, he forsook theater for journalism and started writing for the little magazines (most notably the *Dial*) in which he staked out a position as a highbrow intellectual, disdainful of what Kammen calls "the democratization of theatre" and, in particular, of rude, noisy, lowbrow audiences.[49] But there is nothing like the zeal of the apostate, and in *The 7 Lively Arts* he turned smartly against genteel, highbrow culture. His list of the "lively" arts represents a veritable litany of what passed for popular culture in the 1920s: movies, jazz (and jazz-inflected popular music), vaudeville, musical comedy, comic strips, popular dance, and radio—note the conspicuous omission of the legitimate theater from the list. The musings of a self-styled agent provocateur, the book is divided into twenty-nine short essays, most of which are meditations on a single art form. Considering the book's breadth, Seldes's gift for color and hyperbole, and the fact that several of its chapters were originally written as magazine articles, it is intriguingly contradictory. Nonetheless, Seldes succeeds in setting forth a complex and compelling view of an extraordinarily productive and pivotal moment in U.S. culture.

One of Seldes's signal achievements is his revision and displacement of the highbrow/lowbrow opposition by a three-term system: the great, lively, and bogus arts. The "great arts" are characterized by "high seriousness" of purpose, as exemplified by the work of Aeschylus, Aristophanes, Rabelais, Racine, and Mozart. The lively arts, or "minor arts," in contrast, have as their essence "high levity." This characteristic he finds exemplified by the movies of Charlie Chaplin, the songs of Irving Berlin and Jerome Kern, and, reaching back to a historical antecedent, the commedia dell'arte.[50] The great arts represent a species of what was classified as Europeanized, highbrow culture and Seldes imagines them transcending history (and the vicissitudes of fashion) because they "are related to eternity." A species of universal art, the fruits of the Enlightenment, the great arts attest to "that extraordinary march of mankind which we like to call the progress of humanity" (347). The lively arts, in contrast, are arts of the present ("our moment," "our lives"). They are "fresh and transient," they carry "a given theme to the 'high' point" (347–48). Like the movies, they are "strange and wonderful," "an instrument of miracles" (37–38).

Of the lively arts, the one that Seldes takes as emblematic of America and modernity, is jazz. He not only devotes more space to jazz and the performing arts for which it supplies the "proper music" (vaudeville, musical comedy, and dance) than he does the other lively arts, but also provides more detailed and technically accomplished analyses of it (253). But Seldes, like so many of his contemporaries, seems almost completely unfamiliar with the jazz produced by African American musicians. Otherwise, he never would have claimed that "the negro side of jazz" represents a primitive residue of earlier times that is intrinsically valuable but (with the exception of the music of James Reese Europe) has been superseded by the work of the real geniuses of jazz: songwriters Irving Berlin, Zez Confrey, Cole Porter, and George Gershwin (whom he astutely judges, even at this very early stage in his career, "capable of everything"); and bandleaders Ted Lewis, Vincent Lopez, and especially Paul Whiteman who, he claims, has brought the jazz band to "real perfection" (95, 92, 103). Recognizing that jazz is as much a "symbol" as a cultural practice, he judges it "the characteristic art of our time" and "the only native music worth listening to"

(83–84). In its "unrestraint" and "wildness," it epitomizes the "ecstasy" that sets the lively arts "apart from everything else" (205, 204).

Because Seldes professes an aversion to "two of the most disagreeable words in the language: high- and low-brow," he attempts to place the great arts and the lively ones on equal footing ("there need be . . . no conflict between the great arts and the minor," 349, 347). Yet he is unable to remake completely the cultural dispensation he has inherited. For the difference, he writes, between the two arts "is not the degree of intensity, but the degree of intellect" (319). The great arts may not tower, but they stand, one might say, at least a head above the lively ones, which he admits, represent something of "an opiate" (204). Like a delectable but insubstantial dish, "they trick our hunger for a moment" but "do not wholly satisfy" (204). Thus does Seldes's scheme furtively reinstate the well-established highbrow/lowbrow opposition. But with a difference.

What sets *The 7 Lively Arts* apart from earlier elaborations of the cultural hierarchy is Seldes's third category, "the peculiarly disagreeable thing for which I find no other name than the bogus" (310). The class of things he calls the "bogus arts" is opposed to both the great and the lively. The bogus are watered down and debased, "easier to appreciate" since they "appeal to low and mixed emotions" (349). Into this damnable class he places "vocal concerts, pseudo-classic dancing, the serious intellectual drama, the civic masque, the high-toned motion picture, and grand opera" (311). Seldes condemns them all for being "dull," "pale," "trivial," and "uninspired" (311–14). He sees them as poised between, competing with, and imperiling both the great and the lively. For they represent "pretentious," "genteel," "dignified," "artistic"—and "dead"—versions of the great arts that appeal only to snobs (349, 338, 336). Yet he maintains they are especially dangerous less to the great arts (which are beyond the vagaries of time and taste) than to the lively ones. "They pretend to be better than the popular arts, yet they want desperately to be popular." Representing a feminine imposture, they are "the exact equivalent of a high-toned lady, an elegant dinner or a refined collation served in the saloon" (319). He singles out for special disapprobation the Metropolitan Opera and the legitimate stage. Indeed, for Seldes "the uncommunicative, uninspired, serious-minded intellectual drama" epitomizes the bogus (314). "In producing serious plays," he writes, "we will stand for a second-rateness we would not for a moment abide in the construction of a bridge or the making of an omelette" (133). Although the connotations of *serious* are variable for

Seldes, he almost always means it disparagingly when applying it to the legitimate stage, "where knowing one's job perfectly and doing it simply and unpretentiously are the rarest thing in the world" (255). "Modern serious plays," like St. John Ervine's *Jane Clegg* (an acclaimed 1920 Theatre Guild production), are not only "bad drama"; they make a "spurious appeal to our sentimentality or our snobbery." They pretend "to be a great and serious art when they are simply vulgarizations" (315).

Although Seldes expresses a certain reluctance to employ the word *bogus*, his use reveals an intriguing and unspoken supposition that undergirds his criticism and that of so many American radicals. For the term betrays what I can best describe as *mimetiphobia*, a fear of imitation itself. Significantly, of the lively arts, only three (musical comedy, movies, and comic strips) are essentially representational. And Seldes clearly values these examples of what I am tempted to call the illegitimate stage for the challenge they pose to traditional forms of representation. He esteems vaudeville performers for their technical brilliance and the "immediate contact" they establish with the audience (252). And he insists that he intensely dislikes "refined vaudeville": all those unfortunate, bogus performances when one must endure "the dreariest aesthetic dancing," "painfully polite vocalism," and especially " 'drama,' " replete with its "bad sentimental *acting*" (252–54). Predictably, Seldes loves musical comedy not for its verisimilitude but its musical, choreographic, spectacular, and vaudevillian qualities: "colour, light, sound, movement" and "that particular air of urbanity, of well-being, of rich contentment and interest which is the special atmosphere of musical shows" (172). (It should come as no surprise that he was one of the few critics to appreciate Lawson's *Processional*, calling it "extraordinary" and "the most important play of the year.")[51] Among other genres, Seldes especially admires George Herriman's *Krazy Kat*, the most extravagant and grotesque comic strip of the 1920s and the basis for a popular 1921 ballet by the respected composer John Alden Carpenter, whose program note for the piece is reprinted in *The 7 Lively Arts*. Seldes claims, moreover, that the "greatest mistake" the movies ever made (even in 1924!) was in trying to take "over the realistic theatre" (338). Because "the camera was" developed "as legitimately an instrument of distortion as of reproduction," film is best suited "to the projection of emotion by means *not realistic*" (he accordingly praises the celebrated German expressionist film *The Cabinet of Dr. Caligari* [1920], 339).

For Seldes, the legitimate stage is the emblem of mimesis gone wrong.

Everything that appears upon it represents a bad copy. Indeed, because he seems to espouse an almost Platonic horror of imitation, the very phrase "bad copy" is redundant because there can never be a good or successful copy. On the stage the "desperate effort . . . to create the illusion of reality" suppresses the "essential distortion, caricature, or transposition which you find . . . in a vaudeville sketch" (315). Unquestionably, his contempt is in part the result of his unfortunate equation of mimesis with the theatrical realism of Ibsen, Strindberg, and Chekhov which was imported to the United States at the beginning of the twentieth century and reinforced in the 1920s and 1930s by the tours of the Moscow Art Theatre and the introduction of Method acting. (Realism continues to represent the dominant style of the American commercial theater.) And Seldes particularly disdains the kind of "serious" play, like the ploddingly realistic *Jane Clegg*, which "without wit, or intensity, 'presents a problem' or drearily holds the mirror up to nature" (314). (So much for his former idols, Ibsen and Shaw!) He much prefers the "playing" he discerns in *Caligari*'s "destruction of realism" to theatrical impersonation, that is, "acting" (335). The dogged literalism of the realistic stage ensures the dullness and superficiality of theater and theater artists. For "if a man has anything profound to express he will flee from the theatre where everything is dependent upon actors usually unintelligent and [where everything] is reduced to the lowest common factor of human intelligence" (314).

Not surprisingly, Seldes's mimetiphobia is linked to his fixation on the "lively." Indeed, the other side of mimetiphobia is always a desire for pure, unmediated being; for life; for a transcendent performance that can never be repeated.[52] Seldes's choice of the word *lively* to describe the popular arts is thus no accident. For his title betrays a longing for art before it has been corrupted by re-presentation, an "honest" art, something "fresh and transient." This art, he writes, has a "relevance not only to our life, but to life itself." It enables one "to live fully" in "our moment" (346–47). Indeed, the popular arts are so powerful because they are contemporary, ephemeral, and overwhelming. Thus, for example, the two biggest stars in vaudeville, Al Jolson and Fanny Brice, with "their intensity of action," perform "at the highest possible pressure" like people "possessed by a daemon." Jolson (doubtlessly in blackface) "flings" into a song with "so much energy, violence, so much of the totality of one human being, that you feel it would suffice for a hundred others" (191–92). The legitimate theater, in contrast, is shaped by dead or moribund playwrights whose tedious, old-fashioned plays turn directors and actors into slaves who are supposed to execute faithfully their providential designs.[53] For Seldes, the legitimate stage represents an archaic remnant of an older cultural dispensation ill-suited to the tenor of the modern age.

The antitheatricalism of *The 7 Lively Arts* is extremely selective. Seldes does not, like so many who have penned antitheatrical tracts, cast moral aspersions against the theater or against actors. They may be dim-witted, but they have no monopoly on public lewdness. And he clearly prizes performance for its ostentatiously civic face, its role in the public sphere. He loves its theatricality, or what the German philosopher Walter Benjamin calls its aura: the uniqueness, intense live presence, and charismatic power of actors and of the stage itself.[54] His prejudice thus represents what Martin Puchner calls "an avant-garde theatricalism," a love of theatricality for its own sake, combined with "a modernist anti-theatricalism," a profound distrust of the legitimate stage as a bourgeois institution.[55] He deplores the fact that it has become a forum for "serious" drama, that is, for a shoddy, antiquated art naive enough to believe it is representing real life. On the one hand, like so many American and European avant-gardists, Seldes eagerly champions the theatricality of the modern age, of cities, amusement parks, factories, and of a vast array of innovative and once-disdained art forms. He longs for "a revolution in our way of looking at the arts" which will celebrate (for example) "the damned effrontery" of vaudeville shows and "the shouting song of the Negro" (24, 249, 63). He even argues that "a plea could be made for violence *per se* in the American theatre" as a way to rediscover its "energy" (193). On the other hand, Seldes's antitheatricalism exemplifies a high modernist assault on traditional forms of representation, "a critique of the actual theatre," that is, the "serious" drama of the 1920s. Taking up the "modernist critique of realism, mimesis, and literalism," he argues that the liveliness of legitimate theater has been quashed by its tendency "to prettify and restrain" and deaden (193).[56]

Seldes's idiosyncratic attitude toward theatricality set the pattern for all the American avant-gardists of the 1920s and even some of the more conservative modernists. His championing of the "lively" arts, however, cannot disguise a telling ambivalence toward "the people." Contra the claims of genteel or progressive critics, he insists that the popular arts "do not corrupt" their audiences (204). Yet "the people" are curiously absent from his book. There are almost no references to working-class or petit bourgeois audiences and readers. When he uses first-person plural pronouns, he seems to be appealing to a class of progressive, epicurean, modernist intellectuals (like him), the "we" who "have no leisure" and yet who, "in the presence of great works of art . . . are suspended between the sense of release from life, the desire to die before the image of the supremely beautiful, and a new-found capacity for living" (203). No working-class mugs or tired businessmen need apply, since it is highly unlikely they would have cultivated such powers of discernment or intensely philosophical responses to Aeschylus or Mozart. The few references that Seldes does make to mass audiences are contradictory. On the one hand, he defends the "some twenty million people" who follow the daily comic strips and disdains those snobs who ridicule "the unenlightened millions" who attend musical revues (213, 151). On the other hand, he also disparages "the inexpressive multitudes who have laughed" at Chaplin films "and not wondered why" and the crowds who spread "sharp almond odours" throughout movie houses—the multitudes to whom *The 7 Lively Arts* is clearly not addressed (3). In his love of popular culture but ambivalence toward the people who patronize it, Seldes represents a variation on the ironic, 1920s modernist intellectual who, Edmund Wilson notes tartly, enjoyed "the debauchment of American life as a burlesque show." His was "the attitude of trying to get a kick out of the sheer energy and size of American enterprises, . . . of letting one's self be carried along by the mad hilarity and tragedy of jazz, of living only for the excitement of the night."[57] To this extent, Gorman is certainly correct when he argues that Seldes and the other cultural radicals "were in effect sustaining the distance from the mass public that intellectuals on the Left had opened over the early century."[58] In Seldes's case, however, the primary sign of that distance is not derision but the near erasure of the "class known as lowbrows," the ones who have, after all, "created and admired" the popular arts that Seldes so relishes (350).

The 7 Lively Arts would seem to address itself to two classes of readers: modernist intellectuals like Seldes himself with a deep antipathy to the genteel tradition, and pretentious "middle class" patrons who rely on the approval of "pretentious intellectual[s]" before reaching a verdict on matters cultural and regard the lively arts "as impostors and . . . contemptible vulgarisms" (349–50). These middle-class audiences and intellectuals, of course, are the ones who champion the bogus arts, the snobs who relish "the shoddy and the dull" that passes itself off as art (348). They represent the consumers whom Seldes and so many other American modernists attacked, not the "simple and sophisticated people" at "the two extremes," but those unfortunates who hover "in between," those "who can see nothing without the lorgnettes of prejudice provided by fashion and gentility" (23). Neither highbrow nor lowbrow, they are the chief patrons of the new literary stage, the ones who guarantee its dullness, superficiality, and inconsequence. They are the dupes who disparage popular forms in favor of the "ill-rendered profundity" that has increasingly found a haven in the legitimate theater. Let us call them middlebrow.

THE MIDDLEBROW STAGE

Gilbert Seldes's carving out a middling position in which to place the legitimate theater, between the "simple" and "sophisticated," ties it inexorably to the category "middlebrow," which, Janice Radway notes, "was apparently first mobilized sometime in the 1920s as a way of referring to an increasingly visible group of consumers who enthusiastically bought the diverse products of a growing industry devoted to the marketing of 'culture.'"[59] Although Seldes does not employ the term, his portrait of the genteel, fashionable snob who patronizes the legitimate stage is closely aligned with other descriptions from the 1920s of the passive consumer of standardized art commodities. From the 1920s through the 1950s, the middlebrow was considered to be traditional at heart yet striving to be au courant, a middle-class man or woman with education and social aspirations who, Radway notes, would "read the new book-review sections" in newspapers and subscribe to "innovative magazines like *Time* and the *New Yorker*."[60] Radway usefully identifies the culture with which these people identified not as a "harbinger of new mass cultural forms," but as a distinctive by-product of American modernism, "a separate aesthetic and ideological production constructed by a particular fraction of the middle class offended equally by the 'crassness' of mass culture and by the literary avant-garde."[61] For the middlebrow consumer was routinely described as—and condemned for—being a social-climbing parvenu trying to "preempt . . . the highbrow's function" and "blur the lines between the serious and the frivolous." Unlike the lowbrow, who suffers "immediate pleasure or grief," the middlebrow is the unapologetic consumer and cultural middleman, a "pretentious and frivolous man or woman who uses culture to satisfy social or business ambitions."[62] And because middlebrow culture, as Pierre Bourdieu notes, always references highbrow by offering up either "minor forms of the legitimate cultural goods and practices" or "acceptable versions" of avant-gardist or consecrated works, it promotes confusion between highbrow and middlebrow. Middlebrow consumers are thus always looked down upon by the elite (those possessing large sums of economic and cultural capital) as reactionaries who have developed an "avid but anxious, naïve but serious way of clutching" at a legitimate culture to which their access remains restricted.[63] They are unmistakably the bogus sophisticates that Seldes so berates: the highbrow wannabes, the ones fixated on those dreary and pretentious, "arty conglomerations of middle-high seriousness and bourgeois beauty" (315–16).

Despite the conflicts between the genteel critics and the modernists, the cultural hierarchy in the United States during the 1920s was typically imagined as being clearly delineated and relatively stable. As Kammen emphasizes, "from the 1870s until the 1960s, a great many Americans did in fact believe that cultural stratification existed and they responded accordingly."[64] (This delineation, moreover, at least as far as theater is concerned, has survived largely intact to the present day.) At the top during the 1920s, representing consecrated, highbrow culture, were both large institutions (like opera companies, symphony orchestras, and museums filled with old masters) and smaller, independent artists (like painters, poets, and composers) who vended a restricted body of goods to a high-status public. (Many of the consumers of these goods were in fact other artists.) These independent producers ranged from anticommercial avant-gardists to folk artists. Then as now, highbrow work tends to be wrapped in mystique, trading on its purported authenticity and its refusal to succumb to the commodity form. At the opposite end of the spectrum, captivating the unwashed, largely foreign-born masses, were genres such as jazz, comic strips, nickelodeons, dime novels, and among theater forms, minstrel shows, burlesque, freak shows, circuses, cheap vaudeville, and the like. Although these forms were not mass-produced in the way that cinema was, they were usually deemed lowbrow insofar as they were imagined to be fit for consumption only en masse by the working classes and the petite bourgeoisie.

I have argued elsewhere that what I am labeling the legitimate theater became positioned during the 1920s as a middlebrow form, committed both to artistic and commercial success.[65] This is not to say that all theatrical practices in the United States fell into this category. Paul DiMaggio notes that the noncommercial art theaters (the little theaters whose voice and champion was *Theatre Arts* magazine, first published in 1916) aimed to produce a relatively elite product. "But for a handful of settlement-house, leftist, and rural theatres, the little stages never tried to serve any but a high-status public" and charged admission accordingly, effectively barring "the working or lower middle classes."[66] Though Eugene O'Neill emerged out of the Provincetown Players, his plays were being produced on Broadway by 1920, as the New York–centered legitimate theater and the nationally organized touring companies were in the process of staking out a position somewhere between highbrow and lowbrow. As this "serious" theater was being institutionalized, the critic, playwright, and drama professor Thomas H. Dickinson called for it to strive for moderation, to take up what Dorothy Chansky describes as a dialectical position between "elitism and popular taste."[67] Eschewing equally the "esoteric" and "debased," Dickinson's new theater was to be aimed not at "*Connoisseurs*" ("highbrows") nor at those for whom "theatre is a pastime only" (lowbrows). Its proper audience should be those Seldes disdained, "Theatre-Lovers" with "taste" who "go to the theater to enjoy it and not to judge it" (middlebrows).[68]

During the 1920s, every theater critic weighed in at one time or another on the difficulty of trying perpetually to negotiate the schism between highbrow and lowbrow, art and commerce. Walter Prichard Eaton, the Harvard-educated successor to George Pierce Baker at Yale and longtime contributor to *Theatre Arts* magazine, despaired at the disparity between the "professional theatre of commerce" and what he called the "intellectual and spiritual aristocrat," otherwise known as "the true theatre."[69] And the most famous, flamboyant, and idiosyncratic of the drama critics, George Jean Nathan, who made a career out of terrorizing the many artists he disdained and enshrining the chosen few (most notably Eugene O'Neill), felt that the popular theater must know and respect its place. Because it was an art that "enthrones ignorance," it was suitable only for "the mob."[70] For Nathan, the popular, commercial theater (and specifically musical comedy) was inimical to consecrated culture; because it was bankrolled by "a great savanna of successful business men who are mistaken for and hailed as talented producers," it was a "refuge from art and literature, from beauty and truth."[71]

The middlebrow status of the legitimate stage was confirmed by the renown and power of a "warm and reasonable" tastemaker like Burns Mantle, who was theater critic for the *New York Daily News* from 1922 until 1943.[72] He is best known, however, for his stewardship of the annual *Best*

Plays volumes that he initiated in 1919 and of which he remained editor until his death in 1948. Although one might argue—and many have—with his annual selection of the ten "best" plays (he excluded musicals until the Gershwins' 1931 Pulitzer Prize–winning *Of Thee I Sing*), his series is undeniably representative of Broadway's legitimate offerings. Included among his selections is the vast majority of now canonical plays (or rather, "descriptive synopses" thereof), along with an assortment of long-forgotten pot-boilers and Seldes's "arty conglomerations of middle-high seriousness."[73] In the introduction to the first volume, Mantle maps out his editorial project and his method of play selection. He claims that the collected plays "represent the best judgment of the editor, variously confirmed by the public's indorsement. The intention frankly has been to compromise between the popular success, as representing the choice of the people who support the theater, and the success with sufficient claim to literary distinction of text or theme to justify its publication."[74] His collections thus strike "a sanely considered compromise" between "the popular or so-called commercial theater, which is the theater of the people" and "the 'best' plays judged by the higher literary standards."[75] His "best," moreover, represent a self-fulfilling prophecy, reinforcing the idea that Broadway's most important contributions represent a compromise between lowbrow and highbrow. For his exclusion of musical comedies, light farces, and "experimental" plays guarantees the unremittingly middlebrow character of the theater that has come down to us as representing the "best" of its time.[76]

Mantle's penchant for "compromise," however, conceals the social and cultural struggles taking place in and around the legitimate theater during the 1920s. For with the brisk assimilation of new immigrants, the rapid expansion of the white-collar sector of the workforce, the growth of disposable income and leisure time in which to spend it, the rise of jazz and radio, and the phenomenal efflorescence of a popular culture industry centered in Hollywood, the legitimate theater became a kind of battleground in which a "higher literary" theater was becoming increasingly hostile to and isolated from "the theater of the people." This struggle pitted so-called serious playwrights against commercial producers, art against business, the "literary" against the "lively," and the most influential critics against "a popular theatre," to borrow Nathan's phrase, in which "the best in drama and dramatic literature must inevitably fail."[77] It also pitted a generation of older critics, like Nathan and Walter Prichard Eaton, against a generation of young upstarts, like Gilbert Seldes. For at the risk of oversimplification,

I must point out that much of the "higher literary" theater of the 1920s represented a preserve for upper-middle-class patrons, critics, and playwrights, many of whom had deep roots in American soil and represented what one observer described as "Anglo-Saxon and inherently Protestant" stock.[78] The majority of these partisans, moreover, came from upper-middle-class families and were educated at elite universities, unlike the stars, producers, and defenders of vaudeville, musical comedy, farce, and so forth. So many of those associated with this insurgent popular theater were first- or second-generation Jewish-Americans, like Seldes, Fanny Brice, Al Jolson, the Marx Brothers, Eddie Cantor, the Gershwins, Jerome Kern, Rodgers and Hart, plus a slew of other cultural producers and critics. Critics like Seldes, meanwhile, were intent on launching a revolt that, as C. Wright Mills points out, "was aesthetic and literary rather than explicitly political, . . . an enthusiastic revolt against 'provincial' regional hankerings, against social and ideological proprieties, against gentility in all forms."[79]

The conflict between high and low that defined the legitimate theater during the 1920s set old money against new; a Europeanized cultural tradition against a new vernacular one that was impudently laying claim to the brand names "modern" and "American"; and a well-established, white Anglo-Saxon Protestant elite against young, insurgent, entrepreneurial, often Jewish artists and intellectuals. It is worth noting here that although Nathan came from a Jewish family, he "repeatedly refused to discuss his Jewishness," "obfuscated his family background," and "lived in dread of 'exposure.'"[80] And it is no coincidence that Seldes in *The 7 Lively Arts* chooses Walter Prichard Eaton as the spokesperson for the legitimate theater and a "great antagonist of the movies" in an imaginary debate he pens between Eaton and D. W. Griffith set in the sacred precincts of the "theatre of Dionysos." Although Seldes does not (here and elsewhere) always endorse Griffith's positions, the less sympathetic Eaton is limned as an Apollonian, elitist metaphysician for whom "the past is not dead," who acknowledges "the dullness of the theatre" but who glories in an "invisible and divine" art, and longs to resurrect a humanistic drama that plays to "the imagination of mankind." Griffith, in contrast, ever the Dionysian—and materialist—defines himself as one unafraid of "the very lowest." Unlike Eaton (and the many advocates of a "sacred," legitimate theater), he chooses to embrace what he acknowledges to be "*the* vulgar art," the movies, in the belief that the "popular" and the "grand" need not be antithetical. On the contrary, for Griffith, as for Seldes and the other populists of the 1920s, the machine (here, the movie projector) is a bringer of "miracles," the vehicle of a "Rabelaisian madness" that restores the "grandeur" of the ancient Greek theater. And the "gross caricatures" of movies (as well as of comic strips, vaudeville, and the other lively arts) are "truer than the realism of the theatre." They are true because they represent an art of the people, an alchemical art that turns the debris of the Machine Age, the dregs of modernity, into gold. The cinematic art, Griffith explains, should "have its appeal to the very lowest. But because our roots are in the dung and the mire, do you think there shall be no lovely blossoms on the trees in spring and no fruit?" (27–38).

THREE

FASCINATING RHYTHM

Jazz is the result of the energy stored up in America. It is a very energetic kind of music, noisy, boisterous and even vulgar. One thing
is certain. Jazz has contributed an enduring value to America in the
sense that it has expressed ourselves. It is an original American
achievement which will endure, not as jazz perhaps, but which will
leave its mark on future music in one form or another.

—George Gershwin,
"The Composer and the Machine Age" (1933)

The struggles taking place in the American theater during the 1920s—between the legitimate and the popular, art and commerce, Broadway and
Hollywood, the sacred and the profane, art music and jazz, gentility and
modernism, the upper classes and the working classes, and gentiles and
Jews—were far more than merely fodder for critics and intellectuals. Indeed, every sector of the cultural economy was profoundly impacted by the
tensions and contradictions that arose from them. These struggles, moreover, not only comprised the context for theater in the 1920s; they also
provided the subject matter for countless plays, musicals, and vaudeville

acts (which usually defended one side or the other). Countless pieces of theater during the 1920s were, in one way or another, about the conflict between highbrow and lowbrow. When one considers the considerable overlap between the struggles for legitimation in theater and in music, one figure stands out as emblematic of both the promise and the curse of jazz: George Gershwin (1898–1937). A hero of Broadway, Hollywood, Tin Pan Alley, cabaret, concert hall, and opera house, he is by all accounts the most famous composer the United States has produced. And Gershwin was central, Howard Pollack points out, to the histories of both American music and theater.[1] As Carol Oja emphasizes, for "many white critics and listeners in the 1920s, Gershwin did not just borrow from jazz; he embodied it."[2]

Yet George Gershwin is also the one composer whose cultural status was (and continues to be) the most controversial. His music, both popular songs and concert music, represents not only a hybrid of black and white traditions, but also an attempt to negotiate and even reconcile the schism between highbrow and lowbrow entertainments, art music and jazz, European and American techniques, and upper-class and working-class amusements. Certainly no other musician of the 1920s was as well educated as Gershwin in both popular and classical traditions and compositional methods.[3] Even the terms *popular* and *classical* become extremely problematic when analyzing his work. Is *Porgy and Bess* opera when performed at the Metropolitan but a musical when presented on Broadway? Is the Concerto in F a modernist classic when played by the New York Philharmonic but only light, middlebrow entertainment when performed by the Boston Pops? It is little wonder that champions of the lively arts like Gilbert Seldes and Carl Van Vechten would be fascinated by Gershwin's category-defying compositions or that countless musicians and composers, from W. C. Handy to Maurice Ravel, Fats Waller to Arnold Schoenberg, admired his music and were mesmerized by his brilliant pianism. At the same, given the changes in the definition of jazz between the 1920s and the 1950s, it is not surprising that postwar jazz historians would virtually ignore a body of work that, in its stylistic conventions and modes of production, distribution, and consumption, is sharply distinguished from the music of Louis Armstrong or Bessie Smith.

From an early age, Gershwin aimed to fold jazz into the classical tradition in order to write a uniquely American music. During the 1910s he played, studied, and listened to many kinds of music, and as early as 1922 he attempted to fuse highbrow and lowbrow in his one-act, Negro opera,

The Gershwins' 1924 musical *Lady, Be Good!* Dick Trevor (Fred Astaire) in a
sea of ostrich feathers.

*Credit: Billy Rose Theatre Division, The New York Public Library for the Performing Arts,
Astor, Lenox and Tilden Foundations*

Blue Monday Blues, composed for George White's *Scandals*. Both Gershwin
and White knew the tremendously successful black musical *Shuffle Along*
(1921), and that piece, Pollack notes, "may have helped steer Gershwin toward 'the possibilities of writing an opera for colored people.'"[4] Gershwin,
moreover, was intensely aware, even before *Rhapsody in Blue* (1924), of the
hazards of challenging the highbrow/lowbrow divide. *Blue Monday Blues*,
which Isaac Goldberg refers to as both a "one-act vaudeville opera" and
"black-American *verismo*," was withdrawn after one performance.[5] With
the sensational premiere of *Rhapsody in Blue*, however, he became a light-

ning rod for those anxious about symphonic jazz and the integration of popular and classical traditions. Some critics regarded the piece as the revelatory beginning of a uniquely American, classical music; others as a pretentious, crude, poisonous mulligan stew.[6] As David Schiff emphasizes, "Gershwin's music was premised on a mediation between cultural spheres," spheres that had previously been considered utterly inimical.[7]

Gershwin's published writings repeatedly advocate the indispensability of jazz as "the voice of America" and "the expression of its soul," a miraculous "black and white" hybrid containing "all colors and all souls unified in the great melting-pot of the world."[8] The fantasy of his own jazz as a site of social and cultural miscegenation was widely shared during the 1920s as jazz was not only becoming established as the most popular and distinctively American music but also exerting a tremendous influence (much to the horror of antimodernist music critics) on conservatory-trained American and European composers, from John Alden Carpenter and Aaron Copland to Igor Stravinsky and Maurice Ravel. More than any other musician, George Gershwin personified the revolutionary or scandalous (depending on one's point of view) mixing of high and low. His music was so controversial in classical music circles because it quickly became central to the debate during the 1920s about whether innovation (the sine qua non of art deemed culturally significant) should be rooted in American or European vernaculars. Conservatives, on the one hand, routinely considered Gershwin the purveyor of ill-mannered, low-class, mongrel music and the destroyer of cultural propriety, not least of all because of his unparalleled commercial success. (A British music radio station, Classic FM, calculates that Gershwin earned more in his lifetime, allowing for inflation, than any other composer.)[9] Modernists, on the other hand, like music critic Charles L. Buchanan, considered jazz, especially when worked by educated, "Machine Age" composers like Gershwin, the key to a new American music:

> In one breath our intelligentsia are deploring the fact that our art is a mere sterile replica of European standards, and then when we produce something that is individually spicy and racy and partially indigenous, the same intelligentsia throw up their hands in holy horror because the affair does not approximate European standards. "This is all right insofar as it goes," they say, "but keep it in its proper environment. Segregate jazz; it belongs in the cabaret; how dare it knock at the doors of the sacred temples of sound!"

Like Gershwin, Buchanan envisions an American art that expresses all the voices of the melting pot. It hardly seems accidental, moreover, that in the era of *Plessy v. Ferguson*, Buchanan's critique of a hypocritical intelligentsia implicitly analogizes the segregation of lowbrow from highbrow and of black from white. This champion of new American music especially delighted in Gershwin's Concerto in F (1925), a piece commissioned by Walter Damrosch for the certifiably highbrow New York Symphony Orchestra, which Buchanan deemed "the one composition of indubitable vitality, and authentic progressiveness, that this country has produced."[10] Carl Van Vechten, music critic, controversial author of *Nigger Heaven* (1926), and chief "bohemian impresario to the New Negro Renaissance," abruptly switched his allegiance during the mid-1920s from Europe to America, from high art to the lively arts.[11] Van Vechten lionized Gershwin, another advocate for cultural and racial mixing, and called *Rhapsody in Blue* "the finest piece of serious music that had ever come out of America."[12]

Carol Oja argues that Gershwin's disruptive power "showed both the fragility of the budding modernist scene in America and the degree to which the high-low controversy was central to it."[13] Indeed, all the debates in the 1920s about American modernism (musical or otherwise) seemed to pivot around jazz. And all the debates about jazz were preoccupied (consciously or unconsciously) with questions about the character of national tradition; the fear, in Gershwin's words, that "the American soul" might be "negroid"; the mechanization of cultural production and distribution; and the seemingly inexorable triumph of an art that issued from the working classes.[14] (In a country that has long disavowed the significance of social class, "making hierarchical distinctions about culture," John Seabrook notes, "was the only acceptable way for people to talk openly about class.")[15] Was American modernism a brilliant, nationalist efflorescence or the betrayal of long-standing national traditions? How was it to use popular vernaculars? Was it really as utopian as Gershwin and others maintained, and would it produce a new dispensation in which elite and popular cultures would no longer be constructed as adversaries, poised (like the ruling and working classes) to fight each other to the death? What would a consequential American modernist art be? And what would happen to those undeniably bourgeois forms, like theater, that ranged uneasily from lowbrow to highbrow?

As often happens during times of sweeping social and cultural change, disparate issues tend to be collapsed into one critical problem that is made to stand in for them all. During the 1920s, the signal concern for so many arbiters of taste was race, a category that then included certain groups that were then in the process of becoming separated out as ethnicities. In debates about jazz and the popular theater, the central and often unspoken problem so often came down to the relationship between African Americans and Jews. Jews were the one white, ethnic group that was then almost universally considered to have a privileged relationship to black culture. It was also the social fraction whose musical creativity and economic power most dramatically outweighed its meager representation as a portion of the U.S. population. In the person of composers, performers, writers, arrangers, producers, and publishers, Jews dominated large segments of the popular music, theater, and motion picture industries.

During the 1920s, Jewish musicians and vaudeville entertainers—many of them in literal or figurative blackface—were constructed less as thieves than as the primary intermediaries and popularizers of a musical vernacular that indisputably began as an African American form but of which, for biological and cultural reasons (it was reasoned), Jews have a deeper understanding than any other ethnic group. The model most frequently proffered was thus less appropriative than collaborative. And while the collaboration was undoubtedly theorized in racist terms, both African Americans and Jews were constructed as active and inventive makers of culture. Composer and critic John Tasker Howard, for example, in the first comprehensive survey of American music, noted strong resemblances between Negro and Jewish song. Trying to explain why "the Jew becomes an expert at jazz," he argued the similarities could be traced back to "an ancient relation between Negro and Semitic races on the African continent."[16] Isaac Goldberg maintained that the Jew "was originally much darker than he is today" and has "the sad, the hysterical psychology of the oppressed race." Because Jews and Negroes are both "Oriental," there are profound emotional, psychological, and musical similarities between the "ecstatic songs of the Khassidim" and "the sacred and secular tunes of the Negro." "The simple fact is that the Jew responds naturally to the deeper implications of jazz, and that as a Jewish-American he partakes of the impulse at both its Oriental and its Occidental end."[17] Waldo Frank, meanwhile, provided a more psychological explanation for the resemblances: "the races at once most flexible and most maladjusted—the Negro and the Jew—give the best jazz-masters."[18]

Whether they approved of jazz or not, many commentators in the

1920s regarded it as the emblem of the United States as melting pot. One columnist observed that some people believed jazz is "an expression of Hebrew-Americanism, others think it is an expression of Negro-Americanism, still others think it is pure American, unhyphenated."[19] For jazz to be "pure American," however, the model of national identity needed to be revised and the music's pedigree enlarged. Henrietta Straus contended that jazz is paradigmatic "melting-pot" music whose "now Slavic, now Oriental element" is "due to the fact that many of those who write, orchestrate, and play it are of Russian-Jewish extraction."[20] Composer and critic Virgil Thomson, meanwhile, reserved a special animus for what he called the music of "the melting pot," the "piquant but highly unsavory stirring-up-together of Israel, Africa, and the Gaelic Isles."[21]

George Gershwin aimed to dispel "the superstition that jazz is essentially Negro" by alleging that "its essence" is "no more Negro than is syncopation."[22] Having gained renown as the most innovative maker of what his supporters and detractors alike called jazz, Gershwin voiced some of the most utopian formulations of the 1920s and 1930s. He repeatedly described jazz as the quintessence of a modern, uniquely American syncretism; the "result of the energy stored up" in the nation; a progressive artistic and social force; the voice of "Machine Age America."[23] On the streets of New York, he wrote,

> I heard a concourse of sounds. . . . Old music and new music, forgotten melodies and the craze of the moment, bits of opera, Russian folk songs, Spanish ballads, chanson's [sic], rag-time ditties, combined in a mighty chorus in my inner ear. And through and over it all I heard, faint at first, loud at last, the soul of this great America of ours.[24]

Like so many composers and performers of the period, Gershwin constructed jazz as the most distinctive and important ingredient in musical modernism and the unique voice of a progressive, democratic, melting-pot America.[25] He explained that his ideal was "to express [him]self; then, to express America." But he "felt that it would be one and the same." In other words, he envisioned himself the personification of Machine Age America. American music, meanwhile, "must be a voice of the masses, a voice expressing our masses and at the same time immortalizing their strivings."[26] It is no accident that during the Depression, his apolitical stance seems to have given way to leftist sympathies. Mixing with Diego Rivera and "his radical friends" on a trip to Mexico, Gershwin "discussed at length their doctrines and intentions."[27] Pollack reports, moreover, that some of his nonmusical activities from the mid-1930s "at least suggested support for the anti-fascist Popular Front."[28] How amused Gershwin would have been to discover that in 1953 Senator Joseph McCarthy would brand his music "subversive."[29]

SHUFFLE ALONG

Although the musical comedies on which George and Ira Gershwin collaborated during the mid-1920s are rooted in several different traditions, they owe much to an earlier show that revolutionized the genre. In May 1921, as the theater season was drawing to a close, the all-black musical *Shuffle Along* premiered in a makeshift theater on West Sixty-third Street, taking Broadway by storm and changing the course of American theater history. With music and lyrics by Eubie Blake and Noble Sissle and a book by Flourney Miller and Aubrey Lyles, *Shuffle Along* tells a loosely structured tale of a mayoral election in Jimtown, Mississippi. It made stars of its performers (among whom numbered its four creators), introduced the Charleston to a jazz-hungry and dance-crazy America, broke down barriers of racial segregation, legitimized the black musical, and displaced what Blake described as "mushy, sobby, sentimental love songs" with "lively, jazzy songs."[30] Garnering nearly unanimous positive reviews, it quickly became the biggest hit on Broadway, and the rage of the social elite.[31] *Shuffle Along* also enthralled leading artists and cultural critics, including Langston Hughes, who claimed he enrolled at Columbia University so he could come to New York to see the musical that "symbolized Harlem"; George Jean Nathan, who saw it five times and delighted in what he called the "clogging of coloured feet, the swing and rhythm of coloured bodies, the wild, jungle pulsing of coloured tunes"; and George Gershwin, who was doubtlessly influenced by its songs and comedy.[32] Gilbert Seldes, believing that "*Shuffle Along* had been conceived as an entertainment for negroes," judged it, like all "negro shows," to be "without art," but he and virtually all the other white critics celebrated its "tremendous vitality."[33]

Musical comedy represents a form of theatrical bricolage, combining at the least, speech, song, dance, underscoring (derived in part from melodrama), and spectacle. And because songs perform different dramatic

Act 1, scene 3 of *Shuffle Along*. Flourney Miller and Aubrey Lyles, in black-face, in the grocery store scene.
Credit: *Museum of the City of New York*

tasks, they come in clearly distinguishable types and styles, including bal-lads, choruses, marches, love duets (both serious and comic), operetta airs, as well as specialty numbers: novelty, charm, patter, and list songs. In all musicals, there is a disjunction, more or less distinct, more or less disrup-tive, between speech and song. Yet *Shuffle Along* is unusual even for a mu-sical comedy because it is so frankly a collage, a mixture of disparate con-ventions, comic routines, dances, and songs. Like many early musicals, it undermines the already slim divide between musical comedy and vaude-ville. Both creative teams, Sissle and Blake as well as Miller and Lyles, had acquired reputations as "Colored Vaudevillians," and *Shuffle Along* can be seen as a sequence of vaudeville turns juxtaposed against a fairly standard romance plot that could have come from operetta.[34] Miller and Lyles were best known for blackface comedy that burlesqued Southern small-town life with slapstick and cascades of malapropisms, and the musical's book is an expansion of one of their early routines, "The Mayor of Dixie," that features two dueling, crooked, pratfall-prone candidates. Inserted into the musical is a second routine, a twenty-minute comic fight, "Jimtown's Fisticuffs," that they had developed independently and for which they were justly famous.[35] The songs, moreover, were very similar to (and some cases, identical with) the songs Sissle and Blake had used in their vaudeville act. The dances, however, as performed by skilled soloists and glittering showgirls, were, like the Charleston, new and sensational and were in large part responsible for making the show, in the words of one critic, "A breeze of super-jazz blown up from Dixie!"[36] The chorus was "exceptionally well drilled," and the solo dancers included Tommy Woods, who wowed ticket-buyers with "a slow-motion acrobatic dance," and Charlie Davis, an inspired tap dancer whose "sheer speed and endurance . . . staggered the audience."[37]

The phrase that the makers of *Shuffle Along* used to describe their piece is "a musical mélange" and Robert Kimball lays emphasis on the different "values, musical styles, and cultural influences" that went into it: "It was a series of fragments, bits, individual moments, each valid, brief, and pointed."[38] Its use of preexistent material, moreover, was not confined to comic routines and songs. Even the costumes were recycled, "discards from two flops" that included a sizable cache of "vaguely Orientalish costumes" perfect for the show's "Oriental Blues."[39] Sissle and Blake's songs, moreover, represent clever variations on clearly recognizable styles, including ragtime ("In Honeysuckle Time"), coon songs ("Bandana Days"), blues ("Daddy, Won't You Please Come Home"), operetta-style ballads ("Love Will Find a Way"), and jazz ("Baltimore Buzz"). The characters, too, derive from different theatrical traditions. On the one hand, the romantic leads, Harry Walton and Jessie Williams, who will be allowed to marry only if Harry wins the election, are virtually lifted out of operetta. On the other hand, the two mayoral candidates Sam and Steve, played by the blackface comics Miller and Lyles, derive in part from the antics of the low-comic Tambo and Bones of minstrel shows. They are complemented by Tom Sharper, the political boss (played by Sissle) who functions as a straight man, or, in minstrel-show terminology, the interlocutor, in rela-

tion to the two clowns. The script also numbers among its bit players characters named Uncle Tom and Old Black Joe.

The characters and routines in *Shuffle Along*, however, come filtered
through the comic dialogues and song-and-dance numbers of Bert
Williams and George Walker, the principal reformers of blackface comedy
in the early years of the twentieth century. Indeed, the song "Bandana
Days" may well be a reference to Williams and Walker's 1908 musical,
Bandanna Land. The song itself represents a coon song once removed.
That is, Sissle and Blake use the conventions of an up-tempo plantation
nostalgia number, complete with a verse in the minor mode that modulates
to the major just before the peppy refrain. The highly syncopated refrain,
moreover, looks in two directions historically, backward to ragtime and
forward to jazz. Yet "Bandana Days" can also be seen, I believe, as a sly
satire of plantation nostalgia that even interpolates snatches of "Dixie" into
the release. This song, like so much of *Shuffle Along*, thus authorizes a kind
of double reading. The piece can be interpreted as it was on opening night
by Alan Dale as a simple, "jolly" "'darky' musical comedy" performed by
actors who "reveled in their work."[40] Or it can be seen, as it doubtlessly was
by many African Americans in the audience, as an ironic reinvention of a
racist formula that freely appropriates and satirizes the conventions of both
minstrelsy and musical comedy. If *Shuffle Along* does indeed authorize this
double reading, it represents the persistence of conventions developed by
African Americans at the turn of the century that, David Krasner argues,
responded to "two competing forces: the demands to conform to white notions of black inferiority, and the desire to resist these demands by undermining and destabilizing entrenched stereotypes of blacks onstage."[41]

Perhaps the best example of *Shuffle Along*'s success in jazzing up the
musical is its best-known song, "I'm Just Wild About Harry." It is sung at
the top of the second act after Jessie learns that Harry has lost the election
and that they therefore may not wed. Given its position in the plot, it did
not need to be an up-tempo number. Sissle and Blake could have given
Jessie a blues or torch song to mourn her seemingly lost love. But instead
they give her a lively, heavily syncopated, major-mode jazz tune (in A-B-A'-
C form) which is about the "ecstasy" of requited love and may well be the
only musical comedy ballad that is also a campaign song.[42] Although there
are many features that make it memorable, I want to single out the syncopations on the repetitions of the word "wild" and a blue note on the first
syllable of "ecstasy" as examples of its skillful word painting, its use of mu-

sic to illustrate the sense of the lyric. Yet what I think makes the song most potent is the unexpected leap of a tritone on "about me" at the end of the first eight-bar phrase, which thereby substitutes a gloriously dissonant leading tone for the expected tonic. In the A' section that follows, the tritone is "corrected" to a predictable perfect fifth that lands the melody back on the tonic and leads to a rousing, extended, syncopated coda. It is little wonder that the critics were utterly disarmed by the "lively entertainment" provided by this "excellent score."[43]

Shuffle Along's unique position in the U.S. theater is in part a result of a fortuitous congruence between the musical's plot and its own position in theatrical culture. In other words, it dramatizes the very predicament in which its creators and performers found themselves. Like the mayoral candidates, Sissle, Blake, and company were aiming for success in an extremely competitive arena. Like them, they were black, middle-class entrepreneurs who would be getting a cut of the proceeds. Like them, they knew their success depended on their skill in putting together and promoting a performance that would hold people spellbound. *Shuffle Along* cleaned up in every respect. It was a major moneymaker on the road for three years, helped integrate theaters in the North, and provided a springboard for several of its performers who became among the foremost artists of the age, including Josephine Baker, Florence Mills, Paul Robeson, and William Grant Still. Musical comedy would never be the same.

THE GLORIFICATION OF THE POPULAR GENIUS

Shuffle Along modernized musical comedy by introducing a sparkling mélange of ragtime, operetta, and jazz that did more than carry audiences away. Indeed, Robert Kimball does not exaggerate when he calls it "an epoch-making stage work without which much that has been individual and original in American musical theater would probably never have happened."[44] This mélange permitted a cleverness and dynamism that were relatively new to the Broadway musical. Yes, musical comedy had been lively and tuneful, but jazz allowed the musical to expand its expressive and dramatic range, to play with and ironize the genre's formulas in subtle and creative ways. *Shuffle Along* made jazz and tap dancing obligatory on Broadway and opened the door for a string of inventive black musicals, including Sissle and Blake's follow up to *Shuffle Along*, *The Chocolate Dandies* (1924).

Among those most inspired by *Shuffle Along*'s achievement, one must count George and Ira Gershwin who, beginning with *Lady, Be Good!* decisively detached musical comedy from operetta and consolidated their distinctive brand of song, which, the *New York Times* noted, even "the unmusical and serious-minded will find it hard to get rid of."[45] The critic's reference to the "serious-minded" suggests that he or she was well aware that *Rhapsody in Blue* had preceded *Lady, Be Good!* by ten months and that Gershwin's profile was markedly different from that of other Broadway tunesmiths. And while *Lady, Be Good!* had few highbrow pretensions, its composer remained a touchstone for those concerned about the future of American music. Indeed, Gershwin was never able to escape the cultural and social controversies that swirled around jazz. In *Lady, Be Good!*, however, the Gershwins do not take up these controversies, and the piece remains, in Alan Dale's words, an unusually "delightful," if "quite typical musical comedy."[46] Isaac Goldberg seconds Dale's observation and admits that the Gershwins brought not "radical change" to the formula, but "a distinctive musical personality."[47]

In his discussion of 1920s musical comedy, Goldberg summarizes its conventions and provides one of the more precise contemporary accounts of its form and function. Describing what could be *Shuffle Along, Lady, Be Good!* or dozens of other musicals, he explains that it is based on "a loose story, or 'book'; a skeleton of action" that generally revolves around one or more pairs of young lovers whose coupling is in some way being thwarted.[48] Usually the action pits persons of different generations or social classes against each other, but inevitably youth, sincerity, and true love win out in the end. The characters as a rule are stock comic figures that include the young lovers (the ingénue and juvenile lead), foolish parental figures, an eccentric sidekick or two, as well as other comic foils (many of them clearly derived from vaudeville). The plot is loosely enough constructed to allow the interpolation of songs, routines, and specialty acts. (Scott McMillin describes the books of these musicals as "for-the-moment exercises in nonchalance.")[49] The resulting "hodge-podge" usually begins with an "[o]pening chorus, chiefly to break the ice . . . and to exhibit the female wares."[50] The interpolated numbers, meanwhile, include

Sentimental songs, to which correspond the slower, suaver rhythms of the dance . . . "Hot" numbers—these especially since the jazz invasion—with dance specialties of faster tempo and of more abandoned spirit . . . Happiness songs,—songs to induce forgetfulness of troubles and assurance of better times to come.[51]

To these Goldberg adds other song types: the blues, "a purgative expression of woe that is more sincere among the Negroes than among the whites"; the torch song, "a specialized blue mood in which is sung (by a female) the burning pangs of unrequited love"; the production number, which is "intended for the stage spectacle chiefly"; and the hit, which is "short, pithy, catchy" and "aimed at the public purse."[52] He explains that the alternation among these contrasting types keeps the audience from getting "wearied." Above all, the musical comedy hodgepodge is an expression of "American optimism" and so represents "the glorification of the national popular genius."[53]

The jazz-influenced songs of the late teens and 1920s transformed the conventions that had dominated Broadway and Tin Pan Alley at the turn of the century. Mark N. Grant argues that the arrival of jazz allowed composers and lyricists to write a new kind of song that was especially well-suited to the musical theater. Out went the march, two-step, and waltz (songs in 2/4 or 3/4 time) and in came new, slower, four-beat songs (with accents on the first and third beats) that went by the name "foxtrot." Grant points out that a foxtrot, like "I'm Just Wild About Harry," with its rhythm of one slow step followed by two quick ones, was the perfect form for the new musical dramaturgy that was overtaking Broadway. "It can be made to swing or syncopate, yet it gives off a subtle lilt even when the rhythm is foursquare and unswinging. It can be elegant and romantic or peppy and jazzy with a simple alteration of the basic tempo." Most important, the foxtrot, with its "slower, suaver rhythms," allows for a much more supple relationship between music and words. Grant explains that it

afforded lyricists and book writers an unprecedented expansion of verbal and dramatic possibilities. The backbeats of the foxtrot smoothly glide instead of boom-chucking, thus not distracting too much attention from the lyrics of a song. The four beats provide more space in which a lyricist could unfurl his thoughts, and more room for complex lyrics. . . . Like the African-American blues and the European lied, its predecessors in 4/4 song forms, the foxtrot is built to accommodate and highlight narrative lyrics but, unlike them, does so while kicking up light, bouncy, danceably rhythmic downbeats. . . . It drives by soft sell-

complex wordplay and
4

1 flexible song lyrics de-
elopment of the foxtrot.
e new vernacular of the
1guration of what is uni-
dates the beginning of
als for the Princess The-
dy, Be Good! or to *Show*
like Lorenz Hart, Cole
ld never have developed
insentimentally roman-
,---- ....ut a musical vernacular to match and inspire their words. Philip Furia explains that the challenge the lyricist faces is to fit "words 'mosaically' to music," to work "within musical constraints" or subvert them, and to match the "composer's phrasing with verbal fits (or shrewd misfits)."[55] In transforming the relationship between words and music, jazz, or rather, syncopated dance music in 4/4 time, helped turn musical comedy from enjoyable throwaway entertainment to dazzling throwaway entertainment.

JEWISH JAZZ

Tip-Toes, the Gershwins' third Broadway musical (following *Tell Me More* [1925]) is a virtual anthology of "American optimism." It opened in December 1925 at the apogee of George's early celebrity, six months after he became the first U.S.-born musician to appear on the cover of *Time* magazine and three weeks after he premiered his Concerto in F with Damrosch and the New York Symphony before a jam-packed Carnegie Hall. With a book by Guy Bolton and Fred Thompson and choreography by Sammy Lee, *Tip-Toes* enjoyed 194 performances, a national tour, and successful runs in London, Paris, Montreal, and Australia. Attracting "a large and prominent Broadway audience" on its opening night, it was judged by Alexander Woollcott as having Gershwin's "best score" and being "precisely three times as entertaining" as their previous hit, *Lady, Be Good!*.[56] More recently, John McGlinn has called it Gershwin's "first truly great

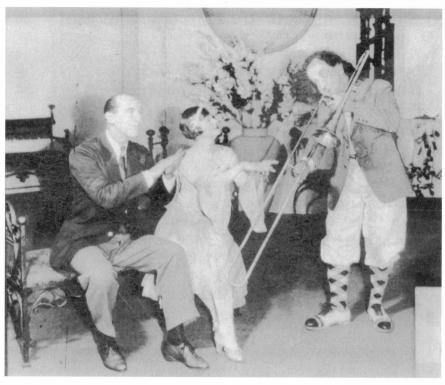

The Gershwins' 1925 musical, *Tip-Toes*, featuring the three Komical Kayes:
Hen, Tip-Toes, and Al (Harry Watson, Queenie Smith, and Andrew
Tombes).
*Credit: Billy Rose Theatre Division, The New York Public Library for the Performing Arts,
Astor, Lenox and Tilden Foundations*

stage score." "[C]areen[ing] into the jazz age," it "encapsulates an entire
era."[57]

    Tip-Toes is set in Florida during the brief but feverish land boom of the
mid-1920s and centers on two couples: the wealthy Rollo Fish Metcalf and
Sylvia, his socialite wife; and the charming Steve Burton, brother to Sylvia
and heir to a glue fortune, and Tip-Toes Kaye, one of the "Komical
Kayes," a three-person vaudeville troupe from New York. Although the
vaudevillians have come to Palm Beach as hired entertainers, they hope to
snare a millionaire for Tip-Toes by passing themselves off as the rich, aristocratic Van Renssalaers. This being a 1920s musical comedy, Tip-Toes
and Steve fall in love at first sight, but at the end of act 1, Tip-Toes suffers

amnesia, after having been nearly run over by a car, and comes to believe she truly is Roberta Calhoun Van Renssalaer. Rollo (who once had a flirtation with Tip-Toes) reveals her true identity to Steve, who fears she is a gold digger and to test her, feigns sudden impoverishment. After several more plot twists, Tip-Toes proves she loves *him*, not his fortune, and Steve offers her an engagement ring and confesses the subterfuge, and the curtain falls while all happily reprise the show's biggest hit, "Sweet and Low-Down."

With its two pairs of lovers, lively chorines, glamorous locale, mistaken identities, displaced New Yorkers, vaudeville routines, and snappy songs, *Tip-Toes* in many ways represents a typical (if unusually skillful and tuneful) example of the mid-1920s musical comedy. Less typical is the piece's high level of musical, lyrical, and dramatic coherence, a full eighteen years before Rodgers and Hammerstein allegedly revolutionized the genre with *Oklahoma!*, which is routinely and misleadingly called the first integrated musical. Philip Furia is correct to note that Ira Gershwin's lyrics are "more integrated into the dramatic context of the show and more closely tied to particular characters" than in any preceding Gershwin musical.[58] More typical—and far more revealing of the struggles taking place in American theater—is the musical's focus on the economic and social obstacles the young lovers face. In fact, the cross-class romance is only one in a series of antagonisms on which the musical is focused. On the level of plot, the upper-class, WASP socialites holidaying in Palm Beach are set against the rootless, indigent vaudevillians. To dramatize these class differences, the writers set the rich swells, decked out in "fashionable and expensive clothes," against the "typical vaudeville actor[s]" sporting "'nifty' clothes."[59] The presence of the Komical Kayes, moreover, authorizes Bolton and Thompson to oppose realistic book scenes for the upper crust to comic routines for the vaudevillians, at least one of whom, "as funny a fellow as one could ask for" (Harry Watson Jr.), seems to have been plucked "from the bosom of the two-a-day."[60] And the Kayes, like Miller and Lyles from *Shuffle Along*, inevitably bring the conventions and energy of vaudeville to their scenes. Al and Hen Kaye, for example, are bona fide clowns who recall the Marx Brothers, whose hit, *The Cocoanuts*, had opened only three weeks before. They shoot out their own outrageous theatrical euphemisms for money ("The maguma! The spondulicks. The cush! The kale. The toadskin!") and perform clearly identifiable shtick: masquerading

The chorus presents the star of the show, Tip-Toes Kaye.
Credit: *Billy Rose Theatre Division, The New York Public Library for the Performing Arts, Astor, Lenox and Tilden Foundations*

as pedigreed sophisticates in knickers and an "old varsity blazer," drinking soup through a straw, and clowning with cap pistols, fright wigs, and an "old battered trombone" (1–9, 1–19, 1–22).

The Kayes, moreover, unlike the WASPy socialites, are implicitly coded as Jews—like so many of the most famous vaudevillians during the 1920s. Although many major vaudeville stars and entrepreneurs were non-Jewish, the majority of headliners, theater owners, and managers were first- or second-generation Jews, from Al Jolson, Eddie Cantor, Sophie Tucker, Fanny Brice, and the Marx Brothers to the Shuberts and Klaw and Erlanger.[61] Indeed, as in musical comedy and motion pictures, Jews figured more prominently in vaudeville during the 1920s than any other ethnic or racial group.[62] Although neither book nor lyrics of *Tip-Toes* features Yiddish slang, Hen does a brief "Dutch" routine in act 1 (1–22), so named, as Robert W. Snyder notes, because many spectators "thought that . . . Yiddish accents sounded German."[63] And in "These Charming People," Al "Van Renssalaer" brags that his invented family fortune "was made in undergarments"—like those of so many Jewish rag trade moguls.[64] Even their surname corresponds to a common Americanization of a German or Slavic Jewish name. The evidence for the performers' actual Jewishness may be circumstantial, but their association with Jewish vaudeville is anything but.

The Kayes are constructed as assimilated Jews in part because of their highly theatricalized mutability, yen for constant performance, and multiple pseudonyms (Lord Canvasbottom, Professor Pierre de Cochon, etc.). As Andrea Most notes,

> After the passage of the Johnson-Reed immigration act of 1924, Jews of Eastern European descent in particular were shunted into an out-of-favor racial category. The danger of being essentialized, locked into an unwanted racial definition was clear: without control over his or her identity, an American Jew was subject to the illogical and dangerous whims of racial science and public persecution. For this reason many Jews resisted racial definitions and clung tenaciously to the notion that one could become an American simply by adopting American culture, language and appearance. The musicals of the 1920s and 30s, many of them written and performed by Jews from immigrant backgrounds, suggest a strong opposition to rigid racial categorizations, advocating instead a more fluid conception of identity.[65]

The basic premise of the musical and the carnivalesque atmosphere of Palm Beach afford the Kayes (and the Gershwins!) unparalleled opportunities to try on an array of upper-crust American identities and in the process to satirize the WASPy, idle rich.

Like all the early Gershwin musicals, *Tip-Toes* dramatizes the cross-class (and arguably cross-cultural) romance by mixing high and low, setting foxtrots ("That Certain Feeling" and "When Do We Dance?") against songs that are closer to operetta ("Nice Baby" and "Looking for a Boy"). The Komical Kayes may not have a monopoly on jazz, but they are unquestionably the personification of the modern, Jewish-dominated, popular entertainment industry whose most important musical contribution in the 1920s was jazz-inflected popular music. As such, they allegorize the position of George Gershwin himself during the mid-1920s, the "young Jew" so-described in the first sentence of *Time*'s profile.[66] A child of a "tenement street," he may have "skinned his knees in the gutters," but he found "a curious music" there that he made "hump along with a twang and a shuffle, hunch its shoulders, and lick its lips."[67] This tenement-born and tenement-

The Komical Kayes.
Credit: Billy Rose Theatre Division, The New York Public Library
for the Performing Arts, Astor, Lenox and Tilden Foundations

bred, successful, rich, "famed jazzbo," whose "success is the typical Horatio Alger story," represented the antithesis of the WASPy socialites of Palm Beach, like Steve, with inherited fortunes.[68] For as Gerald Mast notes, "Gershwin's music seems a metaphor for democratic American creativity itself—the self-taught and self-made man not just as Commercial Success but as Revolutionary Artist."[69] And the musical repeatedly demonstrates the irresistible allure of (Jewish) jazz and popular culture and the success of those, like the Kayes, who exemplify and disseminate them.

Steve's first song, "When Do We Dance?," represents a repudiation of the high, European culture conventionally linked to a genteel fraction of the upper and middle classes during the 1920s. The first part of ⌐ devoid of Gershwin's well-known syncopations and blue notes, soun⌐ it could have been lifted from an operetta:

> I'm fed up with discussions
> About the music of Russians,
> And I'm most unhappy when you talk about art.
> Conversation so highbrow
> Is much too heavy for my brow.

The refrain that follows uses a conventional A-B-A-C form. But its strong rhythmic thrust and syncopation shatter the four-square mood of the verse as Steve implores,

> Let's take a chance, I'm in a trance,
> Getting a thrill in advance.

And although the release features a soaring, lyrical melody line, each phrase begins on a syncopated offbeat:

> Just can't help swaying—I must begin
> When they are playing Kern or Berlin.[70]

Jazz, in other words—or at least a Jewish version of jazz—is thrilling, trance-inducing, and irresistibly appealing to the glue-factory heir from Maine. And the jazz dancer, Tip-Toes, is constructed as the emblem and agent of this seduction, the one on whom Steve "take[s] a chance."

In the many discourses from the 1920s critical of jazz and other new forms of popular culture (like cinema and radio), the latter were conceived as dangerous modes of seduction, a standardized, mass-produced product that a dehumanizing society has made out of primitive beats and grunts, "a thing of . . . modern man-made jungles."[71] In *Theatre* magazine, the editor, Arthur Hornblow, attributed jazz to "the wild tom-tom music of savages in the jungle" that has (regrettably) been taken up and developed "by our own barbarians."[72] One of the most vehement opponents of jazz, Daniel Gregory Mason, a conservative, Harvard-educated composer and critic, considered it an "industrial turmoil, fever, and distress that we can but hope to survive."[73] For these and other antimodernist critics—most of whom had never been near a factory unless they owned it—popular culture (especially jazz and motion pictures) provided an analogue to the assembly lines that were becoming ubiquitous in the American workplace and represented an opium for the "mass man" that was the unwelcome by-product of these assembly lines. As a 1922 critic, William J. Schultz, noted, "The modern *Massemensch* is a creature of paved and lighted streets and grimed air; his dwelling is the tenement and frame house." He "is the patron of the dance hall, of the vaudeville show," and "the musical review." "His music is jazz."[74] As Andreas Huyssen explains, "male fears" of standardization and "an engulfing femininity" were routinely "projected onto the metropolitan masses, who were thought to represent a threat to the rational bourgeois order" as enshrined in highbrow cultural forms.[75] And Janice Radway notes that middlebrow culture in particular was attacked for producing "an undifferentiated mass of passive 'consumers' who were satiated by their indiscriminate absorption of a wholly undifferentiated substance."[76]

Yet the opponents of jazz were not the only ones who imagined it to be machine music. George Gershwin claimed that jazz represents "the nervous energy of modern American life," and he compares it to "the triumph of machinery."[77] He explained that he got the idea for *Rhapsody in Blue* while riding "on the train, with its steely rhythm" and "its rattle-ty-bang."[78] Although Paul Whiteman, the self-proclaimed King of Jazz, also likened jazz to "newer" machines, most of its advocates imagined its thrill as being not mechanical at all, but rather a delivery from regimentation, "the symptom of a glorious release from the bonds of moral constraint."[79] Its alleged emancipatory force, however, also provided the enemies of jazz, and of popular culture more generally, with rounds of moral ammunition. The "weird discordances" of jazz, Hornblow writes, "harmonize with the unbalanced, neurotic, chaotic, unmoral state into which the war plunged the world."[80] Its "crude" lyrics and "discordant" harmonies "provide a stimulant for jaded nerves."[81] Yet as Gershwin put it, it is "as useless to deplore the triumph of jazz as it is to deplore the triumph of machinery."[82]

Daniel Gregory Mason, Arthur Hornblow, and other conservative opponents of jazz were the foot soldiers in a battle between so-called Yankee critics and composers—the old-moneyed, Protestant advocates for a redemptive and genteel musical culture—and their insurrectionary and increasingly numerous, popular, and successful competitors, many of them Jews. MacDonald Smith Moore points out that because of the slippage between "Hebrew Americanism" and "Negro Americanism," both detractors and champions of jazz and musical modernism imagined "the stereotypical 'New York Jew'" as being "identified with a racial tradition midway between Yankees and Negroes." The Yankee classicists deplored this "'spiritual miscegenation'" because it "seemed that Jewish composers intended to obliterate the root distinction between high culture and merely anthropological culture."[83] Tenement-born, self-educated Jews like George Gershwin, in other words, had the impudence to challenge the Ivy League–educated, WASP elite, to lay claim to American modernism, and to seduce the all-too-gullible mob that, like Steve in *Tip-Toes*, is powerless to resist that syncopated beat.

The dangerously seductive and disruptive power of Broadway jazz is wryly attested to in a song from the now-forgotten 1928 musical, *Here's Howe*, with music by Roger Wolfe Kahn and Joseph Meyer and lyrics by Irving Caesar (all of them Jews). The play's show-stopping hit was "Crazy Rhythm," which Gerald Bordman describes as "one of the best and most enduring jazz numbers of the epoch" and which neatly illustrates (and enacts) the conflicting sentiments swirling around jazz in the late 1920s.[84] With a standard A-A-B-A' structure, the song personifies "crazy rhythm" and features a second verse that warns,

Ev'ry Greek, each Turk and each Latin,
The Russians and the Prussians as well;
When they seek the lure of Manhattan,
Are sure to come under your spell.
Their native folk songs they soon throw away,
Those Harlem smoke songs, they soon learn to play.

In the refrain, Harlem's "crazy rhythm" becomes the singer's obstinate antagonist: "Crazy rhythm, here's the doorway, / I'll go my way, you'll go your way." The singer is characterized as a masculine, "high-hat" hero who is rendered so defenseless by his black, déclassé seductress that he cannot help but begin every line of the song (except for two in the release) on a syncopated offbeat. The lyric of the release both explains and performs the power of jazz to sabotage cultural propriety:

When a highbrow meets a lowbrow
Walking along Broadway,
Soon the highbrow,

He has no brow,
Ain't it a shame,
And you're to blame.

Prompting both an unseemly colloquialism and an imperfect end-rhyme, crazy rhythm represents a blasphemous intermingling of high and low. (Kahn could relish this blasphemy. His father was Otto Kahn, one of the richest men in New York and chairman of the board of the Metropolitan Opera from 1908 to 1931.) It is also intoxicating and illicit. "What's the use of Prohibition, / You produce the same condition." With its devilishly catchy, relentlessly repeating musical phrases, the song finally and utterly infects the singer: "I've gone crazy, too."[85]

Among the aforementioned opponents of Jewish jazz, none was more vociferous than Daniel Gregory Mason, the scion of an eminent family of American composers and for many years head of the Columbia University music department. And while his position is uncompromisingly reactionary, it is also unusually revealing of the assumptions that underlay the debates about jazz. (As Bourdieu emphasizes, "nothing more clearly affirms one's 'class,' nothing more infallibly classifies, than tastes in music.")[86] What is at stake for the antimodernist Mason—and for so many champions of jazz—is nothing less than what Mason calls "the American temper," which the genteel Yankee associates with both the New England "Anglo-Saxon" and "the old South" (during the heyday of the Ku Klux Klan!). Because the "Jewish type" is manifestly "foreign," it has allegedly corrupted "our whole contemporary aesthetic attitude, . . . especially in New York," which "is dominated by Jewish tastes and standards, with their Oriental extravagance, their sensuous brilliancy and intellectual facility and superficiality." The "Oriental abandonment to excess" of "Hebrew art" threatens to make "public taste . . . permanently debauched."[87] (The association of Jewish cultures with New York dates back to the first wave of German Jewish immigration in the mid-nineteenth century. A much larger wave of eastern European Jews immigrated to the United States between 1880 and 1925 and prompted a more vigorous anti-Semitism.) Mason, like so many critics of the popular theaters, identifies this "Hebrew" music as a strictly "commercial product" that issues from "business and industrial life." This sanctimonious musical aristocrat, moreover, is even more severe than a Walter Prichard Eaton or George Jean Nathan, pathologizing popular culture by linking jazz's "morbid excitement" to the "fatigue" and "despair" of modern urban life: "It is a symptom of a sick moment in the progress of the human soul."[88] And Jewish jazz was not the only form of popular culture to be singled out for an attack that, after all, was based as much in class antagonism as anti-Semitism. Hollywood, as well, was repeatedly denounced for being, in the words of Henry Ford's notoriously anti-Semitic *Dearborn Independent*, "exclusively under the control, moral and financial, of the Jewish manipulators of the public mind." The latter were imagined, like the "Hebrew" jazz musician, as representing an "Oriental view" hostile to "the Anglo-Saxon, the American view." And movies—like jazz—were so dangerous because of their shameless commerciality, popularity, and ubiquity: "everywhere their lure and lasciviousness have been felt."[89]

The characterization of Jewish-produced popular culture as "Oriental" is a sign of its insinuatingly alien nature that offers an immediate (if unspoken) threat to "Anglo-Saxon" traditions. It is also symptomatic of its conceptualization, even by the champions of jazz, as a mixed art, "an example of miscegenation," the mongrel offspring of Russian Jews, African Americans, Irish, Italians, and other immigrant groups.[90] The construction of George Gershwin during the mid-1920s as a composer of both jazzy Broadway songs and serious concert music meant that he became, for supporters and detractors alike, the personification of cultural miscegenation, of the promiscuous mixture of high and low, white and black, esoteric and popular often characterized during this period as "Oriental." It is hardly by accident that Paul Whiteman's legendary 12 February 1924 Aeolian Hall concert, "An Experiment in Modern Music" (whose finale was *Rhapsody in Blue*), included several "Oriental" pieces, including an "Oriental Serenade" by Victor Herbert (in fact, his last composition), then the leading writer of operettas. Herbert's short piece surprisingly blurs the differences between a musical fantasy of the Orient and Jewish jazz by incorporating so many of the elements that usually characterize the latter: pentatonic scales, wailing saxophones and clarinets, frequent alternation between major and minor modes, generous use of blue notes, and repeated syncopations.[91]

The fantasy of Jewish jazz as a hybrid, "Oriental" form, a scene of madness, seduction, and social and cultural mixing, was widely promulgated even in forms that embraced jazz, especially musical comedy. Kern and Hammerstein's *Show Boat* famously thematizes and performs miscegenation not only in the story of Julie, the tragic mulatta, but also in the aggressive juxtaposition of musical genres, among them operetta, pseudoblues, pseudospirituals, hymns, sentimental ballads, and so-called jungle music (i.e., pseudo-African jazz). Like *Shuffle Along* and *Show Boat*, *Lady, Be Good!* features several different kinds of mixing. It combines comic, operetta-inspired songs (like "So Am I") with the Gershwins' distinctive brand of jazz, including perhaps their most dizzyingly syncopated song, "Fascinating Rhythm," with its "shaking," "hopping," "never stopping" polyrhythms as well as its melodic echoes of the conclusion of *Rhapsody in Blue*. Like "Crazy Rhythm," "Fascinating Rhythm" threatens to "drive" the singer "insane" with its breathless, throbbing, intoxicating beat (from which the release provides only momentary respite).[92] The plot, meanwhile, features another cross-class and miscegenated romance between millionaire socialite Jack Robinson and Susie Trevor, an impoverished aristocrat manqué who disguises herself as a Mexican gold digger, a "[d]ark-eyed señorita" who inspires the chorus boys in a lively, minor-tinged, Mexican dance, "Juanita."[93] And like *Tip-Toes, Lady, Be Good!* mixes musical comedy with vaudeville. Its elaborate plot is several times interrupted by specialty acts, including Cliff "Ukulele Ike" Edwards's rendition of "Fascinating Rhythm," Susie's fandango, and the "[d]iscovery of pianos" in the act 1 finale and the ensuing piano specialty act of Victor Arden and Phil Ohman (who appeared in all the early Gershwin musicals and provided the distinctive pianistic sound so closely associated with the composer).[94] If musical comedy during the Jazz Age was neither "serious" drama nor vaudeville, where did it belong?

"WHEN A HIGHBROW MEETS A LOWBROW"

Throughout the 1920s, critics of popular theater were more exercised by its insistent crossing of categories—its promiscuous mixing of high and low and its defiance of generic boundaries—than its allegedly mass-produced and standardized qualities. George Jean Nathan, predictably, inveighs against the "popular, or mob, theatre," which is degraded, he claims, because "the mob lowers automatically the intelligence of its component individuals."[95] And although he compares the virtuosity of the commercialized "Broadway playwriting type" to that of "the Chicago beef-king" or "the Schenectady electro-mechanical type," he is more disturbed by the Broadway play's "cheap" and "loud" qualities than its standardization.[96] The primary source of anxiety for critics like Nathan or Walter Prichard

J. Watterson "Watty" Watkins (Walter Catlett) surrounded by his señoritas in
Lady, Be Good!
Credit: Billy Rose Theatre Division, The New York Public Library for the Performing Arts,
Astor, Lenox and Tilden Foundations

Eaton was the difficulty of categorizing and ranking the many different
theatrical offerings, drawing clear boundaries between variety entertainments and the legitimate stage, between "whipped cream" and the
"roast."[97] And of all theatrical forms, the one that gave them the most trouble in the 1920s was musical comedy. Burns Mantle excluded it on principle from the "best plays," while Herman J. Mankiewicz noted that "the
only difference between the exceptionally good burlesque show and the
generally poor Broadway legitimate musical offering is that the prices for
the burlesque show are less than half those asked for its more pretentious
brother."[98] Oliver Sayler grouped musical comedy together with motion
pictures and bedroom farces as genres that "dilut[e] the general average of
intelligence and lower . . . the standard of demand."[99] Elsewhere, he shunts

Act 1 of *Lady, Be Good!* Jeff (Cliff "Ukulele Ike" Edwards) tries out his "Fascinating Rhythm."

Credit: *Billy Rose Theatre Division, The New York Public Library for the Performing Arts, Astor, Lenox and Tilden Foundations*

musical comedy off to a chapter dedicated to the "*[h]ors-d'oeuvre* of the theatre," "Revue, Variety and the Dance," in which he characterizes it as the "frisky maiden aunt of the Revue." He argues that these popular forms "are not yet really provocative enough . . . to tempt the taster farther into the theatre" and that the "borderland" between the musical play and the revue "is often dim—in the direction of vaudeville when the revue doesn't sufficiently digest and unify its fund of raw material; in the direction of musical comedy when the latter provides generous leeway to its comedians."[100] For Sayler, the Princess musicals of Jerome Kern and P. G. Wode-

Act 1 of *Lady, Be Good!* Watty Watkins courting Jo Vanderwater (Jayne Auburn).

Credit: Billy Rose Theatre Division, The New York Public Library for the Performing Arts, Astor, Lenox and Tilden Foundations

house (often regarded as "the first series of truly modern American musicals") exemplify this category crisis: "What . . . were the Princess cameos? . . . Musical comedies or revues in miniature?"[101] Both Nathan and Eaton were also anxious that the musical comedy know—and respect—its allotted position in the cultural hierarchy. An "outlet for our trivial moods," "the music show occupies to the theatre and drama the same relationship . . . that alcohol occupies to art: a convivial moment of forgetfulness."[102] Problems arise when this amnesia-inducing tipple unhappily forgets its place and "takes itself with deadly seriousness."[103] The Gershwin musical comedy—with one foot in the legitimate theater and "the sacred precincts" of Carnegie Hall and the other in vaudeville, cabaret, and "cheap dance-hall"—became a cultural sensation in the mid-1920s and a perpetual irritant for playwrights like Eugene O'Neill and the contributors to *Theatre Arts* magazine who were working so hard to establish a literary theater in the United States.[104]

The ability of a musical comedy like *Tip-Toes* to rehearse so clearly the struggle between drama and vaudeville, gentile and Jew, old money and new, is in part the result of its own intermediate position in the American theater during the 1920s, not quite legitimate yet not variety entertainment either. This position, in fact, accounts for the musical's often high level of preoccupation with the struggle between high and low and its concern for its own dubious legitimacy. The work of the Gershwins in particular challenged both genteel and "vulgar" norms of theater and music (and musical theater) by mixing conventions in unpredictable ways. Ira was, after all, the first lyricist to attempt, as Philip Furia points out, to marry formal diction to ready-made clichés, the proper to the colloquial, as a way of defamiliarizing both modes of discourse. For his main interest—and one that betrays his central position vis-à-vis American modernism—was "the medium of language itself—the vocabulary, idioms, and phrasing of American speech." His use of enjambment, contractions, dropped endings, elisions, and other poetic devices allowed him to rag "vernacular phrases against musical ones."[105] Isaac Goldberg praised Ira for mastering the application of words to a "jazz-type melody" that "forces the versifier to follow, in all its twists and turns, a jagged, capricious melodic line" and challenges him "to feats of dexterity."[106] It is little wonder, then, that Lorenz Hart would congratulate the lyricist after the opening of *Tip-Toes* for helping to ensure that "light amusement in this country" will finally lose its "brutally cretin aspect." Ira's lyrics proved to Hart that "songs can be both popular and intelligent."[107] For it was Ira, Deena Rosenberg asserts, who (several years before Cole Porter's first Broadway hit) "made sophisticated song lyrics central to American musical comedy."[108]

George, meanwhile, became celebrated not only for his different modes of composition but also for helping to standardize the paradigm of the thirty-two-bar Broadway song that was no longer merely a frothy confection but, as Linton Martin wrote in 1924, an "elusive, subtle, individual, piquant and plaintive" composition. The writer of a miscegenated, "Oriental" jazz, he "combined the musical heritage of his Eastern antecedents with the syncopated sounds of 42nd and Broadway in rhythmic and harmonic effects [that] bow confidently at Stravinsky and thus arrive at originality."[109] He managed, in other words, against all odds, to make the popular song an original, distinctively American, modernist achievement by adapting and mixing styles. But Gershwin did more than modernize the Broadway song. He was also seen as the man who masculinized the form by rescuing it from "nauseating sentimentality."[110] Goldberg claims that Gershwin's emphasis on tonic and dominant harmonies and his use of extrachordal accented notes in the melody help "to make so many of his songs masculine in effect."[111] According to Goldberg, his compositional technique echoed his "muscular" athleticism and his love of "hard physical work."[112] Indeed, even Gershwin's concert pieces, Goldberg notes, are "as spare as his muscles."[113]

Given the signal importance of personal style for a modernism that maintained a deeply ambivalent attitude toward standardization, Gershwin fashioned himself unique by developing a technique more distinctive melodically, rhythmically, and harmonically than that of his great contemporaries. For white Americans, he was the first jazz auteur, "King George the First of Jazz."[114] Indeed, Gershwin's songs are often instantly recognizable in a way that Kern's or Rodgers's are not. This is due in part to what Alec Wilder sees as the masculine aggressiveness of his music, his tendency toward "the 'hard sell.'"[115] Even more important is "the curious paradox" that Wilder identifies, "that though Gershwin is considered the great 'jazz' song writer, his songs show less syncopation than do those of many other contemporary writers." They are distinguished primarily by their "boldness," "wit," "unexpectedness," and distinctive chromatic harmonies. "Syncopation is only the obvious device."[116] Howard Pollack astutely analyzes what he calls George Gershwin's unique comic voice, which, he argues, is the result of "certain incongruities—the way, for instance, straightforward melodies rubbed up against chromatic harmonies and snappy syncopations, giving the whole an air of mock innocence."[117] This comic voice becomes especially rich, complex, and often ironic when matched with Ira's playful verse.

Tip-Toes and the other early Gershwin musicals introduced a new level of musical and lyrical sophistication to musical comedy by subtilizing and consciously manipulating the conventions of the Tin Pan Alley standard. What, for example, could have been a throwaway song for a secondary comic couple in *Lady, Be Good!*, "We're Here Because," becomes in fact one of the slyest numbers in the show. A sprightly novelty song, based rhythmically and melodically on a two-note snap, it begins by posing the weightiest question of them all:

Philosophers the whole world over often put this query:
"Why are we here?"

After an unexpected harmonic modulation in the verse when the signature question is repeated, the refrain (in A-B-A'-C-A form) begins with that two-note rhythmic germ and provides the jauntiest of answers by enunciating what I am tempted to call the metaphysics of musical comedy:

We're here, we're here, we're here because
I love you and because you love me.

Inflecting the philosophical in a poetically naive way (like a nursery rhyme version of Plato's *Symposium*) and positing romantic love as a species of fun-loving transcendence, the refrain alternates between staccato patter and lyricism, simple harmonization and subtle, fleeting modulations. Although the second verse repeats the music of the first, the lyric veers to a new and rather more internalized subject. At its end, a simple scalar melody accompanies the singer's declaration of his modernity and familiarity with the latest style:

I'm not a bit old-fashioned, so I would be overjoyed
To psychoanalyze the question à la Freud.[118]

Rhyming the father of psychoanalysis with the near-translation of his name, the song achieves its complexity (à la Freud) by virtue of its ingenious variations on a thematic motif (à la Oedipus) and its restless and evocative underlying harmonic structure (à la the unconscious).

The mixture of high and low, of conventions derived from jazz and art music, characterizes Gershwin's concert scores as well as his musical comedies. This is in part why so many representatives of the classical music establishment (from the critics of the 1920s to the *New Grove* [1980]) tend either to denigrate his concert works or damn them with faint praise. Gershwin's concert music is thus useful not only for separating genteel critics from modernists but also for distinguishing between two competing

American modernisms: a universalizing, high, pseudo-European modernism (that expects jazz to stay in its place) and a populist, vernacular, syncretic one (that regards jazz as the key to a distinctive national culture). Raymond Williams emphasizes that because modernism represents "a restless and often directly competitive sequence of innovations," it is "strongly characterized by its internal diversity of methods and emphases." The conflicting responses to Gershwin suggest that these innovations are "always more immediately recognized by what they are breaking from," in this case, the genteel tradition, "than by what, in any simple way, they are breaking towards."[119]

The negative critical assessments of Gershwin's concert pieces always fixate on the same alleged weaknesses. Although Gershwin's works feature attractive thematic material, they lack unity (it is said), are disjointed, and rely on thematic repetition rather than development. For Virgil Thomson, the concert works remain "just some scraps of bully jazz sewed together with oratory and cadenzas out of Liszt."[120] For Paul Rosenfeld, another champion of new music, each of Gershwin's "ambitious products" is (like a vaudeville show) "only very superficially a whole, actually a heap of extremely heterogeneous minor forms and expressions." Each impels the listener "to look forward to some inevitable development" but instead dissipates all tension.[121] Each, the *New Grove* decrees, is "structurally defective."[122]

Among Gershwin's symphonic works, the one most frequently singled out for praise (even by those suspicious of his "ambitious products") is the Concerto in F. Richard Crawford finds it "a convincing whole," while even Rosenfeld pronounces it "the juiciest and most entertaining of Gershwin's concert works."[123] Despite Gershwin's attempt to use a more tightly constructed musical form than the rhapsody (Steven Gilbert convincingly expounds on the piece's unity), the concerto, especially the first movement, resembles nothing as much as a Broadway overture.[124] Its musical vernacular may be more complex, its melodies more chromatic, and its counterpoint thicker, but, as Carol Oja emphasizes, the piece repeatedly uses the kind of "bustling transitions" that link songs in a musical comedy overture.[125] Although the concerto—written concurrently with *Tip-Toes*—commences with a drum roll (like the overture to that musical), its percussive, brassy opening is distinctively modernist, closer to Sergei Prokofiev than Paul Whiteman. (This was the first of Gershwin's concert pieces orchestrated by the composer.) As if proclaiming himself not a "jazzbo" but a serious composer, Gershwin is here staking out a position as *the* American musical modernist. "[A]s I listened," Beverly Nichols wrote in 1927, "the whole of new America was blossoming into beauty before me. The phrases swept up the piano with the stern, unfaltering grace of a skyscraper."[126] Not until measure 28 does a recognizably Gershwin-style, jazzlike melody insinuate itself. This melodic germ, like so many others in the piece, is constructed as a four-bar unit (like those of Gershwin's Broadway songs) in which the initial unit is literally or nearly literally repeated, as it is in the Tin Pan Alley, jazz, and Broadway formulas. Gershwin "stitch[es] together" these germs and consistently uses devices associated with the Broadway overture, including repeated scalar passages, sequences, and insistent upward modulations.[127]

The modular construction of the Concerto in F, and of all Gershwin's concert pieces, links it to a central modernist preoccupation with the fragment and to the fixation on constructing large canvases, poems, or musical works through the use of collage, the appropriation and recombination of shards of images, texts, or music (cubism is perhaps the clearest example of this technique). Although widely attacked for his use of this technique (quite acceptable in Satie, Stravinsky, or Picasso), Gershwin, as jazz critic Abbe Niles recognized, was adept at turning his "supposed deficiencies" into strengths. Niles observed that "ragtime [or jazz] particularly benefits by a simple, well-rounded and brief form—eight or sixteen bars to the strain (in the case of the blues, twelve)." "If the composer presses on into 'development,' does he not risk taking his subject out of the category of ragtime as well as robbing it of one of the very virtues which made it popular . . . ?"[128] Yet for the majority of Gershwin's critics, these "virtues" were in fact vices. The hostility to Gershwin's use of jazz (or pseudojazz) collage in his concert music represents, I believe, more than a high-modernist aversion to popular styles. (According to the Harvard-educated composer Edward Burlingame Hill, the "average jazz tune does not possess the universality of the best type of folk-song.")[129] It also betrays yet another species of modernist antitheatricalism, in this case, an extreme antipathy to program music, Broadway, and the commercial theater. Gershwin freely offered that both *Rhapsody in Blue* and the Concerto in F were imagined as narratives. Indeed, he confesses that he was not able to sit down to notate the *Rhapsody* until he had composed the "definite *plot* of the piece."[130] Nichols discovered in the Concerto in F the "chattering of Broadway chorus girls drinking mint julep[s] at Child's" and "slow, secretive melodies that had in them something of the mystery of vast forests."[131] But Rosenfeld belittled Gershwin as a "Broadway paladin," while Virgil Thomson judged him an "excellent composer for the theatre" but the bane of the "concert room."[132] Hill, too, found Gershwin's "musical comedy . . . unsurpassable." But his "troubles began," Hill wrote, when "he thought to invade the concert hall."[133]

For critics who came out of the genteel tradition (like Mason, Hill, and Eaton) and for those others who championed a universalizing modernism (like Thomson, Rosenfeld, and Nathan), popular cultures that issued from and catered to the working classes—whether jazz, vaudeville, musical comedy, or motion pictures—represented a dangerous insurgency. The product of an industrialized, urbanized, commercialized, multiethnic, and multiracial society, they regrettably express and mimic the miscegenated identities of the men and women who fabricate them. These cultural producers, meanwhile—the illegitimate offspring of the working classes and "Oriental" or, at the least, "foreign" cultures—are upstarts who challenge the social, cultural, and spiritual principles that had long passed as being uniquely American.[134] The challenge of these upstarts is exacerbated by the fact that they, like George and Ira Gershwin, the Shuberts, Fanny Brice, Al Jolson, or the Marx Brothers, ironically embody "the typical Horatio Alger" ideal as expressed through their mastery of capitalist entrepreneurship. The real scandal of the "lively" (i.e., the illegitimate) theater, of which they were emblems, is its claim to be the theater of "the people," the voice and expression of America. Gilbert Seldes, for example, dared extol one of vaudeville's biggest stars, the wild, irreverent, "Cyclonic" Eva Tanguay, who, in the words of a less charitable critic, was neither "talented," "clever," nor "artistic," but merely "flaunted her mediocrity."[135] Yet Seldes has the audacity to proclaim her the "Soul of America" (375). And jazz, he decrees, is not a minority art but the "characteristic expression" of "America" (83). This assertion jibes with Gershwin's own claim that he conceived *Rhapsody in Blue* "as sort of a musical kaleidoscope of America—of our vast melting pot, of our incomparable national pep, our blues, our metropolitan madness."[136] This struggle over the identity and meaning of the nation also helps to explain the vehemence of Mason's indignation over the fact that a composer of art music, Ernest Bloch, "long the chief minister of . . . intoxication to our public," had the gall to title his "thoroughly Jewish symphony" *America*.[137] As Moore explains, the scandal of Jewish jazz is the result of the impudence of eastern European Jews with working-class roots

Act 1 finale, *Tip-Toes*. Steve Burton (Allen Kearns) with Binnie (Gertrude McDonald) and Denise (Lovey Lee) blow that "Sweet and Low-Down."
Credit: Billy Rose Theatre Division, The New York Public Library for the Performing Arts, Astor, Lenox and Tilden Foundations

who "participate in the sacred ceremonies of national autogenesis through culture."[138]

The most famous song in *Tip-Toes*, "Sweet and Low-Down" (reprises of which end each act), functions to celebrate the national dissemination of this aggressive, mongrel, popular culture (and implicitly to thumb its nose at cultural conservatives). The verse begins in the minor mode (only just before the refrain does it modulate to the major), in order to evoke the Blues Café, a jazz cabaret that, "[i]f you're in a crisis," "peps you up like electricity," a café where "the band is blowing blue" (the very word motivates a blue note).[139] The refrain deploys a typical A-A-B-A form and makes its point—which, according to Wilder, "is, in a word, a crescendo"—by using "three rising one-measure phrases" in the A section that mimic the first phrase.[140] For the Blues Café is a site of intense theatricality, imitative spectacle, and nonstop pleasure—of jazz, dancing, singing, and divine consumption ("where the milk and honey flow"). And the band's riffs, like the music of "Kern or Berlin," are trance and "fever" inducing: "You'll dance until you totter." The rising, syncopated phrases sweep up everything in their path, guaranteeing that even "philosopher or deacon," guardian of genteel intellectual or religious probity, "can't keep [his] seat."[141]

As imagined by the Gershwins, jazz, cabaret, dancing, and musical comedy represent challenges and Dionysian alternatives to all the "bogus arts" that Gilbert Seldes so scorns. For of these four lively arts, only the last can be said to be mimetic, and it is so primarily in its book scenes, not in the musical and vaudevillian sections that constitute its main attractions. As such, musical comedy represents a challenge to the legitimate, realistic theater. For the latter's power depends in part on its mimetic and referential precision, its ability to imitate and refer to situations, personalities, and ideas outside the theater. The primary aim of the lively arts, in contrast, is less to represent than to inspire and arouse, to put the spectator, in Alexander Woollcott's words, "under the spell" of a "communicable glow."[142] Undermining the differences between art and life, musical comedy is guaranteed to shatter even "your" resistance and have you uncontrollably tapping your feet and "shouting to the nation," "Blow that Sweet and Low-Down!"[143]

The struggle for legitimation over jazz (and jazz-inflected performances and texts) challenged the U.S. cultural hierarchy, struck a fatal blow to the genteel tradition, and firmly established both a universal, high modernism and its populist alternative as the competing vernaculars of American art. Intriguingly, many of the predictions made by both the proponents and opponents of jazz have come true. Jazz, the "only logical national music," has indeed become both the substance of and the foundation for "real American music," having inspired generations of popular song writers, rock 'n' rollers, blues bands, hip-hoppers, and composers of art music.[144] And the man who imagined himself the voice of mongrel America, George Gershwin, remains in the enviable position of being the first (and perhaps the definitive) crossover artist, appreciated and loved by aficionados of virtually every kind of music. Gershwin thus paved the way for many crossover composers: Duke Ellington, Kurt Weill, Vernon Duke, Leonard Bernstein, Philip Glass, Astor Piazzolla, Wynton Marsalis, Osvaldo Golijov, and many others. Among Gershwin's works, "Summertime" has appeared in hundreds of recorded versions, running from Leontyne Price to Janis Joplin, jazz to reggae, easy listening to hip-hop. Even the classical musical establishment (as exemplified by *Grove*) has in the past twenty-five years changed its stance from patronizing dismissal to patronizing appreciation.[145] The genres most closely associated with 1920s jazz, musical comedy and vaudeville, have constantly reinvented and renewed themselves. Indeed, musical comedy is the only theatrical genre to have been able reliably to find its place over the past hundred years as part of popular culture. In contrast, a legitimate stage devoted to "the finest spoken drama" scorned the working or lower middle classes. The critics and playwrights of the 1920s who tried to install an elitist, heroic modernism and expected jazz to know its place helped to invent a serious drama of no mean consequence. But by keeping at bay both "our great moron population" and the entertainments it cheered, they ended up ensuring that the legitimate theater would become an increasingly inconsequential part of U.S. culture.[146]

FOUR

PANDERING TO THE "INTELLIGENT MINORITY"

> The legitimate stage, vaudeville, burlesque, dime museums, chau-
> tauquas, and penny arcades have all been forced in to the back-
> ground by this modern amusement device [the motion picture] with
> its almost universal appeal to the mass of the people.
>
> —Jesse Frederick Steiner, *Americans at Play* (1933)

The claim that cinema wounded and nearly killed the theater in the
United States is contested by no one. Although relatives and descen-
dants of the comparatively lowbrow theatrical forms lived on and prospered (most notably on radio and television), vaudeville and burlesque, as
institutions, were dead by the end of the 1930s. The legitimate theater, on
the other hand, not only survived (despite Gilbert Seldes) but developed a
canon of significant, "serious" works that are still read and performed. Although Jesse Steiner's assertion is irrefutable, his conflation of every theatrical form into one category is as problematic as his erasure of class differences in the phrase "the mass of the people."[1] In fact the array of public
amusements in the 1920s was plainly hierarchized (as Steiner's sequence

inadvertently betrays) and particular forms, genres, and venues maintained strong class identifications. Thus, for example, the predominantly urban, ethnic, working-class audience that frequented nickelodeons was habitually opposed to the largely middle- and upper-middle-class patrons of the lavish movie palaces of the 1920s. One work that is useful in unpacking "the mass of the people" is the groundbreaking study, *Middletown* (1929), by Robert S. Lynd and Helen Merrell Lynd, the first detailed sociological analysis of an American community (in fact, Muncie, Indiana). By way of example, the Lynds provided a telling example of class-bound consumption in their assessment of magazine subscription patterns, determining that readership of and subscription to periodicals was highly segregated by class. Among the total number of periodicals (122) received by Middletown's families, only 16 percent (20) could boast subscribers from both the business and working classes.[2] Although the Lynds did not—alas!—attempt a similar class-based analysis of theater versus motion picture attendance, their statistics suggest that the consumption of cultural products during the 1920s was closely correlated with class and unusually revealing of social attitudes. As they explain (in their characteristically understated manner), "much may be learned regarding a culture by scrutiny of the things people do when they do not have to engage in prescribed activities" (311).

Yet the Lynds were by no means the only sociologists to neglect the study of audiences in the 1920s. In fact, there are no detailed surveys of audiences for theater, motion pictures, vaudeville, cabaret, and other forms of public amusement (this was long before the development of elaborate marketing surveys or the founding of record-keeping organizations like Theatre Communications Group or the League of American Theaters and Producers). There are no statistical accounts of the class differences between and among potential theatergoers afforded an array of theatrical offerings. On the other hand, there is a wealth of anecdotal information. Most valuable are newspaper and magazine articles about theater, many of which contain revealing portraits of theatrical events and audiences. (Unlike theater critics' near obsession with motion pictures, film critics as a rule paid theater no heed.) Just as important as these portraits, however, are the sets of assumptions underlying these discourses: the implicit and explicit hierarchies of taste to which they appeal; the social, aesthetic, and moral bases for value judgments; the criteria used to distinguish among social classes; and the often stereotyped notions of class-specific behaviors and preferences. Moreover, critics' judgments of audiences and theatrical offerings are strongly affected by their sense of their own privileged status as cultural observers and arbiters of taste.

In this chapter, I shall sift through the discourses that focus on the status of the legitimate theater at the height of the Jazz Age and the theater's vexed relationship to mass culture, especially motion pictures. I aim not to ascertain the exact numerical composition and economic profile of audiences (an impossible task) but the broad, class-based assumptions that obtain and the kinds of pleasures and anxieties that swirl around theatrical entertainments. If chapter 2, with its focus on tastemakers, writes a history from the top down, this chapter aspires to sketch a history from below, all the while recognizing the impossibility of anything even approaching a systematic study. I aim, in short, to comb the discourses about audiences and entertainments in order to perform something like the "social psychoanalysis" that, according to Pierre Bourdieu, sociology attempts "when it confronts an object of taste."[3] Why did the movies hijack working- and middle-class audiences, vaudeville and burlesque fade, and the legitimate stage become a playground for sophisticated, urbanized, well-heeled patrons? To which audiences did the stage and motion pictures cater? Why did so many critics use the phrase *intelligent minority* to describe the audience at which the new commercial art theater aimed its appeal? How did theater audiences behave? How was their constitution policed? And finally, why was the uplifting of the stage essential for the production of a drama that was—and still is—able to pass for serious, if not quite highbrow, art? To answer these questions, I first analyze the conclusions of cultural historians; second, the available statistical data; third, theories of the class system in the United States; and fourth, discourses from the 1920s about the class composition of theater audiences.

HIERARCHIES AND AUDIENCES

Although the hierarchy of theatrical entertainments was clearly defined during the first quarter of the twentieth century, it was always based, as I argued in chapter 2, on a binary opposition between the serious, legitimate stage and everything else. This guaranteed that literary or text-based theater (regardless of its provenance) was granted a degree of prestige denied musical or variety entertainments. Yet both reportage from the period and the work of subsequent historians make it clear that theatrical genres were hierarchized only in part by formal conventions. They also addressed themselves (sometimes deliberately, sometimes not) to particular class fractions, however indistinctly and carelessly those fractions may have been defined in contemporary discourses. The hierarchy of genres, moreover, was very nearly analogous to the hierarchy of social classes. And historians of theater and culture tend to agree about the disposition of both.

According to Marion Wilson, the *New York Tribune* began in 1909 to discriminate among theatrical entertainments by ranking them in a clear-cut hierarchy, with "Comedy and Drama" at the top, followed by "Musical Plays," "Variety Houses," and "Beach and Park."[4] The most elevated and high-priced form, "Comedy and Drama," sold its orchestra seats mostly to those Richard Butsch references as "affluent audiences," the often "inattentive and impolite" few who were repeatedly upbraided by critics. The galleries, meanwhile, at least after 1910, were peopled by increasingly professionalized spectators, "earnest devotees of drama unable to afford orchestra seats," mostly "middle-class and mostly women."[5] Although no cheaper than the legitimate stage, "Musical Plays" were usually able (then as now) to attract larger and less affluent audiences. Nonetheless, there was a considerable range of offerings within this category: the *Tribune*, for example, classified the Ziegfeld Follies not as variety but as musical entertainment. Historically, both musical comedy and the musical revue have always been the most category-defying forms—part play, part variety; part narrative, part spectacle; part drama, part song and dance; part opera, part "leg" show; part art, part glamour. Variety and burlesque were inevitably placed at the bottom because, as Paul DiMaggio notes, they "appealed to audiences of working-class men and [were] shunned by women and the well born."[6] Vaudeville, in contrast, represented a relatively elevated form of variety entertainment because its leading producers (first Tony Pastor and then Keith-Albee) attempted with considerable success to clean up variety by expunging rude language, innuendo, and scantily clad female bodies in order to attract middle-class patrons, especially women and children. The most popular theatrical form, vaudeville, whether big time or small time, was available in almost every city and many smaller towns. But vaudeville was by no means a homogeneous genre. Robert Snyder reports that the ubiquity of theaters and the centralized booking circuits "made possible vaudeville's many-voiced communication" with audiences of almost every class, from newly arrived Jewish immigrants in New York's

Lower East Side to the middle- and upper-middle-class patrons of the big-time vaudeville theaters that increasingly "became central to new business districts for shopping and entertainment." As he notes, vaudeville "spoke in many dialects" because most urban Americans "were too divided by class, race, ethnicity, and gender to find satisfaction in one standardized vaudeville theatre."[7]

The audiences for motion pictures during the first quarter of the twentieth century are only slightly easier to gauge than those for theater. Richard Koszarski points out that "even in the crudest terms, estimates of the number of paid admissions are not reliable" before 1922 because most were mere "extrapolations from federal admission-tax receipts." Not until 1919 were surveys conducted of movie audiences.[8] From the motion picture's introduction in 1898 until the beginning of the nickelodeon era in 1905, most films were screened as part of vaudeville programs. And until the widespread distribution of feature-length films (starting in 1915), the generic boundaries remained indistinct. Early cinema often provided programs of live music, lectures, and other forms of entertainment, while many vaudeville programs (even after 1905) included short films. Because the coupling of a silent film with a prerecorded disc was unpredictable, movie theaters always used some form of live music to accompany films, most frequently organ music. While some large theaters employed orchestras, the smallest had to make do with (overworked) pianists. The musicians inevitably played some combination of popular song, including ragtime; familiar, light classics like the *William Tell* Overture or "The Maiden's Prayer"; original scores made up of stock melodies; and standardized mood music played off of cue sheets. By 1920, Koszarski reports, a "battle was . . . raging"—as it was in so many sectors of U.S. culture—"between populists and classicists."[9] The former endorsed popular music, since the "average motion picture audience is made up largely of people who are unable to appreciate classical music," while the latter deplored the "tawdry" ragtime and jazz that so often accompanied movies.[10] Not until the very end of the silent era did jazz bands become common in urban movie theaters. Miriam Hansen argues that these many requisite "nonfilmic activities" in the early theaters effectively blurred the lines between the media by maintaining "a sense of theatrical presence."[11] At least two surveys from the 1920s indicate that live music, "courtesy," and comfortable seating were greater draws for patrons than the pictures themselves.[12]

Although historians regularly claim "a substantial working class audience" for the many nickelodeons that sprouted up in immigrant neighborhoods, Butsch notes that this is only a part of the story. Nonetheless, the
image has persisted "of the urban nickelodeon as an immigrant refuge
[that] made it inappropriate for middle-class clientele."[13] Hansen points
out that many nickelodeons did indeed offer "a glimpse of cultural otherness" for middle-class observers for whom the "working-class audiences
were perceived as part of the spectacle."[14] Yet by 1910 there were ample
opportunities for middle-class audiences to patronize nickelodeons in relatively upscale business and shopping districts in cities and towns. As with
vaudeville theaters, nickelodeons in different neighborhoods catered to "a
variety of audiences distributed across these venues: the middle class, who
had not previously patronized stage entertainments because of religious
beliefs; more prosperous working-class patrons of melodrama or vaudeville, who abandoned stage entertainment for movies; and the urban working class, who seldom spent anything on entertainment until the movies."[15]
In every social class, young people comprised the largest share of the market. In the mid-1920s, the Lynds found that about two-thirds of high
school students attended the movies at least once a week. And while they
calculated attendance of boys and girls to be "about equal," children of
both business and working class families attended more frequently without
than with their parents (265). Other contemporary studies confirmed that
the "backbone of today's business is the attendance of young people from
seventeen to twenty-three years of age."[16]

The arrival of the movie palace in the second decade of the twentieth
century marked the beginning of a significant change in audiences. Because the palaces cost far more to attend than nickelodeons or small neighborhood theaters, they shifted the class composition substantially upward.
These huge theaters, with spacious lobbies, grand staircases, and sometimes even one-hundred-piece orchestras, were elaborately adorned with
Hollywood-style exotic decors, usually Chinese, Egyptian, Aztec, or Roman. They encouraged people of all classes, including the middle and upper, to "seek escape there from the humdrum existence of daily life, . . .
picked up on a magic carpet and set down in a dream city amidst palatial
surroundings . . . where pleasure hides in every colored shadow and music
scents the air."[17] Given the relatively high prices and the opulent fantasies
that both motion pictures and their palaces aimed to unleash, it is little
wonder that the Lynds found that business-class families in Middletown

attended more frequently than working-class families (265). The up-market movie palace not only competed vigorously with vaudeville but also provided what Koszarski describes as a horrifying "shock to patrons of the legitimate stage."[18] Walter Prichard Eaton complained that while the leading roadhouse in Buffalo was dark, the movie palace teemed, "seating 3000 people, and boasting, beside gilt and plush, a 'symphony' orchestra, and organ and a 'dance revue.' It was full four times a day." Its top price, sixty-five cents, just about matched the cheapest seat for a musical comedy in New York or on the road.[19] After the opening of Broadway's first palace in 1914, a *New York Times* critic was alarmed that "the finest looking people in town would be" forsaking the legitimate stage and "going to the biggest and newest theater on Broadway for the purpose of seeing motion pictures."[20] By 1922, even Emily Post acknowledged that the "best society" sometimes patronized "the moving pictures."[21]

Film historians tend to classify motion picture genres not, like theater, according to a hierarchy of taste but rather of popularity. This mode of classification attests to the status of movies as a box office-driven medium that, because it has an "almost universal appeal to the mass of the people," is less closely linked to the vicissitudes of social prestige than the stage and is less welcoming of interventions by critics or arbiters of taste. The Lynds found comedy the preferred genre, followed by "society films," "heart interest," and "adventure" (266). Other surveys from the 1920s were more detailed because they subdivided the movie audience and used different genre classifications. One 1924 survey, for example, distinguished between foreign and English-speaking spectators, while another from 1928 separated college students out from the general public. Nonetheless, these polls more or less supported the Lynds' findings, indicating that the favorite genres were comedy and melodrama, followed closely by mystery and historical films, and more distantly by "sex drama," westerns, and costume dramas.[22]

The decline in the popularity of theater during the first quarter of the twentieth century (coupled with the scarcity of statistical data) makes it difficult to gauge the exact demographics of spectatorship during a pivotal era in the development of U.S. culture. Nonetheless, there are certain facts and figures that have important implications for the history of both theater and motion pictures. Indeed, as Bourdieu emphasizes, "statistical enquiry is indispensable in order to establish beyond dispute the social conditions of possibility." But statistical inquiry represents only one form of analysis, one moreover that can be interpreted to support contradictory explana-tions. "Because it inevitably looks like a scholastic test," he adds, "it may fail to capture the meanings which this disposition and the whole attitude to the world expressed in it have for different social classes."[23] And while one must attend to facts and figures, these only set the stage for a more complete analysis of the social dimensions of different forms of cultural production.

THEATER'S TRAGIC FALL

After an exhaustive study of Middletown, the Lynds became convinced that the Jazz Age bore witness to the "greatest rapidity of change in the his-tory of human institutions" (5). And they were particularly interested in documenting and analyzing the unfolding economic, social, and cultural revolution. Among the many facets of daily life they studied, leisure activ-ities were especially important in part because of their unprecedented pro-liferation since the end of the nineteenth century as new technologies gen-erated new forms of amusement: motion pictures, radio, phonographs, and automobiles. These latter, they noted, tended to marginalize and supplant the "traditional ways": public speaking, reading, playing musical instru-ments, singing, painting, and theater (225).

The Lynds, like many cultural observers both before and after, detected three decisive changes in the character of leisure activities at the beginning of the age of mass culture: first, the increasing "standardization of leisure-time pursuits"; second, a growing nationalization of culture that mandated the near abandonment of locally produced activities in favor of those "im-ported from without"; and third, a shift from active participation to what they call "passive enjoyment" (309, 271). Yet given the Lynds' systematic survey, it is curious—and revealing—that theatrical activities very nearly fall between the cracks. They note that the "local Chautauqua, lasting less than a week, is rapidly ceasing to be popular" but mention the legitimate stage only in passing in the context of motion pictures (229). Because the Lynds make no mention of a local stock company in Middletown, the only professional theatrical entertainments would have been theatrical compa-nies on tour, despite the fact that "the road" had been nearly wiped out by the mid-1920s. (The number of companies touring nationally declined from an April–December average of 339 in 1900 to 69 in 1923.)[24] Although the Lynds report that three plays were performed at the Opera House in January 1923, three in July, and two in October, they neglect to provide details. But this number is trifling in comparison with motion pictures, for the town had nine movie theaters (divided into "cheaper" and "better" houses) that offered "twenty-two different programs with a total of over 300 performances" every week (265, 263). And almost everybody, it seems, went to the movies (although "business class families tend[ed] to go more often than . . . working class families," 265). Paid admissions to motion pictures for "the 'peak' month of December" totaled 38,000, or "four and one-half times the total population" of Middletown (263–64). Back "in the 1890s," the Lynds noted, elaborately produced popular theater offerings like *The Black Crook* or *Uncle Tom's Cabin*, featuring "fifty men, women, and children" and "a pack of genuine bloodhounds," had "packed the Opera House to capacity" (267). But these were "pale 'sensations'" next to motion pictures and had been almost completely supplanted by them (267).

Extrapolating from the Lynds' figures, Jack Poggi calculates that in 1890, if all of the "125 performances at the local opera house" had sold out, the monthly average attendance would have been a healthy 8,333, a little more than two-thirds of the population. By 1923, however, with only eight touring productions visiting Middletown, he estimates that the monthly average would have shrunk to 2,666. In the interim, however, the town's population more than tripled. So in 1923 the monthly average of "one-thirteenth of the population" that attended the legitimate theater is negligible compared to the "four and one-half times the total population" that turned out for the movies every month.[25] (Because these statistics from the 1920s are based upon the number of paid admissions, they cannot distinguish between those who attended once and those who attended repeatedly.) By Poggi's estimation, the ratio of movie attendance to theater attendance was a staggering 58.5 to 1.

The paltry spectacle of the road show in Middletown in the mid-1920s is confirmed by countless other sources, all of them emplotting the decline of the road as tragedy—the lamentable fall of a once great sovereign. In his comprehensive study of the economics of the U.S. theater, Alfred Bernheim asserts that "it was the legitimate theatre's own mistakes that led to the downfall of the road."[26] He reports poignantly of the swan song of the legitimate theater in the college town of Northfield, Minnesota. At the turn of the century, Otis Skinner, *Uncle Tom's Cabin*, and *A Doll's House* numbered among its offerings. But in 1926 a local writer penned a terse obituary for the legitimate stage: "Nothing but pictures and amateur shows—the end of the spoken drama."[27] Houston, too, his sources told him, "has lost practically all road show business as inferior companies, poor housing facilities and excessive prices have scared the customers away."[28] To chart the theater's eclipse by motion pictures, Bernheim draws a comparison between theater attendance nationally in 1900 and motion picture popularity in 1925. (Although this comparison is somewhat problematic given the development of the media themselves, it still provides a rough idea of the change.) If all the theater companies touring nationally in 1900 played to full houses seven times a week, weekly attendance at the most would be "something less than 2,300,000." His statistics indicate that the theater had been so eclipsed by motion pictures in 1925 that only one person among fifty-seven would choose "the legitimate drama" over "the pictures." Yet as Bernheim makes clear, this remarkable disparity indicates that although movies may have "weaned some people away from the old form of the drama," they must also have developed their own clientele among people who had never attended the theater. He notes ominously that these figures demonstrate that "we have a large population that spends most of its non-working, non-sleeping time watching life unfold itself on a silver screen."[29]

The many reasons for theater's supersession by motion pictures outside New York City have been rehearsed many times.[30] But let me summarize the ones repeatedly cited. First, admission prices for theater during the first third of the twentieth century were many times higher than those for movies. Ticket prices in 1928 for nonmusical plays ranged from $0.50 to $4.40 and for musicals from $0.50 to $6.60 (which represented a 40 percent increase since 1913, adjusting for inflation).[31] In contrast, 99 percent of the motion picture audience paid between ten and forty-nine cents.[32] The low admission cost for movies put them in most direct competition not with the legitimate stage but, Poggi notes, with "'popular-priced' theatrical shows," especially vaudeville, variety, and burlesque. Predictably, these "were the first to suffer."[33] Unlike the theater, the movies always remained, as Steiner puts it, "a low-priced form of entertainment well within the reach of the mass of the people."[34] Second, silent film was far more attractive and accessible to non-English-speaking immigrants and to children than the more linguistically challenging legitimate stage and even vaudeville and variety, which sometimes highlighted wordplay and puns. Third, the widely acknowledged deterioration of the quality of touring companies helped to hasten the road's decline. Fourth, motion picture corporations attempted to disseminate their product as widely as possible and bought up and converted as many legitimate theaters as they could. Fifth, producers typically squeezed theater owners outside New York by asking "for a greater share of the profits from the local theaters than they received from New York theaters" in order to make up for a weak New York run.[35] Sixth, because theater galleries were never filled after 1912, theater owners' already slim profit margins were further reduced.[36] Seventh, the luxuriousness of the movie palace charmed and wooed patrons by enabling them for a few hours to live "in a world far removed from the routine of daily life."[37] Eighth, the film companies were enticing many actors and directors from Broadway by offering them salaries that ranged from two to ten times as much as they earned in the theater. And ninth—and most controversially—many cultural observers argued that motion pictures carried, in Bernheim's words, "a much more universal appeal" than the legitimate drama. People like the movies because "they can grasp the average screen production, intellectually, so much more readily than the average stage production."[38]

The near extinction of the road meant that by the 1920s legitimate theater in the United States had come to mean theater in New York City. "New York is the fountain," one producer wrote, "from which all theatrical blessings, or otherwise, flow."[39] Given the boom in new plays, theater construction, and theater-weeks (the number of weeks one production occupies one theater), it is easy to overlook the many structural problems of the commercial stage. Jack Poggi points out that statistically Broadway's peak season was 1925–26, a season in which 255 productions (including plays, musical comedies, and revues) opened in seventy-five theaters and ran for a total of 2,852 theater-weeks.[40] Assuming an average of eight hundred admissions (in theaters that accommodated between five hundred and seventeen hundred spectators) for seven performances a week, one can estimate that the New York theater attracted 15,971,200 spectators that year. Yet that total is paltry compared with the annual attendance of movies across the country in 1926, which numbered 162 times that figure: 2,600,000,000.[41] Moreover, relative economic prosperity is not necessarily a sign of what Burns Mantle calls a "trend toward new artistic standards." In his roundup of that season, Mantle calls it "just average" and references the large number of plays that fell "with rather a definite thud." The season's highlights, he laments, "were scattered and dim."[42]

Both Bernheim and Poggi carefully document the economic precariousness of the New York stage despite its apparent good health. Poggi argues that "Broadway was in trouble before it felt the impact of the talkies and the crash" and he blames its "collapse" on "three major problems: growing cost, growing risk, and growing competition from the movies."[43] Two other factors that were repeatedly raised in contemporary accounts of the theater's crisis are the explosion of real-estate values and the ubiquity of ticket speculators whose markup could double the cost of attending a hit Broadway show.[44] Bernheim offers a minutely detailed survey of all production costs from a play's option to the transportation of its tattered scenery into storage after a national tour, with estimates for every imaginable expense. Summarizing Bernheim's findings and adjusting for inflation, Poggi reports "a relative increase in production costs" between 1913 and 1928 of 25 to 50 percent coupled with a 20 percent increase in the weekly cost of running a play. These elevated expenses include the price of labor and commodities (from paintbrushes to lighting equipment). The increase in labor costs was due in large part to the success of unions in the theater industries in raising salaries, especially those of the lowest-paid workers. And despite a substantial rise in ticket prices, especially for musicals, producers were not able to make up for the increase in costs. J. J. Shubert (perhaps not the most reliable source) insisted that a show needed weekly grosses of thirty to forty thousand dollars to keep it running "at a fair profit." Those figures dwarf the five to six thousand dollars that he considered "particularly good" at the turn of the century.[45] "Only a few very expensive musicals like *The Ziegfeld Follies*," Poggi observes, "charged prices in keeping with" these ballooning production costs.[46] "Extravagant musical shows," Shubert notes, that would have required fifteen thousand dollars to mount at the turn of the century, would in 1925 take eighty thousand dollars.[47] These cost factors led, among other things, to an intensification of the hit/flop phenomenon (as producers resisted keeping a marginally successful show alive) and an increase in the importance of selling subsidiary rights, especially film rights.

Yet the key to understanding the irresistible rise of theater's expenses and ticket prices during the 1920s, especially in comparison with the movies, is the impossibility (then as now) of mass-producing theater. As a result, it can benefit but little from the continual rise in productivity in virtually every other sector of the U.S. economy. For as William Baumol and William Bowen point out in their now-classic analysis of the U.S. culture industries, output per man-hour throughout the economy "doubled approximately every 29 years" during the first two-thirds of the twentieth century.[48] During the 1920s alone, productivity in the manufacturing sector, for example, rose 52 percent.[49] But because theater remains a business in which the "performers' labors themselves constitute the end product which the audience purchases," productivity remains relatively invariable.[50] (A similar calculus would apply to jazz bands and orchestras of the 1920s.) Yes, there were significant improvements in every kind of stage technology. But these account for a relatively small portion of the expense of mounting a play. (Bernheim notes that actors' salaries "almost invariably claim the largest single slice of the producer's share of gross receipts.")[51] During the first three decades of the twentieth century, theater production costs rose much faster than inflation.[52] And since theater was not subsidized by public or private funds, this increase had to be passed on to consumers. For theater is quite unlike forms of mass culture (like motion pictures) that, because they are highly technology-dependent, revolutionized the mechanics of production. As these mass-produced forms became more sophisticated and efficient, "the cost of providing a given hour of entertainment to each member of the audience . . . dropped precipitously."[53] But theater as an industry cannot benefit from technological advancements or increases in output per man-hour to anywhere near the same degree as mass cultural forms. It will therefore "inevitably experience a growing gap between income and expenditure, even if there is no inflation."[54] Perhaps, if one insists on constructing the history of theater in twentieth-century America as a tragedy, one must locate the cause in its very ontology, its status as an archaic, handmade mode of production quite unlike the mass-produced and mass-distributed forms against which it has had the misfortune to compete.

As always in tragedy, however, adversity produces unexpected rewards. The decline of theater during the 1920s was highly selective and uneven, and the so-called popular-priced forms (like variety, vaudeville, and burlesque) suffered the most because they were vying with motion pictures in admission price. Poggi notes apologetically that "after the triumph of the movies" the "theater probably became *less* democratic. . . . Though the disappearance of the 'popular-priced' shows and the galleries indicates the elimination of the old class lines in the theater, it may also indicate the elimination of part of the audience."[55] In fact, a huge and hugely important class fraction had defected to the movies. If, as I believe, the 1920s was the turning point for the constitution of theater (and motion picture) audiences, for the development both of literary drama and musical comedy, and for the near-fatal decline of the liveliest of the theatrical arts, then the less democratic legitimate stage that emerged by the end of the decade had to work vigorously to retain the class of patrons who could afford it. It was obliged to make its "new artistic standards" of inestimable value. From what classes did these different audiences come, both in New York and Middletown? What, for that matter, was the organization of social classes in the United States during the 1920s? How was class understood? And how was the theater permanently transformed by the influx of that fraction that C. Wright Mills calls "the new middle class"?[56]

SOCIAL STRATIFICATION IN THE JAZZ AGE

Until the stock market crash of 29 October 1929, the 1920s marked the triumph of American modernity, the "prosperity decade," the Age of the Flapper, the New Era. In the face of sweeping social changes—women's suffrage, Prohibition, the near curtailment of European immigration, the increasing depopulation of rural areas, the Great Migration of African Americans to the cities of the north, the proliferation of assembly lines, and the rapid advance of consumerism—the conservative and scandal-ridden administration of Warren G. Harding endeavored to let "normalcy" reign. To that end, three Republican presidents (Harding, Coolidge, and Hoover) vigilantly engineered a revival of laissez-faire capitalism, a weakening of labor unions, and an ever-widening division between rich and poor. This conservative resurgence was in part a reaction to an eruption of left-wing activism (in both the United States and Europe). In 1919, bombs were detonated in eight U.S. cities, and the labor movement, which had acquired a new militancy, launched an "unprecedented series of strikes."[57] Organized labor's insurgence was ended only by the Palmer Raids (1919–21) in which Justice Department officials smashed up the offices of labor unions and socialist organizations and deported communists and alleged foreign agents. Labor was especially hard-hit, and despite the considerable increase in the workforce over the course of the decade, union membership shrank by 16 percent. Unions were forced to change their tactics from confrontation to "class-collaboration," and the number of industrial disputes declined by 73 percent.[58]

Historians agree that, in the wake of the Palmer Raids, the 1920s witnessed rapidly increasing wealth and a "buoyant optimism" that was prompted by "exceptional price stability" and a dramatic increase in output per man-hour. As Coolidge bluntly declared, "the business of America is business."[59] With automobiles, radios, telephones, washing machines, refrigerators, and other new consumer goods flooding the market—as well as an enormous expansion of the credit system—many Americans were able to go on a decade-long shopping spree that ended up doubling the industrial use of electricity and tripling its residential use.[60] A consumer society had been born, one that witnessed a change in emphasis from relations of production to consumption and in which "work was seen as a means to the end of buying more goods."[61] Yet historians also point out that though the 1920s were golden, they were so "only for a privileged segment of the American population."[62] Because of an unprecedented growth in rates of productivity due to the triumph of the assembly line and a decline in total work-hours, "the financial gains of the workforce were extremely modest." (Between 1899 and 1929, production increased 210 percent "while the labor force used in manufacturing and mechanical occupations increased only 50 per cent.")[63] The dividends of this boom (then as now) therefore "went not to the consumer, nor to labour, but to shareholders or other owners in the form of profit."[64] Between 1923 and 1929, the wealth of the top 1 percent grew by 63 percent, while "the income of the lowest 93 percent contracted by 4 percent."[65] Among the working classes, the only fractions to benefit from the boom were "the so-called aristocrats of labor, that is to say, the well-organized skilled craft workers."[66] By the end of the "prosperity decade," 60 percent of American families earned less than the two thousand dollars annually deemed necessary to cover basic necessities, while the income of the wealthiest 0.1 percent was equal to that of the bottom 42 percent.[67] The working classes' failure to protest this settlement was in part a result, Stanley Aronowitz argues, of the emergence of a more compliant workforce.[68] For the massive assembly lines in the giant Ford plant in Highland Park, Michigan, manufactured more than merely fourteen hundred cars a day; they also mass-produced what Terry Smith calls a "new 'Fordized' man" whose "active use of at least some intelligence, fantasy, and initiative" had been broken by the redefinition of work as wholly physical and mechanical. This "Fordized" man was constructed not only directly, in productive processes, but also indirectly, through the pressures exerted by wage policies, the destruction of unions, and corporate propaganda. He was engineered to consent to a draconian ideological settlement and to accept the conservative admonitions propagated by corporations regarding sex, morality, and alcohol.[69]

The relative affluence of the 1920s, the acceleration of technological changes, and the expansion of leisure time had a tremendous impact on the entertainment industries. Among the macroeconomic changes, the most important for both Broadway and Hollywood was the quickening pace of the shift from manual to nonmanual labor. Rising productivity meant that the manufacturing labor force remained nearly stationary while the numbers of those employed in predominantly white-collar and service industries increased sharply. "Nonmanual workers (professionals, wholesale and retail dealers, other proprietors, and clerks and kindred workers) advanced 38.1 per cent from 10.5 to 14.5 million." Both unmarried and married women entered the job market at an accelerated pace and accounted for an increasing portion of the white-collar labor force.[70] The substantial growth in total employment over the course of the decade was thus due almost entirely to the expansion of the nonmanual sector of the economy, the sector that provided the theater, especially the legitimate theater, with a substantial majority of its customers.

If an exact profile of the large class of nonmanual workers in the United States in the 1920s is very difficult to sketch, then that of its small theater-going fraction is nearly impossible to determine. For although the U.S. Census Bureau and other organizations compiled demographic and economic statistics, they reveal little about the relationship between economics and culture. The most detailed, comprehensive, and influential study of class formations in the 1920s is, of course, the Lynds' *Middletown*. Completing their field work in 1925 and publishing their results four years later, the Lynds provided a rigorous anthropology of a representative, "mid-channel sort of American community" (7). Yet even with the wealth of information they collected, the Lynds chose to divide the families of Middletown into only two classes defined in occupational terms: the working class and the business class. The former (71 percent of the population) they identify as those who "address their activities in getting their living primarily to *things*, utilizing material tools in the making of things and the performance of services." The members of the business class (29 percent), in contrast, "address their activities predominantly to *people* in the selling and promotion of things, services, and ideas" (22). This "outstanding cleavage" is thus roughly equivalent to the distinction between the blue-collar and white-collar labor forces and is, the Lynds assert, "the most significant single cultural factor" in the lives of Middletown's families (24).

To divide the American populace between working and business classes represents a somewhat crude dichotomy and is, the Lynds admitted, not "entirely satisfactory" (23). As they note, "there are not just two worlds in Middletown; there are a multitude. Small worlds of all sorts are forever forming, shifting, and dissolving" (479). The Lynds understood that there are few sociological concepts as challenging as social class. The difficulties of theorizing class are in part a result of the oft-noticed fact that Americans do not tend to think in terms of class despite the fact that the United States "was and remains a highly stratified society—especially in terms of class, socioeconomic status, or income."[71] (Indeed, since 1980 the United States has become "the most economically stratified of industrial nations.")[72] This unwillingness to recognize the primacy of class differences has deeply affected American sociology, which in its early years (at the beginning of the twentieth century) did little empirical research on the subject. As Milton M. Gordon notes, a "revival of interest in class phenomena" during the 1920s "took place in almost incidental, and certainly sporadic fashion."[73] Although the eugenics movement (advocating selective breeding) was most influential before World War I, some eminent postwar social scientists still correlated cranial shape and size with intelligence and approvingly cited studies that allegedly verified the intellectual superiority of (highbrowed) white persons to (lowbrowed) Negroes.[74] The Lynds were instrumental in displacing these racist and biologically essentialist theories with a theory of social construction that stresses "the dynamics of the economic class system and the differential distribution of power."[75] The Lynds' approach is usually characterized as *objective* (and closer to a Marxist model of class analysis) because of their emphasis on income and the relationship to the means of production. The next major contribution to scholarship on class in the United States was the work of Harvard-educated sociologist W. Lloyd Warner and his associates. Although they began their empirical research early in the 1930s, they did not publish it until a decade later.[76] Their books are usually characterized as being more *subjective* (and closer to Max Weber than Marx) because of their focus on behavior, social life, values, and attitudes. (They appeared just as a vigorous reaction was being consolidated against the Popular Front and other left-wing social, intellectual, and cultural projects of the 1930s.) Given the shape of U.S. political culture during the Cold War, it is not surprising that their approach remained dominant for several decades.[77]

From the 1920s into the 1960s and beyond, scholarship on class in the United States was always based on an opposition between objective and subjective methods. According to an analysis contemporary with *Middletown*, the former approach is defined by its focus on "the ownership or non-ownership of the instruments of production," "the general standard of living," and the struggles between classes. The latter, in contrast, emphasizes the "community of interest and outlook, rooted in the economic structure of any given period" and is concerned with questions of rank, esteem, point of view, taste, and prestige.[78] Milton Gordon's 1949 essay on theories of social class provides a list of factors that may have been given different names by midcentury sociologists but were used by all of them in some combination. They are *economic power*, which includes income, wealth, and occupation; *status ascription*, which is comprised of class consciousness (feelings of membership and social interest), competitive class feeling, and acknowledged or intuited social status; *group life*, or the awareness of and participation in a social system; *cultural attributes*, which include patterns of behavior and consumption as well as attitudes toward morality, sex, religion, art, sport, and other cultural phenomena; and *political power*, both locally and nationally.[79]

While subjective and objective approaches have often been assessed, no one has composed a more trenchant and productive critique of them than Pierre Bourdieu. "Of all the oppositions that artificially divide social science," he writes, "the most fundamental, and most ruinous, is the one that is set up between subjectivism and objectivism."[80] It is especially sterile, he notes, "in the theory of social classes."[81] He insists that social science must take note of both objective conditions, "material properties . . . that can be counted and measured," as well as "symbolic properties," an individual's perceptions of material properties in relationship. A social class must be understood as a subjective, imaginary construct—which is derived from and reinforced by objective economic and social inequalities—in which individuals and families are grouped together because of shared characteristics and popular stereotypes (of varying accuracy). It is defined, Bourdieu points out, not by a specific property or "chain of properties" (like the ones listed by Gordon), but "by the structure of relations between all the pertinent properties."[82] This structure may appear permanent or changeable, rigid or flexible, depending on the particular properties one emphasizes. Certain properties are commonly imagined as being alterable (occupation, income, or education, for example) and others as essential (race, sex, or family pedigree). Whenever a social scientist constructs an explanatory model that classifies individuals by taking one property, or chain of properties, as primary, he or she will discover that they "always bring with them . . . secondary properties which are . . . smuggled into the explanatory model."[83] For class is not a structure but a *process* performed in multidimensional social space. It is produced through multiple, ever-shifting, and volatile interactions of economic, social, cultural, and political variables. And class position is more a set of probabilities than certainties. For no matter how definitively sociologists are able to classify social subjects, these subjects are always able to make choices that defy and undermine their classification—especially in matters of culture.

During the 1920s, with the triumph of industrialization, a rapidly subdividing labor force, and new restrictions on immigration, the configuration of classes was changing dramatically as the number of class-based divergences increased (the number of professions, for example). I want, therefore, to multiply the classes the Lynds identify by appealing to the work of sociologists working during the next decade. I want to subdivide the working and business classes by attending to qualitative as well as quantitative differences, both objective circumstances and what Bourdieu calls the class habitus, "the internalized form of class condition and of the conditioning it entails."[84] Signifying far more than habit (to which it is obviously related), habitus designates the subject's "cultural unconscious" or "'feel for the game,'" a learned, "'practical sense' . . . that inclines agents to act and react in specific situations in a manner that is not always calculated and that is not simply a question of conscious obedience to rules."[85] A set of predispositions and probabilities, habitus is the primary marker of class.

In their 1941 books, W. Lloyd Warner and associates, investigating different regions, devised the now familiar six-part division of American society. Warner and Paul S. Lunt (studying New England) and Allison Davis, Burleigh B. Gardner, and Mary R. Gardner (the Deep South) described three composite classes—upper, middle, and lower—each in turn subdivided into upper and lower.[86] Although not all the details observed by these researchers can be projected back to the 1920s, the six-category class system does, in fact, provide a more detailed and useful scheme than the Lynds' for analyzing the composition of audiences. (These six categories were already part of "common speech" in 1930.)[87] Particulars may have changed between 1929 and 1941, but class habitus, I believe, remained remarkably consistent. Most important, the class system functions as a kind of self-fulfilling prophecy. Because so many people believe in this imaginary construct, this social abstraction, they endow it with legitimacy and power.

At the top (and this was as true in the 1920s as in 1940) was old money (1.4 percent), "an aristocracy of birth and wealth."[88] This class, however, did not need to possess quite as much economic capital as the class just below it because it had amassed far more social and symbolic capital. These were the people "who [sat] on the boards of directors of businesses and banks," sent their children to Ivy League colleges, and found their names in the *Social Register*.[89] Next were the nouveaux riches (1.6 percent), those whose wealth was the product of their leadership in industry and finance and who aspired to the hallowed position of the old aristocracy (the boundaries of the upper upper class are always the most rigorously policed). Both fractions of the upper class as a rule owned the means of production. Next down the social ladder, the upper middle class (10.2 percent), represented smaller-scale, independent businesspersons, trained professionals (like doctors and lawyers), and upper-level managers, "specialists in business or professional pursuits who make the daily decisions." Career-minded individuals, they were usually American-born by the 1920s ("college [had] rubbed off most of their ethnic characteristics, and business competition [had] completed the job").[90] The lower middle class (28.1 percent)—a particularly fast-growing group in the 1920s—was composed of "clerks and other white-collar workers, small tradesmen, and a fraction of skilled workers," many of whom had completed their high-school education.[91] But they remained " 'semi'—semiprofessional, semimanagerial" and " 'petty'—petty businessmen, petty farmers," petty bourgeois. "More conscious of being in between" than any other class, "they [were] at the bottom of the various ladders that lead upward" (the members of this class were personified by Mr. Zero in Elmer Rice's celebrated play about American business, *The Adding Machine* [1923]).[92] The blue-collared, upper lower class (32.6 percent), in contrast, was "composed of 'poor but honest workers' who more often than not [were] only semi-skilled or unskilled" and for whom there was little possibility of occupational or social advancement.[93] The adjective *routine* is frequently invoked in descriptions of this worker who, for so many writers of the 1920s, epitomized the alienated human robot, "tighten[ing] a few bolts" on an assembly line.[94] Finally, the lower lower class (25.2 percent), not unlike the upper upper, was—and is— the class whose lived reality is most likely to be obscured by highly romanticized (and often, pernicious and phobic) fantasies of otherness. This situation results in part because the lower lower class has far fewer socially legitimate opportunities for self-representation than the other classes. Its constituents are the unskilled laborers who are "thought to be" "lazy" and "shiftless," who *are sometimes said* to 'live like animals.'"[95] During the 1920s, this class was composed largely of "Negroes and foreign-born." It was the least educated and (even in the eyes of many social scientists) most "culturally deficient," the ones most ill-prepared to rise up the economic ladder.[96]

Returning to *Middletown*, I would argue that the upper upper, lower upper, and upper middle classes, and a small fraction of the lower middle class, comprised what the Lynds called the business class (29 percent). As a composite, the business class exceeded the working class in every form of capital. In Middletown's cultural sphere, they were the ones who bought the "current books," were "responsible for most of the organized musical life," drove Buicks rather than Fords, and frequented the Presbyterian church rather than "the Holy Roller" (230, 246, 24). In terms of class habitus, members of the business class were always described by sociologists as ambitious and jealous of their economic and social achievements. They "aspire to the classes above" or "aspire to 'higher things.'"[97] And while they were often sympathetic to the plight of working-class individuals, they were just as likely to exploit them or dismiss them. The Lynds, for example, report one city leader as declaring that "working men don't need unions" because they "are just as well off now as they can possibly be except for things which are in the nature of industry and cannot be helped" (80). Labor, in other words, must follow the laws of "nature" and keep to its place.

The lower lower, upper lower, and most of the lower middle class comprised what the Lynds label the working class (71 percent). While it is difficult to draw generalizations that apply to all its class fractions, this large composite class was by the 1920s gradually becoming more American-born and deskilled. As the Lynds point out, industrial and technological innovations were scheming "to supplant muscle and the cunning hand of the master craftsman" with highly standardized forms of labor (40). Although the blue-collar worker was becoming more and more the cog in the machine, the question of working-class consciousness remained problematic. As Dennis Gilbert and Joseph A. Kahl argue, the increasing specialization of tasks, the relatively high rate of unemployment, the hurdles to union organizing, the fragmentation by racial and ethnic differences, and the obligation to perform (in the Lynds' words) "orderly[,] clangorous[,] repetitive processes" (40) militated against the development of a "homogeneous and combative class consciousness."[98]

The identity and consciousness of this working class was analyzed with great care by the Lynds. But other cultural observers of the 1920s would reference it much less precisely with phrases like "the mass of the people" or "the Common Man."[99] For these were the men and women who were imagined (by those possessing greater economic, cultural, and symbolic capital) as forming a great amalgamated mass, the melting pot, the ones chastened and disdained for their vulgarity by the genteel critics yet embraced and romanticized for their "lively arts" by the modernists. What would be the fate of those entertainments, like legitimate theater, from which the lower class was excluded for economic and social reasons? What class fractions possessed the disposable economic and cultural capital to invest in theater in the 1920s?

FROM TRAGEDY TO MELODRAMA

At the apogee of Broadway's apparent prosperity, *Vanity Fair* (a monthly the Lynds number among "status magazines of the upper class," 259) enlisted a champion of the legitimate stage, Walter Prichard Eaton, to convene "A Discussion, in Seven Parts," published between April and September 1926, on the relationship between theater and motion pictures. That the conclusion of the "discussion" was foreordained is revealed by its subtitle: "The Strangling of Our Theatre: Dangers Involved in the Coming Control, by Film Producers, of the American Stage." (Both Eaton and *Vanity Fair* had far more symbolic and economic capital invested in theater than in film. Eaton was the cheerleader for an elite legitimate theater, while *Vanity Fair* devoted far more coverage to the stage—and in the glamorous first pages of each issue yet—than to any other art form, including motion pictures.) Despite its obvious bias, the symposium provides a revealing portrait of "the professional theatre of commerce," that peculiarly American fusion of art and business, during a key moment in its development.[100] Broadway was enjoying its most lucrative season ever. *Craig's Wife* by George Kelly had just won the Pulitzer Prize for drama, while Eugene O'Neill's *The Great God Brown* scored a glowing review from Brooks

Atkinson, who was beginning his long tenure as theater critic for the *New York Times*. Hollywood, meanwhile, continued to break records. Attendance of motion pictures in the United States averaged 50,000,000 persons per week in 1926 (almost one-half of the nation's population of 117,000,000).[101]

Eaton posed questions about the commercial theater and motion pictures to five respondents: Ralph Block, former theater critic and production manager of the Famous Players–Lasky Film Corporation; John Emerson, president of Actors' Equity Association; Pulitzer Prize–winning playwright Sydney Howard; Brock Pemberton, an independent producer; and theater magnate Lee Shubert. In an introductory essay, Eaton sounded the alarm by warning that "Motion Picture Producers are securing direct control of the drama" through their investments in plays, playwrights, actors, and theaters.[102] Playwrights had already begun to respond to this crisis by forming the Dramatists Guild and in February 1926 drafted a five-year contract "designed to safeguard the playwright's financial and artistic interests in regard to motion picture rights."[103] What other changes, Eaton asks, will the influx of Hollywood money provoke? Does the legitimate stage have a future?

A fierce partisan of an art theater that has, he rhapsodizes, "for twenty-four centuries voiced the highest aspirations, expressed the deepest poetry of mankind," Eaton has a heavy axe to grind (47). As if mimicking Seldes's sardonic portrait of him in *7 Lively Arts*, he makes it clear that by theater he means the legitimate theater at its most majestic, excluding both the non-commercial little theaters and musical comedy and vaudeville. He condemns Hollywood, whose product he deems "cheap, obvious and sensational" and whose investments in the stage he regards as imperiling the latter's sacred mission (48). In presenting himself as a champion of an unapologetically elite, minority culture, Eaton—along with his respondents—was far more representative than one might expect. For his opinions reveal the ideals and beliefs that underwrote the elevation of the "serious" theater during the period when Broadway and Hollywood were painfully (and invidiously) hammering out an economic, social, and aesthetic contract whose major points would remain essentially unchanged for about forty years—until the demise of the studio system and the Hollywood Production Code, the rise of Off Broadway, and the growth of regional theaters in the 1960s. The arguments set forth in these essays also help explain why certain classes of people patronized and esteemed the legitimate theater. The first motion picture to feature sound synchronization (*The Jazz Singer*) was still a year away, but the arrival of the talkie did not fundamentally transform the relations that Eaton and company analyze. Rather, it seems merely to have consolidated a cultural settlement to which the major players had already tacitly acceded. For it is noteworthy that the release of *The Jazz Singer* did not spark a sudden flurry of panicked articles about the impending death of the stage. In fact, it was virtually ignored by the principal periodical devoted to the commercial stage, *Theatre* magazine (which covered movies as well as the stage). For *Theatre* had already published a battery of articles and editorials in the early and middle 1920s that bitterly prognosticated the "strangling" of Broadway at the hands of Hollywood. When *Vanity Fair*'s symposium appeared, the debate had reached its climax and its terminus.

Despite their very different economic and aesthetic investments in the debate, the contributors agree on the intransigence of a cultural hierarchy that ranks the legitimate stage well above motion pictures and Eugene O'Neill well above other playwrights. Although they acknowledge theater to be in the throes of an economic crisis, most seem quite content with the vertical arrangement that guarantees that the " 'movie' is never . . . a real rival of the true spoken drama."[104] Of all the respondents, Ralph Block (perhaps because of his history in both camps) is the most analytical. He recognizes that movies have "been slowly and against great odds developing the art of the motion camera," and he welcomes the "sometimes startlingly brilliant art of screen pantomime." (Even cinema's severest detractors admitted that a few directors and actors—Charlie Chaplin, Ernst Lubitsch, Emil Jannings, and Adolphe Menjou are often cited—had participated in creating a handful of artworks.)[105] He regrets that motion pictures have been "timid and soft spoken, afraid to offend the hierarchy of the arts" and to question their alleged inferiority to the legitimate theater. He emphasizes that both are distinctively modernist practices, "symptoms of an amorphous, confused, speeded up and over-crowded civilization." And he points to an overlap in audiences, to the fact that in "their social aspects they are less than distinct arts." Block also recognizes that the champions of an art theater who dismiss movies as "infamous trash" (like Walter Prichard Eaton or George Jean Nathan) are victims of what can be described only as a phobic response that masks their "fear" with "distaste." He thereby displaces the narrative of the decline of theater as tragedy with a narrative of fear-mongering theater critics recycling outmoded melodramatic conventions. As epitomized by the "astronomical Nathan," "looking far into space," the critics "grew fearful of this giant child of Demos [the People] and predicted dire happenings to the theatre when the movies came of age."[106] Fearing the "scrofulous touch" of motion pictures, they scorned (in Eaton's words) "the great, submerged mass of the workers" or (in John Emerson's) "the congenital and incurable stupidity of the Great Mass" that loves them.[107] In other words, the champions of the legitimate stage as an elite practice, having made cinema their enemy, cannot do without disparaging both the working classes and an abstracted version of the "mass man" that so fascinated and troubled the high modernists.

Unlike the other discussants, Block (a social constructionist *avant la lettre*) seems to recognize that art is a social phenomenon, that any cultural form's claims to universality are always suspect, and that class positions represent cultural performances. He notes, for example, that proud and beleaguered playwriting "craftsmen" decided to take up "the shield of art" only when "society" resolved it "might condescend to go slumming among the 'movies.'" In other words, he sees how calculated and parasitical the relationship is between producer and consumer. He also recognizes the schizophrenic nature of cultural production in a market economy, "the left hand of the . . . dramatist reaching around his back to collect the fee from the movies, while the right gesticulates splendidly to give emphasis to exalted sentiments about the dignity of art." So the outpouring of rhetoric in the 1920s attempting to consecrate the serious theater represents a response to and disavowal of the increasingly commercial status of the legitimate stage. It is also an attempt to rescue the stage from cinema, which is deemed by its detractors a pure commodity and, by the more sanguine Block, "a primitive," that is, not yet fully developed "art attached to the religion of Prosperity—in a new socially and economically democratized world."[108]

According to Block's narrative, elitist theater critics imagine themselves the Cassandras, the frightened, feminine prey of a degraded, mass-produced entertainment machine. Yet the critics in question, notably Eaton and Emerson, envision a considerably more literary scenario that could have been written by Euripides. In John Emerson's view, the legitimate stage heroically guards the temple of Art in order to resist the dangerous incursions of "the great mass of people" who threaten to raze the temple and with it "our national taste for what is fine and beautiful." Despite his full-time service to Actors' Equity, he has no interest in expanding the audience for theater in the United States by trying to compete more aggressively with the movies. Rather, he is delighted that "moron customers" now have a cultural form of their own, and he trembles at the thought they might again invade the sacred precincts of the "finest spoken drama." Untroubled by the decline of the road, he argues that "there never were enough intelligent people in the one-night stands to support good plays." Because the legitimate stage has "gained enormously" by the defections of "the great uncivilized majority," he imagines a happy ending for his Euripidean melodrama: "a real Renaissance" of "the Art Theatre, the forward-looking experimental theatre." In order for this to occur, however, he requires a deus ex machina. Like so many partisans of a Broadway art theater, he argues that it must be subsidized like highbrow cultural forms, opera and symphony orchestras in the United States and opera and repertory houses in Europe.[109] He believes that subsidy will perform three operations: first, retrospectively confirm the art theater's highbrow credentials that date back to time immemorial, second, verify its highbrow status on Broadway (which by 1926 had not been indisputably attained), and third, make up the revenue lost by the defection of fractions of the middle class.

If an invigorated art theater plays the role of the striving hero of Emerson's melodrama, the villain must be the hydra-headed collective subject that goes by many names: "the Great Mass," "Public Taste," "the Great Public," "the untutored mind[s]," the "morons."[110] For Emerson's discourse rehearses a contempt for mass man that links it less to the genteel critics than to George Jean Nathan, Walter Prichard Eaton, and the other champions of the theatrical modernism epitomized by Eugene O'Neill. As such, it clearly represents a phobic response to a fantasy of the working classes as a cowed, irrational, overwhelming mass that threatens the solitary subject and the boundaries of legitimate culture. But Emerson's portrait is more than a fantasy. It is also one among many discourses from the 1920s that asserts an inextricable link between taste and social class. Like many others trying to consecrate an art theater on Broadway, Emerson meticulously categorizes by class both his heroic protagonist (the serious theatergoer) and his dastardly antagonist (the amusement-hungry slob).

Emerson's attack on the non-theatergoing audience, "the Great Public," represents more than just an assault on the lower classes that had by 1926 deserted the legitimate stage and become increasingly scarce even at vaudeville. His dismissive and picturesque evocations of a "soap maker of Pittsburgh" or "Arkansas farm-hand" clearly function as emblems for the upper lower and lower lower classes, respectively. But he seems to reserve a particular animus for those fractions of the middle classes exemplified by the "Kiwaniser or Rotarian" who is "totally guiltless of the slightest understanding or appreciation of contemporary Art."[111] According to the Lynds, these civic clubs were peopled not by working-class but business-class Middletowners. The Rotary, representing the "oldest and most coveted" of the clubs devoted to business development and civic betterment, attracted upper-middle-class and even lower-upper-class members. The Kiwanis, in contrast, designated a more lower-middle-class organization (301). It is revealing, moreover, that the Lynds note in passing that a Rotary meeting they observed included "ten minutes of lusty song" that featured "the latest Broadway hits" (which the members were more likely to know from sheet music or radio than road companies, 302). For in disdaining both "the Great Public" and at least two fractions of the middle class that could afford to go to the theater, Emerson betrays his privileging of connoisseurship and taste above all else. This move allows him (and the theater for which he was a mouthpiece) to distance himself both from popular forms like musical theater and vaudeville and from that portion of the business class which defines itself strictly in terms of the capitalist marketplace—in Emerson's view, the sworn enemy of the art theater.

THE INTELLIGENT MINORITY

Like so many champions of the legitimate stage in the 1920s, both Walter Prichard Eaton and John Emerson (like George Jean Nathan) repeatedly use the phrase *intelligent minority* to describe the audience of "the true spoken drama."[112] The category of intelligence, however, functions as a decoy for these critics. For their concern is less with the mentally acute than with those fortunate enough to have inherited or acquired significant amounts of cultural, educational, and symbolic capital. In choosing this word, moreover, Eaton and Emerson are (consciously or unconsciously) summoning up a history of pseudoscientific eugenics that deems "intelligence" to be "spread more generously in the upper social classes" and believes it to decline steeply as one passes "to the lower ones."[113] Eaton attempts to hijack upper-class prestige by imagining his highbrow theater as catering to a cultural elite comprised of "intellectual and spiritual aristocrat[s]" (48). Emerson, meanwhile, further winnows down the theater audience by estimating the "people of intelligence and good taste" to be, at most, half a million. Given a U.S. population of 117,000,000 in 1926, his imagined intellectual elite would be extremely rarefied, a mere 0.43 percent of the population (a much smaller percentage than the upper upper class or the number of people who attended the legitimate theater that year). Even if one takes into account Emerson's hyperbole, the supporters of a highbrow theater would represent a small fraction of the theatergoing public, a fraction, moreover, that presumably would scorn not only movies but also vaudeville and musical comedy.

Numerous journalistic texts from the 1920s on theater and theater audiences illuminate the details of class status taken for granted by Eaton and Emerson. Eaton himself notes the shift in lower-priced galleries on Broadway, which were peopled (for a 1923 performance of Galsworthy's *Loyalties*) not by the lower classes but "college students" and "middle-aged men and women of serious countenance" who were "distinctly neither time killers nor sensation seekers." This was the audience, he adds, "one used to see at the Boston Symphony," people of "alert and watchful" "intelligence."[114] Playwright Benjamin De Casseres confirms the change from a "Dionysian" to an "Apollonian" audience in the gallery that, he notes, was lately rechristened the Family Circle. This new audience represents diverse fractions of the "middle classes" that "Aspire to Culture," not only "the Student of the Drama," "poets, painters, sculptors, embryo O'Neills and sex-mystics," but also (and most revealingly), "the solid backbone of the nation—proofreaders, rising watchmakers, manufacturers and distributors of pajamas in as yet a small way, and the goodly *hausfrau*." (De Casseres conveniently overlooks the manual and machine laborers who comprised the *real* backbone of the U.S. economy.) The new gallery was taken over, in other words, by a "reflective, sedate, contemplative" audience: a self-styled intellectual elite of connoisseurs; remnants of the old, entrepreneurial middle class; and those C. Wright Mills calls the new middle class, "white-collar people on salary."[115]

Although critics of the legitimate theater agreed about the composition of gallery audiences, which they generally esteemed for their good taste and manners, they provided a more variegated portrait of the affluent downstairs crowd. There are three reasons for this range of opinion. First, as Davis and colleagues note, commentary about class habitus and behavior tends to be much more detailed and nuanced the less social distance obtains between observer and observed.[116] And the critics by and large were closer to the downstairs crowd—by physical proximity, class background, and habits of identification and desire—than to the sober middle-class audience in the gallery.[117] Second, the behavior, taste, and opinions of the clientele downstairs remained controversial. These were the people, after all, whose paid admissions and capital investments sustained the legitimate stage. Yet their rowdiness, late arrival, and inattention were easy and frequent targets for critics. Third, although most of these critics came from upper-middle-class families, they were as a rule far less affluent than the captains of industry with whom they rubbed elbows. Their reportage of the downstairs crowd, therefore, tends to be more ambivalent and judgmental than that of the "solid" middle class upstairs.

During the late 1920s, Cornelius Vanderbilt Jr. contributed a few articles to *Theatre* magazine. Being, as the editor noted, "in a position to know" about "the patronage of 'society,'" Vanderbilt offered that "the best society seem to feel that their presence and approval of the play is necessary to its success."[118] Although those "in society," he writes, could buy no more than one-fifth of the seats, their attendance had a positive impact. "Plenty of evening shirts"—the sign of "refinement" and "culture"— "cheer an actor" and are far preferable to a "rough, uncouth and vulgar-looking" audience.[119] Novelist Mildred Cram also approved the fact that New Yorkers were becoming more like Londoners, "more picturesque than they used to be," with "starched shirt-bosoms" and refined manners.[120] Although other commentators were less willing to equate wealth and "culture," their reportage confirms the patronage of the fashionable "*élite* . . . in flashing tiaras and shirt fronts" as well as "the lobster-fed, hip-flask gentry who come to Broadway to have 'a good time.'"[121] If these upper classes comprised about a fifth of the Broadway audience, then the rest of the downstairs crowd must have ranged from the even-then proverbial "T.B.M. [tired businessman] snatching a hurried smoke while his wife stifles her yawns behind her program" to the "intelligent" and relatively affluent "better grade of professional man or merchant," in other words, representatives of both the new and old middle classes.[122] These white-collared, upper-middle-class fractions likely accounted for a sizable portion, if not the majority of the audience for the legitimate stage.

The importance of the legitimate theater for members of the "Best Society" is confirmed by Emily Post, who dedicates more pages in her *Etiquette* (first published in 1922) to the theater than at any other form of public amusement. Indeed, it is the only entertainment, with the exception of opera, that warrants more than a few words. But the three pages she devotes to comportment at the opera is trifling in comparison with the nine she fills with elaborate prescriptions for the proper behavior before, during, and after a theatrical performance. (Motion pictures merit three dispassionate sentences scattered among 619 pages!) For Post, there is "no more popular or agreeable way of entertaining [New Yorkers of highest fashion] than to ask them to 'dine and go to the play.'"[123] The legitimate theater is far more popular than opera among the smart set, she notes, "because those who care for serious music are a minority compared with those who like the theater" (38). The theater, moreover, represents more than merely a place to see and be seen. Unlike the jaded critics, Post emphasizes that "comparatively few" of the downstairs audience "are ever anything but well behaved." Although some arrive fashionably late, most take going to the theater seriously. They "take their seats as quietly and quickly as they possibly can and are quite as much interested in the play and therefore as attentive and quiet as you [sic] are" (42). Only once does Post reference less elevated forms of theatrical entertainment that clearly represent more casual distractions. She notes, "Older people . . . very often go for a supper to one of the cabarets for which New York is famous (or infamous?), or perhaps go to watch a vaudeville performance at midnight, or dance, or do both together" (45–46). And vaudeville and cabaret clearly do not demand the same sartorial and behavioral refinement as the legitimate stage.

A survey of *Theatre* confirms the fact that the legitimate stage catered to affluent audiences. The most widely circulated theater magazine during the 1920s, it plainly addressed itself to a prosperous and "intelligent minority" that was, however, not quite as Apollonian as the readership of *Theatre Arts* ("the chief journalistic exponent of experiment in theater and drama"), nor as Lucullan as the readership of *Vanity Fair*.[124] *Theatre* covered a wide range of theatrical activities (including drama, musicals, vaudeville, and the amateur stage) as well as motion pictures, opera, and radio. Yet editorial policies clearly favored the "serious" legitimate stage as epitomized by the high-status Theatre Guild (of which Walter Prichard Eaton wrote the official history). Advertisements printed in the magazine during the 1925–26 season suggest that its readers had a good deal of disposable income. They also attest to what seems to be an overwhelmingly female readership, a circumstance that suggests that women were responsible for planning cultural engagements to which they would drag along the tired businessmen with whom they shared bed and board. Full-page advertisements proliferate for posh department stores (B. Altman, Saks Fifth Avenue, Bergdorf Goodman), cosmetics, French perfumes (Lenthéric, Coty, Roger & Gallet, Fioret), furriers, and expensive automobiles (Packard, Chrysler, Lincoln). Yet promotional copy is conspicuously absent for men's fashions (except for an occasional advertisement for Arrow Shirts), posh hotels, jewelers, silversmiths, haute couturiers, and other purveyors of luxury goods to the upper classes.

Vanity Fair, in contrast, catered to a somewhat more well-heeled, well-traveled, and sophisticated readership. Although there is some overlap between the two magazines in advertising copy (for Chrysler, Saks Fifth Avenue, Bergdorf Goodman, and others), *Vanity Fair* also featured ads for posh hotels in New York, Paris, and London; steamship lines offering round-the-world cruises; silversmiths; and haute couturiers. During the mid-1920s, Tiffany & Co. commandeered the first inside recto page of every issue. As a rule, *Vanity Fair* devoted three or four pages in every issue to travel ads listed under the heading, "The Condé Nast Travel Bureau," and to notices for elite finishing schools. One of the most striking differences between the two monthlies is the more obviously masculine readership of *Vanity Fair*. The first twenty pages or so were dominated by ads for upscale men's haberdasheries and automobile manufacturers. Less anxious than *Theatre* about its reader's pedigrees, it was far more hospitable to popular theatrical, musical, and literary cultures—and to jazz. (In the cultural settlement of the 1920s, middle-class women were responsible for maintaining the status quo, while men were allowed to sow their wild oats—sexually and culturally.) *Vanity Fair* featured profiles of stylish modernist artists, performers, and intellectuals; clever caricatures of and stories about the comings and goings of the smart set; and stories and columns by the likes of Aldous Huxley, e. e. cummings, Gilbert Seldes, Carl Van Vechten, and Colette.

Theatre addressed itself to readers less secure of their social position and more puritanical than the modishly permissive *Vanity Fair* readership, theatergoers who were anxious to demonstrate their kinship with "intellectual and spiritual aristocrat[s]" by proving their dedication to highbrow art instead of the more populist entertainments that fascinated critics like Seldes or Van Vechten. It thereby aimed less at the "Best Society" than at upper-middle-class women who could ante up for a "reproduction" of a Worth silken wrap rather than the Paris original.[125] This enticement to mimic the habits, dress, and attitudes of the "Best Society" was replicated elsewhere in *Theatre*, suggesting that its readers hoped to perform upper-class style and etiquette on an upper-middle-class budget. Each issue featured a four-page photo spread of Broadway celebrities like Lynn Fontanne, Gertrude Lawrence, or Irene Bordoni promoting glamorous fashions that readers could purchase: "The irresistible Irene Bordoni, star of *Naughty Cinderella* [1925], selected these models from Lord & Taylor to complete her wardrobe," including "a youthful, white georgette dance frock" and "Chanel's newest sweater suit."[126] (The captions almost always identified the actor with a stage role, even if she also appeared in movies.) Each issue also featured a two-page photo spread of both Broadway and Hollywood stars with their luxury automobiles. Noël Coward, for example, "brilliant English author and actor," is photographed beside his "fine Rolls Royce," bought with "the royalties earned by his play, *The Vortex*." "It was to be expected," the caption continues, "that the dramatist, who denounces sham and tawdriness, would choose a car famous for its quiet distinction and exquisiteness."[127]

Cultural observers of the 1920s agree that not all theatergoers would have lionized a star of the "the true spoken drama" like Lynn Fontanne. For different audiences favored different theaters, ranging from those "where evening dress seems to be a tacit metropolitan conspiracy" to those, in Mildred Cram's words, "where the 'peepul' foregather in the careless brotherhood of the hand-me-down." She categorizes audiences by playhouse, from the tight-knit "brotherhood" of the Garrick (the Theatre Guild's home) to the raucous "crowd" of the Cohan (George M. Cohan's theater), from the hushed "meeting" convened nightly in the tiny Provincetown Playhouse to the boisterous "round-up" that filled the mammoth Hippodrome.[128] Playwright Rachel Crothers took a somewhat different tack, ranking audiences across the nation in what was then the standard vertical hierarchy. On top are the snobbish intellectual and cultural elite who "think that the stage is degenerating" and becoming "vulgar." They are complemented by the aficionados of "the so-called 'Little Theatres'" who are "ignominiously called . . . 'highbrows'" by "the great unwashed." At the bottom is the "largest and the most powerful and important class: those who love the theatre because it amuses them."[129] This latter class seems to correspond to the audience that Eaton observed in a small New England city that was "sound," if "not sophisticated," with an "innate respect for good things."[130] They are the middlebrow "theatre-lovers" that Thomas Dickinson distinguishes from the lowbrow "theatregoers because they have taste, and from the connoisseurs because they go to the theatre to enjoy it and not to judge it."[131] "Theatre lovers" make for an "intelligent audience," representing "the sound core of 'middle class' America" that "the movies can never permanently satisfy."[132]

The professionalized critics, playwrights, and producers were anxious to ensure that at least a portion of the legitimate stage would be granted highbrow status, comparable to subsidized or richly endowed orchestras and opera companies. For the elevation of the stage was the most effective way of distinguishing it from the mass cultural forms that had proliferated so unnervingly and safeguarding both the cultural practices they esteemed and their livelihood. Their testimonies suggest that this relatively highbrow theater had in fact succeeded in winning the patronage of both social and intellectual elites, who were far less likely to be synonymous in the 1920s than they had been in the late nineteenth century. Playwright, critic, and composer Channing Pollock noted that a "very considerable proportion of theatre-goers—I'm not sure that they don't constitute the majority—derive 'entertainment' from the exercise of the mental faculties, instead of from their suspension." "They know," he wrote, "about the big questions of the day, and are more vitally interested in them . . . than in discovering which man will get at the pistol in the table drawer."[133] Even Gilbert Seldes, one year after *The 7 Lively Arts*, attested to this shift, claimed that "the intellectuals (or highbrows or artists) have seriously invaded the *terrain* of their enemy," which is to say, Broadway. His use of a military metaphor here points both to the overheated passions involved in the ongoing struggle between art and commerce and to the large amounts of economic and cultural capital at stake. Slightly revising his assessment of the "serious" theater, he described the 1924–25 season (that included *Desire Under the Elms*) as a "triumph of the art theatre over show business." But he noted that he might alternatively have called it a "secret, and far more insidious, triumph of commercialism over art." In other words, a certain amount of "charlatanism" (old-fashioned dramaturgy and showmanship) proved necessary for the "victory" of "the new and 'artistic.'" Nonetheless, he observed, "the theatre, which began making trials some ten or fifteen years ago, . . . has created . . . an audience upon which it can count" and, in so doing, "has enlarged the radius along which the dramatist can work."[134]

But not all critics were as sanguine as Seldes. A small, if vocal, minority had deep roots in the genteel tradition and remained suspicious of what they saw as a shotgun marriage between art and commerce. For example, the Irish-born playwright, critic, and Theatre Guild stalwart St. John Ervine (whose *Jane Clegg* Seldes dismisses in *The 7 Lively Arts* as tedious, "bad drama," 315), pined nostalgically for the days when the theater was being "produced by men who are primarily lovers of the play." It has instead declined "into sterility and poverty" because it has fallen "into the hands of persons who ought to be peddling peanuts or selling second-hand clothing."[135] Ervine's last phrase is an unmistakable swipe at Jewish producers (like Jed Harris and the Shuberts) who had become increasingly powerful during the 1920s. And although a strain of anti-Semitism can sometimes be discerned in attacks on the commercial theater (as well as jazz and motion pictures), it usually remained far more veiled in *Theatre* magazine than Henry Ford's infamous *Dearborn Independent*. Yet Ervine's antipathy to the new theater represented the last stand of the genteel tradition. Although many modernist critics of the 1920s sometimes regarded art and commerce as adversarial, they usually argued that by the middle of the decade artistic and commercial interests managed—miraculously—to have hammered out something of a peace treaty. This unlikely equilibrium between art and commercialism—as personified by Eugene O'Neill—marked a precedent-setting, if provisional, cease-fire among competing class interests.

In addressing itself to consumers who hailed from different social classes, the theater of the 1920s was a site for what Stuart Hall describes as "a continuous and necessarily uneven and unequal" struggle. If "the field of culture" is indeed the "battlefield" that Hall asserts it is, it is one "where no once-for-all victories are obtained but where there are always strategic positions to be won and lost."[136] In striving nervously to become a forum for "the intelligent minority," the legitimate stage found it necessary to renounce the syncopated cacophony of the Jazz Age. By doing so, it provided the occasion for a social and ideological contest among several class fractions: the upper class; the intellectual and cultural elites; the old, entrepreneurial middle class; and most important, the new, white-collared, salaried, bureaucratized middle class. This contest, moreover, took place on both sides of the footlights. Among the members of the audience, it pitted the affluent against the less well-heeled, epicures against intellectuals. Among playwrights, producers, actors, and other theater professionals, it led to an aesthetic tug of war between the partisans of art and commerce. To claim that the literary drama that emerged in the 1920s is simply the product and precipitate of these struggles is disingenuous. Products of culture are never simple, and no economic model can ever explain all the choices that playwrights or other artists make. Cultural struggle, moreover, is as volatile and unpredictable as class struggle. For the former inevitably takes many forms, and enthusiasts on every side always employ different strategies to outwit their opponents. Yet it is impossible to understand "the triumph of the art theatre over show business"—that is, over musical comedy, vaudeville, and melodrama—without considering how these struggles played themselves out on the level of taste. For each class fraction had developed very particular desires and predilections. "The intelligent minority" wanted more than they got at the movies, while "the lobster-fed, hip-flask gentry" and the "poets, painters, . . . and sex-mystics" were looking for very different kinds of pleasures. Playwrights and producers were faced with the challenge of manufacturing plays for which all these consumers would gratefully plunk down their hard-earned cash.

FIVE

HUMAN COGS AND LEVERS

~~~~~~

> It is the maddening monotony of form and rhythm that makes jazz
> eventually such a cruel bore to the concert-wise auditor. . . . Mr.
> Lopez played twenty numbers yesterday afternoon, and with the ex-
> ception of a waltz song by Irving Berlin, every blessed one of them
> . . . had passed through the stereotyping machine to emerge as stan-
> dard, jazz-finished one-steps, as tinny and characterless and indis-
> tinguishable as a school of Fords.
>
> —Deems Taylor, "Our Jazz Symposium" (1924)

Surveying the changes that roiled the U.S. economy and culture, Robert
S. Lynd and Helen Merrell Lynd reported that "[i]nventions and technology continue rapidly to supplant muscle and the cunning hand of the
master craftsman by batteries of tireless iron men doing narrowly specialized things over and over." These iron men, moreover, were being "merely
'operated' or 'tended'" by "the human worker" in their "orderly clangorous repetitive processes" (40). The Lynds described in detail the change at
a local glass plant where "hand skill" was superseded by a production
process that "occurs without the intervention of the human hand" (40–41).

Instead of glass blowers, "Batteries of . . . Briareus-like machines revolve endlessly day and night, summer and winter, . . . as they pass a ghostly finger at the end of each of their ten or fifteen arms into the slowly revolving pot of molten glass" (41). While illustrating how and why the factory was able to increase its efficiency between 1890 and 1925 by 2,300 percent, the Lynds' dramatic prose is most remarkable for its repeated personification of the machines that have taken over the work of human hands. The machines are less meticulously synchronized assemblies of moving parts than "iron men," "Briareus-like" creatures with "ghostly finger[s]" (Briareus is a giant figure from Greek mythology with one hundred hands and fifty heads). This metaphor betrays their apprehension about what they call "the long arm of the job," the effect of the labor process on the myriad facets of social and psychic life (53). Bestowing bodies on machines, they inadvertently reveal the vexing circumstance of the Fordized human subject who has been transformed into an extension, simulacrum, and slave of the machinery he or she operates. The Lynds emphasize, moreover, that the working classes were not the only people who had become servants of the assembly line. White-collar workers, as well, were "dominated by the necessity for keeping costly machines busy" (44). Given the rise of a corporate structure in which all workers performed ever more specialized tasks, the office worker, forced to operate "his appropriate set of rituals under the rules prescribed by 'business,' . . . seems subject to almost as many restrictions as the machine dictates to the worker who manipulates its levers" (45).

With the triumph of Fordism, the proliferation of mass-produced consumer goods, the explosion of advertising, and the development of new forms of mass media—including commercial radio, sound-synchronized motion pictures, tabloid newspapers, electric signs, and airplane skywriting—standardization took on increasingly ominous overtones during the 1920s. Although many apologists for modernism (like George Gershwin, Gilbert Seldes, and Carl Van Vechten) felt invigorated by a Machine Age that brought an abundance of skyscrapers, washing machines, and public amusements, others (like the Lynds and many left-wing intellectuals) felt distinctly uneasy about what they saw as the irrevocable transformation of the human subject into a commodity. Whether modernist or antimodernist, sociologist or artist, Jew or Yankee, cultural critics consistently displaced their anxieties about an exhilarating, frightening Machine Age onto jazz. Jazz's status as an art that rose from the laboring classes, "its rapid standardization and its speed," its widespread distribution by machine (phonograph, player piano, and radio), and its emphasis on rhythm allowed it to emblematize and embody both "mechanical determinism" and "the revolt of human free-will against" determinism.[1] For its supporters, jazz, with "its freely moving upper designs and contrapuntal figures, . . . its varied syncopations, its superimposed cross-rhythms, [and] its impredictable [sic] accentuations," was the expression of the new energy, "freedom from tradition," and "mechanical invention" that had "been liberated . . . in America."[2] For its detractors, it epitomized "the futility of escape from the hounding tyranny of the machine"; it was, in the words of composer Deems Taylor, a maddeningly monotonous music that "had passed through the stereotyping machine to emerge as standard, jazz-finished one-steps, as tinny and characterless and indistinguishable as a school of Fords."[3]

During the 1920s, a large majority of writers for the legitimate theater dreaded that their work might be seen as having "passed through the stereotyping machine." But several avowedly modernist and politically radical playwrights (like John Howard Lawson and John Dos Passos) embraced a populist and jazz-inspired theater because they felt it could act as an antidote to "art theatre," which remained, they believed, "in a feeble trance totally removed from the rush and roar of things as they are."[4] Several plays, which Darwin Turner in 1959 labeled jazz-vaudeville drama, use jazz prominently in the background or foreground, on stage, in the pit, or in the house. These plays are invariably characterized as prime examples of American expressionism and include Lawson's *Processional, Loud Speaker* (1927), and *The International* (1928), Elmer Rice's *The Adding Machine* and *The Subway* (1929), John Dos Passos's *The Garbage Man* (1923), and Francis Edward Faragoh's *Pinwheel* (1927).[5] Lawson, like so many critics during the 1920s, understood that jazz represents more than just a syncopated thirty-two-bar song. More important, it is "a movement, a rhythm . . . [b]uried underneath"—of which one is perhaps only dimly aware—"a genuine inner necessity" that captures and describes the "reality of America spiritually and materially."[6] Jazz, in short, is the syncopated heartbeat of the "the American processional as it streams about us."[7] Before I analyze the impact of this syncopated heartbeat on the development of American expressionism, however, I want to examine "the long arm of the job." For changes in modes of production that allowed the new middle class to thrive during the 1920s also transformed the character of the social struggles taking place between class fractions in and around the legitimate theater. The upshot of these struggles was a new, literary drama, heavily indebted to German expressionism, which harbored deeply contradictory attitudes to the lower classes, the assembly lines they manned, and the amusements (like jazz) in which they took pleasure.

THE NEW MIDDLE CLASS

The literary theater that was consolidated in the 1920s—simultaneously an art theater and a commercial enterprise—represented a kind of covenant between and among several social classes. Since the working classes had chosen to look elsewhere for their entertainment, the legitimate theater was colonized (on both sides of the footlights) by the old and new middle classes and a fraction of the upper class devoted to the "true spoken drama" or to entertaining their rich friends in the most "agreeable way." Behind the scenes, the makers of theater (playwrights, actors, directors, etc.) were as a rule associated with the old, independent, entrepreneurial middle class. Most of them represented fractions of a residual artisanal economy, those C. Wright Mills describes as "handicrafters and tradesmen of small but independent means."[8] Most tended to work as entrepreneurs in and for a specialized market using their education and other professional skills as capital. These artisans were thought of as being engaged in work that was antithetical to and far more meaningful than the increasingly Fordized, mechanical labor of both blue-collar workers and a substantial proportion of the white-collar workforce. Both collaborating and competing with each other, these skilled laborers were primarily independent contractors by the 1920s, despite the fact that playwrights and actors had been organized into trade guilds and were sometimes employed and even salaried by producing organizations. Their somewhat antiquated socioeconomic status, combined with the widespread (and ongoing) romanticization of the artist as the prime exemplar of nonalienated labor, was responsible for producing the misleading impression that they remained, in Joseph Kahl's words, "outside the class system."[9]

In his analysis of modernist cultural economies, Bourdieu emphasizes that despite protests to the contrary, artists and intellectuals were never really outside the market but represented instead a "dominated fraction of the dominant [middle] class."[10] In a similar vein, Raymond Williams observes that because so many of the modernist rebels (like John Howard Lawson and Eugene O'Neill) hailed from relatively affluent families, they comprised not a proletarian insurgency but an avant-garde of the aspiring and evolving middle class itself. They represented, in short, a collection of "distinctively bourgeois dissidents."[11] In a field as commercialized as Broadway in the 1920s, the work of these dissidents was a source of considerable disquiet for both critics and the artists themselves, uneasy with the fact that the work of art was a commodity. As a result, these artists practiced what Bourdieu calls a "disavowal of the 'economy,'" which, he notes was "at the very heart of the field, . . . the principle governing its functioning and transformation."[12] For with the ascendancy of modernism after World War I, artists aspiring to highbrow status could accrue larger amounts of cultural and symbolic capital the more anticommercial and antibourgeois their work became. In other words, in a modernist regime, economic and cultural capital typically figure in inverse proportion to each other. The more closely theater artists were associated with the "art theater" pole, the more likely they were to have to forgo economic gain (at least in the short term). Alternatively, the closer they moved to the "commercial theater" pole, the more steeply their prestige was likely to decline, at least in the eyes of critics like Walter Prichard Eaton, John Emerson, and George Jean Nathan. This "disavowal of the 'economy'" was evident in frequent complaints about the greed of producers (so-called butter-and-egg men). Artists and critics who championed a commercial stage dedicated to art regularly counterposed the old-time "men of the theatre" who produced because they were "lovers of the play" against a new breed of "swollen-headed speculators . . . totally incapable of understanding that the 'box-office test' of a play is finally the worst test of it."[13]

Yet the combined critical and commercial success of O'Neill proves that the economy of the stage was not wholly predictable and that it was possible to amass both economic and cultural capital concurrently. Indeed, the paradoxical triumph during the 1920s of a commercial theater that was constantly insisting it was really an art theater—directed and supervised by "classless," modernist intellectuals and butter-and-egg men—firmly consolidated the upper-middlebrow status of the legitimate stage. This new theater prospered in part because, unlike motion pictures, it provided a public forum for an upper-middle-class "intelligent minority" of connoisseurs to familiarize itself with and debate the merits of the latest fashions in art, philosophy, psychoanalysis, and literature—and be entertained, to boot.

Unlike the slightly antiquated, if thoroughly up-to-date, middle-class artisans working behind the proscenium arch, Broadway audiences tended to be divided into a downstairs crowd, rich in economic and symbolic capital but with variable amounts of cultural capital, and a gallery audience, richer in cultural capital than economic capital. It seems clear if one extrapolates from the anecdotal reports that the affluent theatergoers could in turn be divided into those more discriminating members of the "Best Society" who were "well behaved" and "attentive" (and "more theatre-wise than they were a few years ago") and those purely social creatures who came to the theater to see and be seen.[14] The downstairs was also peopled with upper-middle-class professionals, "those who love the theatre because it amuses them," and a smattering of well-heeled intellectuals ("the 'highbrows'") who allegedly had better-developed senses of connoisseurship than many of their wealthy brethren.[15] Anecdotal evidence suggests that the range of cultural capital among the gallery audiences was even greater, extending from a cadre of bohemians, educated artists, and intellectuals to a larger and more amorphous grouping of people with "taste" who "go to the theatre to enjoy it and not to judge it."[16]

The closest thing to an A/B comparison of gallery and orchestra audiences is a 1920 essay by writer and sometime playwright W. Lee Dickson in *Theatre* in which he reports attending a "successful mystery-drama" on Broadway two consecutive nights, the first sitting with those who pay "from 55 cents to $1.65" and the next with those who spend "$3.30 or even $4.40" for seats "down front." Unambiguously identifying with and addressing himself to the "you" who pay the high prices (i.e., the putative readership of *Theatre*), he presents contrasting portraits of naive and sophisticated spectators. The first night, he sat in front of "two girls" who "went to enjoy that show—and they did!" Applauding "often and much," they "adored the debonair ease of the hero" and "loath[ed] that sneaking, dark-skinned [sic] villain." "[N]ot the exception, but the general rule," these two "enthusiasts" were completely taken in and charmed by the fictional world of the play. The next night, Dickson "sat with the extravagant many" who, in contrast, represented a more worldly, professionalized audience that appreciated "the villain's *acting*" and was familiar enough with dramatic conventions to know that the "virtuous" would in the end be "vindicated and rewarded." Unlike the enthusiastic balcony audience that "is still loyal to . . . the land of 'make-believe' in the theatre," pens "ninety per cent" of the fan mail, and tells friends "to go and see that show," those "blasé 'down front'" register an "indifference . . . that thousands spent in advertising cannot offset."[17]

Dickson's description of conflict between class formations is indicative of two incompatible modes of spectatorship with which the new theater had to contend as it was seeking legitimacy. Dickson emphasizes, however, that both managers and actors claim that although "the expensive seats . . . defray expenses, . . . it's the 'upstairs' that brings the profit." In other words, the legitimate theater of the 1920s increasingly found it necessary to address itself to a class of spectators with cultural aspirations like the two girls who "don't know where the St. Regis is" but "do know where the 'L' stops."[18] Dickson's portrait, as well as those of many other writers, suggests that the girls in the balcony and a substantial portion of the downstairs crowd represented members of the new middle class: salaried, white-collar employees. This composite class was unusually diffuse and heterogeneous and cut through a wide swath of the labor market, from upper-level "business management" (who could buy seats downstairs) to those practicing "manual routine" (who could only afford the gallery).[19] It was also much the fastest growing class during the early twentieth century, consisting of persons involved not in production, but in service, distribution, coordination, and sales. Between 1910 and 1930 it expanded by 134.6 percent (at the expense of unskilled laborers, farm workers, and the old middle class).[20] For the conspicuous growth of this class was very clearly the result of the proliferation of large corporations and the increasing centralization of the U.S. economy. With the expansion of this class, differences in income between wage-workers and salaried ones began to decline. As a result, occupation became increasingly important as a marker of social status and prestige and, indeed, became "the principal basis of stratification."[21] It was also, the Lynds report, the arena that exhibited "the most pervasive change, particularly in its technological and mechanical aspects" (498). Between 1910 and 1930, professionals (either independent or salaried) increased from 4.4 to 6.1 percent of the total labor force, while clerks and "kindred workers" rose from 10.2 to 16.3 percent. The growth was especially dramatic for women, whose proportions in the professional and clerical groups were "particularly large."[22] The rate of increase in the number of women clerical workers between 1910 and 1930 was three times that of men.[23] By 1930, 42.4 percent of women workers were engaged in professional or clerical labor.[24]

As Mills emphasizes, the office was transformed during the 1920s as it became increasingly Taylorized. "In the six or seven years before 1921," he notes, "at least a hundred new office machines a year were put on the market," including mimeographs, calculators, stenotypes, and switchboards (193).[25] This rationalization of production and distribution dramatically increased productivity and marked the birth "of the 'era of scientific management in the office'" (195). The effect on the white-collar worker was unprecedented. As *The Adding Machine* and Sophie Treadwell's *Machinal* (1928) suggest, offices were filled with workers who were performing ever more specialized and repetitive tasks, from relatively independent and high-status upper-level managers to the lowly clerks, like *The Adding Machine*'s Mr. Zero, who were steadily being replaced by machines. Increasing specialization also rigidified the corporate hierarchy and made advancement more difficult. In many large corporations, Mills reports, "the ideology of promotion—the expectation of a step-by-step ascent, no longer seem[ed] a sure thing" (275). In the mid-1920s, "88 per cent of the office managers questioned in one survey indicated that they definitely needed people 'who give little promise of rising to an executive status,' and 60 per cent stated that there was 'very little opportunity' in their offices to learn, and hence rise" (206). Office workers, in other words, were being turned with ever more regularity into laboring machines, into robots.

Numerous sociologists in addition to Mills testify to the impact of the dynamics of the workplace on white-collar workers, no matter where they stood in the corporate hierarchy. Since routinized work was less likely to be a source of satisfaction and pride than the more individualized forms of labor were for the old middle class, other factors became far more important for the white-collar functionary: income, status, social power, leisure pursuits, and consumption. Because the 1920s boom was fueled in large part by consumerism, it represented the real beginning of commodity culture in the United States, or what Mills calls "the Big Bazaar" (168). This new culture was, in turn, stimulated by an unprecedented surge in print advertising and change in advertising's character. Indeed, by 1920, as James D. Norris notes, "advertisements in popular magazines" regularly used a "consumption ethic" to define "the American dream" in terms of the acquisition of commodities and to distract workers from deadening jobs.[26] And six years later, Calvin Coolidge praised advertising for generating "new thoughts, new desires and new actions." "It is the most potent influence," he exclaimed, "in adopting, and changing the habits and modes of life."[27] Mills, meanwhile, observes that "fashion used to be something for uptown aristocrats." But as the advertisements and photo spreads in *Theatre* and other magazines demonstrate, "the Big Bazaar has democratized the idea of fashion to all orders of commodities and for all classes of worshippers." Fashion, which drives the Big Bazaar, represents a kind of consumerist vanguardism (one copies the more advanced or elite). It produces and fetishizes the category of "the new," "because if you worship the new, you will be ashamed of the old" and strive to replace it with the latest product. Most important, Mills emphasizes that the psychology of fashion involves far more than merely buying the new styles. Rather, in a commodity culture, "it has organized"—and, I would add, colonized—"the imagination itself" (168).

Other sociologists reinforce the importance of fashion, novelty, ambition, and aspiration as key components of the habitus of a large portion of the theatergoing public, especially in its upper reaches. Warner and colleagues characterize this new middle class as "the people who get things done and provide the active front in civic affairs for the classes above them." Despite the fact that social and vocational ascent was becoming increasingly difficult with the rationalization of the workplace, these individuals still "aspire to the classes above and hope their good deeds, civic activities, and high moral principles will somehow be recognized . . . and that they will be invited by those above them into the intimacies of upper-class cliques."[28] Davis and her coauthors note that the members of the upper middle class who are "attempting to rise" socially demonstrate the "greatest emphasis on the display of wealth." "Fine clothes, new cars, well-kept homes, and expensive furnishings," with a stress "on modern styles and values," are "the rule."[29] Kahl confirms that the upper reaches of the new middle class are "interested in the latest styles for their homes, their clothes, their cars, and their thoughts."[30] The accent on display is coupled with a high valuation of education and the drive "to 'improve one's self,' an attitude which has special significance for those individuals who are aware of the possibilities of social mobility." Thus upper-middle-class men and women typically patronize social organizations, including amateur theater groups and music clubs, as well as diverse "community improvement" activities.[31] Especially attracted to elevated forms of culture, they took going to the theater very seriously. When they wanted casual amusements, they could always catch a movie. But when they chose to spend a good deal more money and attend the legitimate theater, they expected, as observers repeatedly noted, to "derive 'entertainment' from the exercise of the mental faculties, instead of from their suspension." Whether they could only afford seats in the gallery or were prosperous enough to be able to sit with the crowd "down front," members of the new middle class with serious social and cultural aspirations became an increasingly important segment of the legitimate theater audience, the professionalized "theatre-lovers" at whom playwrights and producers increasingly pitched their work. Because they did not, however, represent a homogeneous social group, the new middle class tended to fracture (as the conflicting responses to *Processional* suggest) into a more conservative, entrepreneurial, socially ambitious fraction and a more restless, politically progressive, intellectual fraction.

THE ART THEATER THAT WAS ALSO A COMMERCIAL THEATER

During the 1920s the theater initiative that seemed especially attuned to the interests of the new middle class and the upper classes was the Theatre Guild. Founded in 1918 as a commercial, professional company, it was in the words of its amanuensis, Walter Prichard Eaton, "the direct outgrowth . . . of the amateur Washington Square Players" and succeeded against all odds in becoming "the undisputed leader . . . of the American theatre."[32] Governed by a board of directors (like most nonprofits), it dedicated itself to producing "great plays" on a subscription basis and was to be composed "only of artists of the theatre who are experts at their work."[33] As managed by Lawrence Langner, a Welsh-born playwright, the Guild nearly eschewed American work in its early years in favor of relatively highbrow European fare by the likes of Shaw, Molnár, Andreyev, Tolstoy, and Ibsen. Novelist and sometime playwright John Dos Passos observed that "[a]fter the opera the Theatre Guild comes nearest being a theater in the Académie Française sense of the word."[34] Brooks Atkinson, speaking for his fellow champions of a serious theater, claimed it drew "the most intelligent theatregoers in town" and characterized it as "the most civilizing producing organization that Broadway has ever had."[35] In his history of the Guild, Eaton summarizes its mission by claiming that "Guild plays are for the most part the antithesis" of "supposedly popular" plays. "They are . . . plays with a sharp intellectual appeal, or with some edge of wit or style or sophistication setting them off from the ruck." At times "experimental," they are distinguished "chiefly" by "some 'spire of meaning.'"[36] (Eaton's metaphor betrays the Guild's project of consecration and cultural uplift.)

The Theatre Guild, in short, aimed to present "plays of artistic merit not ordinarily produced by the commercial managers."[37] By heavily promoting its mission of uplift to the relatively affluent theatergoing classes who were keen to seek out thought-provoking entertainments, it managed to brand itself the premier producer of high-status theater for middle- to upper-class audiences, with fourteen thousand "loyal season subscribers" in 1925 and more than thirty thousand by the 1928–29 season.[38] It thereby endeavored to fulfill the middlebrow dream by reconciling the competing claims of art and commerce. Arthur Hornblow called it "a genuine art theatre" of "artistic standing and prestige" that miraculously "also prospered financially," while Eaton judged it a "theatre dedicated to enduring dramatic art," free of "either personal or commercial exploitation."[39]

A large preponderance of the Theatre Guild's subscribers almost certainly came from the upper reaches of the white-collared class. Critics repeatedly used words like "very sophisticated and selected" to describe the "intellectuals and ultrafashionables" who attended its offerings.[40] Dos Passos portrayed them as "nearrich business men and their wives."[41] One of the many piqued reviewers of *Processional* who was offended by its use of popular elements characterized the "much-valued Theatre Guild subscribers" as feeling duty-bound "to be very serious and very thoughtful . . . while they mulled the piece over in an effort to discover something of [its] 'deeper significance.'" But these sophisticated theatergoers "were sadly at sea" because they were not "familiar with such low-brow enterprises as burlesque shows."[42] Even if one allows for this critic's annoyance, the Guild's public—whether bureaucrats, salesmen, secretaries, artists, housewives, or the idle rich—was unfailingly judged the most highbrow on Broadway. Amassing a remarkable amount of symbolic capital during the 1920s, the Theatre Guild carved out a distinctive profile for itself and became the envy of many producers. Although, with certain exceptions, it did not start to present American plays until the end of the decade, it did interleave ambitious and challenging work by playwrights like Elmer Rice, John Howard Lawson, and Eugene O'Neill into its anthology of modernist European plays.

The Theatre Guild was also instrumental in, if not exactly introducing expressionism to the American theater (O'Neill and the Provincetown Players were responsible for that), then at least helping to familiarize "sophisticated" New York audiences with the stylistic hallmarks, conventions, and preoccupations of European expressionism. In 1922 it presented

Georg Kaiser's *From Morn to Midnight* and Karel Čapek's *R.U.R.* and two years later, Ernst Toller's *Man and the Masses*. It also produced the two American plays that are regularly cited, along with O'Neill's early work, as the most important American experiments in expressionism, *The Adding Machine* and *Processional*. Julia Walker is certainly correct to note the key position of expressionism for the development of American theatrical modernism.[43] The expressionist insurgency included not only playwrights, but also designers like Lee Simonson, Mordecai Gorelik, and Robert Edmond Jones who were responsible for giving a new look and dynamism to American scene design.

A notoriously slippery term that in the United States referred to almost any form of theatrical experimentation, expressionism was viewed as the impetus for and badge of theatrical modernism. Because it "has been used," Oliver Sayler notes, "precisely as well as in general to comprise all the rebels from realism," it became an emblem of a new art theater seeking to distinguish itself from more traditional forms and styles.[44] Expressionism was welcomed into the American theater in the early 1920s in part because of its skill at addressing the many anxieties of the new middle class about standardization, Fordism, and consumerism. By staging the repressed desires and fears of working men and women, the "violent storm of emotion beating up from the unconscious mind," expressionism sought to capture a dreamlike reality ostensibly truer than everyday reality—an auspicious project in what was, after all, the age of Freud.[45] It focused, in Elmer Rice's words, less on "events" than "their inner significance," using "symbols, condensations and a dozen devices which, to the conservative, must seem arbitrarily fantastic."[46] It "exposed" the "half understood 'hinterland' thoughts," director Philip Moeller declared, "all the yearnings and unknown suppressions, . . . just as an X-ray exposes the inner structure of a thing."[47] Its use of distortion, abstraction, and fragmentation (of character, language, plot, and setting) and its focus on intense emotionality provided an ideal set of conventions for an art theater anxious to embrace a European-inspired modernism and distance itself from both gentility and mass-culture.[48] Expressionism was, in short, a perfect vessel for the Theatre Guild as it was trying to navigate the treacherous waters between commerce and art.

During the 1922–23 season, the Theatre Guild presented two expressionist plays, *R.U.R.* and *The Adding Machine*, one foreign, one homegrown, that explicitly and aggressively take on questions about the stan-

Act 2 of the Theatre Guild's 1922 production of Karel Čapek's *R.U.R.* Robots
storm the island factory that manufactures Rossum's Universal Robots. Scene
design by Lee Simonson.
Credit: Billy Rose Theatre Division, The New York Public Library for the Performing Arts,
Astor, Lenox and Tilden Foundations

dardization and commodification of the human subject and betray the
deepest anxieties, both ontological and political, about "the long arm of the
job." *R.U.R.* is a satirical comedy/melodrama (and parable) about Rossum's
Universal Robots, a company that markets mass-produced, artificial workers "more perfect" mechanically than humans but possessing "no soul" (the
play in fact introduced and popularized the word *robot*, taken from the
Czech word for drudgery).[49] Pointedly critiquing capitalism and the company's greedy shareholders, whose "dividends are the ruin of mankind," the
play stages a "revolution of all the Robots in the world."[50] Given the still
recent Communist revolution in Russia and Karel Čapek's Slavic nationality, *R.U.R.* was taken by some critics to be Communist propaganda. Although the play's fatalism ultimately militates against whatever Marxist

sympathies it might hold, it graphically dramatizes the terror (for those who own the means of production, at least) that could be produced by a unified, enlightened proletariat. For the robots are thinly disguised blue- and white-collar employees, "the mechanical workers of our mechanical civilization—human cogs and levers," who revolt against their taskmas- ters.[51] At the beginning of the play they are caricatures of perfectly disci- plined workers, robots who have "no interest in anything," "no will," "[n]o love, no desire to resist."[52] But like a suddenly revolutionized working class, they quickly become a "mob" that kills all but one of their oppres- sors.[53] Since they are unable to reproduce, however, their extermination of human beings ensures their own imminent annihilation. Although the play "shocked" some spectators with its "audacity," *R.U.R.* secured the longest run of any of the expressionist plays presented by the Theatre Guild. Burns Mantle chose to include this "novelty" among his *Best Plays* "for the same reason"—tellingly—"that we have selected others of the Theatre Guild's list of plays—because it best represents the taste of a theatre-going public that is constantly growing in America, and also because it most credibly represents the progressive continental drama."[54] Perhaps it was the very shock it induced that made it so alluring to this growing, sophisticated au- dience, hungry for provocative encounters in the theater.

In Europe, expressionism (which began in Germany in the visual arts shortly before World War I with Oskar Kokoschka, Wassily Kandinsky, Max Beckmann, and others) was never a populist movement but a cutting edge of the historical avant-garde. A self-consciously revolutionary move- ment, it "rejected, unmasked, and caricatured" the art, mores, pieties, and institutions of bourgeois society. Unapologetically aligned with pacifism, humanitarianism, and socialism, it sought to demolish the canons of beauty and taste that dominated Wilhelminian Germany and Hapsburg Austria.[55] And while some avant-gardisms (like Dada and surrealism) sought to un- dermine the differences between elite and popular cultures (and between art and life), German expressionism did not. Indeed, its link to European elite culture was nowhere more evident than in the music with which it is most closely associated, the atonal, pre-twelve-note works that Arnold Schoenberg wrote between 1908 and 1923. Later in the 1920s, composers like Ernst Krenek, Paul Hindemith, and Kurt Weill (all of whom had writ- ten expressionistic music at the beginning of the decade) started incorpo- rating popular music, notably jazz (or what they believed to be jazz), into their concert works and music theater pieces. But this jazz-inspired music was in fact exemplary of *Neue Sachlichkeit*, or the New Objectivity, the movement that reacted against what it took to be expressionism's irrational excesses.[56] In the United States, on the other hand, expressionism had a much closer relationship to popular cultures. Gilbert Seldes was fascinated by Robert Wiene's *The Cabinet of Dr. Caligari* (1919), the first postwar German film to be shown in the United States (in 1921) and the work that introduced German expressionism to many Americans. But he appreciated its "spectacle," not "the dramatic quality of its story," and he favorably compared the chase scene over the roofs with the Keystone Cops (8). He also pronounced George Herriman's Krazy Kat "our one work in the expressionistic mode," a work "rich with something we have too little of—fantasy" (242, 245).

Because the arrival of expressionism happened to coincide with the debate over the role of native vernaculars in American art, expressionism was somewhat more populist and more favorably disposed toward popular culture than it had been in Europe. (This shift is also indicative of a more positive attitude toward mass production in the United States than in western Europe.) In some quarters, expressionism was considered to be the visual, literary, and theatrical analogue to syncopated dance music. Its association with jazz and vaudeville is borne out most strikingly in *Processional* and Lawson's other plays of the 1920s. But Lawson's work was only one example of the close association between expressionism and jazz during the 1920s. One *New York Times* writer considered the terms *expressionist drama* and *jazz drama* interchangeable, while a critic for the African American journal *Opportunity* declared that "modern expressionism in art is jazz art."[57] Even *The Emperor Jones* (1920) betrays the unmistakable traces of jazz in the constant "beating of the tom-tom" that accompanies the scenes of Jones's regression (antijazz critics habitually considered "the beat of the tom-tom which drives savages into orgiastic ecstasies" to be identical with the "beat of the drum" that underpins jazz).[58] The fact that Stark Young would call an avowedly antijazz, expressionist play like *Beggar on Horseback* "jazz poetry" attests to the fact that even antijazz theater was a form of jazz theater. The latter was branded modernist and progressive as well as standardized and dehumanizing, the paradigmatic art of the Machine Age.[59]

An inspiration and formal model for several playwrights, jazz was repeatedly sublimated in the expressionist theater of the 1920s just as it had been in the concert works of George Gershwin.[60] Lawson emphasizes that his play *The International*, for example, does more than use incidental jazz music. It is "musical throughout," in its underscoring, in the singing voices of actors, and in its use of a chorus, which "is a combination of jazz treatment with the dignified narrative . . . of Greek drama." Lawson designed this play, like *Processional*, to be "a formalized pattern or symphony" in which the "music must have the same quality as the play itself" and the words must fall into "jazz rhythms."[61] Jazz thus inheres in the musical structure, in the speech and chanting, and even in the setting with its rhythmic "series of blocks building up like a futurist impression of mass."[62] American expressionist theater was jazz theater less because it featured syncopated dance music (it often did not) than because it was formally analogous to jazz, a structure in which words, lines of dialogue, speeches, or scenes fell into "jazz rhythms." It is the dramatic version of jazz poetry (of Langston Hughes, Joseph Moncure March, and many others) that literary scholars acknowledge to be a major constituent of 1920s American literature.[63] When one expands one's conception of jazz drama—and understands that what I am calling jazz drama is not necessarily favorably disposed toward jazz music—a number of now canonical American expressionist plays become representative, including Eugene O'Neill's *The Hairy Ape* (1922), Elmer Rice's *The Adding Machine* (1923), and Sophie Treadwell's *Machinal* (1928). Each of these plays employs a colorful, working-class vernacular to compose a modernist stichomythia inflected by repetitive, syncopated "jazz rhythms." (This technique is most ingeniously and vividly used in the first scene of *Machinal*.) Each strings scenes together like the lines of a poem. Most important, each play is centrally concerned with the plight of the working classes in the Machine Age and the standardization and commodification of the human subject, the fear of which was obsessively being displaced onto the musical genre with the strongest working-class associations.

CONSECRATING AMERICAN EXPRESSIONISM

With the possible exception of *The Emperor Jones* and *The Hairy Ape*, the most celebrated American expressionist play is surely Elmer Rice's *The Adding Machine*, which was first produced by the Theatre Guild at the Garrick Theatre. It opened on 19 March 1923, garnering mixed reviews and racking up a "comfortable" seventy-two-performance run.[64] The critics were divided about this "sophisticated nightmare," "[v]ery wise, and very wild, and, so far as we are concerned, very insoluble."[65] A "bitter tasting comedy" that "gives vent to a pessimistic philosophy," it is the story of the wretched life and afterlife of a slavish bookkeeper named Mr. Zero.[66] (Guess the sum total of his life.) A dedicated, henpecked drone, Mr. Zero kills his boss in a fit of rage, is tried, executed, and holidays at the Elysian Fields before fleeing to the big office in the sky, his final stop before reincarnation. Innovatively directed by Philip Moeller and designed by Lee Simonson (who earlier that season had collaborated on *R.U.R.*), *The Adding Machine* was one of "several daring experiments" to open on Broadway that year.[67] Heywood Broun noted that it is "exactly the type of play which justifies the existence of the Theatre Guild," while others judged it watered-down and simplistic. George Jean Nathan called it "a pale copy of German Expressionism," and Stark Young complained that "the dreariest fool can now understand expressionism."[68] Although Charles Henry Meltzer deemed it "the most daring and ingenuous" of the "more 'modern' plays by young Americans," H. Z. Torres fulminated against "this so-called 'expressionism,'" insisting that the play possessed "neither dramatic form nor literary merit," and was "singularly devoid of beauty" and "destructive of national sanity."[69] Burns Mantle dismissed it as yet "another impressionistic [*sic*] study on an American theme" and declined to include it in his *Best Plays*.[70] Only in subsequent years would it be hailed, in Brooks Atkinson's enthusiastic words, as "the classic expressionistic American drama" and "the most original and brilliant play any American had written up to that time."[71]

Like many of his contemporaries working in theater, motion pictures, and Tin Pan Alley, Rice (born Elmer Leopold Reizenstein in New York in 1892), the grandson of immigrants, was raised in a lower-class Jewish household. Because of his humble beginnings, histories and biographies predictably construct him, in Frank Durham's words, as "the hero of the Great American Success Story."[72] A dedicated fan of the legitimate theater in his youth, he (like many of his class) pursued education as the means to upward mobility. He attended New York Law School, graduating with an LL.B. in 1912, but practiced law very briefly, preferring writing to full-time employment. His first play, *On Trial*, "a purely commercial transaction," according to Atkinson (and an early example of the use of flashbacks), was a surprise Broadway hit in 1914, earning him a hundred thousand dollars, then a small fortune.[73] Courted by Samuel Goldwyn, he succumbed to Hollywood's money and glamour (and cowrote two screen-

Scene 3 of the Theatre Guild's 1923 production of Elmer Rice's *The Adding Machine*. The *lumpenbourgeoisie* assembles in Mr. and Mrs. Zero's dining room while Mr. Zero (Dudley Digges) goes to answer the doorbell. Scene design by Lee Simonson.

Credit: Museum of the City of New York

plays) but returned to New York after two discouraging years. Although epitomizing the successful entrepreneur, Rice did not acquire his reputation as a writer for the art theater until *The Adding Machine*, which he wrote in seventeen days and in which he turned to a more experimental form and more explicitly left-wing politics.[74] Rice had from an early age identified himself as a utopian socialist, and he explained that he found utopian fictions especially appealing because they demonstrated "the need for revolutionary changes in human institutions and attitudes."[75] Atkinson honors Rice's self-identification, describing him as "primarily a political person" and a socialist (who in 1935 would become the first New York director of the Federal Theatre Project).[76] Critics in 1923, meanwhile, could hardly miss the "thoroughly experimental" style of the play and its "caustic look at the inhumanity of big business."[77] (It is, in fact, questionable whether the dystopian world depicted in *The Adding Machine* would be susceptible to revolutionary, or indeed, any form of real change.) Rice, in other words, used the association between expressionism and leftist politics to propel his work into the art theater and thereby exchange economic capital for cultural capital. When, in Rice's opinion, the Theatre Guild in the late 1920s reneged on its promise as an art theater by becoming "a large scale commercial producing organization," he pulled up stakes.[78]

If both Rice and the Theatre Guild occupied a contradictory position in the 1920s, it was because of their role in promoting a commercial theater that earned its economic and cultural capital by critiquing the foundations of commercialism. And with its production of *The Adding Machine*, the Guild attempted to stake a claim on a distinctively American brand of art theater. Accordingly, "Mr. Rice became," in Joseph Wood Krutch's words, "the Guild's first American discovery."[79] Yet both Rice and the Guild found it very difficult—some would say, impossible—to maintain the balance between art and commerce. The 1923 critics betrayed a distinct uneasiness with a play that, in Arthur Hornblow's mordant words, if "coming from Prague, would excite the townsfolk to prayer and feasting." "But being the work of an American, and an American, incidentally," who "has come out of the movies" and is therefore "not of the esoteric order, we can expect a merely mild critical reception and a patronizing attitude."[80] In other words, the upper-middle-class patrons of a commercial theater that branded itself an art theater would have welcomed a more Europeanized, which is to say, foreign or abstracted, social critique. But *The Adding Machine* was written by a commercial playwright, a successful Jewish entrepreneur who in fact had once prostrated himself before Hollywood's golden calf. In attacking "specifically American commercialism, industry, and civilization," it perhaps hit a little too close to the bone.[81] It is little wonder that the play would not support a long run.

Yet the very characteristics that sabotaged *The Adding Machine*'s initial success were precisely those that bequeathed its fame to posterity. Atkinson's 1970 commendation of a play much more widely read than produced demonstrates that it exemplifies many of the characteristics that would mark the canonical literary drama of the 1920s and 1930s: the depiction of both a highly particularized social formation and a deeply psychologized individual; a mixture of experimentalism and "realism," "philosophy" and "Broadway accent[ed]" satire; and the propensity to launch "a fierce protest against the meanness and ruthlessness of our social system."[82] It confirms the fact that expressionism proved an ideal vehicle for an American drama seeking legitimation. Expressionism permitted the theater, like the "high art" it aspired to be, to make what was called "a philosophic commentary on life."[83] It loaned Broadway a measure of European prestige. It encouraged playwrights (during the vogue for psychoanalysis) to compose an "intellectual drama . . . built around the workings of the human brain as a starting point, rather than around a story."[84] It broke with earlier dramaturgical models by severely limiting empathy and ensuring that "Curiosity" would supplant "Sympathy in the construction of plays."[85]

Perhaps the most important characteristic of expressionism (both in Germany and the United States) was its production of a different kind of human subject. Like so much modernist art, it replicated a Machine Age everyman who was simultaneously a universal subject, an emblem of modernity, and casualty of industrialization (rather than a highly particularized, three-dimensional character). This modern subject, moreover, was always in the throes of contesting, rejecting, or reluctantly trying to accommodate him- or herself to a mass society that turned people into "human cogs and levers." (Shortly before *The Adding Machine* opened, the *Times* reported "rumors" that the play was "'different'—different in the sense that 'R.U.R.' . . . is different" and that its characters were "automatons, talk[ing] in numbers.")[86] Expressionist drama, in other words, was peopled by stereotypes who were usually designated by occupation, social position, or place in the family hierarchy. (The stereotype machine, invented in 1893, made Braille-embossed printing plates to be used to mass-produce books for the blind.) Walter Sokel emphasizes that the apparently universal hero (who is almost always male) dominates the arclike structure of the typical expressionist play, which, like the medieval Passion play, requires him to serve "as an existential example, a paragon" who undergoes a series of trials before being sacrificed in the end. He is surrounded by stereotypes, by "foils" who "are not so much characters as functions in his mission and martyrdom."[87] Unlike domestic realism, which keeps the protagonist safely within the home (and within a well-made plot structure), expressionism usually constructs a "loosely connected 'life story,' a series of 'stations,' pictures, and situations" through which the protagonist passes.[88]

One of the most controversial aspects of American expressionism, and the one that most clearly demonstrated its decisive rejection of the genteel tradition, was its exploitation of a sexual frankness that was roundly attacked by a number of critics. Indeed, during the legitimate theater's consolidation as art in the 1920s, the dispute over obscenity pitted a puritanical, genteel fraction of the middle class against a more permissive, modernist one. This dispute was repeatedly played out among dueling factions in the audience and among critics, including Arthur Hornblow, the editor of *Theatre*, who was an especially vociferous opponent of sexual frankness. (One of the more intriguing ironies of the era involves the fact that his son, Arthur Hornblow Jr., caused one of the biggest scandals of the decade with *The Captive* [1926], his adaptation of Edouard Bourdet's *La Prisonnière*, whose alleged obscenity helped precipitate the Wales Padlock Law of 1927, which authorized the police to arrest actors and producers of offending productions and shutter their theaters for a year.) Hornblow Sr. believed that the legitimate theater was being "turned into a brothel" and repeatedly inveighed against the "ever-rising tide of stage filth."[89] *The Adding Machine* in particular was censured by him and others for its "profanity" and "its profanation of the dead," so corrosive, one critic believed, of "the moral fiber."[90] Another critic claimed he had "a bad, a very bad, taste" left in his mouth by "one hideous episode" (which the *Times* critic deemed "gratuitously vulgar"), "in which the streetwalker . . . lures a customer to the grave of Mr. Zero."[91] In fact, however, this forthrightness about sex, at least until the passage of the Wales Padlock Law, was crucial in distinguishing a more provocative, "sophisticated" legitimate theater in the age of Freud from mass-produced cultural forms and in appealing to an "intelligent minority," to artists, intellectuals, and upper-middle-class fractions that wanted to be unsettled, aroused, and even shocked.[92]

FORDIZED HUMAN SUBJECTS

Although a large preponderance of the Theatre Guild audience may have come from the upper reaches of the white-collared class, all of their expressionist productions and some of their most celebrated U.S. premieres, including *Liliom* (1921) and *They Knew What They Wanted* (1924), featured characters drawn not from the rich but from the lower ranges of the new middle class and "the mass of the people" below it. This preoccupation with lower- and lower-middle-class characters was, as one might expect, the product of several intersecting theatrical and social histories. Going back to the late nineteenth century, it was an important element of a theatrical naturalism that observed and analyzed the sometimes sensationalized behaviors and psychologies of various marginal demimondes. This approach was continued and fortified in the United States during the Progressive Era by socialist novelists like Upton Sinclair and Frank Norris who sought to expose the dehumanizing force of industrial capitalism and mass production on the working classes. In Germany, naturalism led to expressionism, with its revolutionary ambitions and its incisive and shocking representations of the alienated, exploited, dispossessed, urban proletariat.

In *The Adding Machine*, Rice takes up these traditions in his depiction of Mr. and Mrs. Zero and their friends who (jazz opponents would say) are as indistinguishable from each other as one jazz tune is from any other. John V. A. Weaver in fact commends Rice because he "had taken the trouble to listen with attention" to "the tongue of the masses" and was thereby able to produce a "true characterization" of this class.[93] In Mrs. Zero's long, rambling monologue that comprises the play's first scene, Rice clearly establishes the class habitus of an emblematic lower-middle-class couple just barely maintaining itself above the proletariat. (One reviewer quite exactly described the Zeroes as occupying "the outermost fringe of the lowest middle class stratum.")[94] The first half of her speech is devoted to a disquisition on the cultural form from which the play is especially anxious to distance itself, motion pictures, both because of the art theater's higher aspirations and Rice's own regrettable history in the industry. Mrs. Zero is presented as a typical female moviegoer who prefers "sweet little love stories" to "them Westerns."[95] Throughout her speech she voices her love for the movies (the surest sign of her and their lowbrow status) and her class-based resentment directed against both her more affluent neighbors and her "thin, sallow, undersized" bookkeeper husband who has failed even to obtain a raise in seven years and keeps her at home "slavin' [her] life away" (3, 5). Her picturesque diction, with its dropped final consonants, its colorful idioms, and its grammatical errors, presents a vivid and unflattering portrait of a woman who was described by critics as being "monstrous," "intolerably mean minded, ugly and quarrelsome."[96] An unstoppable chatterer, like a radio or phonograph, she never even concludes her speech, but just "goes on talking as the curtain falls" (6).

Throughout the play, women are machines that spew forth words. "Talk, talk, talk," Mr. Zero says to Daisy, his coworker, "Just like all the other women" (7). The primary consumers and dupes of sentimentalized, mass-cultural forms—to which they clearly provide an analogue—they run on endlessly, threatening hierarchies of gender, propriety, and taste. Women, however, by no means have a monopoly on crassness, stupidity, and volubility. The lower-middle-class men, suffering their own brand of resentment, are small-minded and brutal in a similarly mechanical, unthinking way. (The original manuscript of *The Adding Machine* suggests that Rice subscribed to the view of jazz as dehumanizing. It indicates that the chatter among the identically dressed groups of men and women in the party scene was, like a second-rate jazz band, to have "grow[n] louder and more staccato until it acquire[d] a sort of rhythmic beat.")[97] As if preprogrammed, they are sent into a xenophobic, racist, and jingoistic frenzy by fears of unrestricted immigration and "foreign agitators" of all stripes:

> *All [in unison].* That's it! Damn foreigners! Damn dagoes! Damn Catholics! Damn sheenies! Damn niggers! Jail 'em! Shoot 'em! Hang 'em! Lynch 'em! Burn 'em!

They then launch enthusiastically into the first two lines of the anthem "America" (19).

The Adding Machine provides an extremely critical portrait of the lower middle class as a kind of reactionary *lumpenbourgeoisie*. If nothing else, the characters' numerical surnames and lack of Christian names (except for Daisy, Mr. Zero's object of desire) guarantee that the members of each sex are nearly indistinguishable and that they function theatrically as mass-produced copies. Mr. Zero is a laboring machine who prides himself on never missing a day of work in twenty-five years. In the play's second scene, he prefigures the adding machine that replaces him as he and Daisy are discovered "reading and checking figures to each other in a dreary and monotonous sing-song."[98] Mr. Zero and all his friends are clearly marked as lower middle class by their near obsession with hard work, social respectability, and "wholesome" entertainment (3).[99] One of the "good clean people," Mr. Zero is "shocked" by the mere thought of "smutty stories" by the likes of Swift and Rabelais (two authors likely to be esteemed by Theatre Guild subscribers [53]). A reservoir of sexual repression, he quits the Elysian Fields in disgust when he discovers they're peopled by "a lot of rummies an' loafers an' bums" (53–54).[100] A penchant for depicting the *lumpenbourgeoisie* as other, in fact, is very much tied to the particular habitus of the theatergoing and theater-making upper-middle classes. For Davis and coauthors note that upper-middle-class individuals who are "attempting to rise in the social scale point out beneath them the 'lower middles' as a separate class group and almost invariably attempt to exaggerate their social distance from it."[101] Because Rice, the critics, and the Theatre Guild audiences seem intent on discovering that Mr. Zero represents "a decidedly second-class soul," the play essentializes his subordination as an unalterable biological-spiritual condition that predates his various reincarnations: "The mark of the slave was on you from the start" (58).[102]

Mr. Zero may be in essence a machinelike slave, but he is also constructed as a blameless victim of a literally dehumanizing modernization process that replaces him with an adding machine. This contradiction is representative of the difficulties during the Machine Age in trying to adjudicate (and control the relationship) between industrial and social progress. It is a result of conflicting attitudes, as Raymond Williams points out, toward "the urban crowd as 'mass' or 'masses.'" In one version, these terms emblematize standardization, mechanization, and "deadening uniformity." In another, they "become the heroic, organizing words of working-class and revolutionary solidarity."[103] This contradiction is also symptomatic of a profound ambivalence about the status of the individual, an ambivalence that is echoed in the play's title (which signifies both Mr. Zero and the machine that replaces him) and in the dual identity of the "human cogs and levers" who are both pieces of machinery and Fordized human subjects.

John Howard Lawson's book on playwriting, although not published until 1936, provides a provocative analysis of this contradiction. He contends that there is a "double movement" built into the "dominant ideas" of the legitimate theater's primary audience, the "liberal," "cosmopolitan upper middle class." Noting that this class is always engaged in an imaginary restructuring of their "increasingly chaotic environment," he argues that the theater's "social philosophy" necessarily "reflects"—and distorts—"the relationship between this audience and its environment."[104] On the one hand, modern thought is inextricably bound up with a narrow, consumerist materialism. As a result, the theatergoing class has, as a group, developed a set of "low" "[c]ommercial and moral standards." But because their materialist outlook "provides a partial adjustment to the needs of the everyday world," they have learned to take pleasure in mass-produced entertainments.[105] On the other hand, their materialism (and increased "leisure-time") compulsively produces its opposite, the cultivation of a "[s]piritual" and "esthetic other-worldliness" that "offers (or seems to offer) a means of escape from the sterility of the environment." The trend toward materialism is continually opposed to "the trend toward escape-at-any-price from the very conditions which are the product of narrow materialism."[106]

Lawson quite precisely maps what is arguably the central contradiction inherent in the liberalism of the new middle class (and the Theatre Guild). For liberalism, as an ideology, has been (and continues to be) inflected by the struggle between its political and economic dimensions. On the one hand, political liberalism, taking the sovereign individual as the fundamental social unit, prizes a representative and limited government and, at least in principle, is committed to personal freedom, open-mindedness, and egalitarianism. On the other hand, economic liberalism, historically the dominant form of capitalism, is rooted in private property and champions individual initiative and an unrestricted market. Liberal economists and philosophers of the nineteenth and twentieth centuries tried relentlessly (and ultimately, unsuccessfully) to reconcile the patent contradictions between these two dimensions. Mounting a critique of liberalism from the left, Lawson clearly understood how basic these contradictions were, and he provides examples of the many incongruous ideological positions to which this philosophy gives rise: "on the one hand, all men are created free and equal; on the other hand, certain races are manifestly inferior; on the one hand, money destroys spiritual values; on the other hand, money-success is the only reliable test of character."[107] (The Lynds observed this same contradiction playing itself out in Middletown in many different spheres, especially in attitudes toward religion. "On the one hand, . . . there is a tendency to appraise the fruits of religion by . . . tangible, material measurements." "On the other hand, there is a tendency to value religion for its very remoteness and difference from the affairs of every day, its concern with 'another world, another life'" [402–3]). Rather than confront the "intolerable" social and economic "situation" with a revolutionary solidarity, the cosmopolitan upper middle class looks to an escapist "mysticism which is increasingly emotional and fatalistic."[108] The despairing ending of *The Adding Machine* clearly opts for the subjective over the social and thereby honors this fatalistic mysticism. It acquiesces to what it calls the "super-hyper-adding machine," "the final triumph of the evolutionary process" (60–61). This refusal of the social also brings the play's ideology into line with that of the leading playwright of the age, Eugene O'Neill, in whose work, Lawson notes, the "struggle" against a "modern fate" is always "useless" because fate, being "both in man and outside him," is inescapable.[109]

The Adding Machine may be fatalistic but its contradictions are linked to a social liberalism that was very much a hallmark of the upper middle and upper classes during the 1920s. Although members of the upper middle class jealously guarded and defended their economic initiatives, the social

Scene 4 of *The Adding Machine*. In a court of justice, Mr. Zero pleads his case before a sphinxlike judge.
Credit: Museum of the City of New York

prestige of the class was in part dependent on its commitment to social betterment, its participation in community-based charitable activities and other civic enterprises. Kahl notes that members of the upper classes were often "liberal, for their family position guarantees enough security to permit individualistic expression and variation."[110] The theatergoing classes, especially those "selected" few drawn to the Theatre Guild, would likely have been predisposed to sympathize with the hapless Mr. Zero and his fellow unfortunates, despite the stark differences between their respective outlooks and behaviors. ("Suppose you was me," Mr. Zero pleads while in the dock, "Maybe you'd 'a' done the same thing" [24].) For the play leads them to believe that they were not subject to the same inexorable law that guarantees his slavishness and that of his class. They would hardly have fled in horror from the Elysian Fields, bragged about never missing a day of work in twenty-five years, or "cried [their] eyes out," as Mrs. Eight confesses she did, at a patently lowbrow, woman's weepie like *A Mother's Tears* (4).

Even if one is skeptical of Brooks Atkinson's extravagant claims for *The Adding Machine*, the play represents more than merely an expression of class-based resentment. Many of its first critics remarked on its idiosyncratic mixture of rather poignant and subtext-laden domestic realism (all the scenes of heterosexual coupling and decoupling) with patently theatricalized scenes that were intensified by Simonson's brilliantly off-kilter settings. Among the latter, the most frequently remarked upon was the scene between Mr. Zero and his boss during which "the walls suddenly come alive with a mad dance of a thousand figures." Then, after a blackout, "in the midst of the blackness, you see two sudden, stabbing splashes of scarlet."[111] By using style to separate off the domestic sphere, Rice and his collaborators underline the bourgeois fetishization of the home (and the heterosexuality that is supposed to inhere therein) as a refuge from the public sphere.

As if wanting to emphasize the contradictory aesthetic and social projects of *The Adding Machine*, the Theatre Guild engaged Deems Taylor to write incidental music. Taylor was already acquiring a name for himself as a composer of concert music in a conservative modernist style and would the next year write incidental music for *Beggar on Horseback*. Because he was an opponent of the "maddening monotony" of jazz (despite his composition of *Circus Day* [1925] for Paul Whiteman), he arranged his music for the most elite and austere of ensembles, the string quartet, the one that at least since Beethoven has been most closely associated with *Innigkeit*, or subjective inwardness. Although Taylor composed underscoring for three scenes, the murder, graveyard, and Elysian Fields scenes, Moeller declined to use his music for the last.[112] Percy Hammond reports, however, that for the graveyard seduction scene, an "episode so foul as to be absolutely inexcusable," Taylor composed some appropriately vulgar music, "ghostly jazz music, gay though plaintive."[113] For Taylor, and no doubt, the Theatre Guild audience as well, only an eerie jazz arrangement could possibly complement this "hideous" scene. (In later years, Taylor assiduously followed the upper-middlebrow path to fame and fortune. Although the deans of the classical music establishment recognized that his music was extremely effective—as well as "synthetic and derived"—they branded him an "inordinately clever" "opportunist."[114] He became most widely known, however, as a radio broadcaster and the narrator of Walt Disney's *Fantasia* [1939].)

Just as important as an admixture of styles (realism and expressionism, jazz and string quartet) as a sign of art theater in the 1920s, psychoanalysis had quickly become established as the skeleton key to unlocking the door to the psyche. Although the Freudian vogue started after World War I, it was in full swing by the 1922–23 season, during which W. David Sievers points out, "[n]o fewer than five plays" with clear "Freudian content reached Broadway," including John Colton and Clemence Randolph's *Rain* (1922), the first "conspicuously Freudian play" to attain "the 'smash-hit' category" (648 performances).[115] *The Adding Machine* was greeted as a psychological puzzle by several critics; it was a work whose form and meaning remain "very insoluble."[116] And while Zero himself is not a complete mystery—the contradictions of which he is a symptom are clearly mapped—the allegorical characters are more enigmatic, whether Lieutenant Charles and The Fixer or the matricidal Shrdlu (first played by a young Edward G. Robinson), whose mysterious, unpronounceable name is in fact made up of the series of keys on the second line of a linotype machine and who seems to have wandered in off the pages of one of Freud's more lurid case histories.[117] All of these features work to produce a play that was, in retrospect, constructed as a cornerstone of the American art theater, a play that, "like poetry, unleashes a dramatist's [and spectator's!] imagination."[118] Indeed, the mixture of styles and teasing use of enigmatic situations, characters, and themes have since the 1920s been the hallmarks of a commercial theater in the United States that has attempted to pass as an art theater, from Rice and O'Neill to Tennessee Williams, Arthur Miller, Edward Albee, August Wilson, Tony Kushner, and many, many others.

PROFITLESS OCCUPATIONS

Although *The Adding Machine* works assiduously to construct the *lumpenbourgeoisie* as other, it is unable to disguise the fact that both the upper reaches and the lower depths of the new middle class were fundamentally in the same position vis-à-vis the means of production. Upper-middle-class elitism and attention to fashion, upward mobility, and cultural uplift could not completely banish a deep sense of insecurity, the threat of "the elusive meaninglessness" of life, and the fear of occupational paralysis that the new middle-class worker was increasingly being forced to confront, no matter where he or she stood in the office hierarchy.[119] These anxieties, moreover, were directly linked to modern urban life and to the character and dynamics of the newly Taylorized office in which, as Rice puts it, the "iron collar" of the serf had merely been replaced by "white ones" (59). I suspect that one reason for the play's canonization is its effectiveness in analyzing the position of the theatergoing classes while professing to be dramatizing that of a class fraction well below it in the economic and social hierarchy.

In a brilliantly theatrical moment in *White Collar*, Mills articulates the fears of the new middle-class worker. He also quite exactly describes the social position and function of Mr. Zero, with a directness and eloquence, however, that I suspect would baffle the unlucky clerk. Playing both conscience and devil's advocate, he whispers into the ear of an imaginary white-collar operative and articulates what he or she dared not think.

> You carry authority, but you are not its source. As one of the managed, you are on view from above, and perhaps you are seen as a threat; as one of the managers, you are seen from below, perhaps as a tool. You are the cog and the beltline of the bureaucratic machinery itself; you are a link in the chains of commands, persuasions, notices, bills, which bind together the men who make decisions and the men who make things. . . . But your authority is confined strictly within a prescribed orbit of occupational actions, and such power as you wield is a borrowed thing. Yours is the subordinate's mark, yours the canned talk. The money you handle is somebody else's money; the papers you sort and shuffle already bear somebody else's marks (80).

Performing the very operation it professes to describe, Mills's discourse precisely enacts the ventriloquized "canned talk" whose function it explains. As such, it both attests to and dramatizes the radical dispossession of the new middle-class workers who, because they no longer own the means of production or have any real stake in them, must borrow not only their trade and tools but also their language, authority, money, and inner life. Exemplary middlemen, disciplined and surveilled, these white-collar workers represent "human cogs and levers" in the great bureaucratic machine, displaced, alienated, forever aspiring to an authority (like Zero's autocratic Boss) that remains utterly mystified and inaccessible.

The social structure depicted in *The Adding Machine* signifies more, however, than a critique of class relations. It also inadvertently represents a ghostly image of the theatrical apparatus in the 1920s. In the first part of the play, set among the living, the primary conflicts are strictly binary, between capital (the Boss) and labor (everyone else) and between women and men (in the form of the gendered division of labor). These conflicts are not symmetrical, however, and the battle of the sexes is clearly presented as a displacement and, to some extent, parody of the Marxian class struggle. In the afterlife, however, difference is organized as a three-part system. On the one hand, the not-so-sweet hereafter revises and metaphysicalizes the earthly struggle between capital and labor in the figures of Lieutenant Charles and Mr. Zero, the once and future slave. Charles, though, is himself only a slave, a deputy whose power is a borrowed thing, one who repairs but has no more responsibility for making decisions than the white-collar operative. "You can't change the rules," his canned talk goes. "Nobody can" (59). Nobody, that is, except for the absent, nameless demiurge; the Boss upstairs; the Law. Charles may be his delegate, but he is as much a dupe of the "rotten system" as Zero himself.

In the afterlife, the opposition between the Law and its victims (a.k.a. capital and labor) is disrupted by a third party, the "loafers an' bums" who populate the Elysian Fields and are, Shrdlu says, "so strange, so unlike the good people I've known" (53). Though these "good people" never put in an appearance on stage, Shrdlu's description of them provides an unmistakable portrait of men and women of leisure, an idealized fellowship of artists, the old middle-class entrepreneurs who own and control their businesses. Because they represent nonalienated labor, the opposition between work and leisure no longer obtains. Their work is play.

> They seem to think of nothing but enjoyment or of wasting their time in profitless occupations. Some paint pictures from morning until night, or carve blocks of stone. Others write songs or put words together, day in and day out. Still others do nothing but lie under the trees and look at the sky. There are men who spend all their time reading books and women who think only of adorning themselves. And forever they are telling stories and laughing and singing and drinking and dancing (53).

Unlike the other characters, for whom time is money, and who are held hostage to the dehumanizing rhythms of the machine, the inhabitants of the Elysian Fields need only sit together "an' look at the flowers an' listen to the music" (which most assuredly is not jazz! [54]). Rather than saving time, they expend it as heavenly waste. Rather than invest in the production of commodities to be traded in the marketplace, these artists are involved in "profitless occupations." They have no market to supply with goods, no consumers except the producers themselves. This paradise is a realm beyond capitalism. It is also, apparently, one in which deprivation is unknown. Production and consumption are no longer figured as opposites.

This vision of a realm beyond the marketplace and the commodity, beyond the oppositions between work and leisure, profit and waste, production and consumption, is obviously a utopian fantasy, and a very seductive one at that. It is made possible, however, precisely by the "rotten," materialistic system that Lieutenant Charles oversees and from which it provides an escape despite the fact that there is "no way out" (59). Writing a variation on the central contradiction that Lawson observes in liberalism, Rice proves that the bureaucratic machinery will always produce a fantasy of an "escape-at-any-price." Yet this fantastic realm outside the marketplace is not a mere abstraction. It is populated by clearly recognizable painters, sculptors, songwriters, poets, stargazers, readers, narcissistic women, storytellers, singers, and dancers. (Although this list may challenge the opposition between work and leisure, it predictably reinscribes the binary system of gender.) Note: there are no motion pictures in the Elysian Fields. Or phonographs. Or radios. It is, in short, a realm of artisanal production. A realm of highbrow art. For it is—tellingly—without the one form that most damnably confounds cultural categories: theater. It may be home to different kinds of art and performance (which represent components of theater), but, as in Plato's Republic, theater is banished.

In a stunningly contradictory move, the construction of theater as high art by Elmer Rice and the Theatre Guild required the exclusion of theater from the Elysian Fields—and thus from the realm of high art. This exclusion was symptomatic of the fact that the legitimate stage during the 1920s was typically conceptualized as occupying a kind of median position between mass production and artisanal production, between the hell-on-earth of Mrs. Zero's "sweet little" picture shows and the many blissful, "profitless occupations" of the Elysian Fields (3, 53). Its middling status, however, did not deter the Theatre Guild and modernist playwrights like Rice and O'Neill (along with so many critics) from trying to coax it into the realm of high art, beyond the market, mass culture, and the commodity form. This, of course, was an impossible project. Yet given the makeup of Broadway audiences—ranging from the people of "alert and watchful" intelligence in the gallery to the "better grade of professional man" and "hip-flask gentry" downstairs—this theater was obliged to aim for this impossibility. Both the Guild and its audiences, with their social and occupational anxieties and their cultural aspirations, needed this fantasy of a highbrow legitimate theater as an impossible but "ideal goal," a site that would transcend mass culture and cancel the opposition between art and commerce.[120]

Although *The Adding Machine* leaves no place for theater in the Elysian Fields, it does spin out a fantasy of a fellowship of artists, old middle-class entrepreneurs who bear an uncanny resemblance to the board of the Theatre Guild: six men and women who, in Walter Prichard Eaton's words, forsook "personal desires," to embrace an idea of an elevated theater "with passionate loyalty."[121] In producing *The Adding Machine*, the Guild aimed to commemorate the victory of the heavenly arts over jazz and the infernal movies; and of those flush with economic and cultural capital over the culturally indigent. With "the force of revolution," Eaton proudly announced, the Guild had turned "a business" designed for "the exploitation of artists" into "a university . . . working for the lasting good of education."[122] (It did, in fact, operate a School of Theatre from 1927 to 1930.)[123] It also managed almost single-handedly to revive the road, playing in 1928–29 to thirty thousand subscribers divided among six cities, with three more cities to follow the next season. "It has even invaded London," Eaton exulted, at long last proving the export value of American drama.[124] Brooks Atkinson summed up the achievement of the Theatre Guild in elevating the stage by remarking that it had proven—for at least a few years—that "art had become vastly more successful than commerce."[125]

Not all cultural observers felt as sanguine about the Theatre Guild and its achievements as Eaton and Atkinson. Suspicious of its attempts at consolidating a highbrow theater, John Dos Passos wove a more cynical (and, it seems to me, more historically accurate) narrative. The Guild, he noted

> started as a piece of Greenwich Village revolt that was made a financial success by sheer business ability. . . . [T]hrough its productions of O'Neill and a long series of warmedover [*sic*] European productions, it has given a throbbing Viennese [Freudian] soul and a wan intellectual horizon to a whole generation of suburbanites. Theatre Guild productions with their amber lights, the sophomore philosophies of O'Neill and the Lunts in their eternal boudoir are the nearest thing we have to an American theatrical tradition today.[126]

For Dos Passos, the Guild emblematized not high art but the kind of bogus, sophomoric, upper-middlebrow theater that Gilbert Seldes found so mind-numbingly pretentious. And its main achievement in his eyes was far more pedestrian than its boosters claimed. It managed merely to have "reached the standard of efficiency of any ordinary commercial business."[127]

Predictably, the Theatre Guild's days of financial solvency proved short lived, and its story quickly devolved into melodrama, complete with angry creditors knocking at the front door and unhappy artists ducking out the back. Having decided to build its own Broadway theater (which opened in 1925 and was renamed the August Wilson in 2005), the Guild was forced to take out $500,000 in bonds to pay for it. The expenses of running the Guild Theatre, combined with a substantial bonded indebtedness that had to be serviced, required "an annual expenditure of $90,000." Eaton noted ominously that these ongoing expenses "left no great margin for extravagance in experiment, but demanded, instead, that a considerable proportion of [the Guild's] productions be made to yield the maximum of profit."[128] The Guild, in other words—which, in fact, had *never* been an experimental theater—quickly became, Poggi notes, "indistinguishable from most commercial producing organizations." And like so many other theaters at the beginning of the Great Depression, it suffered "a series of artistic failures and financial disasters" and had to cut back its operations substantially.[129] Many of the actors associated with the Guild decamped to Hollywood in the early 1930s (Claude Rains, Claudette Colbert, Miriam Hopkins), while others reorganized as the Group Theatre (Lee Strasberg, Morris Carnovsky, Luther Adler). By the end of the decade the Theatre Guild was $60,000 in debt and in 1944 was forced to sell its theater, despite the unprecedented success the year before of its new musical play, *Oklahoma!*

Although the Theatre Guild continues to limp along into the twenty-first century, its activity has been reduced to the sponsorship of Theatre at Sea Cruises. (In 2008, for prices ranging between $4,335 and $20,825, passengers could ply the waters of the Mediterranean on board the *Crystal Serenity* and be entertained by the likes of Florence Henderson, Lucie Arnaz, and Lynn Redgrave.)[130] Beginning in the late 1940s, however, its mandate had been taken over by Off Broadway and, across the nation, by newly constituted resident theater companies. With the founding of the Alley Theatre (1947), Arena Stage (1950), the Actors' Workshop (1952), the New York Shakespeare Festival (1954), and several others, a serious, non-profit, professional theater in the United States was reborn. This reawakening led to an "explosion" during the 1960s when the number of companies rose from ten in 1960 to forty by 1966.[131] Although in their early years, many of these theaters forged distinctive artistic profiles, they have since the 1980s become increasingly homogeneous. The nonprofit theaters have gradually developed a kind of nationwide assembly line on which the same plays, especially the Pulitzer Prize–winning play of the preceding season and the latest prestigious British import, make the rounds in productions that aim for a certain level of standardization. This homogeny is in part a response to the decline of government support for the arts and the growing reliance of all these theaters on the largesse of corporations, foundations, and individual donors (large and small), all of which expect their investment of economic capital to yield inoffensive art that possesses verifiable cultural and symbolic capital. This tight-knit economy of production and consumption has, moreover, been increasingly reinforced by privately capitalized investments from producers both large and small. Because more and more work mounted by nonprofit theaters in fact represents a joint venture between commercial and noncommercial producers, the differences between these categories continue to diminish, guaranteeing that the supposedly nonprofit theater will continue to attempt to fulfill the Theatre Guild's mission while delivering "a wan intellectual horizon to a whole generation of suburbanites."

SIX

JAZZ COSMOPOLITANISM

~~~~~~

Contrary to the impression still current in quarters abroad, we are
not wild Indians, Negro mammies or cabaret dancers. We are not
even—all of us—rum-runners or millionaires. How is the American
to be natural, real, racial, alive with the temper of a country which
is so fertile, alive and generally irritating to the universe? How
about jazz and all that? How about Stravinsky and atonality and
red-blooded Americanism? Just answer those questions, if you can.

—Olin Downes, "J. A. Carpenter, American Craftsman" (1930)

At the end of the 1920s, *New York Times* music critic Olin Downes published an essay in *Musical Quarterly* on John Alden Carpenter, the most
celebrated composer of his generation and writer of *Skyscrapers* (1926), the
first American jazz ballet and in its time the most critically admired synthesis of art music and jazz to come out of the United States. Preoccupied, like
so many of his fellow critics, with the relationship between American and
European music, Downes asks what were arguably the most important
questions facing U.S. artists trying to legitimize their art during the Jazz
Age. How do Americans seeking international acclaim banish what

Downes takes to be negative, vernacular stereotypes while still holding on to a "red-blooded Americanism"? How is an artist to be both cosmopolitan and sensitive to what is "racial" (read: African American) in a country so "generally irritating" (read: economically and culturally aggressive) to "the universe" (read: Western Europe and the Americas)? How does jazz relate to "Stravinsky and atonality," the dominant trends in European concert music? What role is jazz to play for artists trying to consecrate American modernism? And how is the critic to separate jazz ephemera—whether music, dance, poetry, or theater—from more serious jazz-inspired works worthy of being exported, canonized, and certified "natural, real" American?[1]

During the middle to late 1920s there were as many answers to these questions as there were U.S. artists in search of a place on a world stage that had changed radically since World War I. Following the devastation of large swaths of Western Europe, the United States had become the world's leading economic power (consuming more electricity than the rest of the world combined) and was exporting not only goods, but also a Fordist mode of industrial production.[2] Along with these economic changes came a revolution in modes of communication and in the production and distribution of intellectual properties that facilitated a dramatic rise in the cultural profile of the United States. While the United States was exporting jazz and motion pictures (in addition to soda fountains and slot machines), it was also producing a new generation of cosmopolitan artists who were attempting to bring a "red-blooded Americanism" to bear on more elitist, that is, European, cultural traditions. In this chapter, I will focus on two of them, composers John Alden Carpenter and George Antheil. Self-styled cosmopolitans, these artists defined the parameters of the struggles for legitimacy in the performing arts during the mid-1920s. Their ballets— which represent radically different Gershwin-inspired exercises in serious, symphonic jazz—are distinguished by ambivalent and contradictory attitudes toward jazz, European aesthetic values and paradigms, and the industrial and social projects of a country so "generally irritating to the universe." I hope to explain why Carpenter was easily and immediately welcomed by the guardians of elite culture while Antheil remained a controversial and often ridiculed figure, not least of all because his *Ballet mécanique* (1926) aroused passions as violent as *Processional* had. Yet ironically, the very qualities that ensured Carpenter's success and Antheil's failure functioned in the long run to secure very different canonical status for each. Carpenter has largely disappeared into the mists of tradition, while for musicologists, Antheil has become a key figure in the development of a cosmopolitan (yet distinctively American) modernism. What do the divergent responses to these men reveal about the relationship between art music and jazz during a crucial moment in the stabilization of the cultural hierarchy in the United States; about attitudes toward the assembly line, standardization, and mass consumption; and about the consolidation of a red-blooded American modernism?

Fascinated by the revolutionary changes wrought by European modernism but committed to making a distinctively American art, both Carpenter and Antheil are noteworthy for the crucial positioning of "racial" elements in their work. Indeed, these elements are in part responsible for their construction as paradigmatically American artists. In analyzing the cultural status of their theatrical works, however, I am interested in far more than the representation of African Americans. I want to understand how the very forms they use enact the central dilemmas of a modernism that strives (after Gershwin) to be both nativist and cosmopolitan and to claim African American, European American, and European descent. But I want to start with an examination of American imperialism, cultural and otherwise, since cosmopolitanism is always defined in relation to imperial systems.

Fredric Jameson, studying the representational economy of European modernism, argues that the aesthetic dislocations and the new uses of raw materials that distinguish modernist art from its nineteenth-century predecessors are in part an effect and displacement of the massive European colonial system that remained, however, nearly invisible to those going about their daily business in London, Paris, or Brussels. He bases this contention on the representational impasse that so many modernist works of art confront and attempt to overcome. This impasse, he argues, is an inevitable result of the fact that under imperialism, "a significant structural segment of the economic system . . . is . . . located elsewhere, beyond the metropolis, outside the daily life and existential experience of the home country." "Unlike the classical stage of national or market capitalism," in which systems of production and distribution are readily discernible and relatively circumscribed, "pieces of the puzzle are missing; it can never be fully reconstructed; no enlargement of personal experience . . . can ever be enough to include [the] radical otherness of colonial life, colonial suffering, and exploitation." Because of these missing pieces, "daily life and existential experience in the metropolis . . . can no longer be grasped immanently;

it no longer has its meaning, its deeper reason for being, within itself." Jameson argues that this sense of alienation, this loss of meaning, leaves its imprint upon and is also produced by modernist art. As a result, the content of modernist art will "always have something missing about it," something "comparable to another dimension, an outside like the other face of a mirror, which it constitutively lacks, and which can never be made up or made good." Metropolitan modernism—with its distortion, fragmentation, and dissonance, its collages, its gaps and missing pieces—must then quite precisely "live . . . this formal dilemma," a dilemma it can neither compass nor solve.[3]

I would like to suggest that the 1920s U.S. version of populist modernism—or what I will call jazz cosmopolitanism—represents a sublimation of minstrelsy, a radical rechanneling and elevation of blackface performance. African Americans function as the missing component, subjects who are impersonated and whose music is purloined but whose works are carefully segregated by the white arbiters of taste and considered valuable only as raw material for European American art. The jazz cosmopolitanism practiced by so many white artists could not do without but could not acknowledge an African American presence. The modernism of Gershwin, Lawson, O'Neill, Carpenter, Antheil, and so many other artists lives this formal dilemma by obsessively asserting, in Gershwin's words, that "Jazz is not Negro" while at the same time needing African Americans and their cultures just as surely as the European imperial powers needed the raw materials provided by their colonial subjects.[4] The analogy between African Americans and colonial subjects was reinforced by the fact that the system of apartheid sanctioned by *Plessy v. Ferguson* in 1896 predated by only two years the formal beginning of the U.S. imperial system in Latin America and East Asia. Although a full-fledged theory of racism in the United States as a form of internal colonialism that contains, transforms, and destroys indigenous values was not fully developed until the late 1960s, turn-of-the-century discourses continually associated African Americans with the inhabitants of U.S. colonies.[5] Political cartoons, for example, repeatedly drew out this analogy by staging a scene in which an exasperated Uncle Sam attempts to discipline U.S. colonies (usually Cuba, Puerto Rico, Haiti, or the Philippines), which are personified by minstrel-derived representations of African American children, presented as pickaninnies, who are imagined as unruly, infantile, bug-eyed, jet-black toddlers with unkempt hair and oversized mouths (sometimes outlined in white).[6]

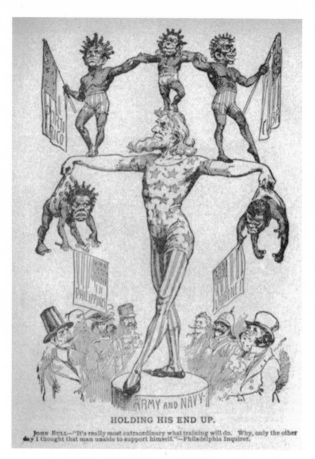

HOLDING HIS END UP.

JOHN BULL—"It's really most extraordinary what training will do. Why, only the
other day I thought that man unable to support himself"—Philadelphia Inquirer.

1899 cartoon, the *Philadelphia Inquirer*. A proud Uncle Sam shows off his
newly acquired colonies—Puerto Rico, Cuba, the Philippines, and the
Ladrone Islands (Mariana Islands)—while being supported by the Army
and Navy.

Given the inevitable slippage in early twentieth-century representations between African Americans and the nonwhite inhabitants of U.S.
colonial possessions, between segregation and colonialism, it is impossible
to determine whether colonial subjects are surrogates for African Americans or vice versa. I would like to suggest that jazz cosmopolitanism is
founded on this equivocation as surely as on the discord between nativism

and internationalism. This is not to say there are not significant differences between these two categories of colonial subjects. If nothing else, the populations of U.S. colonies were literally out of sight, beyond the borders of the mainland, unlike African Americans, who may have been figuratively out of sight (forced to inhabit separate spheres) but were ubiquitous in the metropolis. However, both colonials and African Americans were available in a symbolic repertoire as the embodiments of a fearsome and thrilling primitive vitality indispensable for the enunciation of red-blooded American modernism. Indeed, the thrill of the modern metropolis, especially New York, was predicated in part on the proximity, intermingling, and anonymity of jostling masses of people of different classes, races, and places of national origin. The locus of immigration and exile, anomie and utopia, social discord and revolution, the metropolis was the crucible of jazz cosmopolitanism, the central axis around which a new imperial world system was beginning to revolve.

"THE DIVINE MISSION OF AMERICA"

During the 1920s, the United States was a relative newcomer to the imperialist sweepstakes, at least in comparison with the great European powers. Britain could boast a centuries-old empire of 11.5 million square miles, the United States, less than 200,000 square miles (including Cuba, which was a colony in everything but name).[7] Moreover, while the European colonies were scattered across the globe, those of the United States were either south or west of its borders. Although the United States had long practiced economic imperialism in the Western Hemisphere, it did not begin collecting colonies until the annexation of Hawaii, Puerto Rico, Guam, and the Philippines in 1898 in the wake of the Spanish-American War. Forthright observers confessed that these exploits were the result of a rapidly growing U.S. economy that demanded the fortification and expansion of overseas markets. "American factories are making more than the American people can use," Senator Albert Beveridge declared in 1898. "Fate has written our policy for us; the trade of the world must and shall be ours."[8] And the *Washington Post* concurred, employing a metaphor that betrays imperialism's violent designs: "The taste of empire is in the mouth of the people even as the taste of blood in the jungle."[9] Many U.S. imperialists, however, like their European counterparts, disregarded the economic issues and appealed to a racist theology (not unlike their modern-day descendents) to justify their adventurism. For God, Beveridge decreed,

> has made us the master organizers of the world to establish system
> where chaos reigns. . . . He has made us adepts in government that we
> may administer government among savages and senile peoples. . . . And
> of all our race, He has marked the American people as His chosen na-
> tion to finally lead in the regeneration of the world. This is the divine
> mission of America, and it holds for us all the profit, all the glory, all the
> happiness possible to man.[10]

During the late nineteenth and early twentieth centuries, the primary imperial relationships were imagined to be those not between metropole and colony, but among imperial powers competing for raw materials and markets. "The conflicts of the future," Beveridge candidly admitted, "are to be conflicts of trade—struggles for markets—commercial wars for existence."[11] By the beginning of the 1920s, Sidney Lens notes, a "new imperialism" based on this economic doctrine was "enshrined and virtually unchallenged." "Its purpose was . . . to force other nations, through blandishment or coercion, to grant American business economic advantages" and its government, strategic advantages against all rivals.[12] The United States designed its empire to secure raw materials and develop commercial interests in Latin America and, to a lesser extent, East Asia, and virtually all of its many military interventions and occupations through the 1920s were in these regions, including Mexico, Cuba, Panama, Haiti, the Dominican Republic, Honduras, Costa Rica, Nicaragua, Guatemala, and China. The Caribbean was especially important since U.S. economic interest in the region increased by 345 percent between 1913 and 1929.[13] But American imperialism relied on more than military and economic power. It also cultivated a comprador bourgeoisie, a class of compliant local officials, who would further U.S. interests and their own "with less friction or awakening of outside hostility" than an occupying army.[14] In the discourses of imperialism, the development of a comprador class also provided a way of disavowing what Undersecretary of State J. Ruben Clark recognized to be "violence and oppression" by cloaking it in what was alleged to be a humanitarian "guaranty of . . . freedom, independence, and territorial integrity against the imperialistic designs of Europe." The Monroe Doctrine, he insisted, "states a case . . . not of the United States versus Latin America" but of "the United States versus Europe."[15]

Although the United States could not compete profitably with the European empires for the control of global resources and markets, it vied much more successfully in the arena of cultural imperialism. But only in the fields of popular culture. In the more highbrow performing arts—symphony, opera, and legitimate theater—European artists, styles, and tastes remained in the ascendant. Even by the early 1920s, few American plays, symphonies, or operas had successfully crossed the Atlantic, while throughout the United States, the European canon (and the hierarchy of taste that valorized it) went largely unchallenged, even by modernists like Gilbert Seldes. Thus, most Germans, for example, believed that "America had not produced great artists, musicians, and authors" and that "it lacked first-rate museums, operas, and concert halls."[16] Although disdainful of American elite culture, the large majority of western Europeans was fascinated and enthralled by American popular culture (especially cinema and jazz) because, Richard Pells notes, it "had come to stand . . . for modernity, and for a 'future' that seemed inescapable."[17] Although European motion pictures enjoyed considerable success before World War I, they were eclipsed in the postwar years by American films, which dominated the industry worldwide, much to the dismay of many European critics and intellectuals.[18] Hollywood standardized its product, branded its stars, and glamorized American cars, cigarettes, fashions, gangsters, and nightclubs, and managed to export so many movies featuring the likes of Charlie Chaplin, Buster Keaton, and Clara Bow that its product became the primary vehicle of Americanization. Europeans were fascinated by American style and what they called "'Fordismus,' a savage but riveting and sometimes contradictory mixture of skyscrapers, slums, urban violence, organized crime, smoke-belching factories, Puritanism, sexual licentiousness, and raw human energy."[19] As French novelist Clément Vautel fretted, "America has colonized us through the cinema."[20]

Jazz, considered by Europeans the uniquely American art, aroused more passionate feelings, as it had in the United States, than any other imported cultural practice. It first came to Europe in 1917 with the band of the all-black 369th Infantry Regiment, the "Hellfighters," under the direction of James Reese Europe, which performed widely throughout France. Two years later, the (white) Original Dixieland Jazz Band, touring the United Kingdom, gave a Royal Command Performance for King George V.[21] Composer Darius Milhaud reported that the appearance of a New York jazz band at the Casino de Paris in 1918 "came almost like a cart [sic] of terror, like a sudden awakening," a "shattering storm of rhythm."[22] Milhaud, one of the foremost European champions of jazz, paid a visit to the United States in 1922 and trekked to Harlem to hear the jazz band at the Capitol on Lenox Avenue and to Boston for the jazz band at the Hotel Brunswick, which, he told Gilbert Seldes, was "one of the best he heard in America" (100).[23] He brought black jazz recordings back to France and the next year composed *La Création du monde*, his celebrated exercise in Jazz Age primitivism. But Milhaud was only one among scores of European musicians who were "fascinated and intrigued" by jazz.[24] For as he points out, jazz jibed perfectly with the development of European modernist concert music, with its chromaticism, harmonic and instrumental experimentation, and heavily contrapuntal texture: "it is following the same curve as the rest of contemporary harmony."[25] In Germany, jazz (or rather, a distant approximation of jazz) was all the rage despite the scarcity of jazz recordings and sheet music during the hyperinflation of the early to mid-1920s. Although the Germans were extremely protective of their musical tradition, African American music managed to infiltrate both low and high cultural venues more successfully in Germany than anyplace else in Europe. "The Negroes are conquering Berlin," playwright Ivan Goll declared in 1926.

> They have already filled the whole continent with their howls, with their laughter. And we are not shocked, we are not amazed: on the contrary, the old world calls on its failing strength to applaud them.[26]

At the height of the jazz craze, Ernst Krenek's opera *Jonny spielt auf* (Jonny Strikes Up, 1926), with its minstrel-inspired title character and rather bizarre imitations of American jazz, racked up nearly five hundred performances throughout Germany and western Europe in its first four years and "was granted a box-office success comparable only to the great cinema hits of D.W. Griffith and Charlie Chaplin."[27] Conductors like Leopold Stokowski, Serge Koussevitzky, Ernest Ansermet, and Willem Mengelberg were captivated by jazz. And the list of composers (in addition to Milhaud and Krenek) who experimented with jazz during the 1920s reads like a who's who of European modernists: Igor Stravinsky, Maurice Ravel, Erik Satie, Francis Poulenc, William Walton, Paul Hindemith, Erwin Schulhoff, Kurt Weill, Bohuslav Martinů, Dmitry Shostakovich, plus many, many others. Almost all the European modernist composers born during the last quarter of the nineteenth century found the siren's song of jazz irresistible. The exceptions were for the most part the atonalists (like Arnold Schoenberg and Anton Webern) and those on the geographic periphery who turned instead to the traditional music of their own countries for inspiration (like Manuel de Falla, Ralph Vaughan Williams, and Béla Bartók).

The invasion of Europe by jazz did far more, however, than transform a generation of modernist composers. As it had in the United States, jazz infiltrated many different forms of popular entertainment and fascinated a motley collection of artists, writers, and intellectuals. As Pells notes, Paris was the "primary point of entry, . . . where black musicians, in flight from America's segregated cities, acquired a following in nightclubs, cabarets, and concert halls."[28] Paris was also the site where Europeans (and American expatriates) were most likely to encounter hot jazz. Dance bands in Paris, London, and Berlin quickly adopted the new styles while touring jazz orchestras and entertainers from the United States, both black and white, like Josephine Baker and Paul Whiteman, became European sensations. The new, jazzed-up musical comedy, as well, was profitably imported from New York. Beginning with *Lady, Be Good!* and *Tell Me More*, most of the Gershwin musicals of the 1920s enjoyed successful London runs, as did *No, No, Nanette* (1925), *Show Boat* (1927), and many other Broadway hits. In addition, some Americans wrote musical comedies expressly for the London stage, including the Gershwins (*Primrose* [1924]) and Rodgers and Hart (*Lido Lady* [1926]). While rehearsing *Lido Lady*, Lorenz Hart noted proudly that even the British agreed that "the musical comedy as such is now an American monopoly."

> The English composer strives to imitate American jazz, and because his feet do not touch American soil, he falls just short. Whether we live in the North or the South, the American Negro's music has influenced us. Lacking that influence, the English musical writer can only echo an echo.[29]

As Hart suggests, jazz meant something very different to Americans than to those unschooled in U.S. vernaculars. Being less fraught with both the racial and class-based associations and histories that made it such a contentious practice in the United States, it was abstracted from its social contexts when it reached European shores. Countless European modernists, like the critic Jacques Benoist-Méchin, saw "the arrival of jazz in Europe" as "an event in the history of music." Representing the clamor of the New World, jazz was the only music, he wrote, that "is frankly modern with no concessions to the past." Embodying "the rhythm of the machine," it sweeps away "all our traditions in the outburst of its youth" and helps "free us from our timidities."[30] (Benoist-Méchin was also a "frantic propagandist" for the music of his friend, George Antheil, from whom he no doubt learned about jazz.)[31] For Germans, jazz was an even more generalized phenomenon, "an all-embracing cultural label attached to any music from the American side of the Atlantic, or indeed to anything new and exciting, whether this be the 'jazz time' of American automobiles or 'Maori jazz from New Zealand.'"[32] In Europe, then, jazz became the controversial emblem of a United States that, Pells argues, "had become synonymous with efficiency, advanced technology and industrial dynamism, the worship of machines and assembly lines, 'streamlined' and standardized products, commercialism, mass consumption, and the emergence of mass society."[33]

Although an emblem of modernity, jazz also satisfied the primitivist cravings of European modernists, as it had for their U.S. counterparts. Milhaud (one who "believe[d] heartily in racial traits in art") traced its origin back to "the American Negro," deep in whose nature "[p]rimitive African qualities have kept their place."[34] For his part, Benoist-Méchin, believing jazz songs to be "peopled . . . with luscious black babies, sentimental, smiling and melancholy," saw jazz as a kind of return of the repressed, the product of "an African and millennial lyricism, made up of the most remote and primitive elements" that inexorably resurface. The "racial traits" in jazz, for so many Europeans, were biological and atavistic, linked not to a history of chattel slavery but to a mythologized, primordial Africa, to the intoxicating and terrifying cries issuing from their African colonies. And he seems deeply ambivalent about the possibility that the jazz revolution might inaugurate an anti-imperialist uprising, "cracking" "the old unclean crust . . . everywhere" and spewing forth wild, colonial subjects, "Tartar or Mongol hordes," who would be "discover[ed] . . . camped under the Arc de Triumph [sic] or upon the Place de la Concorde."[35]

Given the American obsession with European culture and the European obsession with a music imagined to be both primitive and millennial, American modernists who sought to elevate and consecrate their art tried to construct jazz both as the raw material—as a lowbrow, disreputable practice—and as a glorious native music that was equal to (or better than!)

European folk music. They tried to paper over this difference by insisting that elite cultural productions could uplift and redeem jazz without purging it of a primitive essence, which, they argued, resided less in an African American specificity than in jazz's status as the music of the melting pot, the first world music, or in George Gershwin's words, "the folk music of the cosmopolitan."[36] Thus the U.S. critic Paul Fritz Laubenstein could speak for many Americans (including Gershwin) when he hailed jazz's "cosmopolitanism," its "unprejudiced appropriation of any usable tune, irrespective of its national source," its mixture of "the Occident" with "the American Negro's banjo, . . . the red man's tam-tam, the Oriental musette, the larger drum of the African and the Spanish castanets."[37] On the other side of the Atlantic, Tristan Tzara wrote simply, "From blackness, let us extract light."[38] Jazz thus became the perfect medium for fashioning a transatlantic modernism that sought to embody universally human principles. American artists were thereby able for the first time to storm the barricades of European culture, and Europeans were able to make an ostensibly universally human art by tapping into a music that was imagined to be particularized and global, unrefined and fashionably cosmopolitan, savage and ultramodern.

For many Americans, jazz provided the entrée to the European market for concert music, popular song, painting, and poetry. But only under certain conditions. For jazz in the United States was a collection of many different kinds of music, from the hottest and most narrowly distributed (i.e., to African Americans and the lower classes) to the sweetest and most widely marketed. As demonstrated by the debate in the United States over symphonic jazz in the wake of *Rhapsody in Blue*'s sensational premiere, some modes of jazz performance were available for elevation to highbrow (or upper middlebrow) art; others were to be relegated to cabaret and vaudeville. In Europe, there was a more narrow range of responses to jazz because jazz was imported very selectively and was seen as an exotic, primitive efflorescence that embodied an American, African American, and "African . . . millennial lyricism." Because jazz in Europe so quickly won over the producers and consumers of both elite and popular arts, it resisted being fixed in cultural hierarchies. Indeed, in Europe even more clearly than the United States, jazz was the form of cultural production that most troubled the boundaries between high and low. Nonetheless, certain class-based assumptions derived from U.S. cultural hierarchies did extend to western Europe. American modernists wanting to prove their parity with their European competitors had to be careful because their use of jazz could be taken to be the sign of an enviable American cosmopolitanism (as with Gershwin and John Alden Carpenter) or of a low-class, gratuitously shocking, pointless savagery (as with George Antheil). It could, in other words, never be known in advance if the appropriation of jazz would lead to the accumulation or forfeiture of high cultural capital.

The jazz cosmopolitanism that was negotiated between the United States and western Europe was more, however, than a cultural settlement. It also represented the translation of an economic imperative into an aesthetic one. It was, in other words, a symptom and sign of the central role of the United States in capitalist globalization between the wars. Given the destruction of European infrastructure during World War I and the unparalleled growth and success of American modes of mass production, U.S. manufacturers began to consolidate economic leadership based not on military might but on their ability to

> produce high-quality goods more cheaply and offer them at lower prices than could most of their European competitors who were still largely craft oriented. As a result, . . . American-made telephones, typewriters, sewing machines, cash registers, elevators, cameras, phonographs, toothpaste, and packaged foods became popular items in the European marketplace.[39]

It is little wonder that jazz was universally identified with modernity, the commodity form, and the Machine Age. For it was the industrial "folk music" of the nation whose Fordized economy was revolutionizing means of production and patterns of consumption worldwide.

The development of a jazz cosmopolitanism is also tied to the increasing worldliness of Americans. The combination of World War I, the greater safety and comfort of oceangoing ships, and the low value of most European currencies relative to the dollar during the 1920s "started a frenzy of transatlantic travel" as a quarter million American tourists, businessmen, students, and expatriates journeyed to Europe every year, pumping three-quarters of a billion dollars into European economies.[40] Most important, many of the foremost U.S. writers, musicians, and artists—the so-called Lost Generation—relocated at least temporarily to Paris. Although the list of novelists and poets is too long to enumerate, few American playwrights took extended stays in Europe during the 1920s (John

Howard Lawson and Eugene O'Neill were two notable exceptions), in part because of their involvement in U.S. productions and because of the difficulty of securing performances of their work abroad, especially outside London. Because musicians could capitalize on the exoticism associated with their use of jazz, Aaron Copland, Cole Porter, George Gershwin, Paul Robeson, John Alden Carpenter, and George Antheil are among the many who were welcomed to Europe and had the opportunity to mix with European composers and musicians as well as Soviet expatriates like Igor Stravinsky, Serge Diaghilev, and Léonide Massine.

In order to legitimize their art and simultaneously stamp it with a national identity, American modernists of the middle to late 1920s chose both to embrace and transcend "racial" music, to combine an American, vernacular cultural nationalism with European-approved styles. This hybridization both reaffirmed and challenged geographical boundaries, allowing American artists—both black and white—to claim an authenticity rooted in jazz's "racial" origins. Yet the very different strategies they used would distinguish those (like Carpenter) whose art would be certified highbrow and who would be made honorary citizens of the world from those (like Antheil) who were condemned to a low-class hell in which races, classes, and types of art were believed to intermix indiscriminately.

JAZZ IN HIGH PLACES

Among performance venues in New York City during the early twentieth century, the old Metropolitan Opera House (built 1883, razed 1967) and Carnegie Hall (built 1890) were the most prestigious. The one housed the most esteemed opera company in the United States, the American home of Enrico Caruso, Claudia Muzio, Nellie Melba, and countless other immortals; the other, New York's two leading orchestras, the Symphony and the Philharmonic (they merged in 1928 to form the present-day New York Philharmonic). These two venues were also the sites for two of the most important events in the ongoing process (that began with Paul Whiteman's "Experiment in Modern Music" in 1924) of legitimizing a jazz-inspired, American, cosmopolitan art. The first was the setting for the enthusiastically greeted world premiere of the ballet *Skyscrapers* on 19 February 1926, with music by John Alden Carpenter (1876–1951), scene design by Robert Edmond Jones, and choreography by Sammy Lee. The second, the site of the catastrophic U.S. premiere of *Ballet mécanique* by George Antheil (1900–1959), the self-styled "bad boy of music," on 10 April 1927. The contrast between these two performances concisely illustrates the differences between a legitimate and an illegitimate jazz cosmopolitanism.

I want to emphasize that although musical compositions were at the center of both performances, their theatrical elements were the decisive factors in their reception. *Ballet mécanique* was not, like *Skyscrapers*, a bona fide ballet, but it was even more extravagantly and controversially theatricalized on the Carnegie Hall stage. The producer of the concert commissioned the scene designer Joseph Mullen to paint two giant backdrops for the performance, and, more important, Antheil enlarged the orchestration of his deliberately shocking score for an immense battery of percussion: ten grand pianos, a player piano, six xylophones, two bass drums, a siren, and an airplane propeller attached to a wind machine. Concertgoers and critics angrily pointed out that these choices turned the concert into an appalling spectacle.

Both Carpenter and Antheil conceived their pieces in Europe and composed them in 1923 and 1924. Both had fallen under the spell of Igor Stravinsky, and *Skyscrapers* and *Ballet mécanique* attest to the influence, in radically different ways, of the Russian's early works, especially *Petrushka* (1911), *Le Sacre du printemps* (1913), and *Les noces* (1923). Carpenter planned his ballet in consultation with Serge Diaghilev, who wanted to produce a "typically American" work for the Ballets Russes, something that would embody "the hurry and din of American life."[41] Diaghilev altered his plans, despite later remarking that the score was "not as bad as [he] expected," and Carpenter signed with the Metropolitan Opera, still hoping the Ballets Russes would stage the European premiere.[42] (In the event, the European premiere of the ballet, renamed *Wolkenkratzer*, took place in 1928 at the Bayerische Staatsoper in Munich.) Antheil, fascinated by what he considered the musicality of machines and the metropolis, wrote *Ballet mécanique* while he was living in Paris (to which he had relocated in 1922) and immersed in the expatriate community in what was then the avant-garde capital of the world. A full generation younger than Carpenter, Antheil unreservedly aligned himself with the "ultramodernists" and, striving for notoriety, quickly became "the new darling of Paris."[43] The first public performance of *Ballet mécanique* at the Théâtre des Champs-Elysées on 19 June 1926 did not quite fulfill his dream. Instead, it incited a near-riot. The "sheer bedlam" unleashed by that performance, however, represented a triumph in comparison with the disastrous New York premiere less than a year later.[44]

The backgrounds of Carpenter and Antheil could not have been more different. John Alden Carpenter was born in Chicago into an upper-class, Republican family that traced its roots back to the fourteenth century and counted Pilgrim John Alden as an ancestor. Graduated from Harvard, he entered the family mill, railway, and shipping supply business, remaining (like Charles Ives) a businessman all his life, a "merchant" who considered music a "recreation,"[45] and lived "the charmed life of the American upper classes," replete with domestic servants and trips to Europe.[46] Carpenter studied in Rome with Edward Elgar (1907–8), and, as John Tasker Howard points out, by "heritage and tradition," he "might easily have been a conservative, if not a reactionary." But Howard ascribes his judicious experimentation to an "economic independence" that allowed him to remain indifferent to the "commercial value of his work."[47] An aristocratic modernist and humanist, Carpenter was widely regarded as not beholden to the market system and, in Olin Downes's words, "the most sensitive, sincere and accomplished American-born composer." Phrases like "personal integrity," "scrupulousness as an artist," "character and temperament," "man of cultivation," and "passion for truth" resound through Downes's essay.[48] While constructing Carpenter as a universal genius, Downes also imagines him to be paradigmatically American, a sophisticated populist in the tradition of Twain and Whitman who, if he were not too polished to be a "flag-waver," "might be our great American prophet."[49] According to Howard Pollack in his authoritative biography of Carpenter, the composer was a "lifelong friend of American popular music" and "showed more enthusiasm" for the music of Cohan, Kern, Berlin, Gershwin, and other songwriters "than for any 'serious' American composer."[50] Although Carpenter cautiously used American vernaculars in his music, only with his ballets *Krazy Kat* (1922) and especially *Skyscrapers* did he turn more resolutely both to jazz and to musical modernism.

George Antheil, on the other hand, was born in Trenton, New Jersey, to petit bourgeois parents of German ancestry. His father owned a small shoe store, and George grew up in an industrial district in Trenton, "across the street from a very noisy machine shop" whose mechanical ostinatos would find an echo in his most notorious piece.[51] In 1920 he began studying in New York with Ernest Bloch and in Philadelphia with Alfredo Casella. More important, however, Antheil succeeded in 1921 in obtaining a patron, Mary Louise Curtis Bok, a wealthy supporter of the arts (who three years later would found the Curtis Institute in Philadelphia). Bok granted him a monthly stipend of the then considerable sum of $150, which enabled him, since he was "planning to become the 'enfant terrible' of the period," to sail to Europe in 1922, from whence he would not return permanently until 1933.[52] Although Antheil and his patron frequently clashed, Bok's largesse freed him to pursue a career as a willful, self-consciously revolutionary, and (some would say) megalomaniacal artist. Mixing with futurists, Dadaists, and cubists, and besieging his patron with requests for money, Antheil explained his goal: "By one stroke I wish to conquer the world."[53] His first European piano recital, in London's Wigmore Hall in 1922, featured several of his own works and established the compositional techniques that would obsess him for the rest of the decade and find their apotheosis in the Carnegie Hall debacle: ragtime, jazz, and machine music.

Despite their very different backgrounds and upbringings, Carpenter and Antheil were fortunate enough to be able to live as gentlemen composers who were not hostages to the marketplace. The beneficiaries of an artisanal economy, they were able to experiment by using American vernaculars in forms that enjoyed unimpeachable European pedigrees. Yet the differences between their works—and their social positions—clearly delineate the opposition between a humanist modernism linked to the declining aristocracy and an avant-gardism of the insurgent bourgeoisie that launched itself in opposition against the commodity status of the work of art, the institutions in which it is consecrated, and the very idea of tradition.[54] The former militated for the autonomy of art, was disdainful or, at best, suspicious of industrialization and mass culture, and remained committed to the rationalism, liberalism, and idea of progress initiated by the Enlightenment. The cosmopolitan modernism of figures like Carpenter, Stravinsky, Eugene O'Neill, T. S. Eliot, and many others sought to remake a universal art by safeguarding the purity of the European (or European American) traditions against the incursions of mass culture, even at the cost of having to incorporate elements of that culture into artworks that aim, sometimes resentfully, to transcend it. Avant-gardisms like Dada, surrealism, and futurism, on the other hand, were always more internationalized than high modernism because of their hostility to parochial (and national) traditions. And they represented a far more radical, and radically negative, insurgency than high modernism. The avant-garde was always, Matei Calinescu points out, "more dogmatic—both in the sense of self-assertion and, conversely, in the sense of self-destruction." Borrowing "elements from the modern tradition," it blew "them up, exaggerate[d] them, and place[d] them in the most unexpected contexts, often making them almost completely unrecognizable."[55] Seeking to destroy the purported autonomy of art, many avant-gardists allied themselves with radical political movements of the left and, in the case of the Italian futurists and Ezra Pound, the right. As Calinescu emphasizes, "Bakunin's anarchist maxim, 'To destroy is to create,' is actually applicable to most of the activities of the twentieth-century avant-garde."[56]

ALL-AMERICAN BALLET

By the time that John Alden Carpenter wrote *Skyscrapers*, he was the most eminent and well-established American composer of his age, renowned for his technical prowess, whimsicality, fluency, "musical refinement," and tasteful use of exotic musical vernaculars, principally Spanish and Negro.[57] Deems Taylor in 1922 described his conservative modernism by its mood, which he found reminiscent of the music of "eighteenth-century France, although the idiom is utterly contemporary."[58] Yet Carpenter's contemporary idiom was then conservatively European, owing far more to the Strauss tone poems, Elgar, Debussy, and Ravel than to Stravinsky, Bartók, or Schoenberg. His first major international success was the fanciful tone poem *Adventures in a Perambulator* (1915), one movement of which, "The Hurdy-Gurdy," uses catches of popular tunes ranging from Berlin's "Alexander's Ragtime Band" to the Miserere from *Il trovatore*, and (foreshadowing *Skyscrapers*) mixes "mystic spiritualism and urban realism."[59] It was a great success in Chicago and other major cities, "became a repertory staple" in the United States, and quickly made the rounds of Rome, Paris, Stockholm, and Berlin.[60] That the most successful and respected works that succeeded *Adventures* are all ballets, *The Birthday of the Infanta* (1919), *Krazy Kat*, and *Skyscrapers*, attests to the fact that Carpenter was widely regarded, in Taylor's words, as a maker of stage music, "America's First Dramatic Composer" (though he never wrote an opera).[61] The theater critic Stark Young commended *Infanta* both for its "modern quality" and the impression it gave that it "was inescapably drama."[62]

Krazy Kat, based on George Herriman's innovative comic strip (an unlikely source for a ballet), was subtitled *A Jazz Pantomime* and, with a scenario by Carpenter and Herriman, was the first of the composer's works to trade in patently lowbrow forms and the first piece of art music to use the word *jazz* in its title.[63] Carpenter's score, however, owes far more to Spanish dance music (replete with castanets), Debussy, Ravel, and Prokofiev than to the hot jazz that had taken Chicago by storm and of which there is some evidence that Carpenter heard in the so-called black-and-tan clubs on the South Side.[64] In *Krazy Kat*, Carpenter spiced up his idiom with blue notes, syncopation, hints of ragtime and fox trot, and a jazz-inspired use of brass and percussion reminiscent of novelty jazz and vaudeville. The ballet was choreographed by Adolph Bohm, a pioneer of modern ballet who had danced with Diaghilev, but was sufficiently able to pass as popular entertainment to be incorporated into the *Greenwich Village Follies* of 1922. The *Follies* that year also featured a drop curtain by Reginald Marsh depicting Village celebrities, a turn by Bert Savoy (Broadway's reigning—and most "outrageously 'camp'"—female impersonator), a skit parodying a Eugene O'Neill play, and a rendition of "Mon Homme" by Yvonne George designed to compete with Fanny Brice's English-language version.[65] Gilbert Seldes commended Carpenter for not fearing "to 'lower [himself]' by the association" with Herriman and for catching "much of the fantasy" of a comic strip he hailed as "our one work in the expressionistic mode."[66] But other critics scolded Carpenter for slumming. Richard Aldrich in the *New York Times* warned that "it behooves Mr. Carpenter to remember . . . that he was graduated in the Class of 1897, Harvard, . . . and that there is still a great deal for him to do in music . . . , and that jazz pantomime is not among it."[67]

Carpenter did not heed Aldrich's warning and in *Skyscrapers* composed his most ambitious and musically progressive piece, far more harmonically daring, jazz-inflected, and frankly modernist than *Krazy Kat*. He wrote the score without a prescribed narrative but as an attempt to capture for the Ballets Russes "the hurry and din of American life, and its association with jazz."[68] Not until the fall of 1924 did Carpenter decide on the title (Le Corbusier would later refer to New York skyscrapers as "hot jazz in stone or steel"), and not until the following spring did he decide to compose a mise-en-scène.[69] For help, he enlisted the collaboration of Robert Edmond Jones, the most influential scene designer of his age and an inventor of the so-called New Stagecraft who had studied in Europe and used abstraction and bold lighting in reaction against the box set and the photographic realism of the prewar theater.[70] The designer of sets and costumes for *The Birthday of the Infanta*, Jones was most strongly "identified . . . with Greenwich Village and Provincetown" and was then (and is now) most celebrated as the scene designer for almost all of Eugene O'Neill's plays between *Anna Christie* (1921) and *Ah, Wilderness* (1933).[71] Carpenter and Jones together devised a scenario that divided the ballet into six scenes (for which Jones designed five sets) that fall into a roughly A-B-A pattern. Although Carpenter insisted the ballet "has no story, in the usually accepted sense," he offered it as "reflecting" the "simple fact that American life reduces itself essentially to violent alternations of work and play, each with its own peculiar and distinctive rhythmic character."[72] Rather than oscillate between work and play, however, the action (like the twenty-four hours of a worker's life) moves from labor (the factory) to leisure (an amusement park) and back to work. According to Olin Downes's review, the ballet begins with a scene of laborers constructing a skyscraper that quickly changes to the exterior of a factory that "devour[s]" workers who "'jazz' or 'strut' for an instant to Mr. Carpenter's engaging rhythms." The central portion of the ballet is set in "'Coney Island'—any Coney Island," with the "workers . . . at play." This scene includes music and dance steps performed by both white and "black, or blacked" performers who were taken from—but are "far from merely literal imitations" of—"the American musical comedy stage, the cabaret, [and] the dance hall." The end of the Coney Island scene presents the dream of a "'White Wings,'" that is, black (or in this case, "blacked") street sweeper, which featured an all-black Harlem chorus directed by Frank Wilson (who had performed in the Jones-designed *All God's Chillun Got Wings* [1924] and was shortly to create the title role in *Porgy* [1927]). Singing "some wordless but . . . half familiar refrain," this chorus marked the first appearance of African American singers on the stage of the Metropolitan Opera. The dream sequence is followed by a return to the opening scene, "the factory doors, the winking lights."[73] *Theatre Arts* noted that this final scene "suggests the building of the city of the future. The spectator is elevated far above the congested streets," watching "the completion of the sky-piercing towers."[74]

To the surprise of some, the original production of *Skyscrapers* allowed the frankly commercial world of musical comedy and vaudeville to infiltrate America's "most conservative musical world."[75] To choreograph the piece, Carpenter and Jones engaged Sammy Lee (né Samuel Levy), "erstwhile member of the 'hoofing' fraternity," "injected direct from

Design by Robert Edmond Jones for scene 2 of the 1926 Metropolitan Opera production of John Alden Carpenter's *Skyscrapers*. Colossal, sinister skyscrapers under construction.
Credit: The Metropolitan Opera Archives

Broadway to give the show the real jazz quality, zip and rhythm."[76] A peerless technician, Lee was the leading Broadway choreographer of the 1920s, during which time he choreographed twenty-six musicals, including *Lady, Be Good!*, *No! No, Nanette!*, *The Cocoanuts* (1925), and (six weeks before *Skyscrapers*) *Tip-Toes*.[77] (A year later he was to choreograph *Show Boat*.) Although *Skyscrapers* was his only venture into classical dance, Lee "was able to use many of his vaudeville routines for the amusement park numbers" and in the skyscraper scenes "even had some of the men swing from girder to girder, as in a trapeze act."[78] Lee's Broadway-derived choreography was set among Jones's inventive sets, all of which, except for the colorful amusement park, featured more or less symmetrical, monochromatic compositions that suggested (rather than literally represented) the inhospitable, industrialized 1920s city: abstracted steel girders, arranged in jagged, triangular patterns (whose exact composition varies from scene to scene) that seemed to rise above the proscenium arch to fashion a kind of tower of Babel that reached up into the heavens. Jones's use of geometrical

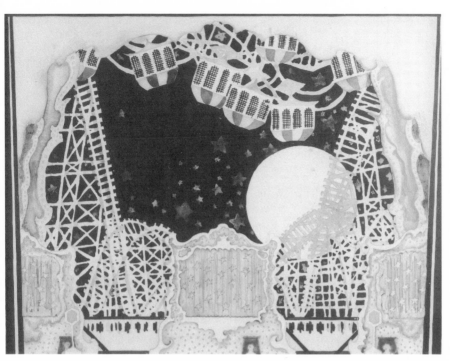

Scene 4 of *Skyscrapers*. "Any 'Coney Island.'"
Credit: The Metropolitan Opera Archives

figures and silhouettes recalled German expressionist and especially Russian constructivist design. These settings (reminiscent of Vladimir Tatlin's model for the *Monument to the Third International* [1919] and anticipating Fritz Lang's *Metropolis* [1927]) made for the most hard-edged designs of Jones's career and provided a rigorous, sophisticated, European, modernist environment for this "all-American ballet."[79]

Like the mise-en-scène, Carpenter's score begins in a severely modernist style (derived in large part from Stravinsky) that exploits relentless ostinatos, biting dissonances, chromatic harmonies, frequent alternations between major and minor modes, repeated changes of meter and key, and bitonal clashes (most notably and jarringly between keys a tritone apart). These techniques are later juxtaposed against a popular style inflected variously by ragtime, coon songs, spirituals, blues, and Tin Pan Alley. The syncopated rhythms of the piece evoke simultaneously the violent cross rhythms of *Le Sacre du printemps* or *Petrushka* and the more temperate and predictable syncopations used in jazz and other popular idioms. Carpenter's colorful and raucous orchestrations are heavy on brass and percussion, including a whistle and two pianos. "Saxophone and banjo," *The Dance* reported, "moan and strum amid the strings and wood-winds that had hushed beneath Melba's soaring golden tones."[80] Or as the *Herald Tribune* announced, "Miss Jazz" was about to "make her bow in the last remaining citadel of classical music in this country."[81]

Carpenter himself was very cautious in the pronouncements he made about jazz. Although he called it "by far the most spontaneous, the most personal, the most characteristic, and . . . the most important musical expression that America has achieved," he was very careful to specify the kind of jazz from which he claimed his work derived, "the rhythmic, harmonious music of . . . Irving Berlin and Jerome Kern."[82] This (Jewish) jazz, "full of character, of pep, of life," is quite distinct from what he called the "sensuous, indecent, ugly jazz that the Broadway cabaret orchestras play" and "appeal only to the vile instincts in human beings."[83] Yet Carpenter found both the purified and impure varieties of jazz deficient, lacking "that element" that he found in spirituals, "the aesthetic qualities necessary to fine music."[84] He therefore sought to keep jazz at a critical distance and argued that *Skyscrapers* represents merely "a reflection [of jazz], with all the exaggeration and distortion a reflection is likely to have."[85]

The mixture of high and low that Carpenter, Jones, and Lee were able to foist off on a suspecting public was warmly received by most of the critics, including many of those who disapproved of jazz in high places, and the ballet remained in the repertoire of the Metropolitan Opera for two years. The critics acclaimed *Skyscrapers* in large part because they believed that it was, as its makers insisted, "a vital expression of fundamental national feeling."[86] Even the reliably conservative Lawrence Gilman commended the use of "purely native choreography and native settings," while Downes called the work "auspicious for the development of a specifically American art form."[87] Gilman insisted that the score redeems jazz because it uses it ruefully; the music "is not parodistic" but "closer to tragic irony."[88]

The alternation between work and play that *Skyscrapers* rehearses is a predictably modernist one. For both terms in fact represent variations on the themes of mechanization and standardization. Carpenter's Coney Island, like the real one in 1926, is immeasurably distant from the bucolic paradise that, beginning in the eighteenth century, romantic artists (and even Elmer Rice with his Elysian Fields) imagined as a refuge from industrializing urban cultures. (The Coney Island amusement park, first built in the late nineteenth century, became an enormously popular and cheap destination for working- and middle-class New Yorkers after 1919, when the subway was extended out to the island.)[89] *Skyscrapers* thus testifies to the ubiquity of mass production and consumption, to the fact that even leisure pursuits by the 1920s had become mechanized and standardized. In representing the city and negotiating the highbrow/lowbrow divide, the ballet was seen as something quite different from a celebration of mass society and culture.

Several critics read *Skyscrapers* as defining a kind of modern, urban tragedy in which, according to Downes, "the dwellers in Manhattan at their work and their play" enact a "broadly human and tragic" predicament. "There is the vibration . . . in this music of exhaustion, of nervous and harried merriment, of heavy dreams, all caught up in a current of electricity and noise and quest."[90] Gilman used the occasion to moralize and condemn "the feverish conformity" and "mechanized joy" that he found "so depressing and pathetic."[91] This critical discourse attests to the fact that *Skyscrapers* was read not as a leftist critique of industrial capitalism (Brock refers to Carpenter and Jones as "tamed revolutionaries," "very demure Bolshevik[s]") but as a humanist tragedy (like *The Waste Land* [1922]) that grieves for a solitary, angst-ridden, alienated everyman, marooned in the frenetic modern city.[92]

I would like to suggest that the reception of *Skyscrapers* as American tragedy depends on more than its attitude toward urban life. The Harlem Negro chorus, "blacked" actors, and its idiosyncratic versions of African American musical forms also contributed to its tragic import. "The Negro Scene," White Wings's dream after he sweeps up the "wreckage" left behind by the dancers, is divided into two parts, the first a "melancholy" choral section in which the chorus, "behind a dimming gauze," sings nonsense syllables that are supposed to evoke a pathos-laden African or antebellum primitivism, and the second a "joyous" jazz dance.[93] The music for the former is a pseudospiritual in the minor mode, spiced up with blue notes and dissonance, suggestive of Gershwin's symphonic scores. Critics maintained that this section provides the piece with its pathos, with "the song of the moaning sons and daughters of slavery," "the true character and the nostalgia of Afro-American music."[94] The dance that follows modulates to C major and represents a kind of symphonic jazz arrangement of what could almost be a jazz or Tin Pan Alley song, complete with verse, refrain, and release. The presence of real African Americans in this scene, however, does not inhibit Carpenter, Jones, and Lee from elsewhere unashamedly using the conventions of minstrelsy. Carpenter weaves Stephen Foster's "Massa's in de Cold, Cold Ground," arranged as if for a carousel, into the din of Coney Island. And shortly before the Negro Scene, the Strutter, a kind of minstrel-derived Zip Coon figure (although not in blackface), using "the gestures of a popular comedian," appears in an oversize black silk hat, dickie, white collar, pants, and cuffs, jumping "over the backs of a half dozen black, or blacked, comedians."[95] Like the Strutter's costume, Carpenter's music is grotesque, a syncopated, lumbering foxtrot that clearly looks back to ragtime. The use of these different (and contradictory) theatrical and musical conventions presages other examples of jazz modernism (like *Show Boat*) that employ African American singers or musicians, white actors in literal or figurative blackface, and jazz or pseudojazz to reconstruct nostalgically the entertainments that diverted the nation.[96] The black chorus, in particular, certainly the most novel feature of the ballet, is exploited for its members' value as entertainers and personifications of a new, jazzed world as well as for the pathos they are able to generate as "throw-back[s] to negro plantation life" and emblems of "an authentic . . . racial note in American musical art."[97]

Rather than acknowledge *Skyscrapers'* incoherence with respect to racial performance, the critics unanimously approved what *The Dance* described as an "all-American triumvirate, which, with the all-American corps de ballet of the Metropolitan, prepared by an all-American mise-en-scène" had put together an "epoch making all-American ballet."[98] For the Americanness of the ballet was achieved not despite but because of this incoherence, that is, the use of contradictory images, persons, codes, and idioms. U.S. national identity was reinforced by *Skyscrapers'* European productions, which both accentuated its Americanness and (perhaps inadvertently) tried to assimilate it to European traditions. The Munich production, for example, which was very warmly received as a representation of "the eternal paradox . . . of American life," used U.S. flags in the Coney Island scene and costumes with stars and stripes while turning the corps de ballet into a Berlin cabaret-style "chorus line of women dressed as sailors."[99] When the score was performed in Paris in 1928, it was greeted as an "authentic voice from the New World."[100]

The success of *Skyscrapers* on both sides of the Atlantic and its triumphant negotiation of the highbrow/lowbrow divide are a testament to the ability of Carpenter, Jones, and Lee to appropriate popular forms. The ballet was seen as a landmark in the construction of an American populist art because Carpenter, rather than being pulled, as Gershwin had, into the mire of popular culture, had ennobled it by "assimilat[ing] jazz style in works of a 'high-brow' character."[101] "Mr. Carpenter," Olga Samaroff noted,

> has used jazz as it should be used. He has not tried to make it a fundamental esthetic of art. He has used it as a vitally distinctive rhythm and color, and given its true nature and scope[,] it has twice the power that it has when an attempt is made to extend that scope beyond its possibilities.[102]

Samaroff's evaluation was seconded by those critics intent on canonizing Carpenter in the pages of *Musical Quarterly*. Borowski praised him as "the most typically American" composer, who had eschewed a distasteful "racial tang" in favor of a "modern" music suffused "with the warmth and beauty that have been the constituents of the finest classic art."[103] That the "finest classic art" was European went without saying. And Carpenter constructed himself a modernist by emphasizing his European pedigree, claiming "that it is advantageous for Americans to study abroad . . . so that they may imbibe first hand knowledge of European traits and also increase their sense of beauty."[104] John Tasker Howard enumerated the many European influences on Carpenter, praised him for his "fine restraint," and absolved him of the fault that so many critics argued hobbled Gershwin, the alleged inability to develop "ideas and material" organically. "In *Skyscrapers*," he wrote, "ideas do not crowd upon each other in such rapid succession that they lack room to show their full contours, to attain their natural growth."[105] Most significantly, Downes lauded Carpenter as the man who has "brought the American composer's technic up to date." He has, "with an immense passion for . . . truth and beauty," "evolved certain clear and admirably developed [European!] forms which enclose American popular musical idioms." It is little wonder that Downes would commend the composer for having in *Skyscrapers* picked up "[t]he 'white man's burden'" and civilized an uncouth musical idiom.[106] In Carpenter's hands, jazz cosmopolitanism was placed at the service of a U.S. empire seeking to disseminate a purportedly native art that would uphold, while bettering, European aesthetic standards. And like the gentlemen imperialists of old, he knew how to keep the natives in their place while exploiting and pilfering their cultural treasures.

ACTS OF PROVOCATION

Unlike Carpenter, George Antheil was—and remains—one of the most innovative and controversial figures in American modernism. A precocious, twenty-six-year-old enfant terrible when *Ballet mécanique* enjoyed its disastrous New York premiere, he relished unsettling, or better yet, assaulting the audiences that attended classical music concerts. One of his early memories sets the stage for his career:

> More than anything else in the world I wanted a piano. . . . [W]hen I was about three years old I wanted to become a musician. Christmas time I was looking for a grand piano for a Christmas present. Not a grand piano, rather, an upright piano. And I stipulated that it was not to be one of these toy pianos that one bought in the toy stores. I wanted a real one. So I made this very clear. And at Christmas . . . I came downstairs and I saw that it was a toy piano. So I didn't say a word; I took it down the cellar and I got a hatchet and I chopped it up. And I like to feel that this has been a symbol of my life . . . . Because if music is not going to be everything that it must be and that I imagined, I feel I want to burn it up.[107]

When Antheil calls this incident "a symbol of my life," he is presumably referring to his enraged destruction of a crude, and embarrassingly bourgeois, plaything that does not compare with the instrument that makes "real" music. And certainly his thorny compositions of the 1920s attest to his loathing of musical pabulum. One would be hard pressed, moreover, to find a composer who so cultivated the pose of the outlaw and whose works, especially *Ballet mécanique*, are as impertinent and violent. Deliberately attacking the figure of the composer as well-behaved aesthete, Antheil styled himself an agent provocateur, or, to borrow the title of his best-selling autobiography, the *Bad Boy of Music*. In that volume, he savors offending music lovers and critics and cultivating an aggressive, arrogant independence of spirit remarkable even among the European avant-gardists who were his fellow travelers during the 1920s. He boasts of buying a "comfortably padded" "holster" from his Berlin tailor early in the decade in which to keep his "thirty-two automatic" that accompanied him "everywhere, especially to concerts." And he attributes his "coolness during various riotous concerts" to a "very simple" reason: "I was armed."[108]

Antheil's violent reaction against gentility, aestheticism, and musical impressionism was far more than just a pose, and it allied him with many celebrated expatriates with whom he sported in Paris. His memoir is rife with reminiscences about the heroes of Jazz Age modernism, including James Joyce, T. S. Eliot, Ernest Hemingway, Igor Stravinsky, Aaron Copland, Virgil Thomson, Ford Maddox Ford, Wyndham Lewis, and Ezra Pound (the last two, it should be noted, were to become fascist sympathizers). Pound even wrote a book to champion the music of his friend.[109] Antheil's 1923 Paris concert debut, for which he was reported to be "fresh from riot upon riot," attracted "the elite."[110] They included Darius Milhaud and Erik Satie, who, like many in the audience of the tony Théâtre des Champs-Elysées, cheered the enfant terrible. Although some relished Antheil's musical radicalism, others were less enthusiastic: "a steely silence" in the auditorium was followed by catcalls, a fistfight, and finally a riot that featured "people in the galleries . . . pulling up the seats and dropping them down into the orchestra."[111] "The audience shouted itself quite hoarse with both indignation with the composer and indignation with the others in the audience who had prevented them from hearing."[112] As Antheil later wrote—without exaggeration—"Paris hadn't had such a good time since the premiere of Stravinsky's 'Sacre du Printemps.'" He had become "notorious in Paris, therefore famous."[113] And, according to Aaron Copland (in 1926), a man of nearly boundless talent: "Antheil is all they claim and more; one needn't be particularly astute to realize that he possesses the greatest gifts of any young American now writing."[114]

Like many of his fellow avant-gardists on both sides of the Atlantic, Antheil was intent on producing a cosmopolitan art of the Machine Age that was far more radical than anything dreamed of by John Alden Carpenter. He confessed that he had embraced "the anti-expressive, anti-romantic, coldly mechanistic aesthetic of the early twenties" even before moving to Berlin in 1922.[115] Ezra Pound encouraged his repudiation of Wagnerian "pea soup" and the "heavy mist[s]" of Debussy in favor of "mechanism," "rhythmic precision," "reiteration," and a contempt for sentimentality: "Antheil is probably the first artist to use machines, I mean actual modern machines, without bathos."[116] Arguing that "music is the art most fit to express the fine quality of machines," Pound described Antheil's world of "steel bars, not of old stone and ivy."[117] Although later abashed by Pound's encomium (in large part, I suspect, because of the poet's collaboration with Mussolini), the composer in 1923 relished being found out by "the world's foremost discoverer of genius."[118] A genius at self-promotion, Antheil constructed himself the messiah of a new age that "finds its rhythms in airplanes and steel." His inspiration, he wrote, proceeded from "intricate machines" with "new arms and legs of steel" that would "reach out and change the entire epoch."[119] One of these new machines apparently was the movie camera; he decided when he began composing *Ballet mécanique* that he wanted "a motion-picture accompaniment to this piece."[120] He sparked the interest of Dudley Murphy, an American cinematographer, who persuaded Fernand Léger to direct a film on which the two filmmakers collaborated, also to be entitled *Ballet mécanique*. In the event, the music and the film were not synchronized (Antheil's piece is some ten minutes longer than Léger's film) and the two exist as independent artworks.

Antheil's aggressive, Machine Age aesthetic jibed all too well with the many avant-gardisms that convulsed European culture after World War I, including Dada, cubism, futurism, and suprematism. One of the most significant correlations, however, was with Italian futurism. Like the futurists, Antheil sought to make a radical break with the long tradition of bourgeois art music and to that end fomented a revolution not only in the production but also in the consumption of music. Like Luigi Russolo and Francesco Balilla Pratella, he worked to extend the range of what could be accounted music, to change the auditor's consciousness of sound and of the newly discovered fourth dimension through which music unfolds: time.[121] And like them, he saw the machine as the primary instigator of this revolution. Parts of Russolo's 1913 manifesto could almost have been written by Antheil a decade later: "THIS EVOLUTION OF MUSIC IS PARALLELED BY THE MULTIPLICATION OF THE MACHINE, which collaborates with man everywhere." Because "pure sound, in its monotony and exiguity, no longer arouses emotion," "IT IS NECESSARY," Russolo wrote, to "CONQUER THE INFINITE VARIETY OF 'NOISE-SOUNDS.'"[122] Both Antheil and the futurists, moreover, were intent on remasculinizing art by scattering the "diaphanous dust cloud" of aestheticism and impressionism with a percussive volley of notes and images.[123] "A pianist's fingers," Antheil wrote, "are both his ammunition and his machine guns."[124]

Despite the similarities between the futurists and the pistol-packin' composer, the latter took pains to distance himself from the former (perhaps in part because of their involvement with Italian fascism as early as 1914).[125] Although Antheil looked forward to the triumph of "orchestral machines with a thousand new sounds" and "sonorities," he insisted these machines would have "nothing in common with the foolish Futurist machines" that "were only and sheerly improvisations of noise intended to imitate automobiles, airplanes, etc. which . . . has nothing to do with music."[126] Unlike the futurists', Antheil's machine music was not to be illustrative or descriptive but abstract, a rigorously organized and mathematical structure that, like his pianism, would represent a translation of the Machine Age itself, in all its hideous glory, into "a synthesis of frenzy and precision."[127]

Given the importance of live performance for Antheil, who planned his concerts to be theatrical happenings, Dada is perhaps an even more important correlation than futurism. Carol Oja emphasizes his debt to Dada, arguably the most radical of all the -isms, to which he had likely been exposed even before he decamped to Europe.[128] Refusing illusionism, symbolism, canons of beauty, and moralizing of all kinds, Dada (like futurism) assaulted the pieties of bourgeois humanism, society, and culture: "We are," Tristan Tzara wrote, "like a raging wind that rips up the clothes of clouds and prayers, we are preparing the great spectacle of disaster, conflagration and decomposition." Ridiculing the idea of "ultimate Truth," Dada blasted psychoanalysis ("a dangerous disease"), logic, systems of knowledge, "slimy objectivity, and harmony, the science that considers that everything is in order."[129] Tzara regretted the fact that Dada "remains within the framework of European weaknesses": "it's still shit, but from now on we want to shit in different colours."[130] As becomes clear from his rhetoric, and as Peter Bürger emphasizes, "shocking the recipient becomes the dominant principle of artistic intent." The most important and effective way of doing so, moreover, was through performance or more exactly, the Dada manifestation—part cabaret, part protestation, part circus, part play, part carnival—which, Bürger notes, "made the provocation of the public [its] avowed aim." Provocation became the prime exemplar of Dada because it produced an *act*, not an object that could be bought and sold. As Bürger emphasizes, the "act of provocation itself," representing a kind of pure decommodification, "takes the place of the work of art."[131] The provocation also takes the place of a moribund theater in which, Tzara laments, "every bourgeois is a little playwright, who invents different subjects and who . . . tries to find causes . . . to give weight to his plot."[132] Considered in light of Dada's ambitions, virtually all of Antheil's early recitals and performances can be seen as acts of provocation, assaults on spectators and the bourgeois playlets that filled elite concert halls. Aware of the real and symbolic violence that permeates the provocation, Antheil, branded "the worst criminal in the realm of art," could never be sure what his recitals would stir up.[133] But he never worried: "I felt for the automatic under my arm and continued playing. . . . *I could always shoot my way out.*"[134]

Antheil also aligned himself with Dada rather than futurism in his use of vernacular traditions. The futurists had little interest in or patience with Italian popular music or theater. Dada, on the other hand, ridiculed the cultural machinery that consecrated some artworks and delegitimized others. More international, or more exactly, transnational than futurism, it embraced vaudeville, puppetry, blackface, and popular music of all kinds. "We are circus ringmasters," Tzara wrote, "and we can be found whistling amongst the winds of fairgrounds."[135] For Antheil the American expatriate, the vernacular tradition meant one thing—jazz—which he found irresistible, because of its modernity and its potential as a destructive force, but problematic, because of its identification with a native land from whose parochialism he had tried to distance himself. Very few of his pieces composed before his removal to Europe in 1922 evince the influence of American popular music. But after arriving in Europe and discovering the rage for *la mode américaine*, he declared jazz to be "one of the greatest landmarks of modern art" and composed several pieces whose titles or musical content reference ragtime or jazz, including "Ragtime Sonata," Symphonie No. 1 (whose final movement is marked "Ragtime"; both 1922), "Little Shimmy," Second Sonata for Violin and Piano, and "Sonata Sauvage" (all 1923).[136] Given the extraordinary popularity of American jazz in Europe, Antheil could no more escape it than he could the Fordist mode of production. His jazz-inflected pieces culminated in *A Jazz Symphony*, written in 1925 on a commission from Paul Whiteman but first performed by W. C. Handy's Orchestra at the same 1927 Carnegie Hall concert that, he wrote in his memoir, turned his life from comedy to tragedy. His association with American vernaculars was so strong that in 1934 David Ewen could assert without fear of contradiction that "Antheil is enormously fond of jazz-rhythms and ragtime effects, which he uses frequently in all of his compositions."[137] That statement, however, is not quite true.

During and after the 1920s, Antheil (along most of his critics) main-

Léger

JAZZ

For the immediate future there will be only two kinds of music, the Banal, and the Mechanistic.

Ragtime embraces the first and is the nucleous of the second.

The first will derive its energy from the pulse of the new people, and the second from the direct environment of these masses; the towers, new architectures, bridges, steel machinery, automobiles, and other things which have a direct functioning, and are aesthetically placed directly apart from the organization of the sentimental which the first includes.

The first will be both sentimental and banal, and will be the artistic reorganization of the new people by a solitary genius. Here organization has the uppermost hand. It will find its energy in the most powerful musical fragments of these people — the most obstinately banal ones.

The second will be purely abstract and will derive its energy from the rhythmic genius of a solitary innovator whose sense of time spaces comes from the present moment of intricate machines which are new arms ands legs of steel and reach out and change the entire epoch. This man must invent new machineries for the locomotion of time, or the musical canvas, in such a way that we have a new musical dimension.

At any rate it is impossible to imagine that we shall go on with innumerable pseudo-Schönbergs, or for that matter Schönberg himself.

A score which presents the illusion of a Mendelssohn with false notes is of no value to a present generation. Everyone knew that something was wrong, Schönberg was dry. The reason is that he had no grip upon spaces, no draughtsmanship that compelled itself.

It is equally as futile to write violin solo sonatas which is now the smartest mode.

Of the others it is difficult to distinguish the sincere classicalists from the downright fadists who profess to gain all their necessity to compose from the last string quartets of Beethoven. To Beethoven and Brahms they add Schönberg. This is the situation in Germany.

Schönberg has not created a single new musical machinery. Strawinsky has, but he belongs to the first group. Auric, Poulenc, and de Falla are lesser stars. Casella is at best when he is sympathetic with Rossini. What Malipiero is trying to do is not always clear; I am not sure that Strawinsky has come more to the point about the music of old Italy with his tiny four-hand piece, "Napololitana" than all of the impressionistic uncertainty of "Pantea". Of one thing I am certain, that the "Espanola" of the same group of four-hand pieces far outdoes anything that has to date come from modern Spain. The last opera of Strawinsky, "Marva" which has to do with an Italian subject, and has arias, duets, and the usual arrangements of an old Italian opera score, is surely the essence and sum of the whole business.

As for the modern Englishmen, they are not so far away from Cyril Scott as they would have us think. In spite of themselves they will forever persist in using the machinery and aesthetic of The Master of Chromatic Siths.

172

The title page of George Antheil's 1922 manifesto, "Jazz," with a drawing by Fernand Léger.

tained that he composed in two different styles, "a synthesized jazz idiom" and machine music. The former he considered something of a diversion, the second a more consequential mode that secured his reputation.[138] Antheil developed this opposition in a 1922 essay entitled "Jazz" (published in Berlin) that is only slightly more coherent than one of Tristan Tzara's Dada manifestos. (It shares the page with a Fernand Léger cubist drawing under which Antheil's one-word title sits like a caption.) Antheil there distinguishes between two kinds of music, "the Banal" and "the Mechanistic." The former corresponds to jazz and ragtime, is "sentimental," and "find[s] its energy" in "the pulse of the new people" and in "the most powerful" and "most obstinately banal" musical fragments. The latter corresponds to "time-space style" and receives its inspiration from "the towers, . . . bridges, steel machinery, automobiles, and other things which have a direct functioning." Although "purely abstract," it "will derive its energy from . . . the present moment of intricate machines."[139]

Antheil's two modes are, I believe, far less distinct than he suggests and are, in fact, mutually constitutive. His "coldly mechanistic" music is inconceivable without his wildly idiosyncratic versions of ragtime and jazz. Even Antheil admits the codependence when he allows that ragtime is "the nucleous [sic]" of "the Mechanistic."[140] And jazz clearly furnishes, or at least inspires, many of the ostinatos that propel his pieces of the 1920s. (The other inspiration, as Antheil often acknowledged, was Stravinsky.) For Antheil, jazz "belongs to America" as surely as it does to "modern life." Four-note jazz phrases "inevitably" evoke "New York or San Francisco" as surely as a fragment of Grieg "brings the fiords of Norway to mind." For Antheil—as for virtually all American modernist composers and critics of the 1920s—"Jazz is [America's] way out to the future."[141]

In his music of the 1920s, Antheil develops a highly abstracted jazz style by elaborating a technique of modular construction that combines idioms that were understood to be both primitive and mechanistic. His music characteristically sets relatively simple, repeated, often diatonic melodies that move in stepwise motion through a narrow compass of notes against (sometimes extremely) dissonant, syncopated ostinatos reminiscent of ragtime, stride piano, jazz, or Stravinsky. Different cells, or what Linda Whitesitt labels "rhythmically activated musical blocks," are set in sequence according to the laws of what Antheil calls "parade-form."[142] And while there are similarities between these cells (they often seem to be disparate variations on a theme that is never quite enunciated), Antheil eschews organic forms, preferring a mode of sudden and jarring juxtaposition comparable to the cinematic jump cut. Nonetheless, his "time-space" pieces are loaned a kind of unity by virtue of a strong rhythmic pulse—a kind of musical unconscious—that underlies, intertwines with, and seems to generate the ostinatos. The dissonance varies from cell to cell and piece to piece, but it usually functions as a musical spice (the extreme version of which is the tone cluster). Unlike Austro-German or impressionist music, Antheil's rarely allows dissonance to serve a harmonic function, that is, to create a harmonic tension that yearns to be resolved. Basing his music on principles of repetition rather than development, Antheil sometimes seems to suspend tonality so that melodies, ostinatos, and tone clusters follow each other "without meaning, top or bottom."[143] Although in some of his pieces the sequence of cells seems to imply a more traditional notion of musical form, he almost always frustrates expectations, preferring repetitive patterns that do not generate a clear sense of forward movement. As if anticipating the music of Steve Reich or Philip Glass—or the late works of John Coltrane—it is governed by principles of repetition, not development.

Like so many of his contemporaries, Antheil turned to jazz as the basis for a cosmopolitan music rooted in American vernaculars. His versions of jazz, however, are far more radical, and far more distant from sweet jazz, than Gershwin's or Carpenter's. Antheil epitomized a European avant-garde that broke aggressively with nineteenth-century conventions. "I refuse to be bound," he wrote, "by any conventions that interfere with my conceptions."[144] No longer interested in composing an "old and rather depressing" French-style concert music that sets "whole-tone scale harmonies jowl-to-jowl with blue Negroidian [*sic*] sevenths and ninths," he repeatedly insisted that jazz is "capable of development into a serious art." Like his fellow avant-gardists, however, Antheil found it necessary to do violence to the vernacular, "to tear apart the elements of jazz and . . . reorganize them." He accordingly expounded a jazz-derived, "time-space" music that takes off from "the 'parade-form'" of jazz, a "stream of melodies which follow one another aimlessly."[145] A piece like the "Sonata Sauvage" (also referred to as "Sonata mecanique") exemplifies his mode of composition during the 1920s, a mode that combines a primitivism derived from ragtime, jazz, and Stravinsky with a hypermodernity associated with subways, jackhammers, and assembly lines.[146] This combination allowed Antheil's music, with its "weird" and "almost barbaric" "mixture of jazz and discords," of "esthetic beauty and sheer cacophony," to be received—especially in Paris—as the "musical expression" of "America's sky-scrapers." "Paris critics," the *New York Herald Tribune* reported, "see in him the composer who, for the first time, has broken with European traditions and created an American national music."[147]

Antheil's ambivalence toward jazz is unsurprising and is linked to an ambivalence toward U.S. culture, primitivism, and "Negro music" that, I have argued, was virtually ubiquitous among European American composers and artists of his generation.[148] Less typical, yet more revealing of the cosmopolitan avant-gardism of the early 1920s, was a profound distrust of the theater and theatricality. For like the Dadaists and futurists (and Gilbert Seldes), Antheil evinced both a modernist antitheatricality and an avant-gardist theatricalism. On the one hand, he showed very little interest in theater or opera either in the United States or Europe and resisted composing a traditional opera or ballet until after the Carnegie Hall debacle. On the other hand, he carefully fashioned his live performances—his "theater"—to be acts of provocation whose consequences could never be known in advance.[149] He relished causing disturbances in concert halls and theaters, if only because it increased the odds of getting in a little target practice. Trying to live out the avant-gardist dream, he aspired to turn life into art and art into life.

Antheil's music, like Stravinsky's, almost always has a theatrical air, and his highly gestural pieces were usually given a one- or two-word descriptive title, even those allegedly "without meaning." During the early 1920s, the titles of his piano pieces often referenced machines (the "Steel," "Roads," and "Airplanes" of "Sonata III" [1922]) or traditional musical forms ("Habañera, Tarantelle, Serenata" [1924]). More scandalously, they evoked primitivist or pseudoprimitivist objects and persons (the "Niggers," "Snakes," and "Ivory" of "Sonata Sauvage"). But as Antheil emphasized time and again, he never attempted, as Stravinsky did, to construct musical narratives or represent literally. Rather, he attempted "to convey the feel" of objects, persons, and traditional musical forms "unconsciously through the medium of music."[150]

Like so many of his fellow avant-gardists, Antheil believed jazz to be intimately connected to the primitive and the unconscious. For him, however, it was less an individual Freudian unconscious than a cultural unconscious, the barely apprehended primitive substrate that allegedly underlies modern civilization, the "African and millennial lyricism" championed by his friend Benoist-Méchin, "made up of the most remote and primitive elements." Like so many of his contemporaries, Antheil imagined he could find the key to unlock the unconscious in the music, bodies, and traditions of Africans and African Americans. A *New Yorker* piece noted that Antheil's "real talent lies . . . in the manner he synthesizes a series of African dance rhythms with the same intellectual precision with which Bach constructed a fugue."[151] During the early 1920s, he made two well-publicized trips to North Africa to discover what he later called "the most interesting authentic ancient music [he] had ever heard."[152] His second junket was little more than a publicity stunt and was cut short when he received a panicked telegram from Sylvia Beach, the owner of Shakespeare and Company: "FOR GOODNESS SAKE GEORGE COME BACK TO PARIS IMMEDIATELY AND DENY THIS IDIOTIC NEWSPAPER STORY LIONS ATE YOU IN AFRICA."[153] A gullible *New York Times* reporter, however, described him as "lost for two months in the Sahara Desert" before emerging "with comprehensive notes on the native music."[154] Antheil's feint of going native thereby succeeded in giving a piece like *A Jazz Symphony* a whiff of primitive authenticity.

Antheil's relationship to African American traditions was even more fraught. A newspaper story published the day of the Carnegie Hall debacle begins with a crude provocation: "Note the importance ascribed to 'niggers.' When George Antheil put them at the head of his list of the things in the United States worthy of musical interpretation, he unwittingly dropped the key to his own biography." Emphasizing Antheil's physical and expressive proximity to "niggers," the article turns him into a kind of musical ethnographer who, it reported, once lived "near the Negro quarter [of Philadelphia] and there, in dingy cabarets, . . . heard jazz for the first time." It also maintains erroneously that he went to Europe "convinced that jazz was the only possible basis for our national music."[155] It is no coincidence that this story should have appeared the day *A Jazz Symphony* received its premiere. Although commissioned by Paul Whiteman, the *Symphony* was returned to the composer, who wrote: "They aint [*sic*] never seen nothing like that before, and hope they never will again."[156] In New York, Donald Friede, the producer of the Carnegie Hall concert, even challenged de facto segregation (with Antheil's blessing) by engaging both white and black musicians. He apparently believed that the African American personnel of W. C. Handy's Orchestra would verify the piece's authenticity. (The orchestra was racially integrated in performance by the presence of the composer at the piano and, in the hall, by the presence in the box seats of the wives and relatives of Handy's musicians.)[157] But because Handy "could not cope with the fantastic intricacies of Antheil's score," Friede dismissed him early in rehearsals and hired Allie Ross, a classically trained African American violinist and conductor, who finally pulled it together.[158]

Antheil was proud of his symphonic jazz and called it "one of the first authentic attempts to synthesize one of our most difficult national mediums."[159] Indeed, the *Symphony*'s "rhythmically activated musical blocks," derived from ragtime, jazz, Tin Pan Alley, and sentimental turn-of-the-century ballads, are submitted to Antheil's decontextualizing, "time-space" ostinato method. Antheil was not wrong to call the piece "hyper-jazz" and to claim it made jazz not respectable, but "jazzier," that is, rowdy and brutish, by referencing not Gershwin, Whiteman, or even Louis Armstrong but "the cheap and almost primitive cafe orchestras" that fascinated him.[160] Through a jarring and violent juxtaposition (and superimposition) of vernacular styles, it establishes what Whitesitt describes as a "honky-tonk atmosphere."[161] With its wailing woodwinds, moaning brass, tinny piano, and clanging percussion winding through a sequence of tunes, the *Symphony* sounds almost like a Dada version of a jazzy Broadway overture, designed to "knock . . . 'em flat, bug-eyed, and nutty."[162]

A THREE-RING CIRCUS

Ballet mécanique represents Antheil's most shocking act of provocation and one of the most remarkable examples of jazz theater. A pounding assault, the most violently repetitive of his pieces, it is, in his words,

> All percussive. Like machines. All efficiency. NO LOVE. Written without sympathy. Written cold as an army operates. Revolutionary as nothing has been revolutionary.[163]

Lasting about twenty-five minutes, the Carnegie Hall version of the *Ballet* puts the din of airplanes, ragtime, throbbing ostinatos, jazz, Stravinsky, and ambient city and factory noises through a sonic meat grinder. Its apparently arbitrary division into three parts is not the result of an inner, formal logic but of the fact that the player piano rolls needed to be changed twice over the course of the performance. As the composer understood, his relentless use of repeated, syncopated rhythmic patterns ensured that the piece would seem radically contemporary, "a macabre sort of jazz," as one Paris reporter called it.[164] Ten years after the Carnegie Hall disaster, Antheil wrote that the "new form" of the piece filled out "a certain time canvas with musical abstractions and sound material composed and contrasted against one another with the thought of time values rather than tonal values."[165] The piece is, in short, the purest and most radical version of his jazz/time-space hybrid. Insisting it has "nothing to do with tonality," Antheil invents a dissonant, ostinato-driven idiom defined by repeated patterns of tone clusters of which, Whitesitt observes, "the tonal implications of tension and repose have been replaced by tensional changes in melodic-rhythmic blocks."[166] Rather than focusing on a tonic as harmonic home, Antheil produces an innovative sense of musical home through the reiteration of distinctive, often ragtime- or jazz-inspired patterns of sonorities and tone clusters. These repeated patterns re-form every three to ten seconds, articulated by musical jump cuts. Despite these jump cuts and over six hundred changes in time signature, the piece maintains a relentless, powerful momentum—until its third part.

Most radically, *Ballet mécanique* is in its last part cut through several times by sudden—and historically unprecedented—bursts of silence, culminating in a sixty-four-beat tacet. In these respites, heralded by electric bells, a well-known Dada contrivance, the music stops dead.[167]

> Here at the end of this composition where *in long stretches* no *single sound occurs and time itself acts as music*; here was the ultimate fulfillment of my poetry; here I had time moving *without touching it*.[168]

There is no structural logic working itself out. The "relationship between part and whole," Bürger notes, "that characterizes the organic work of art" is utterly negated.[169] Contesting the principles of musical development, the third part of the *Ballet* quite literally stages those absences Jameson sees as central to modernist cultural production, those missing pieces of the social and economic puzzle. Sited at the intersection of European and American modernism, of music and theater, of symphony and hot jazz, *Ballet mécanique* is, in Antheil's words, "a dream of niggers, skyscrapers and glittering polished surfaces."[170] It makes audible the silent (because absent) voices of "niggers" and of the colonial subjects whom his friend Benoist-Méchin was not alone in fearing. As might have been expected, the New York critics were incapable of comprehending the piece. Indeed, *Ballet mécanique* comes close to fulfilling Tristan Tzara's Dada injunction: "What we need are strong, straightforward, precise works which will be forever misunderstood."[171]

Antheil always insisted that, as with his other pieces, he was scrupulously avoiding illustration or portraiture: "it ha[s] nothing whatsoever to do with the actual description of factories, machinery." Instead of an illustrative, literal theater, Antheil offers dreams, visions, and evocations couched in metaphor. *Ballet mécanique* is "streamlined, glistening, cold, often as 'musically silent' as interplanetary space, and also often as hot as an electric furnace."[172] It is a "reaction" to New York, "a city composed of parallel lines and dimensions which form beautiful white spaces."[173] It is a construction of "ice blocks," "a solid shaft of steel" that conjures "the dead line, the brink of the precipice."[174] Frigid and infernal, full and empty, white and black, earsplitting and silent, the *Ballet* "writes," to borrow Adorno's word, a "seismogram" of a fearsome reality, of the historical moment when human labor must comply with the machine and the human subject is swallowed up by mass production.[175] It is telling that Antheil's metaphors should reference not human subjects, except significantly, "niggers"—upon whose absence, that is, presence, the piece and the globalized economy are predicated—but a realm of pure objectification, the mineral realm, a world of awesome things.

The Carnegie Hall performance of what Aaron Copland, one of the pianists that evening, called "a visionary experiment" never became the terrifying provocation the composer intended in part because it was sabotaged by a number of choices and accidents that prevented the realization of the social content of the piece.[176] The vast majority of these had nothing to do with the music per se, but with its presentation and with the strategies Donald Friede devised to advertise what the biggest classified ad in the *New York Times* music listings trumpeted as "The Biggest Musical Event of the Year!"[177] Believing "any publicity is good publicity," Friede so aggressively promoted the concert and hyped the nontraditional instruments used in *Ballet mécanique* that the *New York Times* critic imagined he heard and saw quite a few instruments that were quite simply not on the Carnegie Hall stage, including anvils, automobile horns, alarm clocks, torpedoes(!), screw drivers "running in reverse," fan belts, and kazoos.[178] Although Friede wrote that he later realized he was alienating the critics "one by one," he was aided and abetted by the megalomaniacal claims of the composer.[179] A declaration such as "I am the only American-born composer ... who has ever approached even a sensation in any country outside of his own" was bound to, and did, incur critics' wrath.[180] Having planted a wildly exaggerated story in the program about the riotous Paris premiere of the piece during which allegedly "[t]hree hundred frightened American tourists screamed" for the police, Friede and Antheil should not have been surprised that the New York concert was viewed unanimously as an anticlimax.[181] Although some headlines proclaimed, "Boos Greet Antheil Ballet of Machines," most dismissed the concert as a washout: "Expected Riots Peter Out at George Antheil Concert—Sensation Fails to Materialize."[182] The critics ranged from bemused to witheringly contemptuous. In the latter camp, Lawrence Gilman (who the year before had extolled *Skyscrapers*) judged the *Jazz Symphony* a "tame and feeble inanity" and the *Ballet* an "unconscionably boring, artless, and naive" piece of "stupefying length." "[T]he 'hostile demonstration' at the back of the hall," he wrote, "so suspiciously manufactured, . . . died a feeble, fluttering death" before "an infinitely wearied audience" quit Carnegie Hall.[183]

Despite the counterproductive marketing choices, I would like to suggest that the miserable fate of Antheil's New York debut was sealed less by the music than by scenic and performance choices that Friede and Antheil made. Rather than construct the concert as either avant-gardist provocation or elite art event, they inadvertently turned it into an affair that classical music critics could not stomach, a Broadway show. The critic Oscar Thompson described it as "less a concert than a vaudeville act" and judged it accordingly: "stale, tedious, not even funny."[184] The composer Charles Seeger observed that *Ballet mécanique* was "vaudeville," albeit "good vaudeville," while Friede admitted that he had turned "a serious performance into a circus," a position seconded by Antheil, who remembered the concert as a "three-ring circus."[185] One critic noted mockingly that "[a]ll the gals and fellas of the Village were there," while another complained that "[e]lite subscribers of the Beethoven Association and the Philadelphia Orchestra rubbed shoulders with habitués of night clubs and vaudeville artists."[186] For the New York music critics, avant-gardist music and popular theater traditions should never mix. Antheil and Friede had sinned against art by trying to turn Carnegie Hall into the Hippodrome or the Apollo.

According to most chroniclers of the event, however, the real villain of the piece was Joseph Mullen, the scene designer whom Friede hired to remake "the classic and ultraconservative background against which Carnegie Hall concerts were played."[187] Friede commissioned him to paint a backdrop for the *Jazz Symphony* and a cyclorama for *Ballet mécanique*. Although there seem to be no extant photographs of the "gigantic" drops, several descriptions were published.[188] The most detailed remains that of Friede himself, who wrote that the backdrop for the *Symphony* (a design, the *Times* declared, "in negro-jazz vibrations of black, white and silver") "covered the whole rear of the stage" and depicted "a gigantic Negro couple dancing the Charleston, the girl holding an American flag in her left hand, while the man clasped her ecstatically around the buttocks."[189] For the *Ballet*, human beings were virtually eliminated in favor of a "black and white 'constructivist'" composition.[190] The cyclorama featured "a futuristic city of skyscrapers as a background; and in the foreground a series of enormous noise-making machines; . . . in the left-hand corner a more-than-life-size figure of a man jumping off a diving board that seemed to be attached to a curved pipe of the sort generally used in connection with a toilet."[191]

The backdrops violated at least two taboos, first, by its depiction of African Americans in a highly sexualized scene and second, by its oblique scatological reference. Friede reported that when the curtain rose on the "billowing, buttocksy backdrop of the colossal Charleston, the audience roared with laughter." He "had not realized," he wrote, "how utterly incongruous it would seem . . . in hallowed Carnegie Hall." Then during intermission, because he had "miscalculated the space" for the required ten pianos, the stagehands were unable to lower the front curtain and had to "work in full view of the highly amused audience."[192] Most important, these backdrops were responsible for turning Antheil's intended Dada provocation into a knockoff of *Shuffle Along* or the Ziegfeld Follies. Not only was the scene design, in Antheil's word, "tasteless," it also literally illustrated—and thereby impoverished and debased—what the composer had designed to be "the most abstract of the abstract."[193] Although Antheil referred to *Ballet mécanique* as "theater," the stage he envisioned was something radically different from the mise-en-scène that Mullen had designed.[194] To Antheil's horror, the backdrops encouraged the audience (whom Antheil later called "dumb-bells") to expect "pictures of the machine age, . . . a kind of Buck Rogers fantasy of the future."[195] He so detested the Broadway theatricality of the performance that he blamed the backdrops for "single-handedly" sending him "back to Europe broke" and giving "an air of charlatanism to the whole proceedings."[196] (Friede, who in fact paid the bills, blamed the financial loss equally on the "backdrops" and the "twenty-five rehearsals" required for *A Jazz Symphony*.)[197]

The question of illustration also raises the problem of the relationship between Antheil's piece and Léger's film. On the one hand, there are images and techniques used in the film that help one interpret Antheil's piece, if only because the two were constructed at the same time in the same place by avant-gardists reacting to the same historical conjuncture and seeking to reconcile American content with European form. On the other hand, the film is, I believe, best understood as an independent work, not a visualization of Antheil's *Ballet mécanique*. The pieces have at times been coupled, with an edited version of the Antheil serving as soundtrack to the Léger, but neither benefits from this contrived synchronization. Because the cinematic sign and the musical sign are utterly different, the film, unlike the music, cannot escape representation. Even though the Léger uses very rapid cutting and prismatic lenses that often make the imagery difficult to recognize, all of it (including Antheil's hated "pictures of the machine age") can be identified. The musical score, on the other hand, is nonnarrative and nonprogrammatic. With the exception of some ambient sounds (mainly sirens and airplane propellers), it is nonreferential, and its representation is effected through pounding rhythms and an abandonment of tonality, not via two-dimensional, black-and-white images of the real world. Although, for example, one might fancy one hears in the music a busy city street, complete with sirens, automobiles, buses, pneumatic drills, and heavy construction equipment, this impression is produced by purely musical means. Antheil makes no attempt, as some seventeenth- and eighteenth-century composers did, to write instrumental music mimicking cats, cuckoos, church bells, or battles.

There are, however, powerful analogies between the cinematic and musical versions of *Ballet mécanique*. To assert that both are representations of a world of mass production and consumption, a world in which the human subject is made a slave of the machine, is to state the obvious. Yet both pieces were made at a moment when the implications of this process were by no means obvious, when the machine seemed to promise utopia and dystopia in equal measure. Antheil admits as much when he writes in his memoir that "at the time I did consider machines very beautiful." Yet his "idea" for the piece "was to warn the age in which [he] was living of the simultaneous beauty and danger of its own unconscious mechanistic philosophy, aesthetic."[198] To argue that Léger's film seems more explicitly celebratory than Antheil's piece is to fixate on its content, the gleaming machines and metal implements, the smiling face of Kiki of Montparnasse, the amusement park rides. And while the form—the motoric rhythms, the witty juxtapositions imposed by the countless jump cuts—does produce the impression of a frenetic "carnival world of high-key sensations of speed and movement," the film will also disorient a spectator who is not used to nonnarrative cinema or such maniacally fast editing.[199] Léger writes that the rhythms "'persist' up to the point where the eye and the mind of the spectator 'can't take it any more.' We exhaust its visual power at the very moment when it becomes unbearable."[200] Like Antheil's *Ballet*, Léger's uses machine rhythms to unnerve people who were coming to take the assembly line for granted.

The most important and irreducible difference between the Léger and the Antheil is a result of the histories of the different media. Cinema was a relatively novel medium undergoing rapid development in 1924, while orchestral music was seen as obsolescent, rapidly being superseded by popular music and mechanically reproduced musical forms. Thus, the sense of wonder, discovery, and exhilaration in the Léger is a very real effect of a medium reflecting upon itself, a mechanical medium still in the process of developing new technical resources. The Antheil, on the other hand, is a last gambit put forward in a medium whose days of glory were past and whose audiences were progressively shrinking, having fallen prey to the siren's song of what Adorno calls the culture industries. Léger did not need concern himself with the question of whether or not film, as a medium, mattered. Because it did. Antheil, on the other hand, knew that music didn't matter anymore, or at least, didn't matter in the way that it had. And his *Ballet mécanique* is both a recognition of and protest against that obsolescence. Perhaps that is why he sought out a film accompaniment to his piece in the first place and worked to devise a musical equivalent of the cinematic jump cut.

The Léger film was easily reproducible and portable and could be screened almost anywhere. The Antheil, on the other hand, could not become the provocation it aimed to be without live performance. But that performance was rendered virtually impossible on practical and technological grounds. Unlike the Carnegie Hall revision that required ten live pianists, the first version of *Ballet mécanique*, written in 1924, included four groups of player pianos (the composer indicated that he hoped each group would consist of four pianos!). In 1924 it was impossible to synchronize four, let alone sixteen, player pianos (not until 1999 was a computer-coordinated version performed using Disklaviers).[201] So in 1924, Antheil wrote a piece whose genre was obsolete and whose performance was not yet realizable technically. His ambivalence about the "beauty and danger" of the machine (and all it represents) was far more than a matter of personal opinion. Rather, it constituted both the social and technological truth of the piece, its medium poised between a once-glorious past and an unimaginable future.

REFLECTING EARLIER TIMES

The performance of John Alden Carpenter's *Skyscrapers* at the Met in 1926 represented a rear-guard action, an attempt to enliven and renew an old-fashioned form using contemporary musical and theatrical vernaculars. The ballet was up-to-date in its subject matter but looked to the past for its musical rhetoric. It is, like so many examples of symphonic jazz or jazz-influenced concert music of the 1920s, an encounter between highbrow and lowbrow that took up a volatile position in the cultural hierarchy. With the ballet sandwiched between Puccini's *Gianni Schicchi* and Leoncavallo's *I Pagliacci* at New York's most prestigious venue, its makers were attempting, like Gershwin, to enrich and contemporize European musical and theatrical genres by using American vernaculars more authentically than Europeans ever could. They had succeeded, moreover, in producing a ballet that, like *Petrushka*, took a popular theater tradition as subject matter. (Although verismo rather than modernist, *Pagliacci*, about an itinerant commedia dell'arte troupe, also incorporates snatches of vernacular into an elite form.) In analyzing the programmatic works of Stravinsky and his followers, Adorno writes that the "affinity to ballet is no accident in these scores." Works like *Krazy Kat* or *Skyscrapers* represent a kind of dramatic music (as opposed to the absolute music Adorno champions) "that fulfills its function in contexts other than musical." To be fully understood, they require an extramusical narrative or mise-en-scène. Adorno argues that this parasitism effectively reduces dramatic or program music to background music. Deploying his own idiosyncratic version of modernist antitheatricalism, he condemns these genres, finding them "tailor-made for the administered world."[202] If Adorno is to be believed, *Skyscrapers* may set itself up as a relief from and even a cure for the administered, mass-pro-duced world, but ends up rendering it ubiquitous and engendering, in the viewer, to borrow one critic's word, "despair."[203]

Unlike *Skyscrapers, Ballet mécanique* is neither parasitic nor narrative. It is no more a ballet than Strindberg's *The Ghost Sonata* and Tolstoy's *Kreutzer Sonata* are musical compositions. It does not offer a cure for the administered world. On the contrary, Antheil's provocation redoubles and literally hammers home the brutality of a machine-crazy era. Although he described it as a "mad, youthful prank," Antheil also told Mrs. Bok that the piece was "utterly representative of a very interesting period in the world's history."[204] William Carlos Williams recognized the seriousness of the piece and extolled *Ballet mécanique*'s mastery of a new world of noise: "Antheil had taken this hated thing life and rigged himself into power over it by his music."[205] But this attempt to outbatter a battered world was not un-derstood in New York, and the composer was laughed out of town. When he returned to Paris, however, he discovered that his neoclassical Piano Concerto No. 2 had also met with disfavor and incurred the indifference of Ezra Pound: "I am not particularly interested in anything you have done since Ballet Mechanique."[206] He was no longer the darling of Paris. His stock having fallen precipitously, Antheil turned to writing more conven-tionally neoclassical, dramatic music based on American subjects for a more conventional lyric theater. His opera *Transatlantic*, about a U.S. pres-idential election, was a succès d'estime in Frankfurt in 1930, but with the rise of Hitler (and withdrawal of the generous financial support of Mrs. Bok), Antheil and his wife headed back to the United States, finally settling in Hollywood in 1936. Having to support himself for the first time, the composer split his time between writing Hollywood scores (he wrote over fifty for film and television) and concert music, including American na-tionalist, neoromantic program music, and symphonies numbers three through six, many of whose movements have titles that reference U.S. per-sons, places, or events and use local musical vernaculars. He also became an essayist of no mean accomplishment, writing his memoir; contributing es-says to *Esquire* on current affairs, romance, and endocrinology(!); and writ-ing a nationally syndicated, lonely hearts column, "Boy Advises Girl."[207] During World War II, he undertook with the actress Hedy Lamarr to de-velop a design for a radio-directed torpedo that they successfully patented in 1941.

John Alden Carpenter reached the zenith of his career with *Skyscrapers* and though he continued to write into the 1940s, his star, thereafter, also began to fall. His late-nineteenth-century sensibility put him increasingly at odds with twentieth-century musical modernism. Virgil Thomson called his 1942 Second Symphony "comfortable, intelligent, [and] well organized" with "little in it to remember."[208] But perhaps Thomson's most damning judgment—"It is rich man's music, gentleman's composition"—helped, Pollack notes, to "shape the composer's postwar reputation," which has never recovered. Unlike Antheil, Carpenter, the dominant U.S. composer of concert music and ballet during the 1920s, has virtually disappeared from music history, in part because, Pollack observes, "Charles Ives overtook Carpenter" during the 1940s as "the preeminent American composer of their generation."[209] With a kind of nostalgic regret, John Tasker Howard and George Kent Bellows wrote in 1957, six years after Carpenter's death, that he was "once called . . . the most American of composers" and had succeeded "in drawing attention to the American composer and getting European performances and commissions." Although Howard had celebrated Carpenter only sixteen years earlier (in *Our Contemporary Composers* [1941]), he and Bellows effectively wrote his musical obituary: "Today many musicians feel that Carpenter's works are superficial and merely reflect an earlier era, but in his time he was an important musical figure."[210]

A very different fate, however, has befallen Antheil. "It is difficult to take Antheil seriously," Howard noted in 1941, convinced that the bad boy of music was a washed-up charlatan, crank, and opportunist. But Howard's most derisive observation followed: "Hollywood has taken him seriously enough to pay him to write music for the films."[211] Antheil, in other words, sold out what little integrity he had possessed. Dismissed and nearly forgotten in the years after *Ballet mécanique*, Antheil managed to incur the derision of the musical establishment and even a theater critic like George Jean Nathan, who branded him an "inferior artist."[212] Unlike Carpenter, however, who has more or less disappeared into the black hole of music history, Antheil has since his death attracted more and more interest and scholarship. Although quantity is not necessarily an index of cultural import, the *New Grove* (1980) entry on Antheil is twice the length as that on Carpenter.[213] In their histories of U.S. music, both Charles Hamm (1983) and Kyle Gann (1997) devote eight times as much text to Antheil as to Carpenter.[214] In another comprehensive survey, Gilbert Chase (1987) discusses Antheil in some detail, while Carpenter does not even merit a reference.[215]

The difference between the fates of Carpenter and Antheil attests to the problems that arise in canonizing American modernism. For the very qualities that ensured the popularity of the former worked against him in the long run, while the infamy of the latter has proven a mark in his favor. This disparity is in part a result of the rise of a neo-avant-garde after World War II that included John Cage, Merce Cunningham, the Living Theatre, and countless others who can be seen as Antheil's successors. Aesthetic radicalism promptly became much more highly prized than it had been during the Depression and the war, the heyday of a leftist populist nationalism (as epitomized by the Copland ballets *Billy the Kid* [1938], *Rodeo* [1942], and *Appalachian Spring* [1944] and Thornton Wilder's *Our Town* [1938]). Since the 1960s, the interwar avant-garde has become of much greater interest to scholars, producers, curators, and administrators than the conservative modernism of a John Alden Carpenter or Maxwell Anderson. These changes in taste are in part a function of the changing contours of the fields in question. The consecration of the postwar neo-avant-garde made the search for precursors an urgent concern of critics and scholars. This search has benefited figures like Antheil and revived interest in the more experimental and jazz-inflected early works of artists like Aaron Copland, John Howard Lawson, and Langston Hughes. This search has also required a reappraisal of art long associated with primitivism, blackface, and minstrelsy. With the decline of black cultural nationalism since the 1970s, many embarrassing and formerly suppressed remnants of racist cultures have been, if not exactly reclaimed, at least reexamined (in works like Spike Lee's *Bamboozled* [2000]).

The denigration of John Alden Carpenter and rehabilitation of George Antheil are also linked to the continuing contraction of the field of so-called classical music in the United States. As the field has shrunk, the music of a composer like Carpenter, which, even in its heyday, appealed to more conservative upper-middlebrow-class fractions, has been seen as having little more than antiquarian interest. (This development is especially unfortunate for *Skyscrapers*, which would make a splendid addition to the repertoire of the New York Philharmonic.) Antheil's music, on the other hand, which during the 1920s decisively separated the upper-middlebrow sheep from the avant-gardist goats, continues to spark interest. All three versions of *Ballet mécanique* have been recorded, and a 2006 PBS special devoted to Antheil featured a reconstruction and performance of the first version of the piece. Although Carpenter's music was recorded by some celebrated musicians during the 1920s and 1930s, Antheil's has benefited from a spate of recent recordings.[216]

The divergent fates of Antheil and Carpenter suggest that it is impossible to foresee how canons will be constructed. For contemporary musicologists, Antheil marks an important step in the legitimation of an American yet cosmopolitan avant-gardism that did not, however, fully establish itself until after World War II. Carpenter, on the other hand, marks the end of a tradition that enjoyed no noteworthy progeny or renaissance. It is worth bearing in mind, however, that both composers were able to prosper (and to contrive their particular mixtures of jazz and concert music) only because of their relative financial independence. Although Carpenter's inherited wealth relieved him of financial pressures, his social status, as Virgil Thomson argued, perhaps dictated a conservative frame of mind and musical style. Antheil, on the other hand, was in a more precarious position. Coming from a petit bourgeois family, he could not benefit from his social position and so sought out a rich benefactor. In order to encourage the generosity of Mrs. Bok, he "inundated" her with "letters discussing his works" and "compositional aesthetics" and provided her with evidence of his productivity, success, and renown. But because she had "conservative musical tastes," he had to walk a fine line.[217] Although he wanted to make a name for himself as the bad boy of music, Antheil also felt a need to make his way into and through the musical establishment and, indeed, to have his work performed in prestigious venues, like Wigmore Hall, the Théâtre des Champs-Elysées, and Carnegie Hall. He was unable, in other words, to follow through with one of the most important principles of avant-gardism, which is the criticism and sabotage of "art as an institution," of the "productive and distributive apparatus" that underwrites bourgeois art.[218] Although this could be interpreted as his fatal mistake, Antheil, like so many bourgeois avant-gardists, ended up depending upon the generosity of the very people and institutions he wanted to destroy.

The establishment of a jazz cosmopolitanism in the years after World War I meant that, for the first time, European artists, critics, and cultural consumers carefully attended to and absorbed a musical vernacular that came from the United States, a vernacular, moreover, that had modernity stamped upon it. The dissemination of jazz and the development of a generation of modernist artists who could cross the Atlantic with ease opened the door for Americans working in other media: painting, novels, poetry, and even theater. Unlike music, however, plays need to be translated. Unlike novels, which also require translation, plays need to be staged. The success of European—and later, American—expressionism with Theatre Guild audiences proved that educated and relatively prosperous fractions of the middle class could warm to certain trends in European modernism. This development was complemented in western Europe by a growing appetite among elite audiences for U.S. plays that expressed Jazz Age thrills and anxieties—though without stooping to incorporate jazz music. Eugene O'Neill was the man who at long last enabled the American theater to get into the export business.

SEVEN

THE CANONIZATION OF EUGENE O'NEILL

Without criticism, art would of course still be art, and so with its windows walled in and with its lights extinguished would the Louvre still be the Louvre. Criticism is the windows and chandeliers of art: it illuminates the enveloping darkness in which art might otherwise rest only vaguely discernible, and perhaps altogether unseen.

—George Jean Nathan, *The Critic and the Drama* (1922)

There was in the days of Woodrow Wilson in the village of Provincetown, the Players. It begat Susan Glaspell, Robert Edmond Jones, Eugene O'Neill, and many others who, legend has it, created the American theater. The Provincetown Players was born one night in 1915 when a small group of cultural and political progressives summering on Cape Cod gave an impromptu performance of two new plays, *Suppressed Desires* by George Cram Cook and Susan Glaspell and *Constancy* by Neith Boyce. The rest, as they say, is history: "This was the beginning of the Provincetown Players and, in effect, the beginning of modern American drama."[1]

When Daniel J. Watermeier asserts that "the New York stage was set, even primed, for O'Neill's theatrical ascent," he is correct insofar as the producers and administrators of the nonprofit theaters in concert with a group of young playwrights, designers, and critics had set out very deliberately to "revolutionize the theatre," in the words of an editorial in the first issue of *Theatre Arts* magazine.[2] As I have argued, this was less a purely altruistic, self-abnegating campaign for a drama of consequence than a response to the changing shape of the cultural field in the United States and, in particular, to the overwhelming popularity of vaudeville, cinema, and cabarets. Consciously or unconsciously, these men and women understood that the legitimate theater could not compete with these amusements and so needed to remake the entertainments it produced in order to appeal to well-educated, politically liberal, upper- and middle-class fractions said to be "awake artistically and intellectually."[3]

The campaign to elevate, purify, and "revolutionize" the theater was less an economic and political insurgency (like the one being conducted contemporaneously by the Industrial Workers of the World and the Socialist Party of America) than a religious one, a crusade to drive the infidels out of the Holy Land, that is, Broadway. The discourse used in so many of the early documents related to the Provincetown Players and the other little theaters is shot through with sacred metaphors, intimations, and tropes. Although the theologies range from a Hellenistic pantheism to Roman Catholicism, virtually all the young radicals seemed to believe they had a sacred calling, even if this calling was tied to a post-Nietzschean skepticism about established religion and (even) God. Referencing the Judeo-Christian messianic tradition, they sought an artist who would be a redeemer and savior. In their theology, art came to substitute for God, or rather, art became the most exalted conduit for the revelation of intimations of divinity. (Although not aspiring to elite cultural status, like the plays of the Provincetown Players, Samson Raphaelson's *The Jazz Singer* quite precisely dramatizes this process of substitution as well as the fears, anxieties, and pleasures attendant upon the renunciation of faith.) As revolutionaries, the advocates for an art theater looked for inspiration back to holy wars, especially the Crusades, which pitted believers against heretics, persons of European descent against assorted racial, cultural, and (as they would say) spiritual others.

Among the many examples of this discourse, a manifesto of the Provincetown Players' (attributed to Cook) sets forth its aim of re-creating "the communal or religious life" of the "primitive" and "organic human group" in order to restore "a spiritual unity" that reflected the "unity of a pure art."[4] Hutchins Hapgood, one of the founders, declares that the group's plays were "written in a pure spirit," while another early chronicler relates how the Players based their mission on "faith" and the belief that their work had the power to "touch the uttermost depths of material things."[5] I would suggest that this use of religious discourse assisted the so-called art theater in engineering its speedy consecration and that of its saint, demi-God, messiah—take your pick—Eugene O'Neill. Indeed, his almost instantaneous canonization was historically unprecedented. Never before had a U.S. playwright been consecrated so hastily (by 1920, the year of his first Broadway production and Pulitzer Prize), in a critical idiom that has to this day remained remarkably consistent.

The word *canon*, John Guillory notes, was first used in the fourth century C.E. "to signify a list of texts and authors" that early Christian theologians deemed sacred. This "principle of selection" was crucial for reinforcing "the standards of their religious community," codifying what were judged to be the essential truths of Christianity, and most important, "distinguishing the orthodox from the heretical."[6] It was in the late eighteenth century, however, with the breakdown of systems of patronage; the rise of markets for art, music, and literature; the growth of a commercial theater; and the consolidation of bourgeois standards of decorum and taste, that canonization became secularized. Canonization was reconfigured as a process designed to guide the production, distribution, and especially, the consumption of artworks with an eye to what deserved to be immortalized. During the nineteenth century, it became more and more closely linked to the mythologization of the cultural as an autonomous field unconstrained by political or economic forces and the concurrent rise of the purportedly autonomous, visionary artist. Yet as has often been pointed out, canonization is not a mystical but a historical process. It represents an itinerary of cultural legitimation that privileges and excludes certain kinds of texts as well as their makers and consumers; it constructs cultural hierarchies; it tries to sublimate and etherealize the commercial character of art; and it establishes aesthetic, ideological, and moral values and standards that masquerade as disinterested and universal. But the process of canonization is more than a series of feints or an illustration of bad faith. It also consolidates musical, literary, and theatrical forms and vernaculars; it produces a genealogical history that often proves useful for constructing nations, social classes, and other forms of collective (and individual) identity; and it helps to shape, and is shaped by, the markets for literature, music, theater, painting, and other forms of artistic production.

Although canonization does not qualify as a conspiracy, it more often than not functions as a tool of domination. Bourdieu points out that despite the claims of the arbiters of taste, artistic values (like all symbolic systems) are finally arbitrary because there can be no absolute or universal scale of cultural signification and excellence. But the arbitrary nature of cultural values does not mean, David Swartz notes, that these values are "at all arbitrary in their social consequences." Standards and canons function "to differentiate and legitimate inegalitarian and hierarchical arrangements among individuals and groups."[7] But they are effective as modes of categorization only insofar as they direct collective belief. Because the "fields of cultural production are universes of belief," the signature of the canonical author or playwright is invested with a "quasi-magical potency."[8] Indeed, Bourdieu repeatedly emphasizes the analogy between the artistic field and the religious field.[9] (What, after all, is the difference between a pilgrimage to Lourdes and one to Stratford-Upon-Avon? Are they not both shrines to deities who command wide belief? And are not consecrated writers, from Homer to Beckett, still imagined as the high priests of high culture?)

For Bourdieu, canonization is the product of what he calls symbolic violence, a form of manipulation (through language and other symbolic systems) which disguises and dissimulates the power exercised through it. "The establishment of a canon in the guise of a universally valued cultural inheritance," Randal Johnson notes, "constitutes an act of 'symbolic violence,'" that gains legitimacy by concealing "the underlying power relations."[10] Symbolic violence is not, like larceny, for example, a discrete, deliberate, and premeditated act. Rather, it is the inevitable by-product of the operation of systems that classify through the operation of binary oppositions in which one term (e.g., man, white, heterosexual) is privileged at the expense of its supposed contrary (e.g., woman, black, homosexual). All symbolic systems function by grouping persons and properties into opposing classes and they engender meanings and values through a "binary logic of inclusion and exclusion."[11] This logic is indispensable for the operation of canons and hierarchies because the latter always discriminate, Bourdieu notes, between "high (sublime, elevated, pure) and low (vulgar, low, modest), spiritual and material, fine (refined, elegant) and coarse (heavy, fat, crude, brutal), . . . unique (rare, different, distinguished, exclusive, exceptional, singular, novel) and common (ordinary, banal, commonplace, trivial, routine)." These systems of value "find such ready acceptance," he writes, "because behind them lies the whole social order." Yet his simple formulation belies the gravity of his conclusion: this symbolic "network has its ultimate source in the opposition between the 'élite' of the dominant and the 'mass' of the dominated."[12] In other words, canons of taste are structured by a symbolic violence that rationalizes and perpetuates social inequalities. (The exercise of symbolic violence is especially evident in the criticism of the terror of the age, George Jean Nathan.)

The construction of theatrical canons is no innocent occupation, the easy separation of the good from the bad, the timeless from the trivial. Nor is it merely an exercise in brute force. Bourdieu emphasizes that the meaning and consequence of works of art are always mediated by the structure of the fields in which they are positioned.[13] These fields, which designate a relatively circumscribed domain (for example, the legitimate theater or big time vaudeville) have their own laws, conventions, and hierarchies that are only in part dictated by economic imperatives. Although they may owe their most salient characteristics to the class interests they express, they are also always subject to "the specific logic of the field[s] of production" in which they are situated.[14] And cultural practices are always positioned simultaneously in many different fields. In the case, for example, of the original 1920 Broadway production of O'Neill's *The Emperor Jones* these would include nonprofit theater, art theater, the serious Broadway play, minstrelsy, African American performance, and middle-class bohemianism, among many others, each of which could be further broken down into subfields.

An analysis of how a play is canonized is especially difficult because the production process, from first rehearsal to published script, requires so many artists, middlemen, and consumers and participates in so many different fields, each with its own laws and hierarchies. As I have pointed out, theatrical forms during the 1920s were vigilantly hierarchized with the legitimate theater at the top, vaudeville, burlesque, and cabaret at the bottom, and musical comedy somewhere in the middle. The process of canonization worked to consolidate and legitimize this hierarchy, to invent a literary-dramatic tradition, and to construct a genealogy of native drama and literature. (The more highbrow the medium, the greater the need and drive for canonization.) Then, as now, the agents involved in the process of canonization could be divided into six not quite discrete groups:

Creators: playwrights and composers, those whose work could be copyrighted.

Owners of the means of production: producers and theater owners.

Artistic associates: directors, designers, actors, and production staffs.

Administrative middlemen: administrators, tour managers, press agents, the Dramatists Guild, and Actors' Equity.

Distributors: play, trade, and music publishers, record companies, and radio networks.

Consumers: the press, academic critics and historians, the Pulitzer Prize and other awards committees, and of course spectators, readers, and listeners.

Despite the many agents involved in the process of canonization, a handful of critics often become decisive as mediators, referees who manage the sweepstakes that leads to the consecration of the lucky (or cunning) few and the relegation of the vast majority to the margins of cultural history or oblivion. These critics, however, are subject to evolving standards of taste every bit as much as the work they evaluate and re-evaluate. Indeed, the histories of styles, forms, or genres can never transcend their moments of composition. Canonical genealogies are constructed with an eye to what happens to be valued at the time they are written in the belief that the past worth consecrating somehow contains and prefigures the present. Some producers, subjugated from the start, never even enter the sweepstakes, at least not initially. Writers and performers of vaudeville and jazz (whether hot or sweet) and playwrights like John Howard Lawson were regarded during the 1920s either as purveyors of a disposable, popular art or as iconoclasts attempting to overturn canons of taste and pervert the genres they employ. Because they were positioned outside (or on the edge of) legitimate musical and theatrical traditions, it was inconceivable that they could even aspire to canonical status. And although many leading jazz musicians of the 1920s were in fact consecrated after World War II when jazz was refashioned into serious art, John Howard Lawson, unlike George Antheil, never recovered from his notoriety and has vanished from the boards.

For producers working in more certifiably highbrow genres, the persistent remapping of cultural hierarchies means that canonization can never be entirely predictable; what is esteemed one moment may be scorned the next. Among legitimate producers, some, like George Kelly or John Alden

Carpenter, were admired during their lifetimes but then fell, some more speedily than others, into obscurity. Others, like George S. Kaufman or George Gershwin, could gain entrance to the canon by surviving and triumphing over their adulation by the bourgeois multitude and their patronization by the arbiters of high culture. Others, like Sophie Treadwell or George Antheil, could be marginalized during their heyday only to be hailed decades later as revolutionists and prophets. Eugene O'Neill or Igor Stravinsky exemplify a fourth and even smaller group of playwrights, composers, and writers who were so widely and deeply esteemed by intellectual elites during their lifetimes that canonization seemed—and proved to be—preordained.

The differences among these models are a result of the precarious relationship between economic and cultural capital. Virtually all now-canonical modernist art sought, at least when it was made, to distance itself from the marketplace through a denunciation of the mercenary compromises it insisted characterized commercial or popular art.[15] Producers and distributors were prepared to renounce economic capital temporarily in favor of cultural and symbolic capital in the expectation that it would lead in the long run to greater profits. (A mere glance at the current market value of a Picasso oil or a T. S. Eliot first edition will demonstrate how lucrative this strategy proved.) The little theaters, like the Provincetown Players, found it advantageous to disseminate the fantasy that they had utterly transcended the sordid marketplace: they had "no regard for fame, money, or power," no interest in "so-called success"; they never endeavored to treat their audience as "the petted object"; and for them, "[p]ublicity was healthfully and beautifully scorned."[16] (Does not their missionary zeal betray their repressed desire for the power they scorned?) Even after the Players started to transfer work to Broadway, trading in symbolic for economic capital, they tried to maintain this anticommercial (and anti-mass-cultural) pose because it proved to be the surest path in a market economy to the consecration of their theater as a handmade, highbrow art.

Bourdieu emphasizes that the consecration of art is inextricably linked to the prospects of those who produce discourse about it. "Every critical affirmation," he writes,

> contains, on the one hand, a recognition of the value of the work which occasions it, which is thus designated as a worthy object of legitimate discourse, . . . and on the other hand an affirmation of its own legiti-

macy. All critics declare not only their judgement of the work but also their claim to the right to talk about it and judge it. In short, they take part in a struggle for the monopoly of legitimate discourse about the work of art.[17]

Every critical appraisal—and this is especially true of reviews addressed to potential ticket buyers—must assert either explicitly or (more likely) implicitly the expertise of the critic and demonstrate his or her credentials, wisdom, and powers of discernment. The critic must earn the right to judge; he or she must inspire belief in the congregation every bit as much as the artist or the priest.

In the second and third decades of the twentieth century, a new generation of theater critics emerged that was more professionalized, erudite, and sophisticated than its predecessors. It marked a sharp break with earlier critics who, Thomas Connolly notes, fell into two camps, "anonymous puffsters and scholarly, genteel types."[18] The new critics, like their fellow literary modernists, rejected Victorian mores, were unapologetically progressive, and championed European innovations. They also began to encourage U.S. playwrights to write in a style deemed to be distinctively American. Glenn Hughes asserts that "the rise of American criticism" during the twenties was as startling as "the sudden development of American playwriting."[19] It is telling that he should link the two events since playwrights and critics of the 1920s often acted like collaborators. Indeed, they enjoyed a level of symbiosis that was unprecedented in U.S. theatrical culture. O'Neill's success would have been unthinkable without the support and adulation of critics like George Jean Nathan, Brooks Atkinson, and Alexander Woollcott. Similarly, the preeminence of these critics was due in large part to the fact that they promptly and fortuitously affixed their critical reputation to O'Neill's star. They were the ones, after all, who proved their powers of discrimination by claiming to have discovered that O'Neill was "the one dramatic genius that America has produced."[20] Generating self-fulfilling prophesies, they called into being that which they professed merely to be describing.

The older, genteel tradition that was displaced by the 1920s is best exemplified by William Winter (1836–1917), critic for the *New York Tribune* from 1865 until his death and "the most highly respected, and the most widely read theatrical critic in the United States."[21] A patrician, Harvard Law School–educated New Englander, Winter was a stern moralist who wrote a shelf full of books about celebrated actors. He prized English and continental classical drama far more than the new plays that were being imported from Europe, awash as they were with "weakness and sin."[22] Typical of his style was his 1891 admonition to expectant mothers about Sarah Bernhardt's performances in Sardou's *La Tosca*, which, he warned, would be "not only shocking to the nervous system and grossly offensive to persons of true sensibility, but which might . . . inflict irreparable injury on persons yet unborn."[23] Although it is easy to ridicule the puritanical Winter, his attitudes were emblematic of the genteel upper classes to whom the Europeanized literary theater catered and who wanted not subjective, essayistic reviews but, in the words of a contemporary, guides to "the general taste, with its direction and correction."[24]

The key transitional figure between Winter and the full-fledged modernists was James Gibbons Huneker (1860–1921), a Philadelphian who first pursued a career in law before studying piano at the Sorbonne. Beginning in 1891, he wrote theater, music, and art reviews for several New York newspapers, including the *Sun* and the *Times*. Huneker wrote twenty-two books on an extraordinary array of subjects and was hailed at his death as "the Last of the Bohemians." Because he lived during a period of rapidly changing standards, he was able to pioneer a form of criticism that was more essayistic, subjective, and analytical than what had come before in the United States.[25] Unlike Winter, Huneker was a great admirer of Baudelaire, Wagner, and Nietzsche and was able to defend work, like Ibsen's, that "perplex[ed] a spectator's perceptions of good and evil."[26] *Iconoclasts* (1905), his one book on drama, contains insightful examinations (despite its purple prose) of the major European modernist playwrights, including Ibsen, Strindberg, Maeterlinck, and Shaw. Although Huneker was never a strong advocate for a school of U.S. playwriting, he was a close friend and great supporter of younger colleagues like George Jean Nathan who eulogized him as the man who "made possible civilized criticism in this great prosperous prairie" and "taught us cosmopolitanism, and love of life, and the crimson courage of youth."[27] Most important, Huneker cultivated one of the modernist critics' signal attributes, a distinctive personal style perhaps best captured in H. L. Mencken's description of his "talk": "it was chaos made to gleam and coruscate with every device of the seven arts—chaos drenched in all the colors imaginable."[28] This lesson about turning chaos to diamonds was not lost on Nathan, his star pupil.

The emergence of new printing technologies (linotype machines, high-speed printing presses, and rotogravure) at the end of the nineteenth century revolutionized the publishing of magazines and newspapers. Low-cost magazine subscriptions multiplied exponentially, while advertising revenues increased fivefold between 1900 and 1920.[29] These developments helped pave the way for Huneker's children, a generation of theater critics, most of them born in the 1880s, committed to an American modernism. Most were Ivy League–educated, upper-middle-class men (and a few women) intent on discovering and promoting an elevated theater that would provide an American answer to European modernism. Some began their careers working for regional publications, but all ended up writing for either the major New York newspapers or national publications. The most influential tastemakers included Brooks Atkinson (1894–1984), drama critic for the *New York Times* from 1926 until 1960 (except for overseas assignments during and after World War II); Robert Benchley (1889–1939); Heywood Broun (1888–1939); Barrett H. Clark (1890–1953), O'Neill's first biographer; Walter Prichard Eaton (1878–1957), chronicler of the Theatre Guild and George Pierce Baker's successor at Yale; Percy Hammond (1873–1936), *New York Tribune* critic during the 1920s; and Alexander Woollcott (1887–1943), Atkinson's predecessor at the *Times* and member of the Algonquin Round Table.

All these critics, with the exception of Brooks Atkinson, were dwarfed by one figure, the "dean of the critical circle," George Jean Nathan (1882–1958), notorious for his irreverence, worldliness, and caustic wit.[30] Raised in an affluent, middle-class, Jewish household in Fort Wayne, Indiana (his father was a liquor wholesaler), Nathan was particularly adept at rewriting his past in order to style himself an intellectual, dandy, bon vivant, and, in Atkinson's words, the "most flamboyant and the most reckless critic" of his age.[31] Fabricating an upper-class pedigree for himself and studiously denying his Jewish roots, he fashioned an arch persona, complete with "long cigarette holders that could be flicked daintily, a patrician walk, and a formidable manner."[32] And he seemed to relish inventing the most outrageous lies. He maintained that his father owned a vineyard in France and a coffee plantation in Brazil, and although he graduated from a public high school and attended Cornell University, he claimed he had acquired a master's degree from the University of Bologna ("University of Baloney"— get it?).[33] He began working as a critic in 1905 for the *New York Herald* and in 1909 started writing for *Smart Set*, "a cult publication among young intellectuals."[34] Between 1914 and 1924 he served as coeditor (with H. L.

Mencken) of *Smart Set*—which awarded O'Neill his first high-status publication credit—and was able for the first time, Connolly notes, to focus on the theater and pontificate upon "the function of a drama critic."[35] Although he authored over forty books and wrote at one time or another for virtually every major U.S. publication, he did not, except at the very beginning of his career, work as a daily critic. He much preferred writing for weeklies or monthlies in part because this schedule allowed him to review the reviewers. Indeed, critics were as likely to be his whipping boys as playwrights. Having labored to turn his life into a piece of theater and style himself an authority on everything, Nathan is reputed to have provided the model for the reptilian Addison DeWitt in Joseph L. Mankiewicz's *All About Eve* (1950).

Although the critics of the 1920s represented a diverse lot, they were successful in engineering the elevation—and retrenchment—of the legitimate stage. Because most were Ivy League–educated sophisticates who came from the upper reaches of the middle classes, they were suitable spokespersons for the affluent fractions of the theater audience that sat downstairs. But because they were also modernist intellectuals who represented a dominated fraction of the middle class, they were fit deputies for the more bohemian but much less well-heeled audience fractions that sat upstairs. These critics were thus well positioned to be the arbiters of taste for a respectable literary theater newly dissociated from the gewgaws of Broadway and Hollywood. And despite the variations among them—as well as the differences between the predispositions of the downstairs and upstairs crowds—the critics succeeded in championing the very characteristics that made Eugene O'Neill the emblem of the American modernist stage. Indeed, they always managed to discover in him the very qualities they sought. When one reads the reviews of O'Neill's plays from the 1920s, one finds certain words repeated over and over: sincerity, honesty, dignity, intrepidity, depth, tragedy, universality. These were the qualities on which a highbrow literary drama had to be based.

The consecration of the legitimate theater during the 1920s and the policing of generic boundaries were a boon not only to playwrights and producers. Because the legitimate stage could no longer be valued merely as an agreeable public amusement and because the significance of the challenging, new drama was no longer immediately evident to all onlookers, an army of experts was required to interpret the plays and separate the good from the bad, the profound from the shallow. Nathan considered art "a partnership" between artist and critic. Because "everything truly beautiful" represents "something mysterious and disconcerting," criticism is "essential to the interpretation of [art's] mysteries."[36] Because good taste, moreover, was no longer regarded as a universal property, the anonymous review went the way of the horse and buggy. The new critics discovered they could win readers not by appealing to "the general taste" but by cultivating distinctive styles, points of view, and colorful prose. For the first time, Connolly writes, theater critics were becoming celebrities in their own right as "articles about critics and their habits" became much more common.[37] Nathan insisted that "criticism is itself an art," or rather, "an art within an art," and he preferred the term *artist-critic* to the pedestrian *critic*.[38] Indeed, the young "artist-critics" of the 1920s often seemed to be trying to outclass each other to prove their brilliance and powers of discernment by paying humble yet sagacious obeisance to a great play and writing wickedly clever circles around a bad one. Of course, in laboring to institutionalize a new theatrical and critical dispensation, these critics were also working to safeguard their livelihoods by effectively canonizing themselves. Had they failed to secure a distinctive niche for a literary theater, they would have been out of a job.

THE PLAY AS WRITTEN IS THE THING

Eugene O'Neill's critics have often pointed out the unintentional similarities between his plays and the behemoth that devoured the career of his father, James O'Neill. The elder O'Neill bought the rights to *The Count of Monte Cristo* in 1883 and played the role of its hero, Edmond Dantès, more than six thousand times before his retirement in 1912. Despite his son's rebellious assumption of a radically different aesthetic, there are striking correspondences between Charles Fechter's stage adaptation of Alexandre Dumas *père's* 1844 novel and the plays by Eugene O'Neill (1888–1953). The latter's use of plot points, type characters, dramatic structures, rhetorical patterns, sensational curtain lines, asides, soliloquies, coups de théâtre, and so on, owes more than a little to nineteenth-century melodrama and to *Monte Cristo*, in particular.[39] In an early critique of the playwright, Virgil Geddes argues that O'Neill's plays repeatedly evince what he calls "melodramadness." They "do not grow slowly," he notes, "but spread quickly with the decidedly limited and bursting effect of a bombshell." He maintains that this "explosive method" persists in his work, a method that "has long been characteristic of the lower practices of the theatre," that is, melodrama.[40] Although O'Neill went to great lengths to deny the link between his dramaturgy and that of his father's creaky moneymaker, he was even more determined to disavow the connections between his plays and the popular theatrical and musical vernaculars of his own time, especially vaudeville.

James O'Neill's swansong as Edmond Dantès undermined the already slender difference between swashbuckling melodrama and vaudeville in part because the elder O'Neill ended his career playing the vaudeville circuit. Of course, by the end of the nineteenth century, melodrama and vaudeville had become associated because of their unapologetically crowd-pleasing stances and their use of episodic structures, musical interludes, and songs. Melodrama, moreover, frequently incorporated comic routines just as vaudeville did melodramatic skits and one-act plays. Although melodrama did at least pretend to have a plot to knit its episodes together, both genres were unabashedly performer-centered and continually appealed directly across the footlights for the tears and laughter of an audience that was more likely to be working or lower middle class than upper class. In 1911, during the waning days of melodrama, the sixty-five-year old James O'Neill was unable to secure a legitimate theater in which to continue to play the part of *Monte Cristo*'s young, athletic hero. But he was able to obtain a booking with the not exactly highbrow Orpheum Circuit to present a version cut down from four acts to a forty-five minute sprint in which the young and unemployed Eugene reluctantly participated. Arthur and Barbara Gelb refer to it as "a horribly botched affair" that made the elder O'Neill feel "humiliated," both for its ineptitude and because, as part of a "two-a-day," he had to share the bill with "a trained horse act and a group of flying acrobats."[41] Eugene also felt humiliated and candidly remarked that "the 'general frightfulness' of the production reached 'a high spot in the lousiness of my acting.'" He weathered it, in his words, by "never drawing a sober breath until the tour had terminated."[42] And terminate it did, eighteen weeks early, less because of the performance of the superannuated star than because "Mr. O'Neill's support[ing actors] brought adverse comment all along the line."[43]

Following the ignominious end of James O'Neill's career, the younger O'Neill turned decisively against what he considered archaic commercial theatrical formulas, including vaudeville, which epitomized everything against which Eugene's art theater was rebelling. Yet growing up with *The Count of Monte Cristo*, O'Neill learned his lesson only too well and ended up incorporating—while later disavowing—elements of lowbrow genres. At the beginning of his career as a writer, Eugene O'Neill several times toyed with the vaudeville sketch form. His first foray into playwriting, which he wrote in 1913 after he left the Gaylord Farm Sanatorium (where he was recovering from tuberculosis), was a one-act entitled *A Wife for Life*, which Barrett Clark confirms "was written for the vaudeville stage." Clark reports that O'Neill claimed "it was the worst thing he ever did," and Clark intervenes to declare, perhaps a little too confidently, that it "was the first and last play he ever wrote with his eye altogether on the box office."[44] *A Wife for Life* is a short, quasi-tragic skit about love lost and found that takes place in an Arizona mining camp. Its ending evinces what Heywood Broun called (in reference to *The Emperor Jones*) "a little O. Henry dido," a sudden, surprising, and often sentimental reversal of the kind that O'Neill sometimes uses to conclude scenes or acts.[45] In fact, the play reeks not only of vaudeville, but also of silent film. The very simple, graphic action, coupled with O'Neill's vividly descriptive stage directions, suggests a sentimental version of a western, far and away the most popular (and profitable) of the silent film genres.[46] But this was not O'Neill's last flirtation with vaudeville. He confessed to Clark that one of the "rotten" plays (in O'Neill's words) that he wrote for George Pierce Baker the following year, which he later destroyed, he thought "slick enough for vaudeville" but then discovered he had indeed "stolen" the idea "from a successful vaudeville sketch."[47]

O'Neill's final encounter with the Orpheum Circuit was "the unexpected success of *In the Zone* as a vaudeville vehicle" in 1918. Searching for one-act plays to present as part of a vaudeville package, producers Albert Lewis and Max Gordon were quite taken with *In the Zone*, after having rejected *Bound East for Cardiff* as "too highbrow." O'Neill initially rebuffed their offer because, Lewis said, he "thought the vaudeville proposition was degrading." But, Lewis continued, O'Neill "really needed the money" (he was about to wed Agnes Boulton) and so he agreed to the rather generous offer (two hundred dollars in advance with thirty-five dollars per week in royalties). The play was "an immediate success," "toured for thirty-four weeks," and provided the playwright with his "first 'big' money."[48] Discussing this incident a year later, O'Neill characterized it as an example of all he was trying to abandon. He dismisses *In the Zone* as "the least significant" of his works, too "conventional" and "too full of clever theatrical tricks" (despite the fact that he uses comparable "tricks" in virtually every other play). Its "long run . . . in vaudeville proves conclusively to my mind," he adds, "that there must be 'something rotten in Denmark.'" Taking up the mantle of a melancholy Dane and failing to reference the considerable sum he netted, he maintains that the one-act "in no way represents the true me" and, worse yet, is "lacking" in "spiritual import" and a "big feeling for life." Most damnably, it represents "the theater as it is," not as it should be.[49]

O'Neill repudiated his vaudeville hit at a key moment in his career. *Beyond the Horizon* had just been optioned for Broadway, and he was eager to make his mark as an artist, not a commercial hack. O'Neill's repudiation is also linked to his capitulation to the inverse relation that obtains within modernist culture between economic and symbolic capital. "*In the Zone* had made a hit," Clark notes; "how, therefore, could it be good?"[50] Money and "spiritual import," in other words, are antithetical. The playwright's repudiation also betrays the care that an artist must take to use his or her discourse to police this inverse relation. A culture nervously preoccupied with the elevation of the legitimate theater wants to believe that the playwright's "true," etherealized self will have little use for money. He or she should be able to survive on "spiritual import" alone—or be independently wealthy. In order to produce a suitable vehicle for the spirit, the playwright must either suppress commercial vernaculars or keep them at bay. Vaudeville and melodrama were simply too much of the world—and much too lucrative—to find a place in a highbrow, literary theater. So they had to be repudiated with the right hand while the left hand cleansed them of their populist grime: laughter and tears.

Although there are many ways to examine O'Neill's disavowal of the popular, I want to focus on his use of music. One of the more curious contributions to O'Neill scholarship is *The Eugene O'Neill Songbook*, collected and annotated in 1993 by Travis Bogard. Bogard admits up front that, given the playwright's association "with the darkest shades of melancholy and sorrow," an O'Neill songbook "appears to be a contradiction in terms." But he explains that he began his *Songbook* after receiving requests from directors over the years for the music and lyrics to songs that O'Neill quotes or references in his plays. He soon realized, however, that the songs are not merely incidental but "an aspect of the man" and, as such, deserve careful study.[51] (O'Neill scholarship is rife with work that justifies itself by appeal not to the plays themselves but to the playwright.) Bogard also claims that collecting the songs made him even more aware "that [O'Neill's] works have a theatrical integrity comparable to any musical work." But Bogard, in fact, does not mean *any* musical work. Rather, taking his cue from the playwright, he makes it clear that his analogy is with Western art music, especially the symphony. In the afterword to the *Songbook*, titled "The Play as Symphony," he spins out an elaborate series of metaphorical relations between O'Neill's works and the European symphonic tradition that allegedly demonstrates the plays' ineffably symphonic quality.[52]

Bogard's thesis is questionable at best. Cannot the form of any modernist play—or arguably any play—be analogized to musical form by proving that character equals theme, dramatic development equals musical development, setting equals home key, monologue equals aria (with or without cadenza), and so forth? Cannot the four-part structure of *Hedda Gabler* be analogized to that of Brahms's Fourth Symphony? Does not *The Cherry Orchard* practice a characterological counterpoint every bit as complex as Mahler's musical counterpoint? And while these correspondences may shed some light on the plays in question, I suspect they are more useful for actors and directors than for historians and cultural theorists. So I am not going to try to refute (or endorse) Bogard but analyze the assumptions that underlie both his and O'Neill's discourses about music. One of the most striking features of all these discourses is their repeated appeal not to popular music but to Western art music and in particular to the most exalted of musical genealogies, the Austro-German classical tradition from Haydn and Mozart to Beethoven and Brahms. Interestingly, both Bogard and O'Neill are far more eager to demonstrate the kinship of the plays to symphony than to opera (perhaps because operatic melodrama bears far too many resemblances to O'Neill's plays). Indeed, opera as a genre hardly figures in their discourse. According to Bogard, O'Neill's rather substantial collection of recordings did not include any opera (the closest was Debussy's incidental music for Gabriele d'Annunzio's *Le martyre de Saint Sébastien*). The playwright himself kept reiterating his desire to return to his "old idea of using [the] structure of symphony or sonata," and Bogard approvingly cites the playwright's claim that "nearly all of [his] plays" evince an "unconscious use of musical structure."[53] Both men, in short, were intent on proving O'Neill's highbrow credentials by analogizing his playwriting with the most consecrated musical forms. The critic Richard

Dana Skinner takes this one step further by asserting that the succession of O'Neill's plays produces "a larger unity, almost like the movements of a symphony."[54]

Travis Bogard calculates that twenty-nine of O'Neill's fifty plays use music "in significant ways," and he provides a complete list of the period songs the plays reference, songs O'Neill allegedly "remembered with affection" from his youth.[55] Indeed, O'Neill was scrupulous about choosing music that quite exactly corresponded to the place and time represented in his plays. But because so many of his plays are set in the first years of the twentieth century, virtually all the songs he specifies are turn-of-the-century ballads, folk songs, minstrel songs, coon songs, sea shanties, sentimental tunes, or spirituals. Like most songs of the era, the majority are in 2/4 or 3/4 time and major keys. By way of example, the two songs that open *All God's Chillun Got Wings* (1924), the first sung by the white children, the second by the black, were two of the most popular songs of the turn of the century. The first, "A Bird in a Gilded Cage" (1900), is a sentimental waltz by Harry Von Tilzer (the most notable songwriter of the era) and Arthur J. Lamb and the second, George M. Cohan's first big hit, "I Guess I'll Have to Telegraph My Baby: Coon Song" (1898). The first is described by Charles Hamm as a "graceful waltz," while the heritage of the second is stated in its subtitle. (Tellingly, Bogard omits the song's subtitle from the book.)[56] The latter was a remarkably popular genre in the period from about 1890 to the end of World War I. It was usually sung by white singers at a medium to fast tempo, sometimes featuring syncopation, and, Hamm argues, it represented "the last stage of the minstrel song."[57] The coon song, moreover, "was often performed on the vaudeville stage by white female 'coon shouters'" like May Irwin and Sophie Tucker.[58] "I Guess I'll Have to Telegraph My Baby" is in 2/4 time, sung at a medium fast tempo, and is not syncopated. But this is the not the only coon song in *All God's Chillun*. Scene 3 begins with a similar opposition between white and black, setting Irving Berlin's waltz "When I Lost You" (1912) against another coon song, this time "Waiting for the Robert E. Lee" (1912), also in 2/4 time, by Lewis F. Muir and Wolfe Gilbert. All four songs are in the major mode except "When I Lost You," "a melancholy ballad" that was "an enormous hit," which alternates between modes but ends in the major.[59] Both pairs of songs thus deliberately clash: slow against fast, triple time against double, gentility against urban swagger, and middlebrow against lowbrow.

O'Neill's repeated juxtaposition of sentimental waltz against coon song handily musicalizes the racial clash that is this play's theme. But it is important to note that in order to emblematize his African American characters, O'Neill does not opt for ragtime, a form of syncopated music with a far more confidently African American pedigree than the coon song and one whose heyday exactly corresponds to the period represented in the play. And while there is an undeniable family resemblance between the two genres, and while some African Americans did perform coon songs in turn-of-the-century New York, the playwright's choice is symptomatic of his tendency, when portraying African American characters (like Brutus Jones), to appropriate and modify stereotypes, situations, and songs that come out of the minstrel tradition. Like so many of his European American contemporaries, O'Neill looked to minstrelsy (or remnants and reconfigurations of minstrelsy) in part because it was still the most pervasive and influential set of performance practices associated with black, or blacked, culture in the United States. The difficulty in separating white traditions from black during the 1920s, given the long, intertwined histories of racial mimicry, is attested to by the representational idiom of a musical like *Shuffle Along*.

Yet even a play like *All God's Chillun* is far from a sociological tract, and it uses quaintly archaic musical styles in part to provide historical distance. This distance, moreover, was crucial in ensuring that it was interpreted less as a sociological than a spiritual tract by its defenders, like Skinner, who emphasizes its "symbolic" characters, "universality," and preoccupation with "the problems of the soul."[60] Skinner's reading, like so many other contemporary commendations of O'Neill, suggests that playwright and critics had worked out an unspoken agreement that authorized them to take the local for the universal and sententiousness for "spiritual import." O'Neill could thereby be constructed as an arch-humanist and they as interpreters uniquely poised to recognize truth and beauty. O'Neill's repeated turn to the past supports this view, his use of either the mythical past of *The Fountain* (1925) or *Marco Millions* (1928), or more frequently (as in *All God's Chillun*), a vaguely historical turn of the century. The latter was especially important because it permitted him to sketch a period before World War I had institutionalized the assembly line and before the "science that was to have liberated man," Skinner writes, "turned on and crushed him, . . . shattered him with steel or burned him to pulp with the arts of chemistry."[61] Skinner is therefore correct when he notes that "O'Neill is not, in the accepted sense, a poet of his times," at least not when it comes to the literal settings of his plays.[62] However, the construction of the prewar United States as a prelapsarian paradise is very much a response to the anxieties of the Jazz Age, with its profound ambivalence toward modernization and its nostalgia for a time before the triumph of "steel." Like Skinner, the Lynds, and many other commentators, Bogard in the *O'Neill Songbook* erects a barrier between the early twentieth century represented in the plays, "when people carried music within them and brought it alive into their homes, a time when they tapped their feet and sang or whistled in participation," and the degraded, postwar culture "of the mass" that supposedly superseded it.[63] Bogard's romanticization of the former, a participatory, pre-mass-cultural past in which the production and consumption of culture were not diametrically opposed, neatly corresponds to O'Neill's melancholic idealization of a past that never existed.

Bogard's observations suggest that the playwright's nostalgia was never more powerfully expressed than through music. Bogard describes O'Neill's joy at being given a player piano (which he named Rosie) in 1933 on which he delightedly "pedaled through the old piano rolls."[64] Although his acquisition postdated *The Great God Brown* (1926), O'Neill's account recalls his description of the player piano at Cybel's parlor, which "bang[s] out a sentimental medley of 'Mother—Mammy' tunes,'" that is, coon songs.[65] "There sure must have been," O'Neill wrote about Rosie, "an artist soul lost to the world in the New Orleans honky-tonk or bordello she came from."[66] Like so many nostalgic discourses, his turns the player piano into a souvenir of an age that has vanished irretrievably. It also attests to a double loss, the loss of the congenial, privatized public space of the brothel and that of the "artist soul" that once haunted it and has been even more sadly misplaced. In constructing an empty present and full past, O'Neill's nostalgia is the distinctively modernist one that Svetlana Boym describes as "a mourning for the impossibility of mythical return, for the loss of an enchanted world with clear borders and values; it could be . . . a nostalgia for an absolute, . . . the edenic unity of time and space before entry into history."[67] And O'Neill, like so many modernists, held out the possibility that music was uniquely capable of conjuring this fantasy of a prelapsarian past.

O'Neill, however, was very particular about the kind of music to which he would grant the power of nostalgic evocation. Bogard extols the playwright's affection for modernist classics by de Falla, Ravel, and Debussy, as well as his "love for popular music," including "jazz and folk music." Bogard testifies that O'Neill's record collection included many turn-of-the-century albums as well as calypso music, "Songs of the South" (coon songs?), "New Orleans Jazz," songs by Bessie Smith and Louis Armstrong, and many other kinds of popular music.[68] O'Neill's virtual banishment of popular music, that is, jazz, from his plays was due, then, not to lack of familiarity. The only two examples in his plays of what he labels jazz are in *Diff'rent* (1920) and *Dynamo* (1929). In both plays, jazz is heard coming from a Victrola. In the earlier, it is being played at the beginning of act 2 by the grotesque Emma, the fifty-year-old heroine who in the thirty years between acts 1 and 2 has turned into a "laughable," hypocritical, frustrated, lustful, "withered, scrawny woman."[69] In the later play (premiered by the Theatre Guild), the teenage Ada plays "a jazz record" as a signal to her would-be boyfriend that the coast is clear for a planned tryst.[70] In each play, the virtue of the woman with a taste for jazz is questionable at best. In *Diff'rent*, jazz is very clearly a symptom of what Ronald H. Wainscott describes as Emma's "monstrous transformation" from innocent to painted lady between acts.[71] In *Dynamo*, jazz functions as the emblem of a woman Brooks Atkinson describes as a "vulgar jade."[72] The jade in fact was originally played by Claudette Colbert who, if Percy Hammond is to be believed, supplied a lowbrow frisson for a highbrow audience by "providing sex-appeal for those Theatre-Guilders who like a little romance in their clinical entertainments."[73]

Given the difference between turn-of-the-century songs and jazz, I want to argue that jazz is constructed in O'Neill, as it is in the discourse of virtually all antijazz demagogues, as the sign of a degraded modernity, the commodification of the human subject, and the massification and mechanization of culture. In being identified with both the machine (the Victrola) and with woman, jazz is also predictably feminized, positioned as a seductive, cheap, vulgar indulgence in relation to the "good music" that O'Neill insisted he listened to and liked since "earliest childhood."[74] Yet again, in this instance, mass culture is to elite culture as woman is to man. These formulations may be unsurprising, but there is another that is even more revealing about O'Neill's distinctively modernist brand of theatricality. In both *Diff'rent* and *Dynamo*, the mass culture symptomatized by jazz is constructed as a fraud, a feminized imposture, the illegitimate offspring of an obsolete and embarrassing theatricality. In the earlier play, this construction becomes clear in a curious stage direction. In describing the fantastically accoutered, jazz-loving Emma, O'Neill writes: "She resembles some passé stock actress of fifty made up for a heroine of twenty." In other

Act 2 of the 1921 production of Eugene O'Neill's *Diff'rent*. The fifty-year-old Emma Crosby (Mary Blair) buries her face in the sofa, humiliated by her vain attempt at seducing Benny Rogers (Charles Ellis), a man half her age. Benny, meanwhile, confers with his mother (Elizabeth Brown) while the Victrola center stage plays jazz. Design by Cleon Throckmorton.

Credit: Museum of the City of New York

words, Emma embodies not only the excesses of jazz but also the archaic, popular theater emblematized by his father (both at its melodramatic height and in its vaudevillian decline) in which it was not unusual for actors to play characters less than half their age. In *Dynamo*, Ada is also a variation on the painted woman. O'Neill's very first description of her calls for her to be "putting on a heavy make-up of rouge and mascara."[75] And although she is nowhere near as exaggerated as Emma, she is every bit the emblem of grotesque theatricality.

O'Neill's antipathy to mass culture of the 1920s was far more extreme than that of a John Alden Carpenter or Deems Taylor. But neither Carpenter nor Taylor was committed to transforming a vulgar into an elite form of culture. Concert music was already highbrow, and the struggles taking place among composers and music critics were about the position and character of popular American vernaculars in work performed by recitalists and symphony orchestras. Theater, on the other hand, at least until the triumph of the art theaters and their playwrights, had been denied cultural legitimation. So it became all the more urgent for playwrights and

Act 3 of the Theatre Guild's 1929 production of Eugene O'Neill's *Dynamo*. Reuben (Glenn Anders) attempts to introduce a frightened Ada (Claudette Colbert) to the wonders of electricity. Design by Lee Simonson.
Credit: Museum of the City of New York

critics, faced with the flight of multitudes of spectators to the movies, to assert the highbrow credentials of a new, literary theater that was rejecting the shameful theatricality of the popular forms, melodrama, vaudeville, burlesque, and the like. George Jean Nathan predictably berated those who mistakenly approached O'Neill's plays using the "standards of . . . popular drama" rather than those of "aesthetics."[76] O'Neill's aversion to jazz on the stage is also linked to a particular brand of antitheatricalism that was widespread among playwrights and critics of the 1920s. Although he does not harbor the mimetiphobia of a Gilbert Seldes, O'Neill's disdain for the popular represents the inverse of Seldes's high modernist denunciation of traditional forms of representation. Unlike Seldes, who dismisses "serious plays" *tout court*, O'Neill and the other the makers of a literary theater were committed to modernizing the stage and doing away with the melodramatic, vaudevillian detritus. Like many of his colleagues, O'Neill exploited patently theatrical devices such as masks, choruses, and asides. But he steered clear of vaudeville. The lesson of John Howard Lawson's humiliation over the vaudevillian *Processional* would have convinced him if he had not already been a confirmed proponent of "aesthetics."

If Seldes's antitheatricality represents a kind of mimetiphobia, O'Neill's is the opposite: a fear of liveness. Matthew H. Wikander emphasizes that the playwright's distrust of live performance was incited first and foremost by his disdain for and dislike of actors (which O'Neill acknowledged was a result of his experience with *The Count of Monte Cristo*). Hence, O'Neill's notoriously novelistic stage directions that aim to restrict as tightly as possible the actor's ability to make choices. Convinced that actors always misinterpret and pervert the text, O'Neill aimed to foreclose the freeplay of signification: "The play as written, is the thing, and not the way the actors garble it with their almost-always-alien personalities."[77] The play exists not as a blueprint for performance, but as an autonomous artifact. Barrett Clark quotes the playwright as saying,

> I don't go to the theater because I can always do a better production in my mind . . . . Nor do I ever go to see one of my own plays—have seen only three of them since they started coming out. My real reason for this is that I was practically brought up in the theater . . . and I know (. . . too much about) the technique of acting . . . . (Acting, except when rarely inspired, simply gets between me and the play.)[78]

O'Neill envisions a play not as a stimulus for performance, but as a self-contained text, like a poem or a novel, which is staged, that is, interpreted, in the reader's mind. It would be difficult to imagine a declaration that more unequivocally positions drama not as mode of praxis but as a form of literature. Yet this move was consistent with the playwright's relative indifference to the productions of his plays as opposed to his considerable concern for and involvement with their publication. At the apogee of his fame during the early 1930s, for example, he was gratified that books of his plays consistently sold briskly and that he was able to make a "good profit" even on a play like *Dynamo*, "a flat failure in production." Because his "published plays always sold well, often better than highly successful novels," he was able to stake a claim as a producer of plays less for the theater than for the library or study.[79]

O'Neill was rewarded for his emphasis on the dramatic text by being awarded the Nobel Prize in 1936 for his work in the genre called "literature."[80] He had succeeded in establishing a literary drama in the United States worthy to stand next to the canonical European playwrights. And as usual, he was cheered on by George Jean Nathan. The fact that "great drama" is "great literature," Nathan wrote, is "painfully obvious."[81] And Nathan's observation was taken for granted by many. Benjamin De Casseres praised *Strange Interlude* as "a great novel in play form, a unique literary achievement."[82] Joseph Wood Krutch claimed that *Mourning Becomes Electra* "may turn out to be the only permanent contribution yet made by the twentieth century to dramatic literature."[83] And Brooks Atkinson wrote that O'Neill "said in the theatre the things that people were accustomed to seeing only in books."[84] Although George Bernard Shaw intended the label "banshee Shakespeare" to censure O'Neill, at least Shaw was analogizing him to the central figure in the English language dramatic and literary traditions.[85]

O'Neill's construction as a literary playwright is certainly linked to his fear of liveness. Atkinson explained that "Broadway hardly interested him. The life of Broadway he regarded as a steady leeching away of the purity of thought necessary to good work."[86] Atkinson's statement suggests that O'Neill's anxieties were focused not only on actors' misinterpretations. For spectators were also constructed as impressionable chumps who let themselves be carried away by an actor's garbled performance. In that sense, Wikander is correct to note that O'Neill's plays represent "acts of aggression" (although not in the Artaudian way that Wikander suggests).[87] O'Neill's "plodding expository dialogue," his verbalization of unspoken thoughts, the gargantuan lengths of some of his plays, and his often excessively schematic and self-consciously symbolic plotting have the effect of overstating or reiterating the obvious.[88] All these techniques construct the playwright as a kind of tyrannical deity who presides over the theological stage and dispatches edicts to his dim-witted subjects. They rehearse a barely concealed symbolic violence that is directed against all those who choose to interpret or attend his plays and function to identify spectators with actors, about whom O'Neill remarked (in connection with *Strange Interlude*), "If [they] weren't so dumb, they wouldn't need asides."[89]

O'Neill's fear of live performance, patronizing treatment of actors and spectators, and contempt for popular theatrical traditions come together in his antipathy toward the music of the 1920s that epitomized liveness: jazz. Unlike the art music or turn-of-the-century sentimental ballads that O'Neill revered, jazz was at least in part improvisatory. Even bandleaders like Paul Whiteman, who worked closely with arrangers and usually saw to it that parts were written out in detail, did not completely eschew improvisation. The fact that jazz was so closely linked to vaudeville and musical comedy during the 1920s further proved its danger not only to O'Neill's aesthetic but, more important, to the literary drama that he, his fellow playwrights, and the critics were attempting to enshrine. Its indisputable liveness, marketability, working-class and African American associations, and happy refusal to abide by the notes on the page made it the antithesis of everything the commercial theater that was also an art theater was attempting to institutionalize.

SAINT EUGENE

From the very beginning of Eugene O'Neill's career as a playwright, critics have stressed the intimate relationship between man and work. Virtually every essay and book about him (from the 1920s to the present) emphasizes how his plays remain incomprehensible without knowledge of the man, and vice versa. George Jean Nathan writes, "The body of [O'Neill's] dramatic writing reflects him more closely, I venture to say, than that of any other playwright in the present-day American theatre."[90] Benjamin De Casseres exclaims, "everything O'Neill has done has been spun out of his own innards, out of his own hells and heavens."[91] In the very first *New York Times* feature article on the playwright, Alexander Woollcott notes that his review of *Beyond the Horizon* "needs some cross-references to the author's biography" in order to explain the play's content, quality, and method.[92] Barrett H. Clark begins the first edition of the first monograph on O'Neill with the words, "The personality of Eugene O'Neill is quite as extraordinary as his work. Any intelligible discussion of his plays must be based upon some knowledge of their origin during the years when he was groping, though all unconsciously, for a meaning in life."[93] Richard Dana Skinner takes this correspondence between man and work even further by asserting that the succession of his plays represents a "continuous poetic progression," each play "a chapter in the interior romance of a poet's imagination."[94] There are as many more examples as there are flat-out declarations that O'Neill was and is "still regarded as America's finest" playwright.[95]

In what remains the most incisive critical study yet published on the playwright, Joel Pfister analyzes the relationship between man and work, pointing out how carefully attuned O'Neill was "to the cultural role of the modern artist as one who publicly symbolizes a romantic-psychological 'self'" and how well he understood "how to benefit from the equation of his image with 'depth' in the popular mind."[96] Most important, Pfister examines the social and political function that "depth" performed in U.S. culture between the world wars and the playwright's key role in consolidating a particular kind of liberal individualism both in and out of the theater. I want to build upon his work by analyzing the dynamics of O'Neill's canonization as "America's leading playwright" and "the quintessential American dramatist" by turning my attention to O'Neill's critics.[97] I argue that his early critics constructed him a holy man of art—one part saint, one part messiah—whose agonies redeemed the American theater from the tyranny of dreck. Unlike the genuine Christian saints upon whose canonization O'Neill's is modeled, however, the playwright is an unmistakably post-Nietzschean saint, one who does not so much believe as doubt, one whose motto might be "the 'old God [is] dead' and a new one [is] not in sight."[98] Because of his well-known ethnic and religious background, moreover, O'Neill was always being positioned in relation to the Roman Catholic tradition (like a highbrow, Irish rendering of *The Jazz Singer's* Jakie Rabinowitz), a man who renounces the God—and the theater—of his father for the truth of art.[99] O'Neill may have played the apostate, but Walter Prichard Eaton assured his readers that the playwright still possessed a powerful "mystic instinct" and that his plays provide a glimpse of "some higher power suddenly felt, unseen."[100] The narrativizations of O'Neill's life from the 1920s and early 1930s construct his life and work in ways that are remarkably similar to those of medieval lives of the saints. Most important, these hagiographies allowed Eugene O'Neill, the secular saint and savior of the American theater, to burst onto the national stage in 1920 already poised for canonization. Was the American theater not, Barrett Clark asks, "looking for a dramatic Messiah" and was not *Beyond the Horizon*, "with all its shortcomings . . . the first sign of his arrival"?[101]

The narratives of O'Neill's life written since the 1920s are remarkably consistent. This is especially true of accounts of his formative years, the pre-Broadway years, which are always singled out as the decisive ones for understanding the playwright's work. "O'Neill is a man," Clark writes, "who has lived first and written afterward."[102] Of course, O'Neill himself was in part responsible for this because of the way he described his life to journalists, biographers, and critics. The posthumous acclaim of *Long Day's Journey into Night* (1955) reconfirmed that the first twenty-five years of his life were the crucial ones (and further narrowed the focus of many critics to the dynamics of the nuclear family). The most important detail that is left out of the early accounts and that *Long Day's Journey* supplies is, of course, his mother's morphine addiction, which is invariably constructed by critics and the playwright himself as the withheld secret whose discovery was comparable, one critic melodramatically writes, to Oedipus's terrible recognition.[103] The particulars of these accounts hardly vary, moving back and forth from *The Count of Monte Cristo* to *The Moon of the Caribbees*, tuberculosis to suicide attempts, whisky to morphine, nuns to whores, Princeton to Harvard, first wife to second wife, mining in Central America to voyages at sea, Provincetown to Broadway, and Roman Catholicism to Nietzsche, Baudelaire to Strindberg. In fact, the outline of these books, except for the more sordid details about the James O'Neill family, are all present in the first critical biography of the playwright, Barrett H. Clark's *Eugene O'Neill* (1926; revised 1929).

Clark's biography represents an important early example of collusion between critic and playwright. Clark begins the revised version with an intimate, personal recollection of the playwright, and the long introductory, biographical section titled "The Man" is filled with private communications and letters from O'Neill that make it clear that Clark had built a close professional relationship with the playwright and gained his trust. These facts presumably inspire the reader's confidence that Clark is able to separate fact from "legend" in what he admits is an " 'official' " book. He tries to convince the reader that he has been able to maintain a critical objectivity by pointing out that although O'Neill had "O.K.'d the biographical facts he had nothing to do with any judgment I passed on the plays."[104] Clark is also eager to prove his powers of prophecy by quoting one of his own reviews from 1919 that predicts O'Neill's impending recognition as "our leading dramatist" (77).

In *Eugene O'Neill*, Barrett Clark constructs the playwright's life clearly bifurcated by a conversion, a transformation from "wild boy" to dedicated man, doer to thinker, adventurer to philosopher, failure to success, materialist to mystic, wastrel to poet (30). Before, he "had simply not found himself"; after, he was on the road to wisdom and renown (19). The "turning-point" or moment of conversion occurred during his stay at Gaylord Farm Sanatorium in 1913 for "a touch of tuberculosis" (28, 27). (O'Neill himself mythologizes the event in *The Straw* [1921].) There, O'Neill explained, he spent "six months . . . thinking it over. It was in this enforced period of reflection that the urge to write first came to me."[105] He did not need to rouse the will to write, rather it "came to [him]," as Jesus Christ or the Holy Spirit might appear uninvited to a saint-in-waiting. O'Neill imagined his revelatory "jolt" not only in vocational terms but also in moral terms. After he had "just drifted along" for so long, "Retribution overtook me and I went down with T.B. It gave me time to think about myself."[106]

The arrival of O'Neill's "urge to write" was repeatedly constructed like the conversion of medieval saints. Like many of them, O'Neill was transformed after a personal crisis and a confrontation with the possibility of death. Like them, he recovered from a "breakdown," Clark writes, by finding the power to forge a "new life" and dedicate himself to "the most rigid kind of self-discipline" (28, 29, 31). ("He works," Louis Kantor reports, "intensively, eight or ten hours a day, for months at a stretch.")[107] The crucial difference, of course, is that the answer that came to him was not God but Art. And it came in what was by all accounts not an age of faith but an age of doubt. Rather than dedicate himself to God, he would redeem his "aimless, wild, carousing, feverish years" by turning them into the stuff of dramatic poetry.[108] O'Neill's class background, moreover, is by no means irrelevant to his conversion from sinner to saint. In their survey of medieval saints, Donald Weinstein and Rudolph M. Bell point out that despite the valuation of poverty and humility, three-quarters of the lay saints in their sample came from the upper classes in part because conversion depended on a "rejection of the world and its values." Since the "spectacle of reversal, . . . of inversion of worldly status was crucial to the perception of sanctity," saints were virtually obliged to be born into wealth and power.[109] Like these men and women, O'Neill came from an affluent household.

The son of a prince of the theater, he (apparently) voluntarily gave up his riches to associate, Clark notes, with prostitutes, "sailors, stevedores, the down-and-outs" (19). "[I]n the unsocial misfits of our world the young O'Neill found something that he needed, something that was not to be found in normal[!] ladies and gentlemen" (31). Having served an apprenticeship with the "down-and-outs," he was poised to undergo a conversion that would mean appropriating their abjection for his own artistic ends. It was well known, moreover, that O'Neill had not held out against what the Roman Catholic Church would have regarded as a multitude of temptations. But even these could be forgiven or incorporated into the legend. Chastity was never O'Neill's strong suit, but Clark dismisses his first marriage in a few sentences as "a mistake" (17–18). Even his drinking and fraternization with the most ungenteel "unsocial misfits" are explained away by George Jean Nathan in a conversation with Clark: "'Remember, if he hadn't drunk the way he did and mixed with so many kinds of people in those early days we probably shouldn't have had his plays'" (60). Although most female saints were obliged to be compliant and holy in their youth, most male saints would not be saints if they had not first wrestled with temptation, sinned, and repented.

As narrated by Clark, O'Neill's life story recalls the medieval *vitae*, or tales of confessor saints like Paul or Antony, which Alison Goddard Elliott argues comprise hagiographic romances. This form of romance has a four-part structure that Clark's narrative exactly replicates. It begins with a departure, depicting the hero's early life, which marks him or her already as someone "set apart, extraordinary."[110] (Compare O'Neill's privileged, pampered childhood.) This is followed by a perilous journey that is sometimes pictured as a flight from family and hearth but is always figured as a spiritual descent and trial, a "quest into the unknown," a symbolic death.[111] (Compare O'Neill's dissolute years on the road and at sea.) At the end of the journey comes the third stage, the discovery of a place, a relatively isolated site where conversion results from a confrontation with a divine or demonic force. This encounter marks the beginning of the hero's ascent and sanctification. (Compare O'Neill's months at the sanatorium and his encounter there for the first time with the "greatest genius of all modern dramatists," August Strindberg, who, he reports, "inspired [him] with the urge to write.")[112] The final stage is signaled by the translation of experience into text, the construction of narrative, a bearing witness to faith "in word as well as deed."[113] It is usually performed both by the hero who discourses on his or her experiences, and by an outside party, an onlooker who is able to summarize the story and draw a moral from it. (Compare O'Neill's playwriting and Clark's hagiographic tribute.) The role of Strindberg in O'Neill's conversion is doubly significant, because of both Strindberg's role in constructing a Swedish national theater and his own Inferno crisis (1894–96), which similarly divided his life and his playwriting into a before and after.

Accounts of O'Neill's disposition and personality were crucial in reinforcing this construction of the playwright as a secular saint. In detailing a 1926 meeting with the playwright, Barrett Clark characterizes him as humble and ascetic despite his renown. He is a "shy and silent young man" with eyes that "are clear, bright, penetrating, yet infinitely soft" (1). Carol Bird also notes his habit of "keeping out of the limelight" and interprets his eyes as "somber, with a tender melancholy in their dark depths." He is modest and "indifferent to life's superfluities."[114] He "nearly always seems embarrassed," Clark writes, eats only a "frugal luncheon," and is abashed that someone would be writing about him: "A book! Already!" (6, 2). Brooks Atkinson describes him as "liv[ing] in seclusion," always searching for "the ideal place where he could work and think without interruption."[115] He is possessed, moreover, of an undeniably mystical nature that is inseparable from his identity as an artist. Arthur Hobson Quinn titles the chapter about him in his history of American drama, "Eugene O'Neill, Poet and Mystic," while countless other critics emphasize his otherworldly leanings.[116] For these observers, his mystical temperament is signaled less by discourse than by silence. Clark observes that his "silences are long and eloquent" (6) while Bird is fascinated by his "[p]regnant silence" and finds that he projects a "distinct aura." "Waves of silence surge over us," she writes excitedly, but the "silence has told me much. This surely is genius." There is no question but that these characteristics, along with his "illumined look," are coded, as Pfister argues, as signs of fathomless psychological depths. But they are also signs of "[m]agnetism" and spiritual intensity.[117]

Warrior saints, whether male or female, were regarded as having been masculinized by their spiritual vocation. John Kitchen asserts that in hagiographies, "sanctity is expressed in terms of physical, male power; it is the attainment of a victory in a drawn-out contest" waged by a manly fighter whose gender identity "ultimately derives from an adherence to the warrior as the paradigm of Christian sanctity."[118] In biographical discourse,

O'Neill, the warrior for an art theater, remains adamantly masculine, both emotionally and physically. Because both modernism and avant-gardism were coded as masculine in relation both to previous high-cultural movements (gentility and aestheticism) and to popular traditions, O'Neill, like Gershwin and so many other modernists, is figured as a manly rebel fighting against and displacing feminine traditions. Clark emphasizes his athleticism, observing that "[e]xercise is a fetish" for him and that he is "one of the finest swimmers" Clark had ever seen. He wanted, Clark reports, "'to be a two-fisted Jack London 'he-man' sailor, to knock 'em cold and eat 'em alive'" (32). Sayler notes that O'Neill had not succumbed to "flabbiness of muscle" since his days of adventure, while Kantor observes that he loves to "drive his frail red and white kyak [*sic*] . . . out to sea, singing exultantly, while coast guards trembled for his safety."[119] Most important, O'Neill's masculinity is enunciated through his work. Sweeping aside the hyperemotionality of melodrama and the tawdry glitter of vaudeville, "the routine swamps of Broadway," in Nathan's words, O'Neill replaced them with "profound and beautiful thing[s]." "He has no cheapness, even in his worst plays."[120] He is a pioneer, a crusader for a "new and virile kind of romance" that marks a decisive break with the domestic and social drama, comedy of manners, and melodrama of writers like William Gillette, David Belasco, and Clyde Fitch.[121]

The beatification of Eugene O'Neill takes place more or less unconsciously in most of the critical texts on the playwright, through imagery, metaphor, and rhetoric. But in one of the more hyperbolic assessments of the playwright, Richard Dana Skinner, a critic for the liberal Roman Catholic magazine *Commonweal*, explicitly compares O'Neill to a saint. Marshaling a curious hybrid of psychoanalysis and Roman Catholic mysticism, Skinner constructs an argument that one reviewer said was of "extraordinary brilliance and subtlety."[122] He begins by pointing out that saints are converted from "divided selves," in whom a war is waged between sin and righteousness, "into something resembling a peaceful unity of mind and soul." The dramatic poet, "very much like the saint, recognizes himself" in both the sinner and the "ideal person" and he "projects" both "into objective characters." Because of this recognition, Skinner explains, the poet sometimes chooses subjects that are "'gruesome' or 'morbid.'" (O'Neill was often criticized for his allegedly obscene and squalid representations.) "Like the saints," the poet does not fear but "understands" these subjects. But since both know that victory over sin is always provisional, the saint and the poet are constantly in battle and are "plunged again" and again into "darkness and fear." "One reason," Skinner notes, "for assigning Eugene O'Neill an exceptionally high place among the poets of history is precisely because his poetic experiences, as objectified in his plays, correspond with such depth and intensity to the universal pattern of mystical experience so fully described by the saints." Each of his plays, like a stopping point on the road to salvation, represents a "clearly marked stage . . . in the pilgrimage from turmoil to peace." O'Neill may not have been a practicing Roman Catholic, but he was a tortured soul who could not help but dramatize his unending battle with temptation, his "familiar 'dark night of the soul.'"[123]

From the end of the second decade of the century, and long before he became the first playwright, and only the second American, to win the Nobel Prize, O'Neill was constructed as a tormented saint unafraid of dramatizing his most private ordeals, a crusader for an art theater, and the best playwright the United States had ever produced. He quickly and progressively attained preeminence, beginning with the reception accorded even his early one-act plays. By the time *Beyond the Horizon* opened on Broadway, it was hailed as "by far the best serious play which any American author has written for years" and went on to win for O'Neill his first Pulitzer Prize.[124] (It also grossed $117,071 at a time O'Neill "needed the royalties badly.")[125] The superlatives, like the new plays, came "thick and fast."[126] In 1921, O'Neill had five plays produced on Broadway. One can see his step-by-step advancement in Woollcott's reviews for the *New York Times*. In February 1920, Woollcott described *Beyond the Horizon* as possessing "elements of greatness."[127] By the end of that year, after *The Emperor Jones*, he claimed that "for strength and originality [O'Neill] has no rival among the American writers for the stage."[128] By 1922, the year of his second Pulitzer Prize (for *Anna Christie*), O'Neill was already "towering so conspicuously above the milling, mumbling crowd of playwrights."[129] And Woollcott's reviews are by no means exceptional; they represent an accurate gauge of O'Neill's soaring critical reputation. Although some of his plays (for example, *The Straw* [1921], *Welded* [1924], and *Dynamo*), received more negative than positive reviews, they proved temporary setbacks, necessary trials rather than serious obstacles to his consecration.

Another vitally important step in the canonization of O'Neill was the visibility of his plays in Europe. U.S. popular culture, principally cinema and jazz, was all the rage in Europe, and even the work of U.S. novelists (among them Theodore Dreiser, Upton Sinclair, and Sinclair Lewis) had been published in translation. But no playwright had been similarly recognized. Barrett Clark explicitly links O'Neill's preeminence to the fact that "his plays are produced and read in England and France, Germany, Russia, Czechoslovakia, and the Scandinavian countries; two . . . have been seen in Japan" (55). Quinn also commends O'Neill's status as "an international figure," and he and Sayler provide an impressive list of places his work had been performed: Tokyo, Copenhagen, Bombay, Prague, Manila, France, central Europe, and Scandinavia.[130] "*Anna Christie*," Sayler notes, "was a triumph in London."[131] Clark sums up the playwright's achievement by quoting the commendation for his honorary degree from Yale claiming him "the first American playwright to receive both wide and serious recognition upon the stage of Europe" (55). Among more recent historians, Rita Terras points to O'Neill's extraordinary success in Europe. Although not all his plays were acclaimed, she notes that no other playwright "offered European audiences the same mixture of familiar dramatic trends . . . *and* the exoticism of an as yet largely unknown American culture and subculture." No less a high cultural hero than Hugo von Hofmannsthal wrote an appreciation of O'Neill that was published in the United States in 1923. (Despite Hofmannsthal's criticism of a dramatic idiom he finds overly "direct," "simple," and "expected," both Clark and Sayler single out the Austrian's essay as proof of O'Neill's consequence.)[132] That same year, O'Neill's plays were first performed in Berlin. "Between 1923 and 1932," Terras reports, "nine plays were translated by several different translators and also performed" throughout Germany.[133]

As with other international figures (like George Gershwin, John Alden Carpenter, and George Antheil), O'Neill found that his success in the European marketplace was closely linked to his construction, in Sayler's words, as "the personal symbol of our awakening American drama." His status as "our" nationalist figurehead needed no more proof than the fact that "the skyscraper is our contribution to architecture."[134] Casting a more jaundiced eye, Nathan observes that "certain of his plays smell of America as pungently as rotten diplomacy." But he, too, insists that O'Neill's plays are both deeply "American" and "universal."[135] These testimonials are signs that O'Neill's importance is in part a function of his having succeeded in exporting a distinctively U.S. art that was emphatically not the lowbrow stuff of cinema or jazz. His cosmopolitanism was very different from the jazz cosmopolitanism of a Gershwin, Carpenter, or Antheil because his art was not a mixture of highbrow and lowbrow but a high-minded literary production. O'Neill was thus able to take his place beside Dreiser and Sinclair as well as Ibsen and Strindberg, two playwrights who successfully founded national theaters that were also art theaters. His quick acceptance into the European pantheon is no doubt also linked to the fact that his acknowledged influences were all European. He was the stepchild of Schopenhauer, Nietzsche, and Strindberg, not Emerson, Thoreau, and Whitman. He wrote to Nathan from France that "Europe has meant . . . more than I ever hoped it could. I've felt a deep sense of peace here, a real enjoyment in just living from day to day, that I've never known before."[136] During the decade of "Fordismus," O'Neill was thus very well placed to become "a spokesman," Terras observes, for a "country whose pronouncements are taken seriously."[137] It is not by chance that Sayler should compare him to Teddy Roosevelt, Edison, Ford, and Rockefeller. Like the first, Eugene O'Neill was an adventurer and imperialist; like the last three, he was a hugely successful monopoly capitalist who cornered the market on U.S. exports.

O'Neill's acclaim in Europe reinforced the belief that he was indeed the "dramatic Messiah" the theater had been awaiting—and had needed— in order to raise itself above cinema, vaudeville, musical comedy, cabaret, and other cheap entertainments. By the 1920s, the legitimate stage could not compete with them on their own level, and in order to attract an "intelligent minority" willing to pay higher prices to see a play without leggy chorines, it had to become a theater that was dispensing not entertainment but art, a thing beyond price.[138] This priceless artifact, however, was available only to a small minority of theatergoers, the upper classes and selected fractions of the middle class, with a few stray bohemians thrown in. While O'Neill's work was being performed downtown at the Provincetown Playhouse, it drew a more mixed crowd, one that included artistic and political rebels, described by an uptown critic as "not alluringly savory."[139] But by the time it reached Broadway, it needed to attract more well-heeled patrons.

Pfister skillfully analyzes O'Neill's progressive deradicalization and the political ambivalence that works itself out in many of his early plays and makes them more palatable for affluent, liberal spectators. He points out that this ambivalence is linked to the playwright's curious position as an individualist anarchist in the midteens who transforms himself into a liberal convinced that "life as a whole . . . change[s] very little."[140] O'Neill insists he is not a "propagandist" but a dramatist preoccupied with "human beings in conflict."[141] In 1922, he confessed that he had "come to feel so indifferent toward political and social movements of all kinds. Time was," he told Oliver Sayler, "when I was an active socialist, and, after that, a philosophical anarchist. But today I can't feel that anything like that matters."[142] Even his early plays, however, repeatedly take up contradictory positions regarding the possibility and desirability of radical social change. *The Hairy Ape*, for example, authorizes a spectator to read it as an indictment of a cruelly unjust, class-bound society (as some of the upstairs crowd was likely to have done) or as a universal tragedy about the primitive beast that lies at the heart of the modern subject (as much of the downstairs crowd was likely to have done). During the early 1920s, this equivocation is in part a function of the contradictory class positionalities that O'Neill occupied: upper-middle-class landed gentry, son of a prince of the theater, bohemian, political radical, "down-and-out," sinner, saint, dedicated writer, and proud and ambitious artist. (Given his multiple allegiances, is it little wonder that his plays turned out to be so conflicted.) But this equivocation is also a function of and response to the contradictions lived by the class fractions that patronized the legitimate theater, ranging from upper-class swells to Greenwich Village bohemians and radicals, tired businessmen to midlevel managers.

The ability of O'Neill's plays to enunciate opposing positions was—and remains—a large part of their appeal. Spectators are likely to feel flattered when they are able to see their own prejudices and predispositions reflected narcissistically, even if these opinions are at the same time being questioned. Nathan admitted as much when he argued that theater is "a place to which one goes [not] in search of the unexplored corners of one's imagination," but "in repeated search of the familiar."[143] Despite the neat ideological fit between playwright and audience, O'Neill's consecration was only partly his doing. The most crucial part of the task was performed by the new generation of theater critics who were determined to discover and pay obeisance to the "dramatic Messiah." The key figure among these critics was, of course, George Jean Nathan, who, in Atkinson's words, "instantly recognized the ability of the first American dramatist to redeem Broadway from futility."[144] In Nathan's very first review of O'Neill's work from 1918, he praised the playwright in words that seem to set the stage for his later consecration of the dramatic messiah. Nathan wrote that the basic materials of most of O'Neill's work . . . are little more than the materials of ordinary melodrama, yet the approach to these materials and the vivid human portraiture with which they are invested transform them into something at once intriguing and distinguished. In the hands of the Broadway showmaker, an O'Neill play would amount to nothing but a shoddy Guignol shocker; in the hands of O'Neill, the thing takes on a colour and an atmosphere, a sense of something important.[145]

Because Nathan recognized O'Neill's "shoddy" raw materials so clearly, he was all the more intent on setting the playwright apart from the typical showmaker's tawdry melodramas and shockers.

Nathan jealously guarded his personal and professional friendship with the playwright and shared an intimacy that would have been unthinkable to later critics. (Brooks Atkinson, by contrast, "refused to mix in any way with any members of the theatrical profession.")[146] According to Nathan, he and O'Neill had "eaten, drunk, walked, motored, bicycled, slept, bathed, shaved, edited, run, worked, played, even sung" together, and he remained among the first people to whom the playwright sent a manuscript.[147] By 1916 Nathan had established himself as a foremost theater critic and was instrumental in publishing three of O'Neill's one-act plays in *Smart Set* and later securing Broadway productions for *Beyond the Horizon* and several succeeding plays.[148] Over the next twenty years, O'Neill sent him drafts of scripts and often importuned him to intervene on his behalf with producers or directors. Never before or since has there been a closer personal and professional relationship between preeminent playwright and preeminent critic.

The two men had much in common. Both were from nouveaux riches, upper-middle-class families that would have been coded as ethnically marked (Irish and Jewish); learned their trades on the job; and were well traveled and well read. Both earned a great deal of money from their writing. By 1925, Nathan "had become the most widely read and the highest paid drama critic in the world," while O'Neill, during the "ripe years 1920–35," earned almost a million dollars, then a fortune.[149] Nathan lived for fifty years in a suite at the Royalton Hotel on West Forty-fourth Street, a block and a half from Broadway, while O'Neill lived in a succession of impressive houses, including his thirty-acre Brook Farm in Ridgefield, Connecticut; the forty-five-room Château Le Plessis in the Loire valley; the twenty-one-room Casa Genotta at Sea Island, Georgia; and Tao House, his 158-acre estate in Danville, California. Nathan tried to emphasize their bond by claiming that their mothers were friends and had attended the same convent school in Indiana. That claim "is now in doubt."[150] Whether true or false, however, the story is a sign of how strongly Nathan tried to bind himself to the playwright.

Yet O'Neill and Nathan made a decidedly odd couple. The one was famously solemn, the other a wag; the one thrice-married; the other a dandy and sometime roué; the one austere, the other hedonistic; the one a lapsed Catholic, the other a closeted Jew; the one hated vaudeville and popular forms; the other found them exceedingly pleasant entertainments as long as they were carefully cordoned off. But both men were intent on proving that theater in New York was capable of standing next to the eminent national theaters of Europe. The United States did not have the same long history of dramatic literature, but, as befit the first revolutionary nation, it was finally finding its voice in a revolutionary modernism.

The same year that Barrett Clark's *Eugene O'Neill* was published, the first book on Nathan, *The Theatre of George Jean Nathan* by Isaac Goldberg, also appeared. (This was the same Isaac Goldberg who a few years later would write books on George Gershwin and Tin Pan Alley.) The remarkable subtitle of Goldberg's book, *Chapters and Documents toward a History of the New American Drama*, reveals the central role Nathan played in the production and consumption of American modernism. (Even Brooks Atkinson has never had a book written about him.) Although the book includes in its documentary section letters from O'Neill and E. Gordon Craig and satirical scenarios by Nathan and H. L. Mencken, it is devoted to canonizing the forty-four-year-old Nathan as the age's privileged intermediary between playwright and stage and between stage and spectator. Goldberg constructs him as the man whose reviews and essays comprise an authoritative, if idiosyncratic, "history of the new American drama." And certainly it is no coincidence that O'Neill, "Nathan's chief 'discovery,'" is by far the most prominent playwright in the book. Susan Glaspell, Sidney Howard, George Kelly, or Zona Gale do not figure in Goldberg's calculus. Given the book's sweeping claims, it is perhaps not surprising that Goldberg's discourse betrays the symbolic violence that Nathan routinely exercised against less worthy artists. Calling Nathan "a crusader against the crescent," Goldberg evokes the long history of imperialist war waged against the infidel and thereby neatly positions Nathan alongside O'Neill, another holy warrior for art. Emphasizing his subject's verbal aggressivity,

Goldberg argues that "during the years that O'Neill was finding his place in the American theatre," Nathan "served as O'Neill's first line of critical shock troops. He fought against a heavy opposition until the ranks of hostility were broken through." And he imagines playwright and critic as comprising an ideal team, two revolutionaries sweeping aside yesterday's Babbitts, prigs, revelers, and nitwits: "The meeting of the two men was a fortunate conjunction; together they symbolize a new day for the American drama and the American stage."[151]

If O'Neill played the role of the messiah of the stage, Nathan was, in Atkinson's word, a "prophet," who, like John the Baptist, announced the coming of the Lord.[152] Especially adept at "producing a performance of Nathan," he cultivated an image of himself "elegantly dressed, escorting a fetching ingenue toward two-on-the-aisle, row E seats; midnight suppers at the Stork Club; playwrights and directors breathlessly watching his every sneer or smile."[153] If O'Neill was constructed a Catholic saint, Nathan the defiant Hebrew prophet deliberately adopted a satanic image and a "conception of art," Goldberg notes, that was "tauntingly Luciferian" (he was inordinately fond of devil's advocacy).[154] Like O'Neill, Nathan believed politics to be inconsequential. Atkinson reports that "he eliminated politics from his category of adult subjects," declining, as Nathan explained, "to pollute [his] mind with such obscenities."[155] Nathan's motto was "Be indifferent": "When I read some enkindled yogi's indignations over the slaughter of eight thousand Polish Jews, or over the corrupt administration in this or that country, state or city, or over the Ku Klux Klan, . . . I only smile, and wonder."[156] Even if this notorious assertion is mostly Nathan playing Nathan playing agent provocateur, it still betrays an "aristocratic air" and a "contempt . . . for the mob" that were persistently reflected in his attitudes toward art.[157] (It is no surprise that he was repeatedly attacked by the *Daily Worker* and became "the Left's favorite Broadway whipping boy.")[158] Indeed, nowhere was his antipopulist resentment expressed as violently as in his well-known hatred of motion pictures. In a 1925 column Nathan vented his spleen: "[A] thundering flood of bilge and scum," movies are controlled "by men of a complete anaesthesia to everything fine" and "everything potentially dollarless." Their main talent is buying "literature" and "convert[ing] it, by their own peculiar and esoteric magic, into rubbish." Unlike Walter Prichard Eaton and the somewhat more sanguine contributors to the *Vanity Fair* forum, Nathan was convinced that "the moving picture morons have today got their dirty hands around the theatre's windpipe" and are choking it economically. He concludes his column by aiming symbolic violence, blow after blow, at his colleagues. Since the "weapon to save the theatre" rests "in the hands of the dramatic critics of America," the power to drive away "the money-dripping, unschooled, grasping, foul and contemptible gang of motion picture interlopers. . . . Let heads be smashed right and left, and let no mercy be shown."[159]

Nathan's detestation of motion pictures is typical of what his champions, critics, and he himself described as an aristocratic attitude. The theater, he insisted, represents "an aristocracy of beautiful letters, of ideas and wit, of viewpoint and philosophy."[160] And because art is "a matter of individual expression," the "best" theater criticism "must inevitably be personal."[161] Unlike Adorno, who also maintained what is often called an aristocratic stance, Nathan rejected philosophical models and carefully avoiding enunciating a theory of drama, theater, or culture. In fact, he never analyzed the relationship between art and society because for him it is unimportant; art that matters must transcend the social. Preferring the bon mot to analysis, he produced a huge body of idiosyncratic, contradictory criticism that values what he happened to decide at the moment stands the test of "the extrinsic aristocratic soul that is taste and connoisseurship and final judgment."[162] But Nathan of course was the only dependable connoisseur and the sworn enemy of the "herd of hallelujahing song-writers, motion picture actors and Broadway bounders whose illiterate voice is the voice of the illiterate audience whose voice in turn is the illiterate voice of our native popular theatre."[163] Esteeming a drama that addresses itself to "cultivated and artistically sensitive" rather than "inferior persons," Nathan persistently imagined the legitimate theater a monument of high culture. Just as a "dramatist's play" is comparable to a "composer's symphony," so are the great playwrights to be compared to Brahms, Chopin, Wagner, Giorgione, and Michelangelo.[164]

Examples of Nathan's attacks on "inferior persons" of every stripe are legion, and one would be hard pressed to come up with another critic as caustic and, in his own ruthless way, witty. Preferring his own brand of radical libertarianism to any other -ism, he never enunciated a coherent theory of what he calls "the drama," although he does usually commend a particular kind of dialectical playwriting (that dramatizes "us and our opposing ideas") developed by Ibsen, Strindberg, Chekhov, and—of course—O'Neill.[165] He considered women playwrights essentially inferior to men because of their alleged inability to think dialectically. A "woman dramatist seldom succeeds in mastering an economy of the emotions," while "womanish prejudice" makes her think only in absolutes ("Black must be black, white must be white").[166] It should be clear from Nathan's power over Broadway in the 1920s that he excelled most of all as a rhetorician, wielding symbolic violence against playwrights, producers, actors, audiences, and other critics. He was especially adept at constructing elaborate strings of metaphor (that sometimes inflate to allegories) that mobilize malicious and homicidal figures of speech. "[I]t is incumbent upon dramatic criticism," he writes, "to murder out of [the theater] all its mountebanks, shysters, and pretenders."[167] And he deliberately challenged his readers, daring them to disagree with him. He would issue decrees from his bully pulpit at *Smart Set* or *American Mercury* and woe betide anyone who crossed him. Constantly asserting his own authority, he amassed symbolic capital in part by constructing the critic as the playwright's sibling, a "thoroughbred artist" who practices "an art within an art."[168] But he also imagined the critic as a kind of sadistic wife-beater, citing James Branch Cabell approvingly: "It is not possible . . . to draw inspiration from a woman's beauty unless you comprehend how easy it would be to murder her."[169]

Armed with cudgel, pistol, and sword, Nathan achieved his greatest success with his construction of George Jean Nathan as the "prophet" of Broadway and Eugene O'Neill as the man who (in Nathan's scatological allegory) "alone and single-handed waded through the dismal swamp lands of American drama, bleak, squashy and oozing sticky goo, and alone and single-handed bore out of them the water lily that no American had found before him."[170] Although both men survived until the 1950s, they enjoyed their days of greatest glory during the 1920s. O'Neill's career came to a virtual standstill the next decade due to the disastrous Theatre Guild production of *Days without End* in 1934 and his continued "isolation from the theater."[171] And although he won the Nobel Prize two years later, the consensus was that he was finished as a playwright. Nathan, too, achieved his "high point" during the mid-1920s when he had won a large national following as critic for and coeditor of *American Mercury*.[172] Although Thomas Connolly defends his later writing, even he admits that Nathan was "restating and reapplying ideas and attitudes that he had promulgated during the 1910s and 1920s."[173] When both men died (O'Neill in 1953, Nathan in 1958), their *New York Times* obituaries, each of which began on page 1, described them as giants whose lasting achievements dated from a quarter century before their deaths.

Despite a diminishment in the reputations of both men, Eugene O'Neill was universally hailed at his death—even before the premiere of *Long Day's Journey into Night* and his second, posthumous career—as the "greatest playwright in U.S. history."[174] Nathan, meanwhile, was characterized as the man whose name "and the word 'theatre' [had become] almost synonymous."[175] Yet the vaguely circumspect and nostalgic tone of the obituaries suggests that both men had outlived their usefulness. Their most important achievements consisted of "so greatly rais[ing] the standards of play producers" and "determinedly elevat[ing] the tastes of playgoers"[176] But they had accomplished these twin tasks by the mid-1920s, as the legitimate theater was being forced to redefine itself in relation to cinema and other forms of mass culture and to cater more deliberately to the upper and new middle classes. And while it would be misleading to attribute this wholesale cultural transformation to the work of two men, each in his own way epitomized the pure, white "water lily" that blossomed above the "bleak, squashy and . . . sticky goo." Emblems of an elevated, jazz-hating, purebred American culture, they became during the Great Depression the casualties of radical socioeconomic changes that pushed politics to the left and transformed playwriting and performance styles. Neither O'Neill's universalizing humanism nor Nathan's contempt for the left-wing playwrights of the 1930s (dubbed "the little red writing hoods") was bound to win them many converts among the suddenly less affluent theatergoing classes.[177] Nor among playwrights. Nathan was famously scornful of Clifford Odets and described Lawson's plays as being "ridiculously fuddled and amateurish mixtures of Greenwich Village sex and Cherry Lane experimentation on the one hand and of Hollywood theme song and Metro-Goldwyn lot fancy on the other."[178] Nathan's attack betrays not only the bile for which he was renowned but also his lifelong and almost preternatural sensitivity to and scorn for the mixture of highbrow and lowbrow. And while the careful segregation of the one from the other served a useful function during the years when an art theater (that was also a commercial theater) was being consolidated, it became more and more difficult with each passing decade.

The eulogies to O'Neill and Nathan published at their deaths underscored their roles in producing an ineradicable change in U.S. theater.

Brooks Atkinson, borrowing a page from Nathan, monumentalized O'Neill, emphasizing his scale and granitic mien. The words *giant, great, epic, inexhaustible, massive, Promethean, daring, strength, integrity, energy, power,* and *passion* resound through his tribute. At the same time, he aimed to counter O'Neill's image as cold and humorless by emphasizing his amiability, gentleness, sense of humor, boyish relish, and geniality.[179] A combination of Saint Paul and Saint Francis of Assisi, O'Neill was the superhuman playwright who redeemed the theater with his blood, sweat, and tears. Nathan, on the other hand, was eulogized more equivocally in the *Times* by John Mason Brown as "a dazzling showman" and "spoiled child." Despite his idiosyncrasies, however, Nathan still qualified as a "landmark" whose "destructive" style finally proved "constructive." "If he had not possessed this unusual skill, the standards of the American theatre would not be what they are today and the excellence he championed would not be taken for granted."[180]

In working to consolidate a literary theater in the United States that would be "taken for granted" by the 1950s, O'Neill and Nathan led what was figured as a crusade to expel the "mountebanks, shysters, and pretenders" from the temple of art and install in their place a hero possessing "size, stature, daring and strength."[181] Disavowing the commercial character of the Broadway stage, they played major roles in the elevation and transformation of "the drama," redefined as a branch of literature. Given Nathan's unique amalgamation of erudition and arrogance, aristocratic taste and homicidal wit, he was able to appeal to and intercede on behalf of class fractions that in fact had very different interests: the upper class, new middle class, and intellectuals and bohemians. And because his contradictory ideologies were endlessly staged and restaged in his Luciferian prose, he was ideally positioned and equipped to explicate a playwright like O'Neill, whose work virtually demanded some kind of mediation. O'Neill, meanwhile, became the perfect "poet of the individual" for the human subject who had been fashioned an extension, simulacrum, and slave of the machine. Given the decline in leftist activism in the wake of the Palmer Raids (1919–21) and the difficulty of compassing the social and economic complexities involved in the construction of the Fordized subject, it is little wonder that so many artists who catered to elite audiences ended up dematerializing the social, turning politics into psychology and metaphysics. "[O'Neill] is the poet," Skinner wrote, "of the individual soul, of its agony, of its evil will, of its pride, and of its lusts, of its rare moments of illumination, of its stumblings and gropings in surrounding darkness."[182]

A few years after Skinner's monograph, Warner and Lunt's sociological study of "a modern community" included a survey of reading habits divided by social class. According to Warner and Lunt, the upper classes showed a marked preference for books to whose theme they gave the rather vague designation "man's fight against fate" (this genre was second in popularity among this class to volumes about "courtship and family"). Indeed, the preference for books about this fight steadily increased as one ascended the class hierarchy. At the same time, these philosophically inclined upper-class men and women displayed the least interest in "farce and humor."[183] The surfeit of texts from the 1920s extolling the titanic and tragic struggles of O'Neill's characters as well as the playwright's own ordeals (and lack of humor) suggests that he had virtually cornered the market on plays about "man's fight against fate."

Fifty years after his death, George Jean Nathan is little more than a footnote to the history of the twentieth-century stage. During the 1920s his name may have been synonymous with theater but, Connolly reports, Nathan has since his death been "attended to mainly by O'Neillians or Mencken scholars."[184] O'Neill, on the other hand, a figure more admired than loved, remains the great consecrated playwright of the U.S. theater. Despite O'Neill's fall from grace during the last twenty years of his life, Nathan and the other critics of the 1920s successfully paved the way for O'Neill's second, posthumous career by establishing an interpretive framework for his life and work. It is not surprising, then, that after O'Neill's death the critics no longer needed to be the primary agents of what was, in fact, his second canonization. That task was ceded to directors and actors. José Quintero is the key figure, who directed the 1956 U.S. premiere of *Long Day's Journey into Night* and nine subsequent Broadway premieres or revivals of O'Neill plays. Quintero, moreover, was fortunate to be able to enlist the services of some of the most illustrious actors of the era, most notably Jason Robards and Colleen Dewhurst, who are indelibly linked to *Long Day's Journey* and *Moon for the Misbegotten*, as well as Geraldine Page *(Strange Interlude)*, Liv Ullmann *(Anna Christie)*, and many others.

Increasingly, however, O'Neill's preeminence is being defined in literary historical rather than theatrical terms. Although a fixture of modern drama classes, his work has been produced in the United States since 1995 less frequently than that of Tennessee Williams or Arthur Miller. Only two O'Neill plays, *Long Day's Journey into Night* and *A Moon for the Misbegotten*, have been regularly performed by resident theater companies in the United States since 1995, and they are outnumbered by three plays each by Williams and Miller.[185] His academic profile is also changing. According to the Project Muse database, Williams and Miller have each been referenced in scholarly journals since 1997 more than three times as frequently as O'Neill.[186] Yet O'Neill's canonization is even more secure than that of Williams or Miller in part because of the success of critics like Nathan in constructing O'Neill—and by extension, himself—as the great reformer of the stage, the one who rid the legitimate theater of "vaudeville jugglers," "trained dogs," and the disreputable, working-class music that set bodies writhing and brains rattling in skulls.[187] "Jazz has nothing in common," Mitzi Kolisch wrote in 1926, with the work of Eugene O'Neill, who, like other builders of the American "dream," was striving to discover and colonize "another planet where gold is sound and color, and power is loveliness of form." O'Neill's plays represent a repudiation of "the shallow giggling of jazz" and a glorious "expression of the groping and the real struggle of the nation" toward "a grandeur and wisdom to which jazz will forever be blind."[188] Nathan could hardly have put it better.

EPILOGUE

~~~~~~

The theatrical dispensation that critics, playwrights, and producers institutionalized in the 1920s has proven remarkably resilient—even into
the twenty-first century. Legitimate theater in the United States is still regarded as an elitist, intellectual enterprise relative to the vast majority of
Hollywood films, television series, music videos, and other forms of mass
entertainment. Given the ever-widening abyss since the 1970s between the
rich and everyone else, producers and theater owners are able to charge
more and more for this majestic public amusement, up to forty-five times
as much as a movie (with the advent of so-called premium seats that can set
an investment banker back $450). During the early 1920s, the Theatre
Guild attempted to boost the prestige of the legitimate theater by prominently featuring the work of innovative European dramatists. By the end of
the decade, however, the Guild's European playwrights were outnumbered
by their American cousins, chief among them Eugene O'Neill, whose
nine-act "magnum opus," *Strange Interlude* (1928), firmly planted Freud on
the Great White Way and beat the Europeans at their own game. The five-
hour play was an unlikely yet sensational commercial success (playing 426

performances) and netted O'Neill his third Pulitzer Prize. By showing "modern life" to be "convincingly heroic," *Strange Interlude* brought "true tragedy" to Broadway "without imitating Greek or Elizabethan forms."[1]

As if to verify the elevation of the legitimate stage, the Pulitzer Prize committee the next year dropped the stipulation from the guidelines for the award in drama that the winning play should instill "educational value and power" and "rais[e] the standard of good morals, good taste, and good manners."[2] Thanks to the offices of Eugene O'Neill, George Jean Nathan, Brooks Atkinson, and many others, that clause was deemed no longer necessary because the theater had been transformed from a ragtag collection of public amusements to a forum for "true tragedy." Moreover, by 1929, those persons short of morals, taste, and manners had forsaken the theater for the movies. But even the serious theater that remained after the defection of the lower and lower middle classes could not quit aspiring for a prestige it could never confidently own. And the legitimate stage has yet to overcome this inferiority complex. At the beginning of the twenty-first century, as in the 1920s, the commercial and nonprofit theaters continue to envy opera and ballet companies, symphony orchestras, and art museums that retain a more verifiably highbrow patina and are more adept at enticing the social and economic elite to their boards of directors. Now, as then, theater critics and audiences attempt to alleviate this inferiority complex by paying obeisance to British and Anglo-Irish playwrights and directors (like Tom Stoppard, Conor McPherson, and Trevor Nunn) who have nothing new to add to the conversation in the United States about culture, society, or politics yet whose symbolic capital far exceeds that amassed by native artists. The legitimate stage is thus one of the very few cultural arenas in which the world's foremost empire remains colonized by its former ruler.

Since the opening of *Beauty and the Beast* in 1994, large multinational corporations, especially Disney, have invaded Times Square, and the Broadway theater has been nearly taken over by large entertainment conglomerates seeking to capitalize further on their already phenomenally successful properties. This invasion is in part responsible for the fact that Broadway box office revenues and numbers of tickets sold have risen steadily since 2001 despite the fact that the number of new productions has remained steady. During the 2006–7 season, 12.31 million people bought tickets to Broadway shows, while grosses totaled $939 million.[3] As a reaction to the unprecedented success of mass culture spin-offs like *Beauty and the Beast* and *Mary Poppins* (which endeavor to mimic the movies as much as possible), the arbiters of upper-middlebrow taste have taken yet again to promoting an uplifting, serious, ostensibly universal dramatic art whose lineaments can be traced back to the work of Eugene O'Neill and his contemporaries. Indeed, given the rigorous policing of the cultural position of the legitimate theater and the self-consciousness of so many playwrights, the Pulitzer Prize–winning play often arouses a sense of déjà vu. A playwright can hardly be considered serious (or a serious contender for the Pulitzer) unless he or she takes a place in the genealogy of critically approved American dramatists. For most all of these playwrights wrote not against but in concert with their predecessors, especially in regard to their theatrical vernaculars. Sam Shepard may have set Broadway on its ear, but he never undermined its basic values. Thus the predominance of domestic realism. Thus the continuing belief that the nuclear family, with a patriarch at its center, is the primary social unit. Thus the persistence of the literary theater as an upper-middlebrow preserve.

By way of example, the 2008 Pulitzer Prize–winning play, Tracy Letts's *August: Osage County*, seems almost to have been written to specification, dutifully calling up the ghosts of O'Neill, Williams, Miller, Albee, and Shepard. This fact was not lost on the critics, several of whom pointed out the resemblances. In a rave review in the *New York Times*, Charles Isherwood noted approvingly that in *August* "can be heard echoes of other classic dramas about the strangling grip of blood ties—from Eugene O'Neill's 'Long Day's Journey Into Night' to Sam Shepard's 'Buried Child.'"[4] Even *Daily Variety* applauded Letts's "hubris" in daring to write a play that invites "comparison with the work of America's greatest dramatists—Eugene O'Neill's 'Long Day's Journey Into Night' and Edward Albee's 'Who's Afraid of Virginia Woolf?'" as well as "Sam Shepard, Tennessee Williams and a dyspeptic Horton Foote."[5]

Although Broadway continues to make more and more money, its prosperity is due in part to the exclusion of work that producers and critics regard as unsuitable for the increasingly corporatized theater (both commercial and nonprofit) of an increasingly gentrified city. The success of O'Neill knockoffs combined with the seemingly unstoppable British invasion anachronistically reinforces the old cultural hierarchy that had been institutionalized in the theater between the world wars. These varieties of upper-middlebrow drama help to maintain Broadway's distance from Hollywood, on the one hand, and more risky Off Broadway drama, on the other. It works to balance lower-middlebrow fare like *Mamma Mia!*, which has always had a place on Broadway, with "serious" drama. It helps to assuage critics' anxieties about the commercial theater's seemingly inexorable slide into mass culture. It reassures theatergoers out for "an experience" that their most dearly held assumptions and prejudices may be examined but not seriously challenged.[6]

Jazz, meanwhile, has moved further and further from the precincts of Broadway. Soul, gospel, Motown, and hip-hop have replaced it as the styles most frequently employed in black musicals (like *The Color Purple*). Most new white musicals, meanwhile (like *Legally Blond: The Musical*), adopt either a generic, middle-of-the-road rock-pop, or else, in the case of so-called boutique musicals (like *The Light in the Piazza*), take up a sophisticated modernist style that owes more to Debussy and Stravinsky than to Irving Berlin. Nonetheless, the musical theater continues to have a vitality that much of the so-called straight theater sorely lacks. Hearkening back to the days of vaudeville, musicals, even in the largest houses in which they are massively overmiked, are able to establish a more immediate relationship with audiences who are simply more animated, actively engaged, and enthralled than those who frequent straight plays on Broadway. There is no question but that the biggest and most successful shows (like *The Phantom of the Opera*), with their dozens of companies all over the world, represent a new kind of mass production in an industry whose wares used to be handmade. But when one considers that almost everything in the heart of the American empire is now mass-produced, what is the problem? Or are shows like *Legally Blond* and *Hairspray* a symbol of U.S. imperial culture at its most glittering? Are they the native equivalent of gladiatorial combats and chariot races, lavish entertainments designed to keep the wealthy, excited crowds from remembering that every empire must fall?

NOTES

PROLOGUE

1. Benjamin De Casseres, "The Triumphant Genius of Eugene O'Neill," *Theatre*, February 1928, 12.

2. Daniel J. Watermeier, "O'Neill and the Theatre of His Time," in *The Cambridge Companion to Eugene O'Neill*, ed. Michael Manheim (Cambridge: Cambridge University Press, 1998), 33–47.

3. Pierre Bourdieu, "The Production of Belief," in Bourdieu, *The Field of Cultural Production: Essays on Art and Literature*, ed. Randal Johnson (New York: Columbia University Press, 1993), 76.

4. Oliver Sayler, *Our American Theatre* (New York: Brentano's, 1923), 1.

5. Michael Manheim, introduction to *Cambridge Companion to O'Neill*, 1.

6. Gilbert W. Gabriel, "The 'First-Night' Fake," *Theatre*, May 1926, 9.

7. Raymond Williams, *Drama from Ibsen to Brecht* (Oxford: Oxford University Press, 1969), 18.

8. Raymond Williams, *Marxism and Literature* (Oxford: Oxford University Press, 1977), 131.

9. Will Morrissey in *Morrissey & Miller Night Club Review*, 1927 Vitaphone short, restored by the Vitaphone Project.

10. J. Hartley Manners, *The National Anthem* (New York: George H. Doran, 1922), xi, xiv, x.

11. Paul Fritz Laubenstein, "Jazz—Debit and Credit," *Musical Quarterly* 15, no. 4 (1929): 609.

12. Carl Engel, "Jazz: A Musical Discussion," *Atlantic Monthly*, August 1922, reprinted in *Jazz in Print (1856–1929): An Anthology of Selected Early Readings in Jazz History*, ed. Karl Koenig (Hillsdale, N.Y.: Pendragon Press, 2002), 200.

13. See Jacques Derrida, *Of Grammatology*, trans. Gayatri Chakravorty Spivak (Baltimore: Johns Hopkins University Press, 1976), 151.

14. Manners, *The National Anthem*, xii.

15. Theodor W. Adorno, "Cultural Criticism and Society," in *Prisms*, trans. Samuel Weber and Shierry Weber (Cambridge: MIT Press, 1981), 30.

16. Theodor W. Adorno, "Some Ideas on the Sociology of Music," in *Sound Figures*, trans. Rodney Livingstone (Stanford, Calif.: Stanford University Press, 1999), 2–9; emphasis added.

17. See W. Lloyd Warner and Paul S. Lunt, *The Social Life of a Modern Community* (New Haven: Yale University Press, 1941); and Allison Davis, Burleigh B. Gardner, and Mary R. Gardner, directed by W. Lloyd Warner, *Deep South: A Social-Anthropological Study of Caste and Class* (Chicago: University of Chicago Press, 1941).

18. Theodor W. Adorno, *Introduction to the Sociology of Music*, trans. E. B. Ashton (New York: Seabury Press, 1976), 59.

CHAPTER ONE

1. F. Scott Fitzgerald, "Echoes of the Jazz Age," in *The Fitzgerald Reader*, ed. Arthur Mizener (New York: Scribner's, 1963), 324.

2. Isaac Goldberg, *Tin Pan Alley: A Chronicle of American Popular Music* (New York: John Day Company, 1930), 259.

3. Goldberg, *Tin Pan Alley*, 259–60.

4. Anne Shaw Faulkner, "Does Jazz Put the Sin in Syncopation?" *Ladies' Home Journal*, August 1921, reprinted in Koenig, *Jazz in Print*, 153. Koenig's anthology, which collects hundreds of documents from a great variety of magazines, newspapers, and journals, is an invaluable resource for the cultural historian.

5. Manners, *The National Anthem*, ix.

6. William Howland Kenney, *Chicago Jazz: A Cultural History, 1904–1930* (New York: Oxford University Press, 1993), 30, 37, 69, 51.

7. See John Gennari, "Jazz Criticism: Its Development and Ideologies," *Black American Literature Forum* 25, no. 3 (1991): 450.

8. Pierre Bourdieu, *Distinction: A Social Critique of the Judgement of Taste*, trans. Richard Nice (Cambridge: Harvard University Press, 1984), 32.

9. Carl Cunningham, "How's the Business with the Dance Orchestra Boys?" *Metronome*, December 1923, in Koenig, *Jazz in Print*, 265–66.

10. Ashley Pettis, cited in Deems Taylor, "Our Jazz Symposium," *Music News*, 12 December 1924, in Koenig, *Jazz in Print*, 368.

11. Stephen Wise, cited in "Where Is Jazz Leading America?" *The Étude*, September 1924, in Koenig, *Jazz in Print*, 354.

12. A. H., "Is Jazz 'the American Soul'?" letter to *Musical America*, 24 November 1923, Koenig, *Jazz in Print*, 264.

13. Preface to John Howard Lawson, *Processional: A Jazz Symphony of American Life in Four Acts* (New York: Thomas Seltzer, 1925), ix.

14. Brooks Atkinson and Albert Hirschfeld, *The Lively Years: 1920–1973* (New York: Da Capo Press, 1985), 37, 34.

15. Heywood Broun, "The New Play," *New York World*, 13 January 1925.

16. "Going to the Play with the Editor," unidentified source, *Processional* clipping file, New York Public Library for the Performing Arts. Unfortunately, many of the reviews in this file are so tattered that it is impossible to determine their provenance.

17. Alan Dale, "'Processional' Presented by Guild," *American*, 13 January 1925.

18. Percy Hammond, "Some Mysterious Proceedings at the Garrick Theater," *New York Herald-Tribune*, 13 January 1925.

19. H. Z. Torres, "'Processional' Opens at Garrick," *New York Commercial*, 13 January 1925.

20. Burns Mantle, "'Processional' Is a Discordant Jumble," *New York Daily News*, 14 January 1925.

21. Review of *Processional*, *Brooklyn Daily Eagle*, 13 January 1925; review of *Processional*, *Cincinnati Billboard*, 24 January 1925.

22. Broun, "The New Play."

23. Burns Mantle and Carlton Miles, cited in Beverle Bloch, "Searching for 'The Big American Play': The Theatre Guild Produces John Howard Lawson's *Processional*," in *Experimenters, Rebels, and Disparate Voices: The Theatre of the 1920s Celebrates American Diversity*, ed. Arthur Gewirtz and James J. Kolb (Westport, Conn.: Praeger, 2003), 7, 8.

24. Theatre Guild bulletin of 25 February 1925, cited in Bloch, "Searching," 8.

25. Hammond, "Some Mysterious Proceedings."

26. Burns Mantle, *The Best Plays of 1924–25* (New York: Dodd, Mead, 1925), 11.

27. Oliver M. Sayler, *Revolt in the Arts: A Survey of the Creation, Distribution and Appreciation of Art in America* (New York: Brentano's, 1930), 82.

28. Arthur Hornblow, "Editorial: The Red Lamp in the Theatre," *Theatre*, March 1922, 142.

29. George S. Kaufman and Marc Connelly, *Beggar on Horseback* (New York: Boni and Liveright, 1924), 34, 35, 61.

30. Samson Raphaelson, *The Jazz Singer* (New York: Brentano's, 1925), 9.

31. Raphaelson, *The Jazz Singer*, 107, 43.

32. Raphaelson, *The Jazz Singer*, 114–15.

33. Manners, *The National Anthem*, xi.

34. Manners, *The National Anthem*, 141.

35. See "Some Further Opinions on 'Jazz' by Prominent Writers," *Metronome*, August 1922, in Konig, *Jazz in Print*, 202.

36. Alexander Woollcott, "The Play," *New York Times*, 24 January 1922, 22.

37. Burns Mantle, ed., *The Best Plays of 1921–22* (New York: Dodd, Mead, 1922), 8.

38. Manners, *The National Anthem*, 107, 110, 90.

39. Walter Prichard Eaton, "The Strangling of Our Theatre: Dangers Involved in the Coming Control, by Film Producers, of the American Stage," *Vanity Fair*, April 1926, 48, 144.

40. Ludwig Lewisohn (1920), cited in Barnard Hewitt, *Theatre U.S.A.: 1668 to 1957* (New York: McGraw-Hill, 1959), 331.

41. Arthur Hobson Quinn, *A History of American Drama from the Civil War to the Present Day*, rev. ed. (New York: Appleton-Century Crofts, 1964), 200.

42. Eugene O'Neill, *Diff'rent*, in *Complete Plays, 1920–1931* (New York: Library of America, 1988), 27.

43. Sayler, *Revolt in the Arts*, 84; John Emerson, "The Great Public and Its Theatre: The Sixth Article in a Symposium on the Future of the American Stage," *Vanity Fair*, September 1926, 96.

44. Henry F. Gilbert, "Concerning Jazz," *New Music Review*, December 1922, in Koenig, *Jazz in Print*, 220.

45. Mitzi Kolisch, "Jazz in High Places," *Independent*, 10 April 1926, in Koenig, *Jazz in Print*, 463.

46. Max Harrison, "Jazz," *New Grove Dictionary of Music and Musicians*, ed. Stanley Sadie (London: Macmillan, 1980), 9:561.

47. Nicholas M. Evans, *Writing Jazz: Race, Nationalism, and Modern Culture in the 1920s* (New York: Garland, 2000), 14.

48. Fitzgerald, "Echoes of the Jazz Age," 328.

49. Charles Hamm, "Towards a New Reading of Gershwin," in *The Gershwin Style: New Looks at the Music of George Gershwin*, ed. Wayne Schneider (New York: Oxford University Press, 1999), 5–6; Abbe Niles, "Ballads, Songs and Snatches," *The Bookman*, June 1928, in Koenig, *Jazz in Print*, 535.

50. Niles, "Ballads, Songs and Snatches," 535.

51. John Gennari, *Blowin' Hot and Cool: Jazz and Its Critics* (Chicago: University of Chicago Press, 2006), 4.

52. Gennari, "Jazz Criticism," 470.

53. Evans, *Writing Jazz*, 4. Evans features one of the best and most thorough accounts of recent jazz historiography.

54. Evans, *Writing Jazz*, 6.

55. Ted Gioia, *The History of Jazz* (New York: Oxford University Press, 1997), 89.

56. See, for example, Richard M. Sudhalter, "A Racial Divide That Needn't Be," *New York Times*, 3 January 1999, sec. 2, 1+.

57. Gennari, *Blowin' Hot and Cool*, 6.

58. See, for example, Samuel A. Floyd Jr., "African Roots of Jazz" and William H. Youngren, "European Roots of Jazz," in *The Oxford Companion to Jazz*, ed. Bill Kirchner (New York: Oxford University Press, 2000), 7–28.

59. Kenney, *Chicago Jazz*, 26.

60. Langston Hughes, "The Negro Artist and the Racial Mountain," *The Nation*, June 1926, in Koenig, *Jazz in Print*, 479; Gioia, *The History of Jazz*, 95; see also Paul Lopes, *The Rise of a Jazz Art World* (New York: Cambridge University Press, 2002), 52; and Kathy J. Ogren, *The Jazz Revolution: Twenties America and the Meaning of Jazz* (New York: Oxford University Press, 1989), 111–38.

61. Youngren, "European Roots of Jazz," 27.

62. Cesar Saerchinger, "Is Jazz Coming or Going?" *Metronome*, 1 February 1926, in Koenig, *Jazz in Print*, 449.

63. H.B.B., "Jazz," *Life, Letters, and the Arts*, 31 July 1920, in Koenig, *Jazz in Print*, 146.

64. Paul Whiteman and Mary Margaret McBride, *Jazz* (New York: J. H. Sears, 1926), 3.

65. Goldberg, *Tin Pan Alley*, 271.

66. See James Lincoln Collier, *The Making of Jazz: A Comprehensive History* (New York: Dell, 1978); Gunther Schuller, *Early Jazz: Its Roots and Historical Development* (New York: Oxford University Press, 1968); and Frank Tirro, *Jazz: A History*, 2nd ed. (New York: Norton, 1993).

67. Gennari, *Blowin' Hot and Cool*, 5.

68. See Charley Gerard, *Jazz in Black and White: Race, Culture, and Identity in the Jazz Community* (Westport, Conn.: Praeger, 1998), 2.

69. See LeRoi Jones (Amiri Baraka), *Blues People: Negro Music in White America* (New York: William Morrow, 1999), 17.

70. Gerard, *Jazz in Black and White*, xvii.

71. Scott De Veaux, "Constructing the Jazz Tradition," in *The Jazz Cadence of American Culture*, ed. Robert G. O'Meally (New York: Columbia University Press, 1998), 486.

72. Schuller, *Early Jazz*, 62.

73. Youngren, "European Roots of Jazz," 26.

74. Sudhalter, "Racial Divide," 31.

75. See Lopes, *Jazz Art World*.

76. Gioia, *The History of Jazz*, 37.

77. Cited in Kenney, *Chicago Jazz*, 17.

78. Whiteman and McBride, *Jazz*, 33, 15.

79. For analyses of jazz historiography, see Gennari, "Jazz Criticism"; Gennari, *Blowin' Hot and Cool*; De Veaux, "Constructing the Jazz Tradition"; and Evans, *Writing Jazz*, 1–23.

80. Lopes, *Jazz Art World*, 50.

81. See Kenney, *Chicago Jazz*, 11.

82. See Gilman M. Ostrander, *American Civilization in the First Machine Age: 1890–1940* (New York: Harper and Row, 1970), 290–92.

83. See Carol J. Oja, *Making Modern Music: New York in the 1920s* (New York: Oxford University Press, 2000), 314.

84. Collier, *The Making of Jazz*, 78.

85. See Charles Hamm, *Yesterdays: Popular Song in America* (New York: Norton, 1979).

86. I take up the subject of jazz and art music in chapter 6.

87. Gennari, "Jazz Criticism," 464.

88. "Jazz Or—," *Musical Courier*, 7 February 1924, in Koenig, *Jazz in Print*, 273.

89. Gerald Early, "Pulp and Circumstance: The Story of Jazz in High Places," in O'Meally, *Jazz Cadence*, 407.

90. Leigh Henry, "What's Wrong with Jazz," *Musical Opinion*, November 1926, in Koenig, *Jazz in Print*, 493.

91. Gilbert Seldes, *The 7 Lively Arts* (Mineola, N.Y.: Dover, 2001), 95, 98.

92. Cited in "What Effect Is Jazz Likely to Have upon the Music of the Future?" *The Étude*, September 1924, in Koenig, *Jazz in Print*, 352.

93. John Tasker Howard, *Our American Music: Three Hundred Years of It* (New York: Thomas Y. Crowell, 1931), 416, 591.

94. Gennari, *Blowin' Hot and Cool*, 45.

95. Schuller, *Early Jazz*, 192 n. 21.

96. Jane M. Gaines, *Contested Culture: The Image, the Voice, and the Law* (Chapel Hill: University of North Carolina Press, 1991), 120.

97. Copyright Act of 1909, http://www.copyright.gov/history/1909act.pdf (accessed 31 October 2007).

98. E. P. Skone James and Peter Kleiner, "Copyright, United States of America," *New Grove Dictionary*, 4:744–45.

99. Russell Sanjek, *From Print to Plastic: Publishing and Promoting America's Popular Music (1900–1980)* (New York: Institute for Studies of American Music, 1983), 13.

100. Gaines, *Contested Culture*, 130.

101. Lisa Gitelman, "Reading Music, Reading Records, Reading Race: Musical Copyright and the U.S. Copyright Act of 1909," *Musical Quarterly* 81, no. 2. (1997): 285.

102. Gaines, *Contested Culture*, 122.

103. Justice Day, writing for the majority in *White-Smith Music Co. v. Apollo Co.* (1908), cited in Gaines, *Contested Culture*, 130.

104. Goldberg, *Tin Pan Alley*, 267–68.

105. Jeffrey Melnick, *A Right to Sing the Blues: African Americans, Jews, and American Popular Song* (Cambridge: Harvard University Press, 1999), 31, 37.

106. Gitelman, "Reading Music," 279.

107. Gitelman, "Reading Music," 276–77.

108. Lewis A. Erenberg, *Steppin' Out: New York Nightlife and the Transformation of American Culture, 1890–1930* (Chicago: University of Chicago Press, 1981), 196. Doubtless there are many more anecdotes of this sort.

109. Gaines, *Contested Culture*, 118.

110. Gennari, *Blowin' Hot and Cool*, 16.

111. Lopes, *Jazz Art World*, 51, 53.

112. Early, "Pulp and Circumstance," 409.

113. See Oja, *Making Modern Music*, 327; Lopes, *Jazz Art World*, 61.

114. Hamm, "New Reading of Gershwin," 7.

115. Frank Patterson, "'Jazz'—the National Anthem (Part II)," *Musical Courier*, 11 May 1922, in Koenig, *Jazz in Print*, 184.

116. Gershwin, "Jazz Is the Voice of the American Soul," *Theatre*, March 1927, 52B.

117. Gershwin, "The Composer and the Machine Age" (1933), reprinted in *George Gershwin*, ed. Merle Armitage (New York: Da Capo Press, 1995), 225.

118. Edward F. Albee, "Twenty Years of Vaudeville," in *American Vaudeville as*

Seen by Its Contemporaries, ed. Charles W. Stein (New York: Knopf, 1984), 215.

119. Marian Spitzer, "The Mechanics of Vaudeville," *Saturday Evening Post*, 24 May 1924, rpt. in Stein, *American Vaudeville*, 173, 175–76.

120. Walter de Leon, "The Wow Finish," *Saturday Evening Post*, 14 February 1925, rpt. in Stein, *American Vaudeville*, 194, 207.

121. Edwin Milton Royle, "The Vaudeville Theatre," *Scribner's*, October 1899, rpt. in Stein, *American Vaudeville*, 33.

122. George and Ira Gershwin, the verse to "Fascinating Rhythm," from *Lady, Be Good!* (1924); Ira Gershwin, *The Complete Lyrics of Ira Gershwin*, ed. Robert Kimball (New York: Da Capo Press, 1998), 48.

123. Whiteman and McBride, *Jazz*, 33, 130.

124. Caroline Caffin, "Vaudeville Music," rpt. in Stein, *American Vaudeville*, 209.

125. "The Appeal of Primitive Jazz," *Literary Digest*, 25 August 1917, in Koenig, *Jazz in Print*, 119.

126. Cunningham, "How's the Business," 265.

127. "King Jazz and Jazz Kings," *Literary Digest*, 30 January 1926, in Koenig, *Jazz in Print*, 446; U.S. federal budget of $2.9 billion cited in Stephen Moore, "If Congress Won't Cut the Budget, Then Freeze It," http://www.cato.org/dailys/1-13-97.html (accessed 3 January 2006).

128. *Rosalie* (1928) racked up 335 performances, but the music was credited to George Gershwin and Sigmund Romberg and the lyrics to Ira Gershwin and P. G. Wodehouse.

129. The critic for the *Brooklyn Eagle*, quoted in Tommy Krasker, "A Wonderful Party: *Lady, Be Good!*" booklet to recording of George and Ira Gershwin, *Lady, Be Good!*, Nonesuch 79308-2, 1992, 16.

130. W. R., "At the Liberty: 'Lady, Be Good!'," *World*, 2 December 1924.

131. Alan Dale, "Liberty Theatre—'Lady, Be Good!,' a New Musical Comedy Presented by A. A. Aarons and Vinton Freedly," *American*, 4 December 1924. For information about the original orchestrations, see Krasker, "A Wonderful Party," 15–19.

132. Cited in Deena Rosenberg, *Fascinating Rhythm: The Collaboration of George and Ira Gershwin* (New York: Dutton, 1991), 108–10; Gershwin, "Jazz Is the Voice," 52B.

133. Dale, "Liberty Theatre—'Lady, Be Good!'"

CHAPTER TWO

1. Brenda Murphy, "Plays and Playwrights: 1915–1945," in Don B. Wilmeth and Christopher Bigsby, eds., *The Cambridge History of American Theatre*, vol. 2, *1870–1945* (Cambridge: Cambridge University Press, 1999), 289.

2. Jack Poggi, *Theater in America: The Impact of Economic Forces, 1870–1967* (Ithaca, N.Y.: Cornell University Press, 1968), 47.

3. Poggi, *Theater in America*, 48.

4. Hewitt, *Theatre USA*, 333.

5. Manheim, introduction to *Cambridge Companion to O'Neill*, 1.

6. Poggi, *Theater in America*, 30.

7. Brock Pemberton, "What Price Independence? The Future of the American Theatre as Viewed by a Theatrical Manager," *Vanity Fair*, July 1926, 71.

8. Lee Shubert, "All's Right With the Theatrical World," *Vanity Fair*, June 1926, 117; Poggi, *Theater in America*, 53.

9. Cited in Poggi, *Theater in America*, 53.

10. Donald Freedman, "Our Theatre: A Requiem," *Vanity Fair*, March 1926, 49.

11. Edgar Macgregor, "What's the Matter with Musical Comedy?," *Theatre*, July 1922, 120.

12. Richard Butsch, *The Making of American Audiences: From Stage to Television, 1750–1990* (Cambridge: Cambridge University Press, 2000), 122.

13. Cited in Alfred L. Bernheim, *The Business of the Theatre: An Economic History of the American Theatre, 1750–1932* (New York: Benjamin Blom, 1932; 1964), 91.

14. "The Variety Theatres: Sentador's Views on the Decline (?) of this Amusement," *New York Dramatic Mirror*, 18 January 1879, 4.

15. Joseph Jefferson, *The Autobiography of Joseph Jefferson*, ed. Alan S. Downer (Cambridge, Mass.: Harvard University Press, 1964), 312.

16. Jefferson, *Autobiography*, 50.

17. "The Octoroon," *New York Times*, 15 December 1859, 4.

18. Charles Coburn, "Our Theatre Fighting for Its Life," *Theatre*, July 1926, 9.

19. Coburn, "Our Theatre Fighting," 9.

20. Robert McLaughlin, *Broadway and Hollywood: A History of Economic Interaction* (New York: Arno Press, 1974), n.p., 9. This book remains the most comprehensive study of the economic relationship between theater and film.

21. For an excellent account of the field, see John Frow, *Cultural Studies and Cultural Value* (Oxford: Oxford University Press, 1995). See also Tony Bennett, Colin Mercer, and Janet Woollacott, eds., *Popular Culture and Social Relations* (Milton Keynes: Open University Press, 1986).

22. Bertolt Brecht, "Against Georg Lukács," in *Aesthetics and Politics*, ed. Ronald Taylor (London: Verso, 1980), 83.

23. Theodor W. Adorno, "Perennial Fashion—Jazz," in *Prisms*, 128–29.

24. See, for example, Theodor W. Adorno, "Television and the Patterns of Mass Culture," in Bernard Rosenberg and David Manning White, eds., *Mass Culture: The Popular Arts in America* (New York: Free Press, 1957), 474–88.

25. Michael Kammen, *American Culture, American Tastes: Social Change and the 20th Century* (New York: Knopf, 1999), 22.

26. See Frow, *Cultural Studies*.

27. Stuart Hall, "Notes on Deconstructing 'the Popular,'" in *People's History and Socialist Theory*, ed. Raphael Samuel (London: Routledge and Kegan Paul, 1981), 227.

28. Raymond Williams, *Keywords: A Vocabulary of Culture and Society* (Glasgow: Fontana, 1976), 198–99.

29. Peter Burke, "The 'Discovery' of Popular Culture," in Samuel, *People's History*, 216–17.

30. Joan Shelley Rubin, *The Making of Middlebrow Culture* (Chapel Hill: University of North Carolina Press, 1992), 13–14.

31. Lawrence W. Levine, *Highbrow/Lowbrow: The Emergence of Cultural Hierarchy in America* (Cambridge: Harvard University Press, 1988), 221–22.

32. Levine, *Highbrow/Lowbrow*, 219, 230.

33. Paul R. Gorman, *Left Intellectuals and Popular Culture in America* (Chapel Hill: University of North Carolina Press, 1996), 45.

34. Jane Addams, quoted in Gorman, *Left Intellectuals*, 46.

35. See Thomas H. Dickinson, *The Insurgent Theatre* (New York: Benjamin Blom, 1972), 228.

36. Dickinson, *The Insurgent Theatre*, 83.

37. Janice Radway, "The Scandal of the Middlebrow: The Book-of-the-Month Club, Class Fracture, and Cultural Authority," *South Atlantic Quarterly* 89:4 (Fall 1990), 726–27.

38. See Gorman, *Left Intellectuals*, 34–52.

39. Cited in Terry Smith, *Making the Modern: Industry, Art, and Design in America* (Chicago: University of Chicago Press, 1993), 19.

40. Cited in Kammen, *American Culture*, 33–34.

41. Cited in Gorman, *Left Intellectuals*, 55.

42. Hall, "Notes on Deconstructing," 229.

43. Hall, "Notes on Deconstructing," 233.

44. R. J. Coady, "American Art," *The Soil* 1 (January 1917): 54–55.

45. William Wasserstrom, "Van Wyck Brooks," in *American Writers: A Collection of Literary Biographies*, ed. Leonard Unger (New York: Scribner's, 1974), vol. 1, 240.

46. Van Wyck Brooks, "'Highbrow' and 'Lowbrow,'" in *America's Coming of Age* (New York: E. P. Dutton, 1915), 35. Further citations will be noted in the text.

47. See Oja, *Making Modern Music*, 315.

48. Michael Kammen, *The Lively Years: Gilbert Seldes and the Transformation of Cultural Criticism in the United States* (New York: Oxford University Press, 1996), 31.

49. Kammen, *The Lively Years*, 68.

50. Seldes, *The 7 Lively Arts*, 348.

51. Gilbert Seldes, "Producers and Playwrights of 1924–25," *Theatre*, July 1925, 58.

52. See Jacques Derrida, "The Theater of Cruelty and the Closure of Representation," in *Writing and Difference*, trans. Alan Bass (Chicago: University of Chicago Press, 1978), 247.

53. See Derrida, "Theater of Cruelty," 235.

54. See Walter Benjamin, "The Work of Art in the Age of Mechanical Reproduction," *Illuminations*, trans. Harry Zohn (New York: Schocken Books, 1955), 217–51.

55. Martin Puchner, *Stage Fright: Modernism, Anti-theatricality, and Drama* (Baltimore: Johns Hopkins University Press, 2002), 7.

56. Puchner, *Stage Fright*, 7, 11.

57. Cited in C. Wright Mills, *White Collar: The American Middle Classes* (New York: Oxford University Press, 1951), 145.

58. Gorman, *Left Intellectuals*, 81.

59. Janice Radway, "On the Gender of the Middlebrow Consumer and the Threat of the Culturally Fraudulent Female," *South Atlantic Quarterly* 93:4 (Fall 1994), 872.

60. Radway, "Gender of the Middlebrow," 872.

61. Radway, "Scandal of the Middlebrow," 733 n. 7.

62. Russell Lynes, "Highbrow, Lowbrow, Middlebrow," in *The Tastemakers* (New York: Harper & Brothers, 1954), 318, 313.

63. Bourdieu, *Distinction*, 319, 323, 327; see also Rubin, *Making of Middlebrow Culture*.

64. Kammen, *American Culture*, 14.

65. See David Savran, "Middlebrow Anxiety," *A Queer Sort of Materialism: Recontextualizing American Theatre* (Ann Arbor: University of Michigan Press, 2003), 3–55.

66. Paul DiMaggio, "Cultural Boundaries and Structural Change: The Extension of the High Culture Model to Theater, Opera, and the Dance, 1900–1940," *Cultivating Differences: Symbolic Boundaries and the Making of Inequality*, ed. Michèle Lamont and Marcel Fournier (Chicago: University of Chicago Press, 1992), 25.

67. Dorothy Chansky, *Composing Ourselves: The Little Theatre Movement and the American Audience* (Carbondale: Southern Illinois University Press, 2004), 74.

68. Dickinson, *The Insurgent Theatre*, 41, 16.

69. Eaton, "Strangling of Our Theatre," 47–48.

70. George Jean Nathan, *The Popular Theatre*, rev. ed. (New York: Knopf, 1923), 20–21.

71. Nathan, *The Popular Theatre*, 9, 44.

72. Gerald Bordman, *The Oxford Companion to American Theatre*, 2nd ed. (New York: Oxford University Press, 1992), 461.

73. Burns Mantle, "Introduction," *The Best Plays of 1919–20* (New York: Dodd, Mead and Company, 1920), iv; Seldes, *The 7 Lively Arts*, 315–16.

74. Mantle, "Introduction," *Best Plays of 1919–20*, iv.

75. Mantle, "Introduction," *Best Plays of 1919–20*, iv; Burns Mantle, "Introduction," *Best Plays of 1921–22*, iii.

76. Mantle, "Introduction," *Best Plays of 1920–21*, iii.

77. Nathan, *The Popular Theatre*, 21.

78. André Siegfried, *America Comes of Age*, trans. H.H. Hemming and Doris Hemming (New York: Harcourt, Brace, and Co., 1927), 3.

79. Mills, *White Collar*, 146.

80. Thomas F. Connolly, *George Jean Nathan and the Making of Modern American Drama Criticism* (Madison, NJ: Fairleigh Dickinson University Press, 2000), 27.

CHAPTER THREE

1. See Howard Pollack, *George Gershwin: His Life and Work* (Berkeley: University of California Press, 2006).

2. Oja, *Making Modern Music*, 325.

3. See Pollack, *George Gershwin.*

4. Pollack, *George Gershwin,* 270.

5. Isaac Goldberg, *George Gershwin: A Study in American Music* (New York: Simon and Schuster, 1931), 121, 120.

6. For a summary of the reviews, see Goldberg, *George Gershwin,* 148–55.

7. David Schiff, *Gershwin: Rhapsody in Blue* (Cambridge: Cambridge University Press, 1997), 94.

8. Gershwin, "Jazz Is the Voice," 52B.

9. Kirsty Scott, "Gershwin Leads Composer Rich List," *The Guardian,* 29 August 2005. http://arts.guardian.co.uk/news/story/0,,1558516,00.html (accessed 4 December 2007).

10. Charles L. Buchanan, "Gershwin and Musical Snobbery," *The Outlook,* 2 February 1927, rpt. in *Gershwin in His Time: A Biographical Scrapbook, 1919–1937,* ed. Gregory R. Suriano (New York: Gramercy Books, 1998), 44–45.

11. Evans, *Writing Jazz,* 119.

12. Carl Van Vechten, "George Gershwin, An American Composer Who Is Writing Notable Music in the Jazz Idiom," *Vanity Fair,* March 1925, rpt. in Edward Jablonski, *Gershwin Remembered* (London: Faber and Faber, 1992), 36.

13. Carol Oja, "Gershwin and American Modernists of the 1920s," *Musical Quarterly* 78, no. 4 (1994): 655.

14. Gershwin, "Jazz Is the Voice," 52B.

15. John Seabrook, *Nobrow* (New York: Knopf, 2000), 27.

16. Howard, *Our American Music,* 418.

17. Goldberg, *Tin Pan Alley,* 293–94.

18. Waldo Frank, "Jazz and Folk Art," *New Republic,* 1 December 1926, in Koenig, *Jazz in Print,* 498.

19. "Leave 'Jazz' Alone," *Musical Courier,* 26 October 1922, in Koenig, *Jazz in Print,* 210.

20. Henrietta Straus, "Jazz and 'The Rhapsody in Blue,'" *The Nation,* 5 March 1924, in Koenig, *Jazz in Print,* 292.

21. Quoted in Schiff, *Gershwin,* 90–91.

22. George Gershwin, "Our New National Anthem," *Theatre,* May 1925, 30.

23. Gershwin, "Composer and Machine Age," 227.

24. Gershwin, "Jazz Is the Voice," 52B.

25. See George Gershwin, "Does Jazz Belong to Art?" *Singing,* July 1926, rpt. in Suriano, *Gershwin in His Time,* 37–39.

26. George Gershwin, "Fifty Years of American Music," *American Hebrew,* 22 November 1929, 46.

27. George Gershwin, letter to Ira Gershwin, 1935, cited in Pollack, *George Gershwin,* 209.

28. Pollack, *George Gershwin,* 209; see also Hamm, "New Reading of Gershwin."

29. "'Gershwin's Music Subversive' Says Senator McCarthy," *Melody Maker,* 13 June 1953, cited in Pollack, *George Gershwin,* 209.

30. Eubie Blake, quoted in a clipping from an unknown New York newspaper (1921), in Robert Kimball and William Bolcom, *Reminiscing with Sissle and Blake* (New York: Viking Press, 1973), 108.

31. See Kimball and Bolcom, *Reminiscing*, 95.

32. Nathan Irvin Huggins, *Harlem Renaissance* (New York: Oxford University Press, 1971), 288; George Jean Nathan, *The World in Falseface* (New York: Knopf, 1923), 180.

33. Seldes, *The 7 Lively Arts*, 152–53.

34. See Kimball and Bolcom, *Reminiscing*, 138.

35. See Allen Woll, *Black Musical Theatre: From "Coontown" to "Dreamgirls"* (New York: Da Capo Press, 1989), 60, 67.

36. Review in the *Evening Journal*, cited in Kimball and Bolcom, *Reminiscing*, 94.

37. Marshall Stearns and Jean Stearns, *Jazz Dance: The Story of American Vernacular Dance* (New York: Schirmer Books, 1979), 137, 134.

38. Robert Kimball, "*Shuffle Along*," liner notes to *Shuffle Along*, New World Records NW 260 (1976), 4.

39. Kimball and Bolcom, *Reminiscing*, 88.

40. Alan Dale, "'Shuffle Along' Full of Pep and Real Melody," *New York American* (1921), rpt. in Kimball and Bolcom, *Reminiscing*, 99.

41. David Krasner, *Resistance, Parody, and Double Consciousness in African American Theatre, 1895–1910* (New York: Palgrave Macmillan, 1997), 1.

42. Although the title song from the Gershwins' *Of Thee I Sing* is both a ballad and a campaign song, I think of it above all as a pseudo-national anthem.

43. Ibee, "Shuffle Along," *Variety*, May 1921, rpt. in Kimball and Bolcom, *Reminiscing*, 98.

44. Kimball, "*Shuffle Along*," 2.

45. "Adele Astaire Fascinates," *New York Times*, 2 December 1924.

46. Alan Dale, Review of *Lady, Be Good!*, *New York American*, 4 December 1924.

47. Goldberg, *George Gershwin*, 190.

48. Goldberg, *George Gershwin*, 188.

49. Scott McMillin, *The Musical as Drama: A Study of the Principles and Conventions behind Musical Shows from Kern to Sondheim* (Princeton: Princeton University Press, 2006), 18.

50. Goldberg, *George Gershwin*, 188, 185.

51. Goldberg, *George Gershwin*, 188.

52. Goldberg, *George Gershwin*, 189.

53. Goldberg, *George Gershwin*, 189, 188, 186.

54. Mark N. Grant, *The Rise and Fall of the Broadway Musical* (Boston: Northeastern University Press, 2004), 136–37.

55. Philip Furia, *The Poets of Tin Pan Alley: A History of America's Great Lyricists* (New York: Oxford University Press, 1992), 12.

56. "'Tip Toes' Here with Tunes," anonymous review in the *New York Times*, 29 December 1925; Alexander Woollcott, "The Stage: Mr. Gershwin's Latest," *New York World*, 29 December 1925.

57. John McGlinn, liner notes to *Gershwin Overtures*, John McGlinn conducting the New Princess Theater Orchestra, EMI CDC-547977 (1987), 6.

58. Philip Furia, *Ira Gershwin: The Art of the Lyricist* (New York: Oxford University Press, 1996), 51.

59. Music by George Gershwin, lyrics by Ira Gershwin, book by Guy Bolton and Fred Thompson, *Tip-Toes*, typescript, the Billy Rose Theatre Collection, New York Public Library for the Performing Arts, Lincoln Center, 1–2, 1–6.

60. Woollcott, "The Stage."

61. See Robert W. Snyder, *The Voice of the City: Vaudeville and Popular Culture in New York* (Chicago: Ivan R. Dee, 2000), 117–20.

62. See Melnick, *Right to Sing*, 109–10.

63. Snyder, *Voice of the City*, 117.

64. Ira Gershwin, "These Charming People," in *Complete Lyrics*, 70.

65. Andrea Most, *Making Americans: Jews and the Broadway Musical* (Cambridge: Harvard University Press, 2004), 40–41.

66. "Gershwin Bros.," *Time*, 20 July 1925, 14.

67. "Gershwin Bros.," *Time*, 14.

68. "Gershwin Bros.," 14; Nathaniel Shilkret, "George Gershwin—a Tribute," liner notes to his 1938 Gershwin recordings, rpt. in book to *Gems from Gershwin: Magic Key Program*, RCA Victor 09026-63275-2 (1998).

69. Gerald Mast, *Can't Help Singin': The American Musical of Stage and Screen* (Woodstock, N.Y.: Overlook Press, 1987), 67.

70. Ira Gershwin, "When Do We Dance?" in *Complete Lyrics*, 70.

71. J. A. Rogers, "Jazz at Home," *The Survey*, 1 March 1925, in Koenig, *Jazz in Print*, 389.

72. Arthur Hornblow, "The Editor's Uneasy Chair: Jazz Receives a Solar Plexus," *Theatre*, November 1926, 7.

73. Daniel Gregory Mason, *Tune In, America: A Study of Our Coming Musical Independence* (New York: Knopf, 1931), 164.

74. William J. Schultz, "Jazz," *The Nation*, 25 October 1922, in Koenig, *Jazz in Print*, 209.

75. Andreas Huyssen, *After the Great Divide: Modernism, Mass Culture, Postmodernism* (Bloomington: Indiana University Press, 1986), 53.

76. Radway, "Gender of the Middlebrow," 880.

77. Gershwin, "Our New National Anthem," 30.

78. Quoted in Goldberg, *George Gershwin*, 139.

79. See Schiff, *Gershwin*, 89; Goldberg, *Tin Pan Alley*, 259.

80. Hornblow, "The Editor's Uneasy Chair," 7.

81. Schultz, "Jazz," 209.

82. Gershwin, "Our New National Anthem," 30.

83. MacDonald Smith Moore, *Yankee Blues: Musical Culture and American Identity* (Bloomington: Indiana University Press, 1985), 71.

84. Gerald Bordman, *American Musical Theatre: A Chronicle*, expanded ed. (New York: Oxford University Press, 1986), 438.

85. Irving Caesar, Joseph Meyer, and Roger Wolfe Kahn, "Crazy Rhythm," in *Reading Lyrics*, ed. Robert Gottlieb and Robert Kimball (New York: Pantheon, 2000), 220.

86. Bourdieu, *Distinction*, 18.

87. Mason, *Tune In, America*, 159–61.

88. Mason, *Tune In, America*, 162–65.

89. "The Jewish Aspect of the 'Movie' Problem" and "Jewish Supremacy in the Motion Picture World," from the *Dearborn Independent*, February 1921, excerpted in J. Hoberman and Jeffrey Shandler, *Entertaining America: Jews, Movies, and Broadcasting* (Princeton: Princeton University Press, 2003), 51–52.

90. Goldberg, *Tin Pan Alley*, 260.

91. Herbert's "Oriental Serenade" and a reconstruction of the entire concert can be heard on *Paul Whiteman's Historic Aeolian Hall Concert of 1924*, reconstructed and conducted by Maurice Peress, Musicmasters MMD 60113T.

92. Ira Gershwin, "Fascinating Rhythm," in *Complete Lyrics*, 48; see Rosenberg, *Fascinating Rhythm*, 88–97.

93. Ira Gershwin, "Juanita," in *Complete Lyrics*, 53.

94. Music by George Gershwin, lyrics by Ira Gershwin, book by Guy Bolton and Fred Thompson, *Lady, Be Good!*, typescript, the Billy Rose Theatre Collection, New York Public Library for the Performing Arts, Lincoln Center, 1–28.

95. Nathan, *The Popular Theatre*, 21, 33.

96. Nathan, *The Popular Theatre*, 48, 42.

97. Sayler, *Our American Theatre*, 247.

98. Herman J. Mankiewicz, "An Enquiry into Present Day Burlesque," *Vanity Fair*, November 1925, 76.

99. Sayler, *Our American Theatre*, 187.

100. Sayler, *Our American Theatre*, 246, 252.

101. Mast, *Can't Help Singin'*, 58; Sayler, *Our American Theatre*, 252.

102. Walter Prichard Eaton, *The American Stage of To-Day* (Boston: Small, Maynard, 1908), 324; Nathan, *The Popular Theatre*, 81.

103. Nathan, *The Popular Theatre*, 81.

104. Goldberg, *Tin Pan Alley*, 259–60.

105. Furia, *Poets of Tin Pan Alley*, 126, 128.

106. Goldberg, *George Gershwin*, 199.

107. Cited in Rosenberg, *Fascinating Rhythm*, 132.

108. Rosenberg, *Fascinating Rhythm*, 132.

109. Linton Martin, cited in Rosenberg, *Fascinating Rhythm*, 109–10.

110. Gershwin, "Fifty Years of American Music," 46.

111. Goldberg, *George Gershwin*, 37.

112. Goldberg, *George Gershwin*, 53, 11.

113. Goldberg, *George Gershwin*, 11.

114. Goldberg, *George Gershwin*, 3.

115. Alec Wilder, *American Popular Song: The Great Innovators, 1900–1950* (New York: Oxford University Press, 1990), 122.

116. Wilder, *American Popular Song*, 133.

117. Pollack, *George Gershwin*, 330.

118. Ira Gershwin, "We're Here Because," in *Complete Lyrics*, 48.

119. Raymond Williams, "Metropolitan Perceptions and the Emergence of Modernism," in *The Politics of Modernism: Against the New Conformists* (London: Verso, 1989), 43.

120. Virgil Thomson, "The Cult of Jazz," *Vanity Fair*, June 1925, in Koenig, *Jazz in Print*, 413.

121. Paul Rosenfeld, "No Chabrier," *New Republic*, 4 January 1933, in Jablonski, *Gershwin Remembered*, 117–18.

122. Charles Schwartz, "George Gershwin," *New Grove Dictionary*, 7:303.

123. Richard Crawford, "George Gershwin," *Grove Music Online* (accessed 31 March 2006); Rosenfeld, "No Chabrier," 118.

124. See Steven E. Gilbert, *The Music of Gershwin* (New Haven: Yale University Press, 1995), 90–111.

125. Oja, *Making Modern Music*, 321.

126. Beverly Nichols, from *Are They the Same at Home?* in Suriano, *Gershwin in His Time*, 52.

127. Oja, *Making Modern Music*, 323.

128. Abbe Niles, "Lady Jazz in the Vestibule," *New Republic*, 23 December 1925, in Koenig, *Jazz in Print*, 438.

129. Edward Burlingame Hill, "Jazz," *Harvard Graduate Magazine*, March 1925, in Koenig, *Jazz in Print*, 400.

130. Cited in Goldberg, *George Gershwin*, 139.

131. Nichols, in Suriano, *Gershwin in His Time*, 52.

132. Rosenfeld, "No Chabrier," 117; Thomson, "The Cult of Jazz," 413.

133. Hill, "Jazz," 401.

134. Mason, *Tune In, America*, 160.

135. Snyder, *Voice of the City*, 149; Rennold Wolf, cited in Susan A. Glenn, *Female Spectacle: The Theatrical Roots of Modern Feminism* (Cambridge: Harvard University Press, 2000), 63.

136. Quoted in Schiff, *Gershwin*, 12.

137. Mason, *Tune In, America*, 161–62.

138. Moore, *Yankee Blues*, 71.

139. Ira Gershwin, "Sweet and Low-Down," in *Complete Lyrics*, 72.

140. Wilder, *American Popular Song*, 135.

141. Gershwin, "Sweet and Low-Down," 72.

142. Woolcott, "The Stage."

143. Gershwin, "Sweet and Low-Down," 72.

144. Paul Whiteman, cited in D. J., "For Better or Worse," *Musical Digest*, February 1924, in Koenig, *Jazz in Print*, 287.

145. Compare Charles Schwartz, "George Gershwin," 7:302–4 to Crawford, "George Gershwin."

146. Emerson, "Great Public," 65.

CHAPTER FOUR

1. Jesse Frederick Steiner, *Americans at Play* (1933; rpt. New York: Arno Press, 1970), 108.

2. Robert S. Lynd and Helen Merrell Lynd, *Middletown: A Study in Modern American Culture* (New York: Harcourt, Brace, 1929), 240.

3. Bourdieu, *Distinction*, 11.

4. Marion Wilson, Ph.D. diss. " 'Such Fantasy, Such Harlequinade': Ziegfeld,

Class, and the Cultural Hierarchy" (PhD. diss., City University of New York Graduate Center, 2005).

5. Butsch, *Making of American Audiences*, 125, 127.

6. DiMaggio, "Cultural Boundaries," 28.

7. Snyder, *Voice of the City*, 83–84, 103.

8. Richard Koszarski, *An Evening's Entertainment: The Age of the Silent Feature Picture, 1915–1928* (Berkeley: University of California Press, 1990), 25.

9. See Koszarski, *An Evening's Entertainment*, 44.

10. Cited in Koszarski, *An Evening's Entertainment*, 44–45.

11. Miriam Hansen, *Babel and Babylon: Spectatorship in American Silent Film* (Cambridge: Harvard University Press, 1991), 93.

12. See Koszarski, *An Evening's Entertainment*, 30–31.

13. Butsch, *Making of American Audiences*, 141–42.

14. Hansen, *Babel and Babylon*, 65.

15. Butsch, *Making of American Audiences*, 144.

16. Cited in Koszarski, *An Evening's Entertainment*, 26. And this circumstance continues into the twenty-first century.

17. John F. Barry, cited in Koszarski, *An Evening's Entertainment*, 25.

18. Koszarski, *An Evening's Entertainment*, 20.

19. Eaton, "Strangling of Our Theatre," 47.

20. Victor Watson, cited in Koszarski, *An Evening's Entertainment*, 20.

21. Emily Post, *Etiquette* (New York: Funk and Wagnalls, 1924), 1, 40.

22. See Koszarski, *An Evening's Entertainment*, 30–31.

23. Bourdieu, *Distinction*, 40.

24. Poggi, *Theater in America*, 30.

25. Poggi, *Theater in America*, 40.

26. Bernheim, *Business of the Theatre*, 83.

27. Cited in Bernheim, *Business of the Theatre*, 77.

28. Cited in Bernheim, *Business of the Theatre*, 78.

29. Bernheim, *Business of the Theatre*, 87.

30. See especially Bernheim, *Business of the Theatre;* Poggi, *Theater in America;* and McLaughlin, *Broadway and Hollywood.*

31. See Poggi, *Theater in America*, 71.

32. See Koszarski, *An Evening's Entertainment*, 15.

33. Poggi, *Theater in America*, 41.

34. Steiner, *Americans at Play*, 111.

35. Poggi, *Theater in America*, 36.

36. See Poggi, *Theater in America*, 41.

37. Steiner, *Americans at Play*, 110.

38. Bernheim, *Business of the Theatre*, 88.

39. Brock Pemberton, "Broadway and Main Street," *Theatre*, March 1926, 9.

40. Poggi, *Theater in America*, 47, 48, 50.

41. See McLaughlin, *Broadway and Hollywood*, 287.

42. Burns Mantle, "Introduction," *The Best Plays of 1925–26* (New York: Dodd, Mead, 1926), v.

43. Poggi, *Theater in America*, 65–66.

44. See, for example, Pemberton, "Broadway and Main Street," 9.

45. J. J. Shubert, "What It Costs to Put On a Show—and Why," *Theatre*, September 1925, 54.

46. Poggi, *Theater in America*, 67–73.

47. Shubert, "What It Costs," 54.

48. William J. Baumol and William G. Bowen, *Performing Arts—the Economic Dilemma* (New York: Twentieth Century Fund, 1966), 162.

49. Peter Fearon, *War, Prosperity, and Depression: The US Economy, 1917–1945* (Lawrence: University of Kansas Press, 1987) 52.

50. Baumol and Bowen, *Performing Arts*, 164.

51. Bernheim, *Business of the Theatre*, 120.

52. See Poggi, *Theater in America*, 65–71.

53. Baumol and Bowen, *Performing Arts*, 163.

54. Poggi, *Theater in America*, 85.

55. Poggi, *Theater in America*, 89.

56. See Mills, *White Collar*.

57. Stanley Aronowitz, *How Class Works: Power and Social Movement* (New Haven: Yale University Press, 2003), 65.

58. Louis M. Hacker, *American Problems of Today: A History of the United States since the World War* (New York: F. S. Crofts, 1938), 80, 86, 79.

59. Quoted in Allan Nevins and Henry Steele Commager, with Jeffrey Morris, *A Pocket History of the United States* (New York: Pocket Books, 1992), 410.

60. Fearon, *War, Prosperity and Depression*, 19, 48; Aronowitz, *How Class Works*, 69.

61. Aronowitz, *How Class Works*, 69.

62. Irving Bernstein, *The Lean Years: A History of the American Worker 1920–1933* (New York: Da Capo, 1960), 47.

63. H. Dewey Anderson and Percy E. Davidson, *Occupational Trends in the United States* (Stanford: Stanford University Press, 1940), 587.

64. Fearon, *War, Prosperity, and Depression*, 55.

65. Fearon, *War, Prosperity, and Depression*, 67.

66. Hacker, *American Problems of Today*, 80.

67. See Bernstein, *The Lean Years*, 63.

68. Aronowitz, *How Class Works*, 67.

69. Smith, *Making the Modern*, 51, 53.

70. Bernstein, *The Lean Years*, 55.

71. Margo Anderson, "The Language of Class in Twentieth-Century America," *Social Science History* 12 no. 4 (1988): 349–50.

72. Keith Bradsher, "Gap in Wealth in U.S. Called Widest in West," *New York Times*, 17 April 1995, A1.

73. Milton M. Gordon, "Social Class in American Sociology," *American Journal of Sociology* 55, no. 3 (1949): 264.

74. See Pitrim Sorokin, *Social Mobility* (New York: Harper and Brothers, 1927).

75. E. Digby Baltzell, "'Who's Who in America' and 'The Social Register': Elite and Upper Class Indexes in Metropolitan America," in *Class, Status, and*

Power: Social Stratification in Comparative Perspective, ed. Reinhard Bendix and Seymour Martin Lipset (New York: Free Press, 1966), 266.

76. See Warner and Lunt, Social Life of Modern Community; and Davis, Gardner, and Gardner, Deep South.

77. See Baltzell, "Who's Who in America"; and Gordon, "Social Class in American Sociology," 267.

78. Paul Mombert, "Class," in Encyclopedia of the Social Sciences, ed. Edwin R. A. Seligman and Alvin Johnson (1930; rpt. New York: Macmillan, 1966), 3:532.

79. Gordon, "Social Class in American Sociology," 266–67.

80. Pierre Bourdieu, The Logic of Practice, trans. Richard Nice (Stanford, Calif.: Stanford University Press, 1990), 25.

81. Bourdieu, The Logic of Practice, 136.

82. Bourdieu, Distinction, 106.

83. Bourdieu, Distinction, 102.

84. Bourdieu, Distinction, 101.

85. Randal Johnson, "Editor's Introduction," in Bourdieu, Field of Cultural Production, 5.

86. See Warner and Lunt, Social Life of Modern Community; and Davis, Gardner, and Gardner, Deep South.

87. Mombert, "Class," 3:532.

88. W. Lloyd Warner, Marchia Meeker, and Kenneth Eells, Social Class in America: A Manual of Procedure for the Measurement of Social Status (Chicago: Science Research Associates: 1949).

89. Joseph A. Kahl, The American Class Structure (New York: Rinehart, 1957), 188; see also Baltzell, "Who's Who in America," 266–75.

90. Kahl, The American Class Structure, 193–94.

91. Warner, Meeker, and Eells, Social Class in America, 13.

92. Kahl, The American Class Structure, 202–3.

93. Warner, Meeker, and Eells, Social Class in America, 14.

94. Kahl, The American Class Structure, 206.

95. Warner, Meeker, and Eells, Social Class in America, 15; emphases added.

96. Kahl, The American Class Structure, 211.

97. Warner, Meeker, and Eells, Social Class in America, 13, 12.

98. Kahl, The American Class Structure, 65.

99. Warner, Meeker, and Eells, Social Class in America, 13.

100. Eaton, "Strangling of Our Theatre," 47.

101. McLaughlin, Broadway and Hollywood, 287. It is impossible to know how many attendees were repeat customers.

102. Eaton, "Strangling of Our Theatre," 48.

103. McLaughlin, Broadway and Hollywood, 76.

104. Eaton, "Strangling of Our Theatre," 47.

105. See, for example, Benjamin De Casseres, ""Are the Pictures and Stage Antagonistic?" Theatre, January 1928, 23.

106. Ralph Block, "The Worm Turns," Vanity Fair, August 1926, 58, 86.

107. Block, "The Worm Turns," 86; Eaton, "Strangling of Our Theatre," 47; Emerson, "Great Public," 96.

108. Block, "The Worm Turns," 58, 86.

109. Emerson, "Great Public," 65, 96.

110. Emerson, "Great Public," 65, 96.

111. Emerson, "Great Public," 65.

112. Emerson, "Great Public," 96; Eaton, "Strangling of Our Theatre," 48. For another example, see Coburn, "Our Theatre Fighting," 9, 58.

113. Sorokin, *Social Mobility*, 304.

114. Walter Prichard Eaton, "Audiences," *Theatre Arts*, January 1923, 22.

115. Benjamin De Casseres, "From 'Peanut Gallery' to 'Family Circle,'" *Theatre*, May 1928, 16, 66; Mills, *White Collar*, 63.

116. See Davis, Gardner, and Gardner, *Deep South*, 71.

117. See Eaton, "Audiences," 22.

118. "Editor's Note," *Theatre*, April 1927, 14; Cornelius Vanderbilt Jr., "Do the Socially Elect Make a Play Successful?" *Theatre*, April 1927, 14.

119. Vanderbilt, "Socially Elect," 14.

120. Mildred Cram, "Behold, the Audience!" *Theatre*, July 1922, 78.

121. Gilbert W. Gabriel, "The 'First-Night' Fake," *Theatre*, May 1926, 9; Arthur Hornblow, "Editorial," *Theatre*, March 1922, 142.

122. Cram, "Behold, the Audience!" 78; Channing Pollock, "Not for Pleasure Only," *Theatre*, March 1923, 8.

123. Post, *Etiquette*, 38; further references will be noted in the text.

124. Ronald H. Wainscott, *The Emergence of the Modern American Theater, 1914–1929* (New Haven: Yale University Press, 1997), 104.

125. Advertisement for Arnold, Constable & Co., *Theatre*, April 1926, 63.

126. "Fashions: As Introduced by the Leading Women of the Stage and Screen," *Theatre*, March 1926, 45.

127. "Cars for the Players' Playtime: Automobiling Is a Popular Recreation of the Hard-Working Actor," *Theatre*, February 1926, 47.

128. Cram, "Behold, the Audience!" 78.

129. Rachel Crothers, "Four Kinds of Audiences," *Drama*, May 1920, 273–74.

130. Eaton, "Audiences," 25.

131. Dickinson, *The Insurgent Theatre*, 16.

132. Eaton, "Audiences," 25.

133. Pollock, "Not for Pleasure Only," 8.

134. Seldes, "Producers and Playwrights," 9, 58.

135. St. John Ervine, "'The Theatre Is Perishing!'" *Theatre*, March 1929, 20.

136. Hall, "Notes on Deconstructing," 233.

CHAPTER FIVE

1. Laubenstein, "Jazz—Debit and Credit," 609.

2. Laubenstein, "Jazz—Debit and Credit," 609; Llewelyn C. Lloyd, "Jazz and the Modern Spirit," *Monthly Musical Record*, November 1926, in Koenig, *Jazz in Print*, 490; Gilbert, "Concerning Jazz," 221.

3. Laubenstein, "Jazz—Debit and Credit," 609; Taylor, quoted in "Our Jazz Symposium," 366–67.

4. Preface to Lawson, *Processional,* ix.

5. See Darwin T. Turner, "Jazz-Vaudeville Drama in the Twenties," *Educational Theatre Journal* 11, no. 2 (1959): 110–16.

6. Preface to Lawson, *Processional,* viii.

7. Preface to Lawson, *Processional,* ix.

8. Mills, *White Collar,* 5.

9. Kahl, *The American Class Structure,* 217.

10. Johnson, "Editor's Introduction," in Bourdieu, *Field of Cultural Production,* 15.

11. Raymond Williams, "The Politics of the Avant-Garde," in *The Politics of Modernism,* 56–57.

12. Bourdieu, "The Production of Belief," 79.

13. Ervine, "The Theatre Is Perishing," 20.

14. Post, *Etiquette,* 42; W. Lee Dickson, "The Audience Upstairs," *Theatre,* September 1920, 100.

15. Crothers, "Four Kinds of Audiences," 273–74.

16. Dickinson, *The Insurgent Theatre,* 16.

17. Dickson, "The Audience Upstairs," 100.

18. Dickson, "The Audience Upstairs," 100.

19. Anderson and Davidson, *Occupational Trends,* 584–85.

20. Anderson and Davidson, *Occupational Trends,* 592.

21. Kahl, *The American Class Structure,* 65.

22. Alba M. Edwards, *Sixteenth Census of the United States, 1940: Population: Comparative Occupation Statistics for the United States, 1870 to 1940* (Washington, D.C.: Government Printing Office, 1943), 187.

23. Anderson and Davidson, *Occupational Trends,* 592.

24. Edwards, *Sixteenth Census,* 183.

25. See Anderson and Davidson, *Occupational Trends,* 590.

26. James D. Norris, *Advertising and the Transformation of American Society, 1865–1920* (New York: Greenwood, 1990), xvi–xvii.

27. Cited in Ostrander, *American Civilization,* 223.

28. Warner, Meeker, and Eells, *Social Class in America,* 13.

29. Davis, Gardner, and Gardner, *Deep South,* 68, 77.

30. Kahl, *The American Class Structure,* 194.

31. Davis, Gardner, and Gardner, *Deep South,* 77–78.

32. Walter Prichard Eaton, "The Significance of the Theatre Guild," *Theatre,* July 1925, 12; Walter Prichard Eaton, *The Theatre Guild: The First Ten Years* (New York: Brentano's, 1929), 3.

33. Lawrence Langner, cited in Mark Fearnow, "Theatre Groups and Their Playwrights," in Wilmeth and Bigsby, *Cambridge History of American Theatre,* 357; and in Poggi, *Theater in America,* 123. For a comprehensive early history, see Eaton, *The Theatre Guild.*

34. John Dos Passos, "Why Write for the Theatre Anyway?" *New Republic,* 1 April 1931, rpt. in John Dos Passos, *Three Plays* (New York: Harcourt, Brace, 1934), xiii.

35. Atkinson and Hirschfeld, *The Lively Years,* 210.

36. Eaton, *The Theatre Guild*, 4.

37. Lawrence Langner, cited in Poggi, *Theater in America*, 123.

38. Eaton, "Significance of Theatre Guild," 12; Eaton, *The Theatre Guild*, 4.

39. Arthur Hornblow, "Olla Podrida," *Theatre*, August 1923, 7; Eaton, *The Theatre Guild*, 5, 7.

40. H. I. Brock, "American Dance of Life Rhymed to Jazz," *New York Times*, 1 February 1925, SM18; see also Joseph Wood Krutch, "Jazz of the Spirit," *The Nation*, 28 January 1925, 100; Margaret O'Leary, "Plays from Bohemia," *New York Times*, 10 September 1922, BRM4.

41. Dos Passos, "Why Write for the Theatre," xiii.

42. Review of *Processional, Cincinnati Billboard*, 24 January 1925.

43. See Julia A. Walker, *Expressionism and Modernism in the American Theatre* (Cambridge: Cambridge University Press, 2005).

44. Sayler, *Our American Theatre*, 208.

45. Kenneth MacGowan and Robert Edmond Jones, *Continental Stagecraft* (1923), quoted in David Fanning, "Expressionism," *Grove Music Online* (accessed 21 July 2006).

46. Elmer Rice, "A Note from Elmer Rice," *New York Times*, 1 April 1923, X2.

47. Philip Moeller, "From the Producer," *New York Times*, 25 March 1923, X2.

48. See Walker, *Expressionism and Modernism;* Wainscott, *Emergence of Modern American Theater*, 91–140; and Mardi Valgemae, *Accelerated Grimace: Expressionism in the American Drama of the 1920s* (Carbondale: Southern Illinois University Press, 1972).

49. John Corbin, "The Play: A Czecho-Slovak Frankenstein," *New York Times*, 10 October 1922, 24; Karel Čapek, *R.U.R. (Rossum's Universal Robots)*, trans. and adapted P. Selver and Nigel Playfair, in the Brothers Čapek, *R.U.R. and The Insect Play* (London: Oxford University Press, 1961), 9.

50. Čapek, *R.U.R.*, 66, 53.

51. Corbin, "The Play," 24

52. Čapek, *R.U.R.*, 22.

53. Čapek, *R.U.R.*, 84.

54. Burns Mantle, *The Best Plays of 1922–23* (1923; rpt. New York: Dodd, Mead, 1969), x.

55. Walter H. Sokel, ed., *Anthology of German Expressionist Drama: A Prelude to the Absurd*, rev. ed. (Ithaca, N.Y.: Cornell University Press, 1984), x.

56. See Stephen Hinton, "Weill: *Neue Sachlichkeit*, Surrealism, and *Gebrauchsmusik*," in *A New Orpheus: Essays on Kurt Weill*, ed. Kim Kowalke (New Haven: Yale University Press, 1986), 61–82.

57. "About Books, More or Less: In the Matter of Jazz," *New York Times*, 18 February 1922, in Koenig, *Jazz in Print*, 168; "Jazz," *Opportunity*, May 1925, in Koenig, *Jazz in Print*, 409.

58. Eugene O'Neill, *The Emperor Jones*, in *The Emperor Jones, Anna Christie, The Hairy Ape* (New York: Vintage, 1972), 30; Don Knowlton, "The Anatomy of Jazz," *Harper's*, March 1926, in Koenig, *Jazz in Print*, 458.

59. Stark Young, "Beggar on Horseback," *New Republic*, 5 March 1924, 45.

60. See Gershwin, "Does Jazz Belong to Art?" 13.

61. John Howard Lawson, *The International* (New York: Macauley, 1927), 7; Lawson quoted in Henrietta Malkiel, "Awaiting the Great American Opera: How Composers Are Paving the Way," *Musical America*, 25 April 1925, in Koenig, *Jazz in Print*, 407.

62. Lawson, *The International*, 8.

63. See Ryan Jerving, "Early Jazz Literature (and Why You Didn't Know)," *American Literary History* 16, no. 4 (2004): 648–74.

64. Atkinson and Hirschfeld, *The Lively Years*, 23.

65. Percy Hammond, "The Theaters," *New York Tribune*, 20 March 1923.

66. Alexander Woollcott, "Shouts and Murmurs," *New York Herald*, 20 March 1923.

67. James Craig, "The Adding Machine," *Evening Mail*, 20 March 1923.

68. Heywood Broun, "At the Garrick Theatre," *New York World*, 21 March 1923; George Jean Nathan, *Testament of a Critic* (New York: Knopf, 1931), 124; Stark Young, "Marketing Expressionism," *New Republic*, 4 April 1923, 164.

69. Charles Henry Meltzer, "Plays Modern and Near-Modern," *Theatre*, July 1923; H. Z. Torres in the *New York Commercial*, cited in Atkinson and Hirschfeld, *The Lively Years*, 26.

70. Mantle, introduction to *Best Plays of 1922–23*, 15.

71. Atkinson and Hirschfeld, *The Lively Years*, 22; Brooks Atkinson, *Broadway* (New York: Macmillan, 1970), 215.

72. Frank Durham, *Elmer Rice* (New York: Twayne, 1970), 16.

73. Atkinson, *Broadway*, 274.

74. See Rice, "Note from Elmer Rice," X2.

75. Cited in Durham, *Elmer Rice*, 30.

76. Atkinson, *Broadway*, 274.

77. Broun, "At the Garrick Theatre"; Atkinson, *Broadway*, 275.

78. Cited in C. W. E. Bigsby, *A Critical Introduction to Twentieth-Century American Drama*, vol. 1, *1900–1940* (Cambridge: Cambridge University Press, 1982), 130.

79. Cited in Durham, *Elmer Rice*, 54.

80. Arthur Hornblow, review of *The Adding Machine*, *Theatre*, May 1923, 19.

81. Wainscott, *Emergence of Modern American Theater*, 125.

82. Broun, "At the Garrick Theatre"; Woollcott, "Shouts and Murmurs"; Craig, "The Adding Machine"; Meltzer, "Plays Modern and Near-Modern," 9.

83. Crichton Clarke, "A Philosopher Looks at the Playsmiths," *Theatre*, July 1927, 16.

84. Richard Bennett, "What's Wrong with the Theatre?" *Theatre*, May 1924, 50.

85. Clarke, "Philosopher Looks at Playsmiths," 16.

86. "Gossip of the Rialto," *New York Times*, 11 March 1923, X1.

87. Sokel, introduction to *Anthology of German Expressionist Drama*, xxi.

88. Sokel, introduction to *Anthology of German Expressionist Drama*, xxi.

89. Arthur Hornblow, "Better the Blue Pencil Than the Padlock," *Theatre*, June 1925, 7.

90. Torres in the *New York Commercial*, cited in Atkinson and Hirschfeld, *The Lively Years*, 26.

91. Meltzer, "Plays Modern and Near-Modern," 9; "'Adding Machine' Replaces Poor Zero," *New York Times,* 20 March 1923, 34.

92. See John Houchin, *Censorship of the American Theatre in the Twentieth Century* (Cambridge: Cambridge University Press, 2003), 72–116.

93. John V. A. Weaver, "The American Language Play," *Theatre,* June 1925, 12.

94. Craig, "The Adding Machine."

95. Elmer Rice, *Three Plays* (New York: Hill and Wang, 1965), 3.

96. Meltzer, "Plays Modern and Near-Modern," 9; Woollcott, "Shouts and Murmurs."

97. Cited in Walker, *Expressionism and Modernism,* 178.

98. "'Adding Machine' Replaces Poor Zero," *New York Times,* 34.

99. See Kahl, *The American Class Structure,* 202; and Davis, Gardner, and Gardner, *Deep South,* 77.

100. Davis, Gardner, and Gardner, *Deep South,* 77.

101. Davis, Gardner, and Gardner, *Deep South,* 68.

102. Broun, "At the Garrick Theatre."

103. Williams, "Metropolitan Perceptions," 42–43.

104. John Howard Lawson, *Theory and Technique of Playwriting* (New York: G. P. Putnam's Sons, 1936), 83–84, 100.

105. Lawson, *Theory and Technique,* 99.

106. Lawson, *Theory and Technique,* 99.

107. Lawson, *Theory and Technique,* 105, 106.

108. Lawson, *Theory and Technique,* 101, 100.

109. Lawson, *Theory and Technique,* 132.

110. Kahl, *The American Class Structure,* 193.

111. Woollcott, "Shouts and Murmurs."

112. Taylor, quoted in "Our Jazz Symposium," 366; see James A. Pegolotti, *Deems Taylor: A Biography* (Boston: Northeastern University Press, 2003), 95.

113. Arthur Hornblow, cited in Houchin, *Censorship of American Theatre,* 86; Hammond, "The Theaters."

114. Howard, *Our American Music,* 488; John Tasker Howard, *Our Contemporary Composers: American Music in the Twentieth Century* (New York: Thomas Y. Crowell, 1941), 27–28.

115. W. David Sievers, *Freud on Broadway: A History of Psychoanalysis and the American Drama* (New York: Cooper Square Publishers, 1970), 72–73. Sievers provides a plausible Freudian reading of *The Adding Machine,* 147–49.

116. Hammond, "The Theaters."

117. Walker, *Expressionism and Modernism,* 179.

118. Woollcott, "Shouts and Murmurs."

119. Joseph Wood Krutch, introduction to John Howard Lawson, *Loud Speaker* (New York: Macaulay Company, 1927), x.

120. Eaton, *The Theatre Guild,* 6.

121. Eaton, *The Theatre Guild,* 5–6.

122. Eaton, *The Theatre Guild,* 6.

123. Fearnow, "Theatre Groups," 360.

124. Eaton, *The Theatre Guild*, 4.
125. Atkinson, *Broadway*, 211.
126. Dos Passos, "Why Write for the Theatre," xiii.
127. Dos Passos, "Why Write for the Theatre," xxi.
128. Eaton, *The Theatre Guild*, 88–89.
129. Poggi, *Theater in America*, 131.
130. See http://www.theatreatsea.com/index.html (accessed 10 May 2008).
131. Poggi, *Theater in America*, 213–14.

CHAPTER SIX

1. Olin Downes, "J. A. Carpenter, American Craftsman," *Musical Quarterly* 16, no. 4 (1930): 445.
2. Hacker, *American Problems of Today*, 75.
3. Fredric Jameson, "Modernism and Imperialism," in Terry Eagleton, Fredric Jameson, and Edward W. Said, *Nationalism, Colonialism, and Literature* (Minneapolis: University of Minnesota Press, 1990), 50–51.
4. Gershwin, "Our New National Anthem," 30.
5. See, for example, Robert Blauner, "Internal Colonialism and Ghetto Revolt," *Social Problems* 16, no. 4 (1969).
6. See Lloyd C. Gardner, Walter F. LaFeber, and Thomas J. McCormick, *Creation of the American Empire: U.S. Diplomatic History* (Chicago: Rand McNally, 1973), 222, 303; and 1899 political cartoon, "Holding Up His End," http://en.wikipedia.org/wiki/History_of_United_States_overseas_expansion (accessed 19 August 2006).
7. See Sidney Lens, *The Forging of the American Empire* (New York: Thomas Y. Crowell, 1971), 196.
8. Cited in Paul F. Boiler Jr., *American Thought in Transition: The Impact of Evolutionary Naturalism, 1865–1900* (Chicago: Rand McNally, 1969), 219.
9. Cited in Lens, *Forging of American Empire*, 176.
10. Cited in Boiler, *American Thought in Transition*, 220.
11. Cited in Lens, *Forging of American Empire*, 178.
12. Lens, *Forging of American Empire*, 234.
13. Hacker, *American Problems of Today*, 45.
14. Hacker, *American Problems of Today*, 44.
15. Cited in Hacker, *American Problems of Today*, 47.
16. Mary Nolan, *Visions of Modernity: American Business and the Modernization of Germany* (New York: Oxford University Press, 1994), 112.
17. Richard Pells, *Not Like Us: How Europeans Have Loved, Hated, and Transformed American Culture since World War II* (New York: Basic Books, 1997), 11.
18. See Robert A. Armour, "Film," in *Handbook of American Popular Culture*, ed. M. Thomas Inge (Westport, Conn.: Greenwood Press, 1989), 448.
19. Pells, *Not Like Us*, 11.
20. Cited in Frank Costigliola, *Awkward Dominion: American Political, Economic, and Cultural Relations with Europe, 1919–1933* (Ithaca, N.Y.: Cornell University Press, 1984), 177.

21. Paul Oliver, "Jazz Is Where You Find It: The European Experience of Jazz," in *Superculture: American Popular Culture and Europe*, ed. C. W. E. Bigsby (Bowling Green, Ohio: Bowling Green State University Popular Press, 1975), 140–41.

22. Darius Milhaud, "The Jazz Band and Negro Music," *Living Age*, 18 October 1924, in Koenig, *Jazz in Print*, 358.

23. See John Willett, *Art and Politics in the Weimar Period: The New Sobriety, 1917–1933* (New York: Pantheon, 1978), 89.

24. Milhaud, cited in V. B. S., "Jazz, Says Darius Milhaud, Is the Most Significant Thing in Music Today," *Musical Observer*, March 1923, in Koenig, *Jazz in Print*, 235.

25. Milhaud, "Jazz Band and Negro Music," 359.

26. Cited in Michael J. Budds, "The New World Enriches the Old," *Jazz and the Germans: Essays on the Influence of "Hot" American Idioms on 20th-Century German Music*, ed. Michael J. Budds (Hillsdale, N.Y.: Pendragon Press, 2002), 11.

27. J. Bradford Robinson, "Jazz Reception in Weimar Germany: In Search of a Shimmy Figure," in *Music and Performance during the Weimar Republic*, ed. Bryan Gilliam (Cambridge: Cambridge University Press, 1994), 108.

28. Pells, *Not Like Us*, 14.

29. Lorenz Hart, *New York Times*, 17 October 1926, rpt. in *The Complete Lyrics of Lorenz Hart*, ed. Dorothy Hart and Robert Kimball (New York: Knopf, 1986), 78.

30. J. Benoist-Méchin, trans. Sam Putnam, "Jazz Band," *Musical Courier*, 21 February 1924, rpt. in Koenig, *Jazz in Print*, 278.

31. George Antheil, *Bad Boy of Music* (Garden City, N.Y.: Doubleday, Doran, 1945), 142.

32. Robinson, "Jazz Reception," 113. See also Alan Lareau, "Jonny's Jazz: From *Kabarett* to Krenek," Budds, *Jazz and the Germans*, 19–59.

33. Pells, *Not Like Us*, 11.

34. V. B. S., "Jazz, Says Darius Milhaud," 223; Milhaud, "Jazz Band and Negro Music," 360.

35. Benoist-Méchin, "Jazz Band," 278. It is worth noting here that during World War II Benoist-Méchin was an eager supporter of the Vichy government and in 1947 was condemned to death for his collaboration with the Nazis (the sentence was commuted and he was released from prison in 1954).

36. Cited in the *New York Times*, 15 March 1925, in Koenig, *Jazz in Print*, 399.

37. Laubenstein, "Jazz—Debit and Credit," 609.

38. Tristan Tzara, "Note on Negro Art," in *Seven Dada Manifestos and Lampisteries*, trans. Barbara Wright (London: John Calder, 1977), 57.

39. Pells, *Not Like Us*, 9.

40. Mark Rennella and Whitney Walton, "Planned Serendipity: American Travelers and the Transatlantic Voyage in the Nineteenth and Twentieth Centuries," *Journal of Social History*, 38, no. 2 (2004): 372; Hacker, *American Problems of Today*, 129.

41. John Alden Carpenter and Philip Hale, cited in Howard Pollack, *John Alden Carpenter: A Chicago Composer* (Urbana: University of Illinois Press, 2001), 213.

42. Cited in Pollack, *John Alden Carpenter,* 218.

43. Antheil, cited in Linda Whitesitt, *The Life and Music of George Antheil, 1900–1959* (Ann Arbor, Mich.: UMI Research Press, 1983), 67; Antheil, *Bad Boy of Music,* 134.

44. Bravig Imbs, cited in Whitesitt, *Life and Music of Antheil,* 25.

45. Cited in Pollack, *John Alden Carpenter,* 31.

46. Pollack, *John Alden Carpenter,* 41.

47. Howard, *Our Contemporary Composers,* 35.

48. Downes, "J. A. Carpenter," 443–44.

49. Downes, "J. A. Carpenter," 444–45.

50. Pollack, *John Alden Carpenter,* 21.

51. Antheil, *Bad Boy of Music,* 13.

52. Whitesitt, *Life and Music of Antheil,* 7.

53. Cited in Whitesitt, *Life and Music of Antheil,* 70.

54. See Peter Bürger, *Theory of the Avant-Garde,* trans. Michael Shaw (Minneapolis: University of Minnesota Press, 1984).

55. Matei Calinescu, *Five Faces of Modernity: Modernism, Avant-Garde, Decadence, Kitsch, Postmodernism* (Durham, N.C.: Duke University Press, 1987), 96.

56. Calinescu, *Five Faces of Modernity,* 117.

57. Felix Borowski, "John Alden Carpenter," *Musical Quarterly* 16, no. 4 (1930): 455, 456.

58. Deems Taylor, "America's First Dramatic Composer," *Vanity Fair,* April 1922, 59.

59. Pollack, *John Alden Carpenter,* 110.

60. Pollack, *John Alden Carpenter,* 120.

61. Taylor, "America's First Dramatic Composer," 59, 106.

62. Cited in Pollack, *John Alden Carpenter,* 185–86.

63. See Pollack, *John Alden Carpenter,* 195.

64. See Pollack, *John Alden Carpenter,* 198–99.

65. Bordman, *American Musical Theatre,* 373–74, Anthony Slide, *The Vaudevillians: A Dictionary of Vaudeville Performers* (New York: Arlington House, 1981), 134. Savoy was killed when he was struck by lightning in 1923. According to blakstone.com: "The story of his death is legendary and, by all accounts, absolutely true: on June 26, 1923 Savoy and two friends were walking along the shore at Long Beach watching an upcoming storm when a thunderclap prompted Savoy to squeal 'Ain't Miss God cuttin' up somethin' awful?' He was immediately struck dead by a bolt of lightning." http://blakstone.com/Dragstravaganza%20Site/Minor%20Luminaries.htm (accessed 9 June 2007).

66. Seldes, *The 7 Lively Arts,* 240–42.

67. Richard Aldrich, "Music," *New York Times,* 21 January 1922, 16.

68. Philip Hale, quoted in Pollack, *John Alden Carpenter,* 213.

69. Cited in Pollack, *John Alden Carpenter,* 218.

70. See Mary C. Henderson, "Scenography, Stagecraft, and Architecture," in Wilmeth and Bigsby, *Cambridge History of American Theatre,* 504.

71. H. I. Brock, "Jazz Is to Do a Turn in Grand Opera," *New York Times,* 14 February 1926, SM5.

72. Quoted in Fred Austin, "'Skyscrapers': America Produces Its First Jazz Ballet," *The Dance*, April 1926, 25.

73. Olin Downes, "'Skyscrapers' Here with 'Jazz' Score," *New York Times*, 20 February 1926, 15.

74. Review of *Skyscrapers*, *Theatre Arts*, March 1926, 189.

75. "The Descent of Jazz upon Opera," *Literary Digest*, 13 March 1926, 24.

76. Brock, "Jazz to Do Turn," SM5; Austin, "Skyscrapers," 58.

77. See Frank W. D. Ries, "Sammy Lee: The Broadway Career," *Dance Chronicle* 9, no. 1 (1986): 1–95.

78. Ries, "Sammy Lee," 49–50.

79. Austin, "Skyscrapers," 58.

80. Austin, "Skyscrapers," 25.

81. "Society Awaits Jazz Ballet at the Metropolitan," *New York Herald Tribune*, 14 February 1926, 1.

82. "Feste," "Ad Libitum," *Musical Times*, 1 September 1925, in Koenig, *Jazz in Print*, 347; Carpenter, cited in Pollack, *John Alden Carpenter*, 199.

83. Carpenter, cited in Pollack, *John Alden Carpenter*, 199.

84. "Jazz Is Assuming Prominence as an American Music Idiom, Declares *Skyscrapers*' Composer," *Musical Digest*, 23 November 1926, in Koenig, *Jazz in Print*, 490.

85. "Society Awaits Jazz Ballet," 15.

86. Olga Samaroff, critic for the *Evening Post*, quoted in "Descent of Jazz upon Opera," 24.

87. Gilman quoted in "Descent of Jazz upon Opera," 25; Downes, "'Skyscrapers' Here with 'Jazz' Score," 15.

88. Gilman quoted in "Descent of Jazz upon Opera," 25.

89. See David Nasaw, *Going Out: The Rise and Fall of Public Amusements* (Cambridge: Harvard University Press, 1993).

90. Downes, "J. A. Carpenter," 446.

91. Gilman quoted in "Descent of Jazz upon Opera," 25.

92. Brock, "Jazz to Do a Turn," SM5.

93. Brock, "Jazz to Do a Turn," SM5; in the song "In Dahomey" from *Show Boat*, Kern and Hammerstein parody (and implicitly critique) the use of nonsense syllables to evoke a primordial Africanness.

94. Review in *Outlook*, cited in Pollack, *John Alden Carpenter*, 232; Borowski, "John Alden Carpenter," 465.

95. Downes, "'Skyscrapers' Here with 'Jazz' Score," 15.

96. See Lauren Berlant, "Pax Americana: The Case of *Show Boat*," in *Cultural Institutions of the Novel*, ed. Deidre Lynch and William B. Warner (Durham, N.C.: Duke University Press, 1996), 399–422.

97. Carpenter, cited in Pollack, *John Alden Carpenter*, 232; Downes, "J. A. Carpenter," 448. It should be noted that Ravel used a chorus in his ballet *Daphnis et Chloé* (1912).

98. Austin, "Skyscrapers," 58.

99. Pollack, *John Alden Carpenter*, 239–40.

100. Review in the *Paris Times*, cited in Pollack, *John Alden Carpenter*, 242.

101. Edward Burlingame Hall, "Jazz," *Harvard Graduate Magazine*, March 1925, in Koenig, *Jazz in Print*, 400.

102. Samaroff, quoted in "Descent of Jazz upon Opera," 24.

103. Borowski, "John Alden Carpenter," 466.

104. "Jazz Assuming Prominence," 490.

105. Howard, *Our Contemporary Composers*, 38.

106. Downes, "J. A. Carpenter," 447.

107. Interview with George Antheil at his home, conducted by Truman Fisher for KPPC-FM radio, Pasadena, Calif., 1958. From *Antheil Plays Antheil*, Other Minds 1003/4-2 (2000).

108. Antheil, *Bad Boy of Music*, 5.

109. Ezra Pound, *Antheil and the Treatise on Harmony* (Chicago: Pascal Covici, 1927).

110. Caesar Searchinger, cited in Whitesitt, *Life and Music of Antheil*, 19.

111. Antheil, *Bad Boy of Music*, 132–33.

112. Searchinger, cited in Whitesitt, *Life and Music of Antheil*, 19.

113. Antheil, *Bad Boy of Music*, 133–34.

114. Aaron Copland, *Copland on Music* (Garden City, N.Y.: Doubleday, 1960), 145–46.

115. Antheil, *Bad Boy of Music*, 8.

116. Pound, *Antheil*, 40, 48, 54, 51.

117. Pound, *Antheil*, 53, 62.

118. Antheil, *Bad Boy of Music*, 117.

119. Antheil, cited in Whitesitt, *Life and Music of Antheil*, 69–70.

120. Antheil, *Bad Boy of Music*, 134.

121. See Flora Dennis and Jonathan Powell, "Futurism," *Grove Music Online*, http://www.grovemusic.com.ezproxy.gc.cuny.edu/shared/views/article.html?from =search&session_search_id=891323486&hitnum=8&section=music.10420 (accessed 7 December 2007).

122. Luigi Russolo, trans. Victoria Nes Kirby, "The Art of Noise," in Michael Kirby, *Futurist Performance* (New York: E. P. Dutton, 1971), 167–68.

123. Pound, *Antheil*, 40.

124. Antheil, *Bad Boy of Music*, 67.

125. See Kirby, *Futurist Performance*.

126. Antheil, cited in Whitesitt, *Life and Music of Antheil*, 69.

127. Hans Heinz Stuckenschmidt, cited in Herbert Henck, trans. Eileen Walliser-Schwarzbart, liner notes to *Conlon Nancarrow, George Antheil: Piano Music*, Herbert Henck, piano, ECM 1726, 2001.

128. See Oja, *Making Modern Music*, 77–78.

129. Tristan Tzara, "Dada Manifesto 1918," in *Seven Dada Manifestos*, 3–13. See also Mel Gordon, ed., *Dada Performance* (New York: PAJ Publications, 1987).

130. Tristan Tzara, "Monsieur Antipyrine's Manifesto," in *Seven Dada Manifestos*, 1.

131. Bürger, *Theory of the Avant-Garde*, 18, 56.

132. Tzara, "Dada Manifesto 1918," 4.

133. Unidentified New York newspaper article, 10 April 1927, New York Pub-

lic Library for the Performing Arts at Lincoln Center. I have been unable to determine the clipping's provenance. Judging from the typeface (and its conservative bent), I believe it may be from the *Herald-Tribune*.

134. Antheil, *Bad Boy of Music*, 132–33.

135. Tzara, "Monsieur Antipyrine's Manifesto," 1.

136. George Antheil, "Jazz," *Der Querschnitt* I/II/2 (1922), 173. All the pieces, except the Second Sonata and Symphonie No. 1, are written for piano.

137. David Ewen, *Composers of Today: A Comprehensive Biographical and Critical Guide to Modern Composers of All Nations* (New York: H. W. Wilson, 1934), 6.

138. See 1954 interview with Antheil cited in Whitesitt, *Life and Music of Antheil*, 111.

139. Antheil, "Jazz," 172.

140. Cited in Whitesitt, *Life and Music of Antheil*, 112; Antheil, "Jazz," 172.

141. George Antheil, "Jazz Is Music," *Forum*, July 1928, in Koenig, *Jazz in Print*, 538.

142. Antheil, "Jazz Is Music," 537.

143. Antheil, "Jazz Is Music," 537.

144. George Antheil, "In the Mode Americana," *Musical Digest*, 5 April 1927.

145. Antheil, "Jazz Is Music," 537–38.

146. See the catalog of Antheil's music in Whitesitt, *Life and Music of Antheil*, 200–201.

147. *New York Herald-Tribune*, Paris edition, January 1924, cited in Whitesitt, *Life and Music of Antheil*, 20–21. According to Whitesitt, Antheil had underlined the last sentence quoted from the newspaper article.

148. Antheil, "Jazz Is Music," 538.

149. Untitled Antheil manuscript, cited in Whitesitt, *Life and Music of Antheil*, 105.

150. Antheil, "In the Mode Americana."

151. From "Talk of the Town," *New Yorker*, 24 April 1926.

152. Antheil, *Bad Boy of Music*, 125.

153. Antheil, *Bad Boy of Music*, 171.

154. "Composer Brings Electric Bells and Propellers to Play Here Music Europe Fought Over," *New York Times*, 8 March 1927, 27.

155. Unidentified New York newspaper article, 10 April 1927.

156. Letter to Ezra Pound, cited in Robert M. Crunden, *Body and Soul: The Making of American Modernism* (New York: Basic Books, 2000), 333.

157. See Antheil, *Bad Boy of Music*, 194.

158. Donald Friede, *The Mechanical Angel: His Adventures and Enterprises in the Glittering 1920's* (New York: Knopf, 1948), 53.

159. Antheil, *Bad Boy of Music*, 194.

160. Antheil, "In the Mode Americana"; the original versions of both *A Jazz Symphony* and *Ballet mécanique* can be heard performed by Maurice Peress conducting the New Palais Royale Orchestra and Percussion Ensemble on MusicMasters CD 01612-67094-2, 1992; Antheil, "Jazz," 173.

161. Whitesitt, *Life and Music of Antheil*, 113.

162. Letter to Ezra Pound, cited in Crunden, *Body and Soul*, 333.

163. Antheil to Stanley Hart, cited in Oja, *Making Music Modern*, 80–81.

164. Elliot H. Paul, "'Ballet mécanique' Is Successful as Musical Interpretation of Age," *Chicago Tribune*, Paris edition, 18 July 1926, cited in Whitesitt, *Life and Music of Antheil*, 26.

165. Antheil, letter to Nicholas Slonimsky, cited in Whitesitt, *Life and Music of Antheil*, 105.

166. Antheil, cited in Whitesitt, *Life and Music of Antheil*, 104; Whitesitt, *Life and Music of Antheil*, 108.

167. See Oja, *Making Music Modern*, 83. These sections obviously anticipate the silence (filled with ambient noise) that John Cage composed in his *4'33"*.

168. Untitled Antheil manuscript, cited in Whitesitt, *Life and Music of Antheil*, 105.

169. Bürger, *Theory of the Avant-Garde*, 56.

170. Charles M. Prager, "A Riot of Music," *New York Herald Tribune*, 10 April 1927.

171. Tzara, "Dada Manifesto 1918," 11.

172. Antheil, *Bad Boy of Music*, 139–40.

173. Antheil, "In the Mode Americana."

174. Antheil, *Bad Boy of Music*, 139; Antheil, cited in Whitesitt, *Life and Music of Antheil*, 104; Antheil, cited in Oja, *Making Music Modern*, 84.

175. Adorno, *Sociology of Music*, 180.

176. Copland, *Copland on Music*, 146. The composer Colin McPhee was another pianist that evening.

177. Display advertisement for the concert published in the *New York Times*, 20 March 1927, X9.

178. Friede, *The Mechanical Angel*, 50; "Antheil Art Bursts on Startled Ears," *New York Times*, 11 April 1927, 23.

179. Friede, *The Mechanical Angel*, 56.

180. "George Antheil Tells about His Modern 'Ballet Mecanique,'" *New York World*, 27 February 1927.

181. Cited in Whitesitt, *Life and Music of Antheil*, 32.

182. "Boos Greet Antheil Ballet of Machines," *New York Herald Tribune*, 11 April 1927; Olga Samaroff, "Expected Riots Peter Out at George Antheil Concert—Sensation Fails to Materialize," *New York Evening Post*, 11 April 1927.

183. Lawrence Gilman, "Music," *New York Herald Tribune*, 11 April 1927.

184. Oscar Thompson, *Musical America*, 16 April 1927, 7.

185. Charles Seeger, cited in Oja, *Making Music Modern*, 93; Friede, *The Mechanical Angel*, 56; Antheil, *Bad Boy of Music*, 193.

186. Cited in Oja, *Making Music Modern*, 92.

187. Friede, *The Mechanical Angel*, 49.

188. Antheil, *Bad Boy of Music*, 193.

189. "Antheil and His 'Noise,'" *New York Times*, 10 April 1927; Friede, *The Mechanical Angel*, 49.

190. "Antheil and His 'Noise.'"

191. Friede, *The Mechanical Angel*, 49.

192. Friede, *The Mechanical Angel*, 59.

193. Antheil, *Bad Boy of Music,* 193; Antheil, letter to Slonimsky, cited in White-sitt, *Life and Music of Antheil,* 106.

194. Antheil, cited in Whitesitt, *Life and Music of Antheil,* 105.

195. Antheil, letter to Slonimsky, cited in Whitesitt, *Life and Music of Antheil,* 106.

196. Antheil, *Bad Boy of Music,* 193.

197. Friede, *The Mechanical Angel,* 57.

198. Antheil, *Bad Boy of Music,* 140.

199. Standish D. Lawder, *The Cubist Cinema* (New York: New York University Press, 1975), 149. Lawder offers a detailed analysis of film, 117–67.

200. Cited in Lawder, *The Cubist Cinema,* 131.

201. See *Ballet mécanique and Other Works for Player Pianos, Percussion, and Electronics,* University of Massachusetts Lowell Percussion Ensemble, cond. Jeffrey Fischer, EMF CD 020, 2000.

202. Adorno, *Sociology of Music,* 191–92.

203. Alice Holdship Ware, cited in Pollack, *John Alden Carpenter,* 237.

204. Letter, 27 April 1927, cited in Whitesitt, *Life and Music of Antheil,* 41.

205. Cited in Whitesitt, *Life and Music of Antheil,* 40.

206. Letter to Antheil, 30 October 1927, cited in Whitesitt, *Life and Music of Antheil,* 41.

207. See Whitesitt, *Life and Music of Antheil,* 56.

208. Thomson cited in Pollack, *John Alden Carpenter,* 365.

209. Pollack, *John Alden Carpenter,* 407.

210. John Tasker Howard and George Kent Bellows, *A Short History of Music in America* (New York: Thomas Y. Crowell, 1967), 229.

211. Howard, *Our Contemporary Composers,* 257–58.

212. Nathan, *Testament of a Critic,* 58.

213. See Sadie, *New Grove Dictionary.*

214. See Charles Hamm, *Music in the New World* (New York: Norton, 1983); Kyle Gann, *American Music in the Twentieth Century* (New York: Schirmer Books, 1997).

215. Gilbert Chase, *America's Music: From the Pilgrims to the Present* (Urbana: University of Illinois Press, 1987).

216. As of 9 July 2007, Amazon.com lists 34 different recordings of Carpenter's music versus 52 of Antheil's. Many of Carpenter's, moreover, are collections of historical recordings that feature only a song or two of his recorded in the 1930s by singers like Lawrence Tibbett or Kirsten Flagstad.

217. Whitesitt, *Life and Music of Antheil,* 6–7. Although she gave him money beginning in 1921 for nineteen years, she stopped her monthly stipend checks in 1932.

218. Bürger, *Theory of the Avant-Garde,* 22.

CHAPTER SEVEN

1. Bigsby, *Critical Introduction,* 9.

2. Watermeier, "Theatre of His Time," 47; Sheldon Cheney, "Editorial," *Theatre Arts,* November 1916, 48.

3. "Foreword," *Theatre Arts*, November 1916, 3.

4. Cited in Sayler, *Our American Theatre*, 74.

5. Hutchins Hapgood, introduction to *The Provincetown Plays*, ed. George Cram Cook and Frank Shay (Cincinnati: Stewart Kidd, 1921), 6; Edna Kenton, "The Provincetown Players and the Playwrights' Theater," *Billboard*, 5 August 1922, 6.

6. John Guillory, "Canon," in *Critical Terms for Literary Study*, ed. Frank Lentricchia and Thomas McLaughlin (Chicago: University of Chicago Press, 1990), 232.

7. David Swartz, *Culture and Power: The Sociology of Pierre Bourdieu* (Chicago: University of Chicago Press, 1997), 86.

8. Bourdieu, "The Production of Belief," 82, 81.

9. See Pierre Bourdieu and Loïc J. D. Wacquant, *An Invitation to Reflexive Sociology* (Chicago: University of Chicago Press, 1992), 86.

10. Johnson, "Editor's Introduction," in Bourdieu, *Field of Cultural Production*, 20.

11. Swartz, *Culture and Power*, 84.

12. Bourdieu, *Distinction*, 468.

13. Pierre Bourdieu, "The Market of Symbolic Goods," in Bourdieu, *Field of Cultural Production*, 132.

14. Pierre Bourdieu, *Language and Symbolic Power*, ed. John B. Thompson, trans. Gino Raymond and Matthew Adamson (Cambridge: Harvard University Press, 1991), 168–69.

15. See Bourdieu, "The Production of Belief," 79.

16. Hapgood, introduction to Cook and Shay, *The Provincetown Plays*, 6; Kenton, "Provincetown Players," 6, 13.

17. Bourdieu, "The Field of Cultural Production," in *Field of Cultural Production*, 35–36.

18. Connolly, *George Jean Nathan*, 47.

19. Glenn Hughes, *A History of the American Theatre, 1700–1950* (New York: Samuel French, 1951), 406.

20. Benjamin De Casseres, "Eugene O'Neill: From Cardiff to Xanadu," *Theatre*, August 1927, 10.

21. Charles J. McGaw, "William Winter as a Dramatic Critic," *Educational Theatre Journal* 4, no. 2 (1952): 115.

22. William Winter, cited in McGaw, "Winter as Dramatic Critic," 117.

23. William Winter, *New York Tribune*, 5 February 1891, cited in McGaw, "Winter as Dramatic Critic," 117–18.

24. Charles Frederic Nirdlinger, cited in Connolly, *George Jean Nathan*, 46.

25. See Claude de Crespigny, "Huneker," *American Speech* 2, no. 11 (1927): 451–52.

26. Winter, cited in McGaw, "Winter as Dramatic Critic," 116.

27. Cited in Connolly, *George Jean Nathan*, 50.

28. Cited in Connolly, *George Jean Nathan*, 49.

29. Gary Cross, *An All-Consuming Century: Why Commercialism Won in Modern America* (New York: Columbia University Press, 2000), 32–34.

30. Hughes, *History of American Theatre*, 413.

31. Atkinson, *Broadway*, 159.

32. Atkinson, *Broadway*, 159.

33. See Connolly, *George Jean Nathan*, 23–44.

34. Tice L. Miller, "Nathan, George Jean," in *Cambridge Guide to American Theatre*, ed. Don B. Wilmeth and Tice L. Miller (Cambridge: Cambridge University Press, 1993), 326.

35. Connolly, *George Jean Nathan*, 82.

36. George Jean Nathan, *The Critic and the Drama* (New York: Knopf, 1922), 3.

37. Connolly, *George Jean Nathan*, 58.

38. Nathan, *The Critic and the Drama*, 4–5.

39. See John Henry Raleigh, "Eugene O'Neill and the Escape from the Château d'If," in *O'Neill: A Collection of Critical Essays*, ed. John Gassner (Englewood Cliffs, N.J.: Prentice-Hall, Inc., 1964), 7–22.

40. Virgil Geddes, *The Melodramadness of Eugene O'Neill* (Brookfield, CT: Brookfield Players, 1934), 6–7.

41. Arthur Gelb and Barbara Gelb, *O'Neill* (New York: Harper and Row, 1962), 176–77.

42. Gelb and Gelb, *O'Neill*, 177.

43. *Variety*, 14 February 1912, cited in Gelb and Gelb, *O'Neill*, 185.

44. Barrett H. Clark, *Eugene O'Neill: The Man and His Plays*, rev. ed. (New York: Robert M. McBride, 1929), 66.

45. Heywood Broun, "The Emperor Jones," *New York Tribune*, 4 November 1920.

46. See Koszarski, *An Evening's Entertainment*, 182–83.

47. Eugene O'Neill, cited in Clark, *Eugene O'Neill*, 39.

48. Gelb and Gelb, *O'Neill*, 373–74.

49. Letter to Barrett Clark, cited in Clark, *Eugene O'Neill*, 78.

50. Clark, *Eugene O'Neill*, 78.

51. Travis Bogard, *The Eugene O'Neill Songbook* (Berkeley, Calif.: East Bay Books, 1993), preface, http://www.eoneill.com/library/songbook/preface.htm (accessed 16 August 2007). The book is out of print but available online.

52. Bogard, *The Eugene O'Neill Songbook*, "Afterword: The Play as Symphony."

53. O'Neill, cited in Bogard, "Afterword: The Play as Symphony."

54. Richard Dana Skinner, *Eugene O'Neill: A Poet's Quest* (New York: Russell and Russell, 1964), 3.

55. Bogard, *The Eugene O'Neill Songbook*, preface.

56. See Bogard, *The Eugene O'Neill Songbook*, *All God's Chillun Got Wings*.

57. Hamm, *Yesterdays*, 309, 321.

58. Sam Dennison, "Coon Song," *Grove Music Online*, http://www.grovemusic.com.ezproxy.gc.cuny.edu:2048/shared/views/article.html?from=search&session_search_id=913223275&hitnum=1&section=music.51218 (accessed 20 August 2007).

59. Wilder, *American Popular Song*, 95.

60. Skinner, *Eugene O'Neill*, 131, 135.

61. Skinner, *Eugene O'Neill*, 19.

62. Skinner, *Eugene O'Neill,* 7.

63. Bogard, *The Eugene O'Neill Songbook,* "Foreword: A Musical Heritage."

64. Bogard, "Foreword: A Musical Heritage."

65. Eugene O'Neill, *The Great God Brown,* in *Complete Plays, 1920–1931,* 492.

66. Letter to Robert Sisk of 18 October 1937, cited in Bogard, "Foreword: A Musical Heritage."

67. Svetlana Boym, *The Future of Nostalgia* (New York: Basic Books, 2001), 8.

68. Bogard, "Foreword: A Musical Heritage."

69. O'Neill, *Diff'rent,* 28, 27.

70. Eugene O'Neill, *Dynamo,* in *Complete Plays, 1920–1931,* 827.

71. Ronald H. Wainscott, *Staging O'Neill: The Experimental Years, 1920–1934* (New Haven: Yale University Press, 1988), 66.

72. J. Brooks Atkinson, "The Play," *New York Times,* 12 February 1929, 22.

73. Percy Hammond, "The Theaters: Dynamo," *New York Herald Tribune,* 12 February 1929.

74. Cited in Clark, *Eugene O'Neill,* 15.

75. O'Neill, *Dynamo,* 830.

76. Nathan, *The World in Falseface,* 79.

77. Cited in Matthew H. Wikander, "O'Neill and the Cult of Sincerity," in Manheim, *Cambridge Companion to O'Neill,* 221.

78. Cited in Clark, *Eugene O'Neill,* 56.

79. *"As Ever, Gene": The Letters of Eugene O'Neill to George Jean Nathan,* ed. Nancy L. Roberts and Arthur W. Roberts (Rutherford, N.J.: Fairleigh Dickinson University Press, 1987), 149.

80. Roberts and Roberts, "Introductory Essay," *"As Ever, Gene,"* 129.

81. George Jean Nathan, "Literature and Drama" (1928), in *A George Jean Nathan Reader,* ed. A. L. Lazarus (Rutherford, N.J.: Fairleigh Dickinson University Press, 1990), 67.

82. De Casseres, "Triumphant Genius of O'Neill," 62.

83. "Eugene O'Neill Dies of Pneumonia; Playwright, 65, Won Nobel Prize," *New York Times,* 28 November 1953, 22.

84. Brooks Atkinson, "Eugene O'Neill: America's Greatest Dramatist Changed the Character of Our Theatre," *New York Times,* 13 December 1953, X5.

85. Cited in Roberts and Roberts, "Introductory Essay," *"As Ever, Gene,"* 171.

86. Atkinson, "Eugene O'Neill," X5.

87. Wikander, "Cult of Sincerity," 232.

88. Wikander, "Cult of Sincerity," 220.

89. O'Neill to Lawrence Langner, cited in Gelb and Gelb, *O'Neill,* 650.

90. George Jean Nathan, "Eugene O'Neill," from *The Intimate Notebooks of George Jean Nathan* (1932), in *The World of George Jean Nathan,* ed. George Jean Nathan and Charles Angoff (New York: Knopf, 1952), 31.

91. De Casseres, "Triumphant Genius of O'Neill," 12.

92. Alexander Woollcott, "Second Thoughts on First Nights: The Coming of Eugene O'Neill," *New York Times,* 8 February 1920, XX2.

93. Barrett H. Clark, *Eugene O'Neill* (New York: Robert M. McBride, 1926), 1.

94. Skinner, *Eugene O'Neill,* xi.

95. "Eugene (Gladstone) O'Neill," in Wilmeth and Miller, *Cambridge Guide to American Theatre*, 354.

96. Joel Pfister, *Staging Depth: Eugene O'Neill and the Politics of Psychological Discourse* (Chapel Hill: University of North Carolina Press, 1995), 10.

97. Manheim, introduction to *Cambridge Companion to O'Neill*, 1.

98. "The Trouble with Brown," *Time*, 7 December 1953, obituary for O'Neill. http://www.time.com/time/magazine/article/0,9171,890754,00.html (accessed 24 August 2007).

99. My thanks to Alan Ackerman for this insight.

100. Walter Prichard Eaton, "Eugene O'Neill," *Theatre Arts*, July 1920, 287.

101. Clark, *Eugene O'Neill* (1929), 98.

102. Clark, *Eugene O'Neill* (1929), 59.

103. Stephen A. Black, "'Celebrant of Loss': Eugene O'Neill 1888–1953," in Manheim, *Cambridge Companion to O'Neill*, 6.

104. Clark, *Eugene O'Neill* (1929), 3, 10.

105. Cited in Clark, *Eugene O'Neill* (1929), 13.

106. Cited in Gelb and Gelb, *O'Neill*, 231.

107. Louis Kantor, "O'Neill Defends His Play of Negro," *New York Times*, 11 May 1924, XX5.

108. Sayler, *Our American Theatre*, 30.

109. Donald Weinstein and Rudolph M. Bell, *Saints and Society: The Two Worlds of Western Christendom, 1000–1700* (Chicago: University of Chicago Press, 1982), 199.

110. Alison Goddard Elliott, *Roads to Paradise: Reading the Lives of the Early Saints* (Hanover, N.H.: University Press of New England, 1987), 77.

111. Elliott, *Roads to Paradise*, 103.

112. Eugene O'Neill, "The Nobel Prize Acceptance Letter," in *The Unknown O'Neill: Unpublished or Unfamiliar Writings of Eugene O'Neill*, ed. Travis Bogard (New Haven, CT: Yale University Press, 1988), 427.

113. Elliott, *Roads to Paradise*, 185.

114. Carol Bird, "Eugene O'Neill—the Inner Man," *Theatre*, June 1924, 9.

115. Atkinson, "Eugene O'Neill," X5.

116. See Quinn, *History of American Drama*, 165–206.

117. Bird, "Eugene O'Neill," 9.

118. John Kitchen, *Saints' Lives and the Rhetoric of Gender: Male and Female in Merovingian Hagiography* (New York: Oxford University Press, 1998), 105.

119. Sayler, *Our American Theatre*, 30; Kantor, "O'Neill Defends His Play of Negro," XX5.

120. Nathan, *Testament of a Critic*, 27, 98.

121. Sayler, *Our American Theatre*, 36.

122. Oral Sumner Coad, review of Arthur Hobson Quinn, *A History of the American Drama: From the Civil War to the Present Day;* and Richard Dana Skinner, "Eugene O'Neill: A Poet's Quest," *American Literature* 8, no. 3 (1936): 329.

123. Skinner, *Eugene O'Neill*, 25–32.

124. Heywood Broun, "'Beyond the Horizon' by Eugene O'Neill a Notable Play," *New York Tribune*, 4 February 1920.

125. "Eugene O'Neill Dies of Pneumonia," 22.

126. Alexander Woollcott, "The Play," *New York Times*, 29 December 1920, 17.

127. Woollcott, "Second Thoughts," XX2.

128. Alexander Woollcott, "The New O'Neill Play," *New York Times*, 7 November 1920.

129. Alexander Woollcott, "Eugene O'Neill at Full Tilt," *New York Times*, 9 March 1922.

130. See Quinn, *History of American Drama*, 165; and Sayler, *Our American Theatre*, 28.

131. Sayler, *Our American Theatre*, 28.

132. Hugo von Hofmannsthal, "Eugene O'Neill," *Freeman*, 21 March 1923, rpt. in Gassner, *O'Neill*, 28; see Clark, *Eugene O'Neill* (1926), 109–10, and Sayler, *Our American Theatre*, 41–42.

133. Rita Terras, "A Spokesman for America: O'Neill in Translation," in *Eugene O'Neill's Century: Centennial Views on America's Foremost Tragic Dramatist*, ed. Richard F. Moorton Jr. (New York: Greenwood Press, 1991), 87, 92. See also Virgina Floyd, *Eugene O'Neill: A World View* (New York: Frederick Ungar, 1979).

134. Sayler, *Our American Theatre*, 27–28.

135. Nathan, *Testament of a Critic*, 99.

136. Roberts and Roberts, *"As Ever, Gene,"* 84.

137. Terras, "A Spokesman for America," 87.

138. See Bourdieu, "The Production of Belief," 74.

139. James Patterson, "Off the Record," *Billboard*, 15 April 1922.

140. Sayler, *Our American Theatre*, 42.

141. Cited in Pfister, *Staging Depth*, 155. See also 105–85.

142. Sayler, *Our American Theatre*, 42.

143. Nathan, *The Critic and the Drama*, 67–68.

144. Atkinson, *Broadway*, 160.

145. George Jean Nathan, "The Chewing Gum Drama," *Smart Set*, January 1918, 134.

146. Arthur Gelb, cited in Connolly, *George Jean Nathan*, 35.

147. George Jean Nathan, *Passing Judgments* (New York: Knopf, 1935), 118–19.

148. See Isaac Goldberg, *The Theatre of George Jean Nathan: Chapters and Documents toward a History of the New American Drama* (New York: Simon and Schuster, 1926), 77–78.

149. "George Jean Nathan Dies at 76; Dean of Broadway Drama Critics," *New York Times*, 8 April 1958, 30; "The Trouble with Brown."

150. Connolly, *George Jean Nathan*, 31.

151. Goldberg, *Theatre of Nathan*, 75, 24, 78.

152. Brooks Atkinson, "Account Closed: Death of G. J. Nathan Finishes an Era," *New York Times*, 27 April 1958, X1.

153. Goldberg, *Theatre of Nathan*, 6; Connolly, *George Jean Nathan*, 13.

154. Goldberg, *Theatre of Nathan*, 84.

155. Atkinson, "Account Closed," X1.

156. Nathan, *The World in Falseface*, xxii.

157. Goldberg, *Theatre of Nathan*, 5.

158. Connolly, *George Jean Nathan*, 14.

159. Nathan column from 1925, cited in Goldberg, *Theatre of Nathan*, 19–24.

160. George Jean Nathan, *The Popular Theatre* (New York: Knopf, 1918, rev. 1923), 18.

161. Nathan, *The Critic and the Drama*, 23, 21.

162. Nathan, *The Critic and the Drama*, 17, 30.

163. Nathan, *The Popular Theatre*, 12.

164. Nathan, *The Critic and the Drama*, 50, 18.

165. Cited in Goldberg, *Theatre of Nathan*, 122.

166. George Jean Nathan, cited in Constance Frick, *The Dramatic Criticism of George Jean Nathan* (Ithaca, N.Y.: Cornell University Press, 1943), 54–55.

167. Cited in Connolly, *George Jean Nathan*, 123.

168. Nathan, *The Critic and the Drama*, 16, 5.

169. Nathan, *The Critic and the Drama*, 5–6.

170. Nathan, cited in Atkinson, *Broadway*, 161.

171. Roberts and Roberts, "Introductory Essay," *"As Ever, Gene,"* 125.

172. Connolly, *George Jean Nathan*, 121.

173. Connolly, *George Jean Nathan*, 113.

174. "The Trouble with Brown," *Time*.

175. "George Jean Nathan Dies at 76," 1.

176. "George Jean Nathan Dies at 76," 1.

177. Cited in Connolly, *George Jean Nathan*, 101.

178. Nathan, *Passing Judgments*, 170–71.

179. See Atkinson, "Eugene O'Neill," X5.

180. John Mason Brown, "Critic's View of a Critic," *New York Times*, 13 April 1958, X3.

181. Atkinson, "Eugene O'Neill," X5.

182. Skinner, *Eugene O'Neill*, 10.

183. Warner and Lunt, *Social Life of Modern Community*, 433.

184. Connolly, *George Jean Nathan*, 111.

185. See Theatre Communications Group's Theatre Profiles. The Williams plays are *The Glass Menagerie, A Streetcar Named Desire,* and *Cat on a Hot Tin Roof,* and the Miller, *All My Sons, Death of a Salesman,* and *The Crucible.* http://www.tcg.org/tools/profiles/member_profiles/main.cfm?CFID=7866158&CFTOKEN=43264180 (accessed 7 September 2007).

186. According to Project Muse, as of 29 November 2007, there are 42 references to O'Neill compared with 153 for Williams and 150 for Miller.

187. Nathan, *The World in Falseface*, 79.

188. Kolisch, "Jazz in High Places," 463.

EPILOGUE

1. Joseph Wood Krutch, "A Modern Heroic Drama," *New York Herald Tribune*, 11 March 1928.

2. John Hohenberg, *The Pulitzer Prizes: A History of the Awards in Books, Drama,*

Music, and Journalism, Based on the Private Files over Six Decades (New York: Columbia University Press, 1974), 102.

3. See the Broadway League season statistics. http://www.broadwayleague .com/index.php?url_identifier=season-by-season-stats-1 (accessed 10 April 2008).

4. Charles Isherwood, "Mama Doesn't Feel Well, but Everyone Else Will Feel Much Worse," *New York Times*, 5 December 2007, E1.

5. David Rooney, "August: Osage County," *Daily Variety*, 5 December 2007, 10.

6. Todd Haimes, artistic director of Roundabout Theatre, quoted in Robin Pogrebin, "Nary a Drama on Broadway," *New York Times*, 28 December 1999, E5.

INDEX

Page numbers in italics refer to figures.

mass production and, 199
modernism in, 209
musical aspects of, 208–10
ostinato, use of, 209
ragtime, use of, 208, 209
set design, 211–13
syncopation, use of, 209
vaudeville, influences, 211
world premiere (Théâtre des-
Champs-Elysées), 186–87
Ballet mécanique (film) (Léger), 200,
213–14
Ballets Russes, 186, 190
Bamboozled (Lee), 218
"Bandana Days" (*Shuffle Along*) (Blake,
Sissle), 75
Bandanna Land (Williams, Walker), 75
coon song, use of, 75
Baraka, Amiri (LeRoi Jones), 24, 26, 29
Bartók, Béla, 181, 189
Baudelaire, Charles, 229, 247
Baumol, William, 114
Beach, Sylvia, 207
Beauty and the Beast (musical), 266
Beckmann, Max, 151
Beethoven, Ludwig van, 236
Beggar on Horseback (Kaufman and
Connelly), 14, 19, 152
incidental music (Taylor), 164
jazz, characterization of, 19
Beiderbecke, Bix, 30
Belasco, David, 251
Bell, Rudolph M., 248
Bellows, George Kent, 217
Benchley, Robert, 230
Benjamin, Walter, 57
Benoist-Méchin, Jacques, 181, 182,
206, 209
Bergdorf Goodman, 133
Berle, Milton, 36
Berlin, Irving, 23, 53, 85, 101, 138,
187, 189, 194, 237, 268
Cocoanuts, The, 81
Bernhardt, Sarah, 44
Bernheim, Alfred L., 42, 111–15
Bernstein, Leonard, 102
Beveridge, Albert, 177
Beyond the Horizon (O'Neill), 41, 235,

245, 247, 252, 256
Billy the Kid (Copland), 218
Bird, Carol, 250
Birthday of the Infanta, The (Carpenter),
189
Birth of a Nation, The (Griffith), 1
blackface, 10. *See also* coon song; min-
strelsy
Bamboozled (Lee), use of, 218
imperialism and, 175
Jazz Singer, The (Raphaelson), use
of, 19
Jewish American performers, 33, 70
Jolson, Al, 56
Miller, Flourney and Aubrey Lyles,
74
Processional (Lawson), use of, 17
Shuffle Along (Blake, Sissle), use of,
74–75
Skyscrapers (Carpenter), use of, 196
Blair, Mary, *241*
Blake, Eubie, 7, 9, 16, 28
Blake, Eubie, and Noble Sissle
Chocolate Dandies, The, 76
Shuffle Along, 4, 67, 72–76, 77, 79,
81, 90, 212, 238; "Bandana Days,"
75; blackface, use of, 74–75; bur-
lesque, influences, 74; coon song,
use of, 74; "I'm Just Wild About
Harry," 75–76; jazz, use of, 74;
minstrelsy, satirization, 75; musi-
cal comedy, satirization, 75; op-
eretta, influences, 73, 74, 76; rag-
time, use of, 76; song types, 74;
vaudeville, influences, *73*
Bloch, Ernest, 99, 187
America, 99
Block, Ralph, 125, 126, 127
Blue Monday Blues (Gershwin), 67
Bogard, Travis, 235, 236, 237, 239
Bohm, Adolph, 190
Bok, Mary Louise Curtis, 188, 216,
219
Bolton, Guy and Fred Thompson
Tip-Toes (book), 79
Bordman, Gerald, 87
Bordoni, Irene, 134
Boulton, Agnes, 234

Corbusier, Le, 190
Cotton Club, 4, 23
Count of Monte Cristo, The (stage adaptation by Fechter), 232, 234, 243, 247
Coward, Noël, 134
Craig, E. Gordon, 257
Cram, Mildred, 131, 134
Crawford, Richard, 97
"Crazy Rhythm" (Kahn, Meyer, Caesar), 87–88, 90
Création du monde, La (Milhaud), 180
Crosland, Alan
  Jazz Singer, The (film version), 126
Crothers, Rachel, 134
Crouch, Stanley, 24
cubism, 98, 200
cultural hierarchy. *See also* audiences; social class
  class positioning, avant-gardism, 218; burlesque, 2, 4, 22, 35, 60, 106, 148, 225, 242; Carpenter, John Alden, 218; cinema, 18, 99, 109, 125; comic strips, 60; Gershwin, George, 183; jazz, 86, 102; minstrelsy, 43, 60; modernism, 100, 136; musical comedy, 4, 10, 91, 92, 94, 95, 99, 102, 125, 129, 137, 225; O'Neill, Eugene, 237; revue, 92; Taylor, Deems, 164; theater, 10, 170, 267; Theatre Guild, 148; vaudeville, 2, 4, 10, 43, 60, 92, 94, 99, 102, 125, 129, 137, 183, 211, 225, 242
  highbrow vis-à-vis lowbrow, 47–49, 51, 90–102
  middlebrow, 21st century culture, 267; Dos Passos, John, on, 169–70; theater, 59–64, 134–35, 142; Theatre Guild audiences, 148
cummings, e. e., 133
Cunningham, Merce, 218

Dada, 188, 200, 201, 202, 204, 206, 208, 209, 210, 212. *See also* Tzara, Tristan
  avant-gardism and, 151
  modernism and, 188

vaudeville and, 202
Dale, Alan, 17, 39, 75, 77
Damrosch, Walter, 69, 79
Dance, The (magazine), 196
d'Annunzio, Gabriele
  Martyre de Saint Sébastien, Le, 236
Davis, Allison, 121, 130, 146, 160
Davis, Charlie, 74
Days without End (O'Neill), 260
Dearborn Independent, 89, 136
Debussy, Claude, 39, 189, 190, 199, 239, 268
  Martyre de Saint Sébastien, Le, 236
De Casseres Benjamin, 2, 130, 244, 245
Desire Under the Elms (O'Neill), 52
De Veaux, Scott, 26
Dewhurst, Colleen, 263
Diaghilev, Serge, 185, 186, 190
Dial (magazine), 49, 52
Dickinson, Thomas H., 48, 61, 134
Dickson, W. Lee, 143, 144
Diff'rent (O'Neill), 14, 22, 240, 241
DiMaggio, Paul, 60, 106
Doll's House, A (Ibsen), 111
Dos Passos, John, 140, 147, 148, 169, 170
  Garbage Man, The, 140
  middlebrow culture, on, 169–70
  Theatre Guild, social analysis of, 169–70
Downes, Olin, 172, 173, 187, 191, 194, 195, 197
"Downhearted Blues" (Bessie Smith), 13
Dreiser, Theodore, 253, 254
Du Bois, W. E. B., 25
Duke, Vernon, 102
Dynamo (O'Neill), 240, 241, 242, 244, 252

Early, Gerald, 29
Eaton, Walter Prichard, 9, 22, 61, 62, 63, 88, 91, 93, 99, 109, 124–25, 126, 127, 128, 129, 130, 132, 134, 142, 147, 148, 169, 170, 230, 246, 258. *See also* Theatre Guild, history of
  economic history of 1920s, 116–18

Moeller, Philip, 149, 154, 164
Molnár, Ferenc, 147
"Mon Homme" ["My Man"] (Yvain),
190
Monroe Doctrine, 178
Moon for the Misbegotten, A (O'Neill),
263
Moon of the Caribbees, The (O'Neill),
247
Moore, MacDonald Smith, 86, 99
Morton, Jelly Roll, 23
Most, Andrea, 83
Motown, 268
Mourning Becomes Electra (O'Neill), 244
Mozart, Wolfgang Amadeus, 53, 58,
236
Muir, Lewis F., 237
Mullen, Joseph, 186, 211–13
Murphy, Brenda, 40
Murphy, Dudley, 200
Murray, Albert, 24
musical comedy, 1, 6, 76–79, 96, 113.
   See also Gershwin, George and Ira;
   Shuffle Along (Blake, Sissle)
   African American performers, 76
   American genre, as, 78
   burlesque and, 91
   cinema and, 91
   class positioning, 4, 10, 91, 92, 94,
      95, 99, 102, 125, 129, 137, 225
   comedians in, 92
   Concerto in F (Gershwin),
      influences, 97
   conventions, 77, 80, 81
   Eaton, Walter Prichard, on, 93
   Gershwin, George and Ira and, 10
   jazz and, 4, 8, 14, 15, 16, 34, 37, 42,
      89, 245
   Jazz Singer, The (Raphaelson),
      influences, 19
   Jewish American performers, 63, 82
   legitimate theater and, 2, 3, 19, 39,
      45, 100, 116, 254
   London, in, 181
   Nathan, George Jean, on, 61, 93
   operetta and, 77
   performance practice, 15
   ragtime and, 29

revue and, 106
satirization in *Shuffle Along* (Blake,
   Sissle), 75
Seldes, Gilbert, on, 52, 53, 55
Skyscrapers (Carpenter), influences,
   191
syncopation, use of, 79
theater and, 130
ticket prices, 109
vaudeville and, 90, 268
Muzio, Claudia, 185

Nathan, George Jean, 10, 72, 90, 99,
   126, 128, 142, 228, 229, 258–60,
   266
Antheil, George, on, 217
DeWitt, Addison (*All About Eve*), inspiration for, 231
Hollywood, on, 261
O'Neill, Eugene and, 255–58
posthumous reputation, 263
symbolic violence of, 225, 259–60
vaudeville and, 257
National Anthem, The (Manners), 5, 6,
   14, 20–21, 21
musical comedy, characterization of,
   21
revue, characterization of, 21
nationalism
American cultural nationalism,
   67–69, 99
black cultural nationalism, 26, 27;
   decline, 218
imperialism and, 177–79
populist nationalism, 218
*New Grove Dictionary of Music and Mu-
   sicians*, 22, 30, 31, 96, 97, 217
New York Dramatic Mirror, 42
New York Herald, 230
New York Herald Tribune, 206
New York Shakespeare Festival, 170
New York Times, 20, 77, 109, 125, 152,
   172, 190, 207, 210, 245, 252, 260,
   267
New York Tribune, 106, 228, 230
Nichols, Beverly, 98
Nietzsche, Friedrich, 34, 229, 247, 254
Nigger Heaven (Van Vechten), 69

Niles, Abbe, 98
No, No, Nanette (Youmans, Harbach, Caesar), 181
Noces, Les (Stravinsky), 186
Norris, Frank, 158
Norris, James D., 145
Nunn, Trevor, 266

O'Neill, Eugene, 9, 10, 61, 94, 126, 128, 136, 142, 148, 149, 162, 165, 168, 185, 188, 190, 220, 221–64, 266, 267
  Ah, Wilderness!, 191
  All God's Chillun Got Wings, 22, 191, 237, 238; coon song, use of, 237; spirituals, use of, 22
  Anna Christie, 191, 252, 253, 263
  anti-theatricalism of, 243–45
  Beyond the Horizon, 41, 235, 245, 247, 252, 256
  Bound East for Cardiff, 234
  canonization, 245–50
  class positioning, 237
  coon song, use of, 238
  critical reception, 2–3
  Days without End, 260
  Desire Under the Elms, 52
  Diff'rent, 14, 22, 240, 241
  Dynamo, 240, 241, 242, 244, 252
  early life, 232–35, 247–49
  Emperor Jones, The, 25, 152, 225, 234, 252
  Europe, reception in, 252–54
  Fountain, The, 238
  Great God Brown, The, 124; coon song, use of, 239
  Hairy Ape, The, 153, 255
  Ibsen, Henrik and, 21
  In the Zone, 234, 235
  jazz and, 235–43, 264
  Long Day's Journey Into Night, 247, 261, 263, 264, 267
  Marco Millions, 238
  masculinity and, 250–51
  mass production and, 254, 262
  minstrelsy and, 237–38
  modernism in work of, 175, 239, 251
  Moon for the Misbegotten, A, 263

Moon of the Caribbees, The, 247
Mourning Becomes Electra, 244
Nathan, George Jean and, 255–58
Nobel Prize, 244, 252, 260
O'Neill Songbook, The (Bogard), 235–37
politics of, 254–55
popular song, use of, 237
posthumous reputation, 260–64
Pulitzer Prize, 41, 266
ragtime and, 238
Shakespeare, William and, 21
Shaw, George Bernard and, 21
Sheridan, Richard Brinsley and, 21
spirituals, use of, 237
Strange Interlude, 41, 244, 245, 263, 265, 266
Straw, The, 248, 252
vaudeville and, 233–35, 243, 257
Welded, 252
Wife for Life, A, 234
O'Neill, James, 232–34
O'Neill Songbook, The (Bogard), 235–37
Odets, Clifford, 261
Ohman, Phil, 90
Oja, Carol, 66, 69, 97, 201
Oklahoma! (Rodgers and Hammerstein), 81, 170
Oliver, King, 23
On Trial (Rice), 154
operetta
  musical comedy and, 77
  Shuffle Along (Blake, Sissle), influences, 73, 74, 76
  Tip-Toes (Gershwin, George and Ira), influences, 83, 85
Opportunity (magazine), 152
Original Dixieland Jazz Band, 28, 179
  "Livery Stable Blues," 27, 28
Orpheum Circuit, 234
Our Contemporary Composers (Howard), 217
Our Town (Wilder), 218
Page, Geraldine, 263
Pagliacci, I (Leoncavallo), 215

Palais Royal Orchestra, 13
Palmer Raids, 14, 116, 262

vaudeville (*continued*)
  Skyscrapers (Carpenter), influences,
    191
  stars, 56, 99
  theater and, 3, 10, 19, 39, 130, 222,
    254
  ticket prices, 115
  Tip-Toes (Gershwin, George and Ira),
    influences, 82–83
Vaughan Williams, Ralph, 181
Vautel, Clément, 179
Verdi, Giuseppe
  Trovatore, Il, 189
verismo, 67, 215
Very Good Eddie (Kern), 79
Von Tilzer, Harry, 237

Wagner, Richard, 229, 259
Wainscott, Ronald H., 240
Wales Padlock Law, 158
Walker, George, 75
Walker, George and Bert Williams
  Bandanna Land, 75
Walker, Julia, 149
Waller, Fats, 66
Walton, William, 180
Warner, W. Lloyd, 8, 119, 121, 146,
    263
Waste Land, The (Eliot), 195
Watermeier, Daniel J., 2–3, 221
Watson, Harry, *80*, 81, *83*
Weaver, John V. A., 159
Weber, Max, 119
Webern, Anton, 181
Weill, Kurt, 102, 151, 180
Weinstein, Donald, 248
Welded (O'Neill), 252
"We're Here Because" (*Lady, Be Good!*)
    (G. and I. Gershwin), 95–96
West, Mae, 36
"When Do We Dance?" (*Tip-Toes*)
    (G. and I. Gershwin), 84–85
White, George, 67
Whiteman, Paul, 23–24, 25, 26, 27, 30,
    34, 37, 53, 86, 89, 97, 164, 181,
    185, 202, 207, 208

improvisation, use of, 245
Palais Royal Orchestra, 13
Whitesitt, Linda, 204, 208, 209
Whitman, Walt, 49, 187, 254
Who's Afraid of Virginia Woolf? (Albee),
    267
Wiene, Robert
  Cabinet of Dr. Caligari, The, 55, 56,
    152
Wife for Life, A (O'Neill), 234
Wigmore Hall, 188, 219
Wikander, Matthew H., 243, 244
Wilder, Alec, 95, 100
Wilder, Thornton
  Our Town, 218
Williams, Bert, 33, 50, 75
Williams, Bert, and George Walker
  Bandanna Land, 75; coon song, use
    of, 75
Williams, Raymond, 4, 45, 46, 97, 141,
    161
Williams, Tennessee, 41, 165, 264,
    267
  Glass Menagerie, The, 20
Williams, William Carlos, 216
Wilson, August, 165
Wilson, Edmund, 58
Wilson, Frank, 191
Wilson, Marion, 106
Wilson, Woodrow, 221
Winter, William, 228–29
Wodehouse, P. G., 93
Wolkenkratzer. See *Skyscrapers* (Carpen-
    ter)
Woollcott, Alexander, 20, 79, 101, 228,
    230, 245, 252

Youmans, Vincent, Otto Harbach and
    Irving Caesar
  No, No Nanette, 181
Young, Stark, 154, 189
Youngren, William H., 25, 27
Yvain, Maurice
  "Mon Homme" ["My Man"], 190

Ziegfeld Follies, 4, 106, 114, 212